THE PARLEMENT OF PARIS

J.H. SHENNAN

SUTTON PUBLISHING

First published in 1968 by Eyre & Spottiswoode (Publishers) Ltd

First published in this revised paperback edition in 1998 by
Sutton Publishing Limited · Phoenix Mill
Thrupp · Stroud · Gloucestershire · GL5 2BU

British Library Cataloguing in Publication Data
A catalogue record for this book is available from the British Library

ISBN 0 7509 1830 6

Cover picture: The *Lit de Justice* held in the Parlement on the Majority of Louis XV (1710–74) 22 February 1723 (oil on canvas) by Lancret, Nicolas (1690–1743), Louvre, Paris, France. (Lauros-Giraudon/ Bridgeman Art Library)

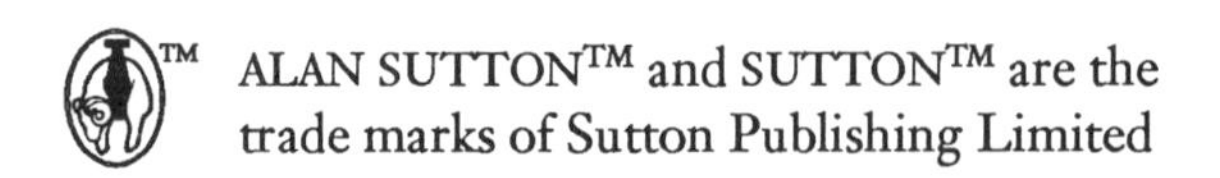

Typeset in 10/12.5pt Janson.
Typesetting and origination by
Sutton Publishing Limited.
Printed in Great Britain by
MPG, Bodmin, Cornwall.

. . . les actes de cette haute magistrature traduisent,
dans leur ensemble, l'histoire de
France, son gouvernement, son administration,
sa justice, ses moeurs. . . .

E. BOUTARIC (ED.), *Actes du Parlement de Paris*,
I, lxxx

For my grandchildren,
on both sides of the Atlantic

Contents

Preface to Second Edition

The Parlement of Paris was first published in 1968. At that time it was a subject attracting the attention of few historians. A group of French legal historians, writing in the nineteenth and early twentieth centuries, including Aubert, Beugnot, Boutaric, Ducoudray, Flammermont, Guilhiermoz, Glasson, Langlois and Maugis, had published editions of *parlementaire* records and studies of the court's political role over various periods of its long history. There were few further significant contributions before the 1950s, though one should mention the prescient work of Roger Bickart on the parlements and the developing notion of national sovereignty in the eighteenth century, and Roger Doucet's two-volume work on the Parlement's relations with Francis I. From 1950, however, interest in the Parlement of Paris began to quicken. In France, François Bluche and Jean Egret were at work on social and political studies of the eighteenth-century court and its members, as was Franklin Ford in the United States where Lloyd Moote also was embarking upon his research on the seventeenth-century French magistracy. Since the 1960s, publications have increased dramatically as scholars on both sides of the Channel and of the Atlantic have continued to explore a wide variety of *parlementaire* themes. This author's debt to a roll of distinguished scholars may be inferred from the new introduction and footnotes, and from the revised bibliography printed in this edition which, as well as incorporating the original bibliography, lists the major contributions of the last thirty years.

In the light of the new material now available, it is reasonable to ask whether the decision to reprint the original text of *The Parlement of Paris* can be justified. That decision has been taken in the belief that readers will find it more convenient to assess the significance of later work when reviewed in an extensive introduction rather than woven into the existing text. In addition, however, the essential theme of *The*

Parlement of Paris, its preoccupation with the long struggle between the king as supreme judge and his sovereign court over the nature and limitations of political authority – what one reviewer called its 'theoretical underpinning' – remains a compelling unifying theme.

Introduction to Second Edition

The Court of Law

The emergence of a separate institution, the Parlement of Paris, from the *curia regis* defies precise documentation. Gradually, however, the nature of that process is becoming clearer. More is known, for example, about the work of one of St. Louis's chief legal advisers, Pierre de Fontaines, both in strengthening the king's judicial authority and in contributing to the development of French jurisprudence. Fontaines was the first layman in France to seek to apply the principles of Roman law to customary law, and the first to compose a treatise in French on customary law, *Conseil à un ami*. He also argued that an appeal to the king was always admissible if there was evidence that customary law had been ignored.[1] From this time too the method of judging appeals became more sophisticated with the development of the *enquête*. This was a procedure whereby two members of the Parlement, one layman and one cleric, were dispatched to the scene of contention with orders to collect the testimony of those in dispute and of any witnesses. The senior chamber of the Parlement, the *Grand' Chambre*, then validated the enquiry and sent the written evidence to the chamber of *Enquêtes* for judgement. Finally, that verdict had to be formally registered as a decree (*arrêt*) of the court.[2] This was the procedure in place by the reign of Philip V in the early fourteenth century though before that date his father, the powerful Philip IV (the Fair), had during his long reign encouraged the development of a more professional outlook among his judges as well as the evolution of

[1] Quentin Griffiths, 'New Men among the Lay Counselors of Saint Louis' Parlement', 255–7; see also the same author's article, 'Les origines et la carrière de Pierre de Fontaines'; and C. van Dievoet, 'La *Somme Rurale* de Boutillier et la jurisprudence du parlement de Paris'.

[2] J. Kicklighter, 'Appeal Procedure in the Medieval Parlement of Paris', 38 et seq.

more efficient court procedures.[3] Indeed, throughout this formative period in contrast to the early history of the English parliament, it was the king's role as judge that provided the crucial stimulus. In Thomas Bisson's words, 'What survived in France from the pivotal 1250s and 60s was . . . the strong impress of a justiciar-king'.[4]

The ordinance of 1345, promulgated by the first Valois king, Philip VI, has long been seen as the final act in the establishment of a permanent Parlement. A French historian, Françoise Autrand, has recently gone further. She contends that that date marks the birth of the *milieu parlementaire* when the lawcourt acquired all the hallmarks of distinction and distinctiveness: stability of membership and of size of establishment, a regular salary for the judges, and the ability to exercise control over the competence of new recruits. From the fifteenth century the Parlement's growing sense of its own identity and importance was reflected in the fact that the members of the court wore legal uniform (though it was not standardized for some time to come).[5]

The question of how the Parlement recruited its members during this early period of its history has been the subject of some scholarly disagreement. Autrand maintains that by the middle of the fifteenth century the court's sense of corporate solidarity was the result of the increasing dominance of successive generations of the same families. This state of affairs was achieved through the device of resignation *in favorem*, whereby a judge was permitted to give up his office to a kinsman. Autrand points out that between 1469 and 1483 half the resignations from the Parlement were in favour of relatives, more and more of sons, and that that proportion rose to two-thirds between 1483 and 1498.[6]

However, Christopher Stocker has expressed some reservations about this interpretation. He points out that the practise of resignation *in favorem* was not a device that allowed family members to do what they pleased with their offices, but was a royal privilege only extended to individuals enjoying the king's favour. He also challenges the extent of vertical family recruitment, emphasizing instead patron-client relationships as a means to preferment (the patron increasingly being the king himself).[7] Stocker had

[3] Joseph R. Strayer, *The Reign of Philip the Fair*, 210.
[4] Thomas N. Bisson, 'Consultative Functions in the King's Parlements', 372.
[5] Françoise Autrand, *Naissance d'un Grand Corps de l'État*, 16, 21, 136.
[6] Ibid., 104.
[7] Christopher Stocker, '*Parti*, Clientage and Lineage in the Fifteenth-Century Parlement of Paris', 17.

touched upon these issues in an earlier article, published in 1973. In it he claims that of more than one hundred nominees recommended for election to the Parlement during the successive reigns of Charles VIII, Louis XII and Francis I, only twenty-five were related to former magistrates, and that election was generally viewed by the court as a means of keeping undesirable applicants out, including for example, those lacking in professional competence.[8] In this article Stocker also criticizes the argument put forward by Roger Doucet, that elections were primarily intended to produce *parlementaire* family dynasties able to defend the political interests of the *haute bourgeoisie* by transforming the Parlement of Paris into a permanent constitutional check upon the authority of the crown.[9]

There are two main thrusts to Stocker's argument. First, he maintains that in renaissance France the enthusiastic pursuit of royal offices in the Parlement and elsewhere was primarily driven by the opportunity thus afforded to acquire honours and privileges. These belonged to each office-holder and were part-honorific, part-material. They included exemption from most forms of taxation, notably the *taille*, the *gabelle*, the *aides* and (in the case of clerical counsellors), the *décime*; freedom from both the obligation to billet troops and to attend for service in the *ban et arrière ban*.[10] In his comments on recruitment to the court Stocker is surely right to emphasize the individual's quest for privilege rather than any oligarchic conspiracy. He is equally convincing when he dismisses ideas of constitutional checks and balances as anachronistic when applied to the early sixteenth century.[11] His second major thrust relates to the continuing significance of patron-client relationships. In this area he foreshadows important later research that has given this theme new and deserved prominence.[12] Some offices did entail obligations of service to great magnates, and that was still the case at the time of the Fronde.[13] Indeed, it would be grossly misleading not to acknowledge that for much of the early modern period, the 'royal administration was in part a great clientage network built upon personal allegiances, full of private enterprise'.[14]

[8] Christopher Stocker, 'The Politics of the Parlement of Paris in 1525', 202–3.
[9] Ibid., 201; see also R. Doucet, *Etude sur le Gouvernement de François Ier*, II, 300.
[10] Christopher Stocker, 'Office as Maintenance in Renaissance France', 35.
[11] Stocker, 'The Politics of the Parlement of Paris in 1525', 210.
[12] See in particular Sharon Kettering, *Patrons, Brokers and Clients in Seventeenth-Century France*, *passim*.
[13] Orest Ranum, 'Money, Dignity and Self-esteem in the Relations between Judges and Great Nobles', *passim*.
[14] Stocker, 'The Politics of the Parlement of Paris in 1525', 211.

The problem is one of striking the right balance and of not underplaying the importance of the Parlement's growing *esprit de corps*. In his article on 'The Politics of the Parlement of Paris in 1525', Stocker recognizes that the judges in the court were heirs to a tradition which acknowledged that the king's chief function was to dispense justice to his people. In judging on the king's behalf each magistrate attracted to his office great dignity and kudos. It was therefore in the interests of all the members of the Parlement to maintain their court's high reputation in order to preserve the worth of their own offices.[15] Yet the corollary must also be true, namely that membership of such an exclusive organization, however achieved, inevitably produced a strong sense of corporate identity. Stocker does not claim 'that the magistrates had no sense of identification with the Parlement and no sense of their corporate identity and interests. It is evident that they did, for they expressed this clearly in both word and deed.'[16] It is worth noting in this context the observation of Lawrence Bryant, that from the second half of the fifteenth century the Parlement began to equate its favoured place in the royal entry processions into Paris with its precedence in government as a fourth estate of the realm, representing Justice.[17] With similar reasoning the Parlement decided in 1461, upon the death of Charles VII, to continue in session, thereby defying the convention that its authority had to be reconfirmed by each new king. The Parlement thus claimed for itself, symbolically at least, the right to dispense royal justice, that quintessential obligation of French kingship, unfettered by the short-term considerations of individual rulers.[18] However, Stocker's insistence upon the importance of the patron-client relationship and upon the value of royal office to the individual holder must be given due weight in any analysis of the judges' attitudes towards their court.

From the early sixteenth century this already complex situation was further complicated when sale of office began to feature as a regular aspect of *parlementaire* recruitment. This procedure reached its defining moment in

[15] Stocker, Ibid., 205.

[16] Stocker, '*Parti*, Clientage and Lineage in the Fifteenth-Century Parlement of Paris', 18.

[17] Lawrence M. Bryant, '*Parlementaire* Political Theory in the Parisian Royal Entry Ceremony', 16–18.

[18] Ralph E. Giesey, 'The Presidents of Parlement at the Royal Funeral', 27–8. In the same era the Parlement also asserted that the king's sovereign justice should reside in one body only, namely in the Parlement permanently based in Paris. It also attacked the royal use of the *Grand Conseil* as a means of circumventing normal judicial procedures. In seeking thus to preserve its unique judicial role the court was also buttressing its political authority. See Christopher Stocker, 'Office and Justice: Louis XI and the Parlement of Paris', 377, 380–2.

1604 with the establishment of the *paulette* or *annuel*. The effects of this new tax were not dramatic or immediate. The tendency for offices in the court to become hereditary in a single family grew, in particular because of the prize of permanent noble status. In the first century of the Parlement's existence, a new kind of personal nobility was being acquired by the judges, based upon their function of public service, the chief characteristic of nobility. 'To live nobly' was to serve the king in whatever capacity he required. Therefore, although tensions between old and new nobility existed in the Parlement, there was no novelty in the recognition of the new men's noble quality.[19] Four years before the introduction of the *annuel* the king recognized the principle of *patre et avo consulibus*, which would transform the personal nobility acquired through membership of the court into permanent noble status for those families who provided three generations, father, son and grandson, as successive holders of an office in the Parlement. Clearly, the *annuel* improved the prospects for such family enterprises, a fact that helps to explain the transformation in the court's previously hostile attitude towards venality.[20] Yet there was no interruption during the four decades following the introduction of the *annuel* to the influx of newcomers, and the court continued to recruit members without family connections down to the very end of the *ancien régime*.[21] Nevertheless, although family links never became preponderant, a kind of social exclusiveness was emerging. In the two decades after the Fronde, the court's membership was drawn overwhelmingly from among the scions of the judiciary, with the sons of non-judicial officials and *bourgeois* much less prominently represented.[22] The ethos within the Parlement was noble and professional (since 1644 the judges in the court had all been granted full membership of the *noblesse de race*), and that social cohesiveness, allied to institutional pride, reinforced the sense of *esprit de corps* and made the Parlement a formidable force.[23]

[19] Autrand, op. cit., 248, 267.

[20] William Doyle, *Venality. The Sale of Offices in Eighteenth-Century France*, 12; Christopher Stocker, 'Public and Private Enterprise in the Administration of a Renaisance Monarchy', 24.

[21] Mark Cummings, 'The Social Impact of the Paulette', 336–7. Note, too, the comment of Jean Egret, 'L'aristocratie parlementaire française à la fin de l'ancien régime', 14: '*L'aristocratie parlementaire, à la fin de l'ancien régime, n'est pas une caste, fermée aux hommes nouveaux et aux idées nouvelles.*'

[22] Albert N. Hamscher, *The Parlement of Paris after the Fronde*, 38–44.

[23] Under the pressure of religious war in sixteenth-century France the judges of the Parisian sovereign courts had developed the ideal of the 'perfect catholic magistrate', as a unifying model for society, which also contributed to the distinctive ethos of the *noblesse de robe*. See Colin Kaiser, 'Les cours souveraines au XVIe siècle', 27–9.

However, this social homogeneity identified in the second half of the seventeenth century had been challenged earlier in the century when, following the introduction of the *annuel*, the price of offices in the Parlement rose. The office of counsellor, which cost about 21,000 *livres* in 1600, had reached 102,000 *livres* by 1629 and 120,000 *livres* eight years later.[24] A number of explanations have been offered for this spectacular inflation, including the introduction of the *annuel* itself, which certainly provided the office-holders with greater security. However, there were other causes too. One was the disparity between the selling price and the official valuation upon which the *annuel* tax was based. A lay counsellor's office, for example, was still only valued in 1665 at 24,000 *livres*, attracting an *annuel* of 400 *livres*, whereas its true selling price was 120,000 *livres*.[25] There was therefore increasing competition for office from very wealthy candidates willing to pay inflated prices at a time when few new offices were being created. In particular, the sons of tax-farmers and financiers perceived a way of achieving instant social acceptability. The magistrates were resolutely hostile to these monied newcomers on social grounds and, from the period leading up to the outbreak of the Fronde, on political grounds too. Indeed, in October 1648 the Parlement issued a decree excluding tax-farmers, financiers and their children from office in the court. Eventually, in 1665, Louis XIV acted to reduce the maximum price of offices in the Parlement, fixing that of a lay counsellor at 100,000 *livres*. This stabilization of prices had the long-term effect of further unifying the court's social base, for when the possession of immense wealth ceased to be the most significant factor in the pursuit of office, magistrates preferred to hand on their offices to their heirs or to sell them to fellow professionals who had reached a suitable point in the judicial hierarchy.[26]

The seventeenth century also witnessed a further extension of the magistrates' control over their own offices. The *annuel* expired every nine years, thereby enabling the king periodically to curb the independence and excesses of his office-holders. That was the theory at

[24] Cummings, op. cit., 341.

[25] Ibid., 350.

[26] Hamscher, op. cit., 14–25; Robert Descimon has also pointed out that the inflationary spiral in the cost of high *parlementaire* office fed a matching rise in the value of dowries brought to the presidents *à mortier* and the *gens du roi*, and of those provided for their daughters by them. By this measurement these members of the Parlement were, by the second half of the seventeenth century, moving into the same social orbit as the dukes and peers. Robert Descimon, 'La haute noblesse parlementaire parisienne', 361–5.

least, though in practice the permanent lack of financial resources forced the government to treat renewal of the *annuel* as a mechanism for raising additional revenues. In 1638, for example, all *parlementaire* offices were reassessed in order to yield a higher *annuel*. However, the members of the Parlement were generally treated more favourably than other office-holders (a fact that played its part in the outbreak of the Fronde in 1648). The *annuel* was abolished in 1709 in favour of a government levy of 12.5 per cent of the office's value whenever the office changed hands. That legislation was revoked in 1722 but members of the Parlement and of the other sovereign courts remained free of the *annuel*.[27]

By the beginning of the eighteenth century, therefore, the judges in the Parlement of Paris had acquired a high level of independence from the crown based upon their ownership of office; and with it a strong sense of identity compounded of shared social status and common membership of an élite, high-profile organization. One effect of this gradual metamorphosis was to remove from the court old patronage-client links that had once threatened the effective implementation of royal policies. By the same token, however, the crown's ability to control the Parlement was also put at risk. The eighteenth century was to witness a protracted period of legal warfare as the court strove with a range of political and quasi-constitutional arguments to deflect the will of its royal master.

During the eighteenth century the price of offices in the Parlement declined from the inflated figures of Louis XIV's mid-reign. However, the extent of that decline is far less remarkable when measured against the base-line of 1726, the date when stability was finally restored to the value of the *livre* after a quarter-century of constant readjustment.[28] An additional explanation for the reduction in the value of a counsellor's office in the court – down to under 35,000 *livres* by the mid-century – has been provided by William Doyle. He points out that between 1710 and 1790 there were only some 150 ennoblements among the 1,250 magistrates in the various parlements. In other words, only those who were already noblemen usually contemplated purchasing a *parlementaire* office.[29] Indeed, of the seventy-seven magistrates who entered the Parlement after January

[27] Doyle, op. cit., 43–50.
[28] Ibid., 211; Egret, op. cit., 14.
[29] William Doyle, 'The Price of Offices in Pre-Revolutionary France', 835–8. It is important to stress again, however, that this growing exclusiveness was based upon shared membership of the second estate, not upon narrow familial links.

1771, only eight were not at least second generation nobles, and a high proportion had far longer noble ancestry.[30] With this narrowing of demand a fall in prices was likely. Nevertheless, the value of offices in the court during the final decades of its existence did not fluctuate spectacularly. Because the Parlement was the flagship of the *noblesse de robe*, its offices would always remain for some an attractive social investment.

Conversely, the publicity accompanying the court's prolonged conflict with the government probably had some adverse effect upon the perceived value of *parlementaire* office. This conflict can also be linked directly to the decline in the volume of legal business passing through the court. Some of that loss can be attributed to the unwillingness of litigants to put their cases in the hands of the very young judges of the chambers of *Enquêtes* and *Requêtes*, whose high-profile political activities suggested a lack of gravitas. Because the minimum age of reception into the court was so low some of those admitted were not old enough to benefit from dowries or the ownership of estates. They needed, therefore, to make some financial profit from their office. With judicial business drying up, some of them chose to sell their offices and look elsewhere for financial rewards, unlike those whose wealth and new-found leisure in the exercise of their judicial functions allowed them to indulge in full their noble life-style.[31]

The growth of venality had a number of other effects upon the Parlement's membership, which were damaging to the highest lawcourt in the land. The growing problem of under-age magistrates was exacerbated by considerations of family investment. Royal letters of dispensation circumventing the minimum age requirement of twenty-five for a counsellor and forty for a president became routine in the seventeenth century rather than extraordinary. It followed that many judges lacked legal training and experience.[32] Other abuses too crept in with the venal system. Some magistrates tried to recoup the cost of the investment in their office by dragging out the judicial process in order to increase their financial return, or by refusing to take criminal cases, which on the whole did not pay well.[33] These were among the many judicial abuses that Colbert tried to address in the Civil Code of 1667. In

[30] François Bluche, 'Les magistrats des cours parisiennes au XVIIIe siècle', 94–7.

[31] Colin Kaiser, 'The Deflation in the Volume of Litigation at Paris', 316, 326–7; Doyle, *Venality*, 233.

[32] Cummings, op. cit., 344–5.

[33] John A. Carey, *Judicial Reform in France before the Revolution of 1789*, 11–14.

order to expedite justice in the courts and make it less expensive, this legislation updated and shortened the procedures. The judges' opportunities for claiming fees were thereby reduced, and any failure to implement the new regulations would invite litigants to sue for damages.[34] Though Louis XIV and Colbert had some success in reforming judicial procedures, they failed in their attempts to reduce the number of age-dispensations, to limit nepotism within the court, or to improve the quality of the judges' legal education. The overriding reason for failure was financial; the crown simply could not afford to overlook valuable sources of income, including of course the sale of office itself.

There is, however, another side to the coin. The Parlement itself was not averse to all reform. It took a number of procedural initiatives in the decade preceding the publication of the Civil Code. In 1658 it required judges to deal with criminal cases even if those involved could not afford the fees, and in the interests of saving litigants' time and expense the court introduced a number of oral, in place of written, procedures. The Parlement also recognized at this time the inadequacies of its members' legal training, and attempted to restore the proviso that magistrate-candidates should be qualified as barristers.[35] Indeed, from the reign of Louis XIV the barristers were setting the professional pace in the Parlement. Official lists of graduate apprentices appeared from the 1680s but the graduates had then to serve two more qualifying years before being recognized as fully practising barristers. In an age when knowledge was beginning to be classified and talent recognized, barristers were taking a leading position among the intellectual élite.[36] In the eighteenth century this was the profession producing the best jurists. In the opinion of Cardinal Fleury they were a more learned company than the judges.[37]

Yet the magistrature as a whole belonged to a culture of erudition. The unprofessional and unedifying conduct of some young counsellors gave a misleading impression of an essentially learned society steeped from the fourteenth to the seventeenth century in the works of pagan and Christian antiquity, Roman history, and the writings of Saints Augustine, Thomas Aquinas, and Bernard of Clairvaux. By the eighteenth century paintings as

[34] Hamscher, op. cit., 172 et seq; see also Roger Mettam, *Power and Faction in Louis XIV's France*, 258–68.

[35] Hamscher, op. cit., 165, 192–3.

[36] Martine Acerra, 'Les avocats du parlement de Paris', 214, 225.

[37] Michel Antoine, 'Sens et portée des réformes du chancelier de Maupeou', 57.

well as books were forming part of magisterial collections. As the century progressed two trends emerged. First, collecting paintings became the pastime of an élite group who clearly appreciated the investment potential of their acquisitions. After 1750 their investments, which were likely to include the works of painters from northern Europe as well as from Italy, were valued by reference to the artists' reputation: in the words of the eighteenth-century connoisseur Pierre-Jean Mariette, '*les collectioneurs achètent des noms et non plus des oeuvres*'.[38] Secondly, by the end of the eighteenth century most magistrates subscribed to the view that it was more important to possess a good library than a collection of paintings.[39] Finally, it should be noted that *parlementaire* libraries did not exclusively reflect current orthodoxies. In the late fourteenth and early fifteenth centuries the heretical writings of John Wyclif were collected, and in the eighteenth the new ideas of the Enlightenment found a prominent place.[40]

Indeed, the magistrates began to deploy the language of the *philosophes* in their increasingly rancorous feud with the king's government. At the heart of that quarrel was the issue of whether the crown's legitimacy continued to depend upon its adherence to a political system that before the end of the eighteenth century had become discredited and irrelevant.

The Political Institution

Among the most influential work bearing upon the history of the Parlement to have been published since 1968 is that of the American historian Sarah Hanley.[41] Her thesis, briefly stated, is that the ceremony of the *lit de justice*, at which the king presided in person at a *parlementaire* session, was a sixteenth-century invention begun by Francis I, for which there were no medieval precedents. When the king had visited his lawcourt in earlier times such occasions were described as royal *séances*. Hanley argues that the

[38] Olivier Bonfait, 'Les collections des parlementaires parisiens au XVIIIe siècle', 28.

[39] Ibid., 33.

[40] Françoise Autrand, 'Culture et mentalité: les librairies des gens du parlement', *passim*; Daniel Roche, 'Noblesses et culture dans la France du XVIIIe siècle', 24–5: '*C'est dans les hôtels de la magistrature parisienne et provinciale que les arts, la philosophie et les sciences font de bons scores . . . la plupart ne sont pas restés indifférents au changement.*'

The libraries of the members of the Maupeou parlement (1771–4) similarly reflected the *parlementaire* interest in the Enlightenment. See J. Félix, *Les Magistrats du Parlement de Paris*, 41–2.

[41] Professor Hanley's major work, *The Lit de Justice of the Kings of France*, was published in 1983. She has also published a number of related articles before and after that date.

two functions served quite different purposes. The royal *séances* were concerned with judicial matters, reflecting the king's role as the source of justice in his state; the *lits de justice* pertained to constitutional issues involving public law, which it was also the king's obligation to defend.

Hanley's thesis, though ingenious and scholarly, has not been universally accepted. The leading historian of Francis I's reign, R.J. Knecht, maintains that the particularities surrounding the *lit de justice* of 1527 are best explained by reference to the contemporary circumstances. These relate primarily to disputes over the Concordat of Bologna, which the Parlement had registered unwillingly and with qualifications in 1518. The Concordat, agreed two years earlier between the king and Pope Leo X, gave each participant some advantage. Francis acquired greater control over the Gallican Church because the previous traditional system of election to ecclesiastical benefices, restated in the Pragmatic Sanction of Bourges (1438), was replaced by one of royal nomination; while for its part, the Holy See welcomed the reduction of the Gallican Church's independence from Rome and the restoration of the payment of annates, the papal tax on benefices. As a doughty defender of the Gallican tradition the Parlement's opposition to the implementation of the Concordat was predictable. The king responded by evoking disputed matters on this issue to another sovereign court, the *Grand Conseil*, which still formed part of the royal entourage. When Francis I was taken prisoner by the emperor, Charles V, after the defeat of Pavia, the Parlement added considerably to the difficulties of the regent, Louise of Savoy, by challenging the government over both the Concordat and the policy of evocation. It was to be expected therefore that upon his return the king would demonstrate, in as authoritative a fashion as possible, the plentitude of his power. In Professor Knecht's view that was precisely what the *lit de justice* of July 1527 was intended to achieve.[42]

This historians' debate focuses attention on the fundamental fact that the role and authority of the crown was evolving. However, the nature of evolution makes precise definition at any stage of the process difficult to sustain. Thus, Hanley's statement that 'Francis I had convoked a *lit de justice*, not a royal *Séance* or the Estates . . . and he intended to effect a separation of functions there', suggests a strategy consciously designed to

[42] R.J. Knecht, 'Francis I and the "Lit de Justice"', 53–83. See also the same author's *Francis I*, 51–65, 182–3, 199–201.

change not only the relationship between king and Parlement but the nature of royal authority itself.[43] She backs up this argument by suggesting that the king's displeasure, causing him to prorogue the assembly of July 1527, was brought about by the failure of the chief spokesman on the Parlement's side, President Guillart, to acknowledge that the court was in fact participating in a *lit de justice*. Knecht's alternative explanation for the president's silence reflects more convincingly the lack of definition about the limits of royal authority: 'Could it be, however, that the president was simply not aware of the distinction Professor Hanley was to draw nearly five centuries later between a royal *séance* and a *lit de justice*?'[44]

Conversely, one of the strengths of Professor Hanley's work is its subtle demonstration of the difficulty in disentangling later modes of discourse about historical events from contemporary perceptions. The transformation in meaning of the phrase *lit de justice* itself provides an interesting example. From its original usage in the late 1380s as a description of the decorative draperies cordoning off the king's space when he visited the Parlement, it had within a quarter-century come to denote a particular kind of *parlementaire* session.[45]

Writing about the politics of the Parlement in 1525, Christopher Stocker considers the relationship between the king and his court as essentially holistic. The magistrates had inherited a long tradition of political thinking whereby the king's judicial responsibility was viewed as the highest of all the obligations of kingship in the secular sphere.[46] That judicial character had to inform all royal actions, not least pronouncements made by the king as guardian of the public law of the realm and as legislator, two functions that were self-evidently inseparable from his quintessential role as supreme judge. The members of the Parlement, whose sovereign court dispensed royal justice at the highest level, were bound therefore to judge political matters presented before them, in judicial terms. Conversely, the judicial ethos of French kingship was so strong that even a century and a half later Louis XIV was still prepared to pronounce judicial verdicts on matters of foreign policy.[47]

[43] Hanley, op. cit., 81.

[44] Knecht, 'Francis I and the "Lit de Justice"', 68.

[45] Hanley, op. cit., 15–23; see also the present author's review of *The Lit de Justice of the Kings of France* in the *English Historical Review*, 101 (1986), 717.

[46] Stocker, 'The Politics of The Parlement of Paris in 1525', 205.

[47] Ibid., 211; J.H. Shennan, *Liberty and Order in Early Modern Europe*, 28.

What was in fact impinging upon the late fifteenth- and early sixteenth-century scene was the slowly emerging concept of the modern state on whose behalf other than normal judicial criteria had on occasion to be invoked. 'Reasons of state' were difficult to justify in a regime so profoundly judicial in character, as the Parlement, representing that tradition, frequently observed. Yet state security sometimes required actions to be taken that, by their nature, risked undermining the authority of the king-judge. The battle thus joined between the king and his court continued down the years. It was, however, a battle fought on common ground, not one based on conflicting ideologies.

An area of increasing controversy in this period concerned the relationship between the spiritual and temporal powers, the Gallican Church and the French state, over both of which the king was the supreme ruler. At the end of the fifteenth century, the Parlement achieved a victory for the secular power by means of the appeal *comme d'abus*, a device allowing it to judge appeals against decisions of an ecclesiastical judge, and especially effective in matters relating to the liberties of the Gallican Church. In its remonstrances of 1525 the Parlement sought to protect its position vis-à-vis the spiritual power by requesting the king not to appoint laymen to any of the clerical offices in the court. By maintaining its mixed membership, lay and clerical, the Parlement could reasonably claim to exercise ecclesiastical as well as secular jurisdiction.[48] Francis I was inclined to limit the court's intervention in ecclesiastical affairs because of the turbulence created among the magistrates in the wake of the Concordat of Bologna.

The Parlement supported the Pragmatic Sanction of Bourges as the legal statement definitively regulating the relationship between the French Church and the Papacy. Its own jurisprudential record, which was also by definition that of the king, reflected that position. When Francis I overturned the Pragmatic Sanction in favour of the Concordat the Parlement's opposition was based upon the argument that what was most at risk was the king's own judicial authority. For the Pragmatic Sanction had been freely registered with due ceremonial after widespread legal consultations, whereas the presentation of the Concordat to the court was accompanied by threats and intimidation. The fact was that a significant part of Francis's calculations had been to effect a rapprochement with the pope as a means of furthering French ambitions in Naples. Thus political

[48] Stocker, 'The Politics of the Parlement of Paris in 1525', 200.

justice, or reason of state, threatened to weaken the king's overarching authority as the chief judge, whose pronouncements were lodged in the registers of his sovereign court of Parlement.[49] The Parlement did not challenge the king's authority during the last twenty years of Francis's reign with the robustness it had displayed in 1517–18 and 1525–7; yet neither did the king ever discount the Parlement's political significance. His prolonged efforts to persuade the court to register the Concordat of Bologna, detailed in Knecht's definitive account of the reign, bear testimony to that fact.[50]

Religious issues, or political issues with fiercely religious overtones, dominated most of the remaining years of the sixteenth century, especially in Paris.[51] The opposing royal and *parlementaire* arguments about legislative rights were regularly replayed. In 1561, for example, the chancellor, Michel de L'Hôpital, informed the court that kings were entitled to amend laws when the public good so required, with at best only a purely advisory role for the Parlement, which could certainly not refuse to register the new measures. Replying on behalf of the magistrates, President Saint-André maintained that the registration of laws was not simply an act of obedience, but represented a necessary part of the legislative process.[52] In May 1563, Charles IX attended the Parlement for the registration of an edict levying exceptional taxation upon the French Church. This measure, deemed necessary in the national interest, was to raise funds for a campaign to drive the English out of Le Havre. On this occasion a constructive compromise was reached: the king brought the legislation to his court, his chancellor explained its importance, and the Parlement registered the edict without demur. Although this session dealt with a piece of legislation concerning the public interest and not with 'ordinary judicial business', Hanley insists that it was a royal *séance* and not a *lit de justice* (she takes issue with an earlier historian, Glasson, for having given it that nomenclature).[53]

[49] Shennan, *Liberty and Order in Early Modern Europe*, 47–9.

[50] Knecht, *Francis I*, 55–63.

[51] Recently, historians have begun to give more weight to the importance of the religious conflict *per se* rather than portraying it as simply a weapon in the struggle between noble factions. See, for example, Barbara B. Diefendorf, *Beneath the Cross. Catholics and Huguenots in Sixteenth-Century Paris*; and in particular, the recent posthumous volume by Nancy Lyman Roelker, *One King, One Faith. The Parlement of Paris and the Religious Reformations of the Sixteenth Century*.

[52] For an analysis of L'Hôpital's turbulent relationship with the Parlement, see S.-H. Kim, 'The Chancellor's Crusade: Michel de L'Hôpital and the *Parlement* of Paris', 1–29.

[53] Hanley, op. cit., 59, 150–7.

A similar scholarly disagreement concerns Charles IX's successor, Henry III, and his manner of dealing with the Parlement. Professor Hanley states unequivocally that 'Henry III (1574–89) never convoked a *lit de justice* assembly'.[54] Mack P. Holt disagrees. He is concerned to demonstrate that the royal device of using a *lit de justice* to enforce unpopular legislation was not pioneered by Henry IV in 1597, as Hanley maintains, but by Henry III in the 1560s.[55] In a telling footnote he underlines the danger of over-precise categorization in analysing a dynamic relationship characterized by a degree of imprecision; 'Hanley has chosen to distinguish two different types of royal visits to the Parlement: the "royal *séance*" to describe visits when the registers of the court do not specifically mention or describe a *lit de justice* ceremony, and a "*lit de justice* assembly" when such a ceremony is explicitly mentioned in the court's registers . . . contemporary accounts including the Parlement's own registers made no such distinction and the terms "royal *séance*" and "*lit de justice* assembly" were not used by contemporaries'.[56] Holt concludes that Henry III did in fact employ the *lit de justice* procedure to force legislation through an unwilling Parlement even though contemporary accounts of such occasions lacked exactness. In view of his implication that linguistic imprecision reflected a similarly imprecise procedure, and of his acceptance that there had been 'numerous disputes and confrontations between the king and the court long before 1559 . . . over such issues as alienation of the royal domain, excessive fiscal demands, Gallican liberties of the French church', it is surprising that Holt should accept Hanley's conviction that the first *lit de justice* did not take place until 1527.[57]

Professor Hanley has responded to the Holt hypothesis by arguing that the contemporary journals of Pierre de l'Estoile and Jacques-Auguste de Thou, upon which Holt places heavy emphasis, are unreliable and error-strewn, and are not supported by the best source, the Parlement's own registers.[58] However, one of Professor Holt's main arguments is that in this period the court's registers were a particularly unreliable guide to what took place between the king and the Parlement. This was because of the Parlement's wish to assert its own standpoint and to play down the

[54] Ibid., 212.
[55] Mack P. Holt, 'The King in Parlement: the Problem of the *Lit de Justice*', 508.
[56] Ibid., 509, fn. 7.
[57] Ibid., 507, 515.
[58] Sarah Hanley, 'The French Constitution Revised', 49–50.

alternative *thèse royale*. The increasingly animated tug-of-war between the two protagonists threatened to produce an all or nothing end-game. Yet ultimately, the magistrates, who derived their powers from the king as chief justiciar, could not defend an independent role for themselves if the king chose to implement his authority in person in his court. In acting in that way he was properly exercising his right of *justice retenue*.

However, there were political advantages for the crown in acting with rather than against the Parlement. The case for joint occupation of the middle ground was well made by a sixteenth-century judge, Etienne Pasquier, who observed that 'as soon as any ordinance is published and verified in the Parlement the French people immediately obey it . . . as if such a body was the link which connected the obedience of the subjects to the commands of their prince. This is no small consequence for the greatness of our kings, who for this reason have always respected this company greatly, even when at first encounter its opinion did not completely and in all ways conform to that of the king's.'[59]

Throughout the Wars of Religion the policy of the Parlement of Paris remained resolutely hostile to the Huguenot cause, and the 'increasingly animated tug-of-war' just referred to was the result of the crown's equivocation. The Parlement opposed the edict of Amboise (1563), which ended the first religious war, only agreeing under duress to register it provisionally. Charles IX had his revenge six months later when he chose to mark his majority by holding a *lit de justice* in the Parlement of Rouen, and to have the edict of Amboise unconditionally registered there. This dual threat, to the court's pre-eminence among the parlements and to its role in registering royal legislation, quickened the development of a more far-reaching *thèse parlementaire* designed to challenge the crown's authoritarianism.

It is difficult to assess precisely the Parlement's part in the events leading to the Saint-Bartholomew's Day massacre of 24 August 1572. The argument has been put forward that the court's well-known intransigent hostility to Protestantism and its protracted constitutional wrangles with Chancellor L'Hôpital, allied to events immediately preceding the massacre, had the effect of detonating a massive explosion of popular violence in Paris. Those events included what may have been the Parlement's first judicial strike, lasting from 16 to 26 August, and provoked by an edict

[59] Holt, op. cit., 522.

imposing a heavy tax upon solicitors serving in royal courts. The Parlement's opposition raised the already high political temperature in the capital as did the court's absence, whether voluntary or involuntary, from the wedding between Henry of Navarre, the future Henry IV, and Marguerite of Valois, the sister of Charles IX. The marriage ceremony, which took place in Paris on 17 August, put into sharp focus the deep religious division that the crown was seeking to reconcile and on the subject of which the Parlement maintained its uncompromisingly anti-Huguenot stance.[60] Later, the court's attitude to the Protestant Henry of Navarre become more equivocal, culminating in the split between those magistrates who remained in Paris as supporters of the Catholic League and those who at the behest of Henry III in 1589 joined the alternative Parlement at Tours. But the fanaticism of the people of Paris, which had been revealed in the slaughter of 1572, become more rather than less virulent in succeeding years. On 12 May 1588, the Day of the Barricades, the Catholic mob once again took control, and forced Henry III to flee from his capital.[61] It has been argued that the Parlement's long-running battles with Henry III played their part in provoking that event in the same indirect way as the Parlement's earlier opposition had helped to prepare the ground for the Saint-Bartholomew's Day massacre. [62]

In the mid-seventeenth century the Parlement was once more implicated, this time far more directly, in an outburst of popular rebellion, the Fronde. This upheaval was the culmination of a further half-century of

[60] J.-L. Bourgeon, 'La fronde parlementaire à la veille de la Saint-Barthélémy', 87. The evidence is inconclusive both on the nature of the court's judicial strike and on why it failed to attend the wedding. See Kim, op. cit., 22, who emphasizes the relationship between the judges' religious stance and their constitutional opposition: citing L'Hôpital's complaint, that the Parlement's remonstrances about the edicts of pacification 'would give false encouragement to disturbers of peace, and that their resistance to royal authority rendered more difficult the enforcement of the edicts'. On the subject of the Parlement's total commitment to the Catholic cause as demonstrated in its public pronouncements it is important to note that a minority of magistrates held a different opinion. The solemn assembly of 9 June 1562, at which all the members of the court were required to swear their adherence to the Catholic faith, revealed that twenty-seven failed to do so. Their motives were mixed. By no means all of them were Huguenots though some were linked to Protestants by bonds of kinship or friendship, while others simply favoured a policy of tolerance. However, the court's official position remained unaltered, and even the opposition of one or two senior judges to the imposition of the death penalty for heresy was based upon expediency rather than principle. See Linda Taber, 'Religious Dissent within the Parlement of Paris', 685–97.

[61] Myriam Yardeni, *La Conscience nationale en France pendant les Guerres de Religion*, 201–22.

[62] Bourgeon, op. cit., 88.

tension between the crown and the court, the latter seeking to maintain the primacy of the normal judicial procedures, the former, particularly after Cardinal Richelieu's rise to power, concentrating upon the need to take extraordinary actions when the interests of the state so required. This was a quickening of the protracted struggle about how the king should exercise his role of chief justiciar in order to ensure the maintenance of a just regime. As the unique source of justice in France he was entitled both to delegate his authority (*justice déléguée*) and to reclaim it (*justice retenue*). Yet there was a convincing argument, enthusiastically propounded by the Parlement, that by circumventing the normal judicial channels the king risked weakening his own authority: 'great kings, established by God, cherished and revered by the people, . . . gladly leave their subjects the liberty and security which is most commonly found before ordinary justices.'[63] The Parlement's quarrel with the king over his employment of *justice retenue* encompassed a range of royal practices: evocations to the *Grand Conseil, lits de justice,* the use of provincial parlements to register government legislation. In the seventeenth century the Parlement faced a more sustained assault upon its powers of delegated justice, in the form of royal commissioners.

All commissioners were given complete freedom to act on the simple authority of the royal seal. Their powers were temporary, limited to specific functions, and could be revoked at the king's will. Their number and influence increased dramatically during the 1630s with the rise of the ubiquitous *intendants*, the stormtroops of the cardinal's new state service.[64] Richelieu understood how the principle of royal *justice retenue* could be applied to the policy of strengthening the power of the state without exceeding the limits of royal authority.[65] His most ambitious project in this regard was the setting up of the *Chambre de l'Arsenal,* a body consisting of fifteen commissioners, six of whom were members of the *Grand Conseil.* Their first meeting took place on 10 September 1631 when they assembled, according to the *Gazette de France*, 'for several affairs important to the state'.[66] This body was never organized as a regular court, it kept no official record, and there was no appeal against its verdicts. It was an instrument of political justice.

[63] J.H. Kitchens, 'Judicial *Commissaires* and the Parlement of Paris', 338.
[64] A. Lloyd Moote, *The Revolt of the Judges*, 44–8.
[65] Kitchens, op. cit., 331.
[66] Ibid., 335.

In an effort to counter what it perceived as an abuse of judicial authority, the Parlement in turn found itself forced to overstate its case, thereby contributing on the pattern of previous encounters, to a dangerous lurch towards confrontation. By the end of November the court had forbidden the judicial officers in the capital to obey the commissioners of the *Arsenal*; by mid-December the King's Council had annulled the Parlement's judgement and required the officers to obey the commissioners under pain of a heavy fine and loss of office. Five of the Parlement's ringleaders were suspended. The episode, and the court's resistance, came to an end when Louis XIII received a *parlementaire* deputation at Metz. This was the celebrated occasion on which he attempted to reduce the Parlement to the status of a simple law court 'established solely to judge between *maître Pierre* and *maître Jean*', adding ominously, 'I will return you to your proper role; and if you persist in your actions, I will cut your nails to the quick'.[67]

J.H. Kitchens observes that the crown and the Parlement were both willing to embrace extreme positions in the course of this dispute. Yet both were also content to see a degree of ambiguity restored as soon as possible. Richelieu's instinct was for compromise with the magistrates whenever possible, and shortly after the confrontation at Metz the cardinal successfully interceded with the king for the release of the five suspended judges. After the death of Richelieu and of Louis XIII the Parlement sought and received letters-patent revoking the powers of the *Chambre de l'Arsenal*. However, the succession of the minor king, Louis XIV, foreshadowed the emergence of renewed difficulties, more threatening to the stability of the state than any dispute since the Wars of Religion.[68]

The Fronde represented a further development of the internecine conflict at the heart of the early modern state. This conflict was caused by the tension between the ruler's twin obligations: to preside over a lawful regime and to guarantee the subjects' security. In France the king's authority was legitimized by the fundamental law of succession that identified him as the rightful heir. Any illegal action by the crown, therefore, posed as serious a threat to the established order as did that from external aggressors. It was, however, the latter threat that loomed largest in post-renaissance Europe as the rise of competing royal

[67] A. Lloyd Moote, *Louis XIII. The Just*, 229.
[68] Kitchens, op. cit., 341–3; Moote, *The Revolt of the Judges*, 41, 63.

dynasties set state against state and made the defence of frontiers the essential theme of government.[69] It was not the case that French kings and their ministers were seeking to introduce a new, absolute form of government while the Parlement strove for a constitutional balance – such a scenario is quite anachronistic. The reality owes far more to pragmatism. As warfare became more expensive and professional, the government had no alternative but to seek extra resources where it could find them, irrespective of the old legalities. The idea of the abstract state to which government and governed alike owed loyalty had not yet emerged, so that there was no clear justification for actions that were thoroughly at odds with the role of the king as chief justiciar. In addition, political decisions had to be presented in the same legal and moral terms as those governing ordinary human relations; as indeed they still are since any other justification would seem inadmissably anti-social. In the seventeenth century the effect was simply to underline the extent of the divergence from acceptable government practice.

It was fitting that the forum in which these contradictory tendencies were confronted should be the Parlement of Paris. It is true that in 'this corporation ridden society' the court had its own axe to grind, namely the need to protect that function, the dispensing of justice, which provided its members with their prestige and income.[70] Nevertheless, the Parlement was also the institution whose history and registers bore most cogent witness to the validity of traditional forms. Its members did not become revolutionaries during the Fronde. Their world view remained at one with that of the government as each side tried to come to terms with the novel concept of change.

Thus the chancellor, Séguier, sought to reassure the Parlement that neither the regent, Anne of Austria, nor her late husband, Louis XIII, had chosen to violate the law. More exactly, in the light of the Habsburg threat, they had been forced to take emergency measures to protect the country's security. Séguier added that such measures would not outlast the military conflict – not the last time that such assurances would be given by the government.[71] The Parlement responded by devising its own strategy.

[69] Hanley, *The Lit de Justice of the Kings of France*, 231–43 and 307–15, draws attention to the emphasis upon dynasticism in the mode of discourse adopted at the two *lits de justice* held in 1610 and 1643 to mark the beginning of the minorities of Henry IV and Louis XIII.

[70] Orest Ranum, *The Fronde*, 68.

[71] Moote, *The Revolt of the Judges*, 85–6. See below, 287.

At the *lit de justice* of January 1648 it deferred to the regent's will, and therefore to the king's absolute authority, by registering a number of financial edicts. However, it succeeded in maintaining its opposition to them by means of later remonstrances grudgingly accepted by the regent, which had the effect of further deferring the implementation of the unpopular legislation. With this 'halting exercise in legalism', the royal judges found a way to oppose the royal will without being accused of rebellion or treason.[72] It was a similar story when the sessions in the *Chambre Saint-Louis* were in full swing. Though the Parlement believed that it had the power to issue *arrêts* enforcing existing laws that had been evaded by the use of administrative decrees (its decision to abolish the intendencies being its most dramatic move in this area), it also accepted that some matters lay exclusively within the king's jurisdiction. These included, for example, the granting of state leases to the hated tax-farmers, and any reduction in the level of the *taille*.[73]

The point has been made that the *parlementaire* Fronde was more a rebellion in favour of corporate interests than a moderate reform movement.[74] Since the Parlement's judges were members of the greatest corporation in France they were indeed unlikely to act against their own self-interest. Their hostility towards the *intendants*, for example, owed something to their sense of grievance at the loss of appelate jurisdiction over matters that were now being judged in the final instance by these new administrative agents of the crown. Nevertheless, their actions also reflected a wider constitutional interpretation of their role, which they wisely preferred not to define too precisely. In Lloyd Moote's judgement, the reforms emanating from the *Chambre Saint-Louis* 'stemmed from complex grievances which cannot be written off as being purely selfish and calculating'.[75]

The period between the ending of the Fronde and the death of Louis XIV's chief minister, Cardinal Mazarin, in 1661 was one of continuing low-level confrontation between the government and the Parlement. Put more positively, it was a time when the court's concept of its political role came close to being realized. In financial matters, for example, it resisted a royal decree intended to devalue the coinage. This legislation was sent, in 1655, to the *Cour des Monnaies* despite the Parlement's claim that it should consider any proposed

[72] Ibid., 117.
[73] Ibid., 145–6.
[74] Richard Bonney, 'La fronde des officiers', 339.
[75] Moote, *The Revolt of the Judges*, 170.

law affecting the national interest. Plenary sessions of the court, remonstrances and a judicial strike followed, to be met by the exile of prominent *parlementaire* opponents of the act. Eventually the government climbed down and sent a new law to the Parlement. This was duly registered yet badly enforced because the magistrates remained hostile to the devaluation in principle. Their opposition encouraged the public to have nothing to do with the new coins and the government initiative foundered. This episode was characteristic of the relations between the protagonists over financial matters at this time. The Parlement was further encouraged by the government's apparent acceptance of the fact that fiscal policies aimed at meeting the demands of war should be of limited duration. It certainly increased its opposition to such extraordinary measures after the signing of the Treaty of the Pyrenees with Spain in 1659.[76]

This period also witnessed the first stirrings of the great Gallican-Jansenist dispute, which would periodically preoccupy the Parlement during the remainder of its existence. Few of the judges had any sympathy with Jansenist theology but the court as a whole was jealous of its particular right to intervene in ecclesiastical matters by means of the appeal *comme d'abus*, and of its general supervisory role as guardian of the liberties of the Gallican Church. Thus in 1653 the archbishop of Sens appealed *comme d'abus* against an anti-Jansenist papal bull, *Cum Occasione*, which condemned five propositions allegedly found in Jansen's *Augustinus*. The archbishop argued that the bull could not be law in France because it had not been approved by a council of French bishops, nor registered by the Parlement. A second bull, *Ad Sanctam* (1657), required all the French clergy to sign a Formulary of submission under pain of heresy. Although the small ginger group of Jansenists within the Parlement led the opposition, few believed that the court's hostility to registering the bull was motivated by pro-Jansenist sentiment. Even the episcopal leader of the anti-Jansenist camp, Archbishop Marca of Toulouse, remarked that 'the officials who compose [Parlement] have not lost the zeal and piety of their predecessors . . . who registered the bull against Luther'.[77] *Ad Sanctam* was finally registered at a *lit de justice* held in December 1657, at which the *Avocat-Général*, Denis Talon, emphasized the Gallican position

[76] Hamscher, op. cit., 90–6.

[77] Ibid., 114. See also the same author's 'The Parlement of Paris and the Social Interpretation of Early French Jansenism', 392–410. Our understanding of the role of the Parlement in the second half of the seventeenth century owes a great deal to the researches of Professor Hamscher.

by stating that 'the bulls against Jansen should be administered through the authority of the king, who is the arbiter in these matters'.[78]

A key factor in this quarrel with the Jansenist tendency was, and would continue to be, the appeal *comme d'abus*, one of the most potent weapons in the Parlement's armoury. Those ultramontane clerics who looked externally to Rome for guidance were most likely to be cited, and the Parlement had no inhibitions about receiving the appeals. Even the registration of *Ad Sanctam* did not resolve the matter of the Formulary since its enemies remained free to take their opposition to the Parlement. Indeed, at this time pressure was brought to bear upon Louis XIV by clerical opponents of the Jansenists, to deprive the court of its right to receive appeals *comme d'abus*. Fouquet, the king's superintendent of finance, responded by pointing out that 'the appeals *comme d'abus* . . . are a part of French tradition and . . . cannot be denied without undermining royal authority'.[79] This was a perceptive and prophetic observation.

Recent historians of Louis XIV's reign, in particular of the period of his personal rule (1661–1715) when he governed without a first minister, have detected a more settled and constructive relationship between the king and the Parlement than an earlier generation of scholars, preoccupied with the rise of absolutism, would allow. The rapport between the Parlement and the King's Council is a case in point. Disputes between the Parlement and the Privy Council (that section of the King's Council responsible for evoking disputed legislation to another court, or for nullifying judgements pronounced in the Parlement or in other sovereign courts) had been commonplace before and immediately after the Fronde. Such disputes concerned controversial issues like extraordinary royal taxation and the work of the provincial *intendants*. When Louis XIV took over the reins of power he set about removing that particular source of irritation. Further research is required if we are fully to understand the reasons for the reconciliation between the king and his Parlement but undoubtedly the example of cooperation and goodwill emanating from the royal Council had its effect upon the court's judges.[80]

Also important were the shared interest in judicial reform of king and Parlement, the evidence that the government was 'prepared to accept the

[78] Hamscher, *The Parlement of Paris after the Fronde*, 115.

[79] Hamscher, 'The Parlement of Paris and the Social Interpretation of Early French Jansenism', 407.

[80] Albert N. Hamscher, *The Conseil Privé and the Parlements in the Age of Louis XIV*, 147–8.

hereditary transmission of posts as a fact of life', and the initial period of peace that removed the need for extraordinary revenues.[81] It was likewise significant that for the first time in generations the magistrates were dealing directly with the sovereign rather than with a regent or first minister. Most important of all, however, was Louis XIV's own sense of the need for a *via media*. Although it is undoubtedly the case that during his reign the political activity of the Parlement decreased (until the concluding years when the Gallican-Jansenist dispute was rekindled), the king nevertheless revealed a preference for working with rather than against traditional institutions like the Parlement.[82] The effect was to change the outlook of the members of the court as over time they became accustomed to a cooperative rather than a confrontational relationship with the government.

It is important in this context to revisit the celebrated legislation of 1667 and 1673, which for some historians marked the Parlement's final humiliation. Roger Mettam, who has scrutinized these royal pronouncements, offers a different interpretation. In the Civil Ordinance of 1667 Louis attempted to quicken the process whereby royal decrees were registered by the sovereign courts. If the court was accompanying the king it had six days in which to offer remonstrances before registration; if the court and the king were in separate locations the permitted time in which remonstrances would be allowed was six weeks; if, finally, the king was present in his *lit de justice* registration would be instantaneous. These provisions were accepted without demur by the Parlement. The royal letters-patent of 1673 went further in requiring registration to take place before any remonstrances could be received. However, the Dutch War had recently begun and the conventional argument, that in extraordinary times extraordinary measures were necessary, was accepted by the court. The Parlement, which had found no reason to remonstrate since 1667, did not interpret this royal act as 'a sudden return to the illegalities of Mazarin'.[83] Mettam makes a final telling point: the 1673 legislation referred only to letters-patent, leaving ordinances, edicts and declarations still subject to the time-frames indicated earlier in 1667.[84]

[81] Mettam, op. cit., 260.

[82] Hamscher, *The Conseil Privé and the Parlements in the Age of Louis XIV*, 151. See also the same author's chapter on 'Parlements and Litigants at the King's Councils during the Personal Rule of Louis XIV', 190–222.

[83] Mettam, op. cit., 267.

[84] Ibid., 266–8. Mettam goes on to argue that the legislation of 1667 and 1673 was aimed primarily against the provincial sovereign courts. For succinct definitions of the various legal forms, see G. Cabourdin and G. Viard, *Lexique Historique de la France d'Ancien Régime*.

From this time until the closing months of the reign, war or the threat of war vied for Louis XIV's attention with a series of religious battles waged against internal and external foes, notably the pope and the Jansenists. These twin preoccupations reached their climax at about the same time. On 8 September 1713, when negotiations to end the War of the Spanish Succession were taking place at Utrecht, Pope Clement XI promulgated the bull *Unigenitus*, thereby signalling 'the beginning of one of the largest and most impassioned conflicts of the ancien régime – a conflict that was to occupy a place of central importance in religious politics during much of the eighteenth century'.[85]

On the day after Louis XIV's death the Parlement of Paris regained in full measure its political influence. It owed its immediate recovery to the circumstances surrounding the king's death. The new monarch, Louis XV, was only five years old so a period of regency had to follow, and the Parlement found itself centrally placed to manouevre the duke of Orléans into the office of regent. Viewed more broadly, however, the Parlement's new-found authority owed as much to the crisis that the country faced following Louis XIV's death. This crisis had at least three elements. First, the Bourbon dynastic principle, so carefully elaborated and stage-managed by Louis XIV, was under attack.[86] Philippe of Anjou, Louis XIV's grandson, had been recognized as king of Spain at the Peace of Utrecht, but only on condition that he renounced his claim to the French throne. Yet by the time of Louis XV's accession Philippe was, according to French fundamental law, the next in line to succeed, should the minor king not survive. Few in France believed that in that event Philippe would not seek to claim his inheritance. The second element of the crisis was financial. After decades of war France faced financial disaster in 1715. The War of the Spanish Succession in particular had finally laid bare the total inadequacy of the French dynastic state to support the costs of a world-wide conflict. Its unsophisticated procedures for raising revenue belonged to a Europe of competing princes, not of rival national interests. The third part of the crisis concerned the peace of the Church, which had once more been sundered, this time by the bull *Unigenitus*. The issue of Jansenism, with which the bull sought to grapple, had ramifications that went far

[85] B. Robert Kreiser, *Miracles, Convulsions and Ecclesiastical Politics in Early Eighteenth-Century Paris*, 15.

[86] Hanley, *The Lit de Justice of the Kings of France*, 330–2; Herbert H. Rowen, *The King's State*, 75–121; Peter Burke, *The Fabrication of Louis XIV*, *passim*.

beyond the matter of a theological dispute; in threatening the prestige and authority of the French Church and state it added another voice to those already questioning the nature and extent of royal government.[87]

Indeed, the regent and the Parlement faced a fourth crisis compounded of these three and of other elements too. It would be a mistake to compare the minority of Louis XV with that of his great-grandfather, Louis XIV, because in the seventy years separating the two periods the power of central government had continued to develop in a way likely to provoke hostility once the dominant figure of the king himself had disappeared. The power of the state was concentrated increasingly upon the waging and financing of war.[88] Yet that very focus was guaranteed to reveal how ill-matched Louis XIV's ambitions seemed to the culture of the state over which he presided. The increasing demands made by French kings on their subjects were only justified traditionally by the need to restore or preserve the security of the realm. Gradually, however, these demands came to assume a greater control over the country's resources than could be justified in a dynastic system. Richard Bonney puts the matter thus: 'The political system could be justified in terms of the need for supreme national effort and sacrifice. . . . But what of the system after 1672, 1688, or 1702? . . . The argument of "necessity" and the need for domestic sacrifice must have appeared threadbare by the last years of Louis XIV's personal rule.'[89] A similar contemporary observation was made by Archbishop Fénelon: 'Have you carefully examined whether your people needed war in which you have become involved? It may only have concerned some claim to a succession affecting you personally; your people may have had no real interest in it.'[90] In fact, Louis's foreign policy was not limited to self-glorifying personal projects. Matters of European security were at stake, but the discourse of the time required him to negotiate and act in the language of dynasticism, thereby drawing further attention to the discrepancy between action and its justification. This discrepancy provoked a variety of responses during the regency of the duke of Orléans. All these responses demonstrated the need to tether French monarchical authority to clear principles, though there was little

[87] J.H. Shennan, *Philippe, Duke of Orléans: Regent of France*, 21 et seq.
[88] Hamscher, *The Conseil Privé and the Parlements in the Age of Louis XIV*, 151.
[89] Richard Bonney, *Political Change in France under Richelieu and Mazarin*, 451.
[90] Quoted in Shennan, *Liberty and Order in Early Modern Europe*, 25.

agreement over what these principles should be. Prominent among the competing voices was that of the Parlement of Paris.

The regency opened with a dramatic escalation of the *affaire du bonnet.* This dispute had its roots in the mid-seventeenth century. It appeared only to concern a number of quarrels over precedence between the presidents of the Parlement and the peers who joined the king in the *Grand' Chambre* for *lits de justice* and other state occasions. In fact it was the outward sign of an incipient constitutional struggle reflecting the views of Fénelon and other members of the entourage of Louis XIV's late grandson, the duke of Burgundy, in favour of the political restoration of the old nobility.[91] The Parlement, which represented the institutional vanguard of the *noblesse de robe,* had no intention of allowing the peers to further their ambitions. On 2 September 1715, therefore, when the duke of Orléans was proclaimed regent in the Parlement, the votes of the peers were ignored on the grounds that they had not observed the correct procedure over the *bonnet.* Nor did the court's record include the traditional formula indicating the peers' presence on such occasions: '*la cour suffisamment garnie des pairs*'.[92] The appointment of the regent was an affair of the highest constitutional and political significance, and in seeking to maximize its own role the Parlement was also depriving the peerage of any formal standing in the matter. There followed a flurry of memoranda as the peers tried to persuade Orléans that they alone had the right to judge such public affairs in the Parlement, the magistrates only deriving their right to speak from the presence of the peers. The Parlement and members of the non-peerage nobility responded by arguing in favour of the legal equality of all the members of the second estate, whether robe or sword. Orléans finally acted in favour of the Parlement by issuing a declaration in May 1716 that imposed silence upon the dispute until after the king's majority.

No sooner had that particular argument ceased than another erupted, the *affaire des princes.*[93] The protagonists in this squabble were on one side the Condé princes of the blood, led by the duke de Bourbon, and on the other the dukes du Maine and de Toulouse, illegitimate sons of Louis XIV whom the old king, fearful of a dynastic crisis, had declared eligible to succeed to the throne with the quality of princes of the blood. The affair

[91] Harold A. Ellis, *Boulainvilliers and the French Monarchy,* 58–64. See also Nannerl O. Keohane, *Philosophy and the State in France,* 332–46.

[92] Ellis, op. cit., 123.

[93] Ibid., 170–7.

began in August 1716 with a petition from the Condé princes which immediately raised the issue of French fundamental law, that contract with the French nation which guaranteed the line of succession and which, they argued, Louis XIV had violated. Part of the royal bastards' response was to appeal to the Estates-General as arbiter. In fact, it was the Parlement of Paris that came closest to playing that role, for in June 1717 Maine and Toulouse brought their protestation before the court. The Parlement voted not to accept it and several weeks later registered the regent's edict depriving them of their right to succeed to the throne. In the course of this registration the first president made the point that the Parlement was the only court competent to discuss great matters of state.

In both these episodes the various adversaries appealed to a limited Parisian public opinion by printing and circulating their petitions and memoranda. The audience was small but the subject matter – who had the right to speak for the nation on such fundamental issues as the royal succession and the appointment of a regent – was potentially damaging to royal authority. The question of public opinion has attracted a good deal of scholarly attention in recent years, much of it inspired by the seminal work of the German sociologist Jurgen Habermas. His interest, however, was in a public that critically debated political issues, a development which Habermas believed only began to happen in France during the second half of the eighteenth century.[94] Yet long before then, stimulated by the growth of printed material, appeals to an inchoate and fractured public opinion had started to appear in order to countenance or oppose the threat of despotic government. Joseph Klaits has demonstrated how Louis XIV's minister, Torcy, skilfully used propaganda techniques to justify French foreign policy during the closing years of the reign. Thomas E. Kaiser has concentrated on two figures at work during the succeeding regency, the *abbé* de Saint-Pierre and the financier John Law, in order to explore the dilemma of how to recruit public support for the despotic power of the state.[95] Behind these examples loomed the question of the nation's welfare, of how and by what agency it should be safeguarded.

With its longstanding political claims, the Parlement of Paris was particularly well placed to play a leading role in this developing debate, for

[94] Jurgen Habermas, *The Structural Transformation of the Public Sphere*, 67.

[95] Joseph Klaits, *Printed Propaganda under Louis XIV*, *passim*; Thomas E. Kaiser, 'The *Abbé* de Saint-Pierre, Public Opinion, and the Reconstitution of the French Monarchy', 618–43; 'Money, Despotism, and Public Opinion in Early Eighteenth-Century France: John Law and the Debate on Royal Credit', 1–28.

eighteenth-century France remained very much a judicial society in which 'the experiences of the law courts were central to the way in which political action was conceptualized'.[96] The Parlement's clash with John Law provided an early opportunity for assessing what middle ground remained between the concept of the absolute power of the state and the traditionally accepted limitations upon government action. Law hoped originally to carry an ill-defined public with him on the basis of enlightened self-interest, especially in that area where public confidence was most needed – support for credit in the form of paper money. However, he was gradually forced by events to the position of defending despotic authority in the imposition of his 'system'. 'It is this despotic authority', he wrote, 'which is so much feared by individual enterprises opposed to the real or apparent good of the State, but which becomes such a strong and powerful support for a public affair that cannot be hurt without undermining all parts of the State.'[97] Before these extreme views were expressed, the Parlement had already fallen out with Law during 1718 over a decision to devalue the coinage. In their remonstrances the magistrates argued that French kings had only ever changed the value of money after acquiring the nation's support following the necessary consultation. They also made clear their belief that at this time the Parlement provided the only channel of communication with the people.[98] They were ultimately to lose their battle with Law but during the summer of 1718 they demonstrated, as they had done earlier over the *affaire du bonnet*, their awareness of a public to be persuaded to their point of view. On 20 June, when all the Parlement's chambers were assembled in plenary session, the First President had to block a proposal that the court's recent representations to the regent and his response should be printed and distributed. At the same time magistrates' individual speeches were being spread anonymously among the populace. Then the court approved a judgement forbidding the distribution and circulation of the newly devalued money. This decree was posted in the Great Hall of the *Palais de Justice* where it attracted much attention as many came to read and copy it. Finally, having been summoned on 26 August to a *lit de justice* at the Tuileries Palace where Law's victory was to be given formal expression, the members of the

[96] David A. Bell, 'The "Public Sphere", the State, and the World of Law in Eighteenth Century France', 933.

[97] Quoted in Kaiser, 'Money, Despotism, and Public Opinion in Early Eighteenth-Century France: John Law and the Debate on Royal Credit', 18.

[98] Ibid., 13.

Parlement sought to arouse the sympathy of the public by solemnly processing to their destination via a circuitous route through the capital.[99]

John Law's 'system' finally collapsed in 1720, the year in which the Parlement registered a compromise declaration on the subject of *Unigenitus*. During the subsequent decade the Jansenist problem did not trouble relations between the Parlement and the government. In March 1730, however, the First Minister, Cardinal Fleury, used the mechanism of a *lit de justice* to enforce the registration of a new declaration that pronounced Unigenitus to be a dogmatic judgement of the Universal Church and a law of the French Church and state. This decision provoked such discord that it is worth reflecting on each side's motivation. Writing in 1970 Jean Egret stressed the cardinal's longstanding hostility to the Jansenists less on the grounds of their alleged heresy than of their threat to the king's authority. For Fleury, support for *Unigenitus* was a matter of state security. Despite the opposition of the Parlement therefore, Fleury '*attaquait méthodiquement et inlassablement les adversaires de la Bulle*'.[100] More recently, Peter Campbell has published an important volume dealing with *ancien régime* politics in the age of Fleury, which casts new light upon the *parlementaire* battles of those years. He does not dispute the proposition that Fleury viewed Jansenism as a threat to royal authority, but he denies that the 1730 declaration represented an extreme departure from earlier policy. Rather was it part of a war of attrition that had been waged successfully since 1720.[101] Campbell notes a degree of flexibility in the cardinal's willingness to permit a certain lack of clarity over the bull's status, avoiding the phrase 'rule of faith', which would have made *Unigenitus* binding upon all the faithful. But he also insists that Fleury had no illusions about the likely hostility of the *parlementaire* response.[102] Why then did he act as he did, and why was the court's reaction so violent?

It is important not to underestimate the high level of emotion aroused by *Unigenitus*. For its enemies it was both legally and doctrinally a discredited document, yet one that was being used as an instrument of persecution by its supporters. Shortly before the publication of the 1730 Declaration, apocalyptic scenes at the Parisian cemetery of Saint-Médard

[99] A full account of these events is to be found in the *Archives Nationales, Série* U416 Section 30, f.3, and in the printed *Gazette de la Régence*.

[100] Jean Egret, *Louis XV et l'Opposition Parlementaire*, 31.

[101] Peter R. Campbell, *Power and Politics in Old Regime France*, 241.

[102] Ibid., 245. See the comment on 'rule of faith' in John Rogister, *Louis XV and the Parlement of Paris*, 53.

confirmed the Jansenist party's potential for provoking instability and disorder.[103] In identifying the members of the *parti janséniste* in the Parlement and analysing their role during this crisis, Dr Campbell has added significantly to our understanding of events. This was a small group of some fourteen magistrates who almost invariably took the lead in debate, avoiding reference to specifically religious matters but seizing upon the broader issues, free speech for the Parlement, the threat of evocation, the crucial importance of the appeal *comme d'abus* (which Fleury's declaration had prohibited in matters concerning *Unigenitus*). They were helped on occasion by the ministry's ill-judged responses: the use of *lettres de cachet* to prevent debate, for example, and the refusal to allow plenary sessions of the chambers to discuss matters arising from the bull were actions bound to foster *parlementaire* solidarity.[104] Campbell also points to other determinants of the Parlement's relationship with government in the crisis of 1730–2, which are not revealed in the formal records: the headstrong attitude of members of the chambers of *Enquêtes*; the First President's inability to provide a strong steer on behalf of the ministry; the organization of a pro-government group within the court. He summarizes the situation as one typical of *ancien régime* politics: 'apparent confrontation mitigated by clandestine manoeuvres'.[105] The overarching conclusion of Campbell's analysis is that Fleury's policy embraced a rejection of Gallicanism, something that the Parlement with its particular legal tradition could never accept.[106] It is possible to extend that conclusion further and to argue that reason of state imposed its own obligations that were not subject to traditional limitations.

In the second half of the eighteenth century the conflict between the crown and the Parlement intensified. The subjects under dispute did not change nor did the protagonists' rules of engagement, but the discourse began to acquire a new edge and gradually the magistrates became more self-confident as the crown became increasingly the prisoner of faction. The attitude of Louis XV himself provides the key to the changing relationship. After Fleury's death in 1743 the king resisted appointing another first minister. Thereafter, he presided over a divided Council in

[103] Kreiser, op. cit., *passim*.

[104] Campbell, op. cit., 249–53. See also his Appendix 2: 'The identity of the magistrates in the *parti janséniste*'.

[105] Ibid., 264.

[106] Ibid., 257.

which rival groups vied for power and government policy became the predilection of those temporarily in the ascendant. Another important change also took place. Louis began to appoint as secretaries of state in the major ministries representatives of the old sword aristocracy. The effect of this shift was to underline the personal nature of Louis's government, thereby making it immediately vulnerable to accusations of despotism; whereas the growth of a state machine guided by a single hand had previously helped to justify arguments based upon reason of state.[107]

Julian Swann has made a number of significant contributions to our understanding of the Parlement's history during the third quarter of the eighteenth century. He also identifies a small number of Jansenist magistrates active in the Parlement in the mid-1750s, who led the court's opposition in the interminable arguments over *Unigenitus* and the limits of episcopal authority; and like Campbell, he observes their ability 'to camouflage their Jansenism by generous use of judicial maxims and historical precedent'.[108] They were greatly assisted by the policy of the new archbishop of Paris, Christophe de Beaumont, who was appointed in 1747. He forbade the administration of the sacraments to those who were unable to prove their unequivocal acceptance of *Unigenitus*. The effect of this policy was to raise the level of conflict between the Parlement and the spiritual powers to a new level. The Parlement's interpretation was that refusal of the sacraments was likely to produce a situation in which 'the safety and tranquility of the public are violated or concerned'.[109] This would make the matter a *cas royal* and subject exclusively to lay jurisdiction. Paris was filled with contradictory judgements emanating from the Parlement and the King's Council, the first prosecuting pro-*Unigenitus* clergy, the second annulling these prosecutions. Pamphlets and printed *parlementaire* remonstrances raised the emotional temperature further.[110]

When the king rejected the Grand Remonstrances the Parlement went on strike and its members were then sent into exile for some fifteen

[107] Julian Swann, *Politics and the Parlement of Paris under Louis XV*, 46–52.

[108] Ibid., 103. It should be noted that Rogister, op. cit., 18–21, 176, disputes the significance of the part played by a small Jansenist ginger group in influencing the court's decisions. Although he acknowledges that the events leading up to the Grand Remonstrances of 1753 support such an interpretation, he regards them as wholly exceptional.

[109] Cited in Roland E. Mousnier, *The Institutions of France under the Absolute Monarchy*, I, 506. See also Rogister, op. cit., 142.

[110] Dale Van Kley, *The Damiens Affair and the Unraveling of the Ancien Régime*, 112–15. See also the same author's *The Jansenists and the Expulsion of the Jesuits from France*, 50–6.

months. Upon their return they registered a royal declaration in September 1754 imposing silence upon the religious controversy. However, the zealots on both sides were not interested in compromise. Two months later a Jansenist magistrate denounced a new case of refusal of the sacraments. The court sought the archbishop's cooperation only to be advised by Beaumont to cease meddling in ecclesiastical affairs.[111] Once more the Parlement was embroiled in a high-profile public dispute in which it again played its traditional anti-despotic role. As usual the king found himself uncomfortably in the middle. Eventually he had recourse to the pope, Benedict XIV – in the light of the history of *Unigenitus* not the most promising way of ending the dispute – who produced an encyclical, *Ex omnibus* (October 1756), which two months later formed the basis of a royal declaration. This declaration, registered at a *lit de justice* in December, limited refusal of the sacrements to juridically convicted opponents of *Unigenitus* and, significantly, still resisted declaring the bull a rule of faith. Unfortunately for the magistrates, it was accompanied by another declaration that was intended to curtail the Parlement's freedom of action in such matters as the time governing the presentation of remonstrances, and the procedures to be followed when plenary sessions of the court were convened. As a result all the members of the *Enquêtes* and *Requêtes*, and a substantial number of *Grand' Chambriers* resigned and a further protracted period of legal warfare ensued.

It is tempting to depict this period of the 1750s as marking a decisive moment in the Parlement's relations with the crown as its criticisms developed into a constitutional programme. Certainly the spirited *parti janséniste* regularly took advantage of the king's indecision and of the competing ministerial factions (each with its supporters in the Parlement), to goad the court into producing outspoken remonstrances that were duly printed and read by an excited Parisian public.[112] The Jansenist lawyer Adrien Le Paige was a particularly fertile source of constitutional ideas, notably of the so-called *union des classes*, according to which all the parlements in the kingdom formed part '*d'un seul et unique Parlement, les divers membres d'un seul et unique Corps*'.[113] Such an idea

[111] Swann, op. cit., 101–2.

[112] Julian Swann, 'Parlement, Politics and the *Parti Janséniste*: the *Grand Conseil* Affair', 435–61, demonstrates this process convincingly in his discussion of the Parlement's juridictional quarrel with an old rival.

[113] Remonstrances of the Parlement of Paris, August 1756, quoted in Egret, *Louis XV et l'Opposition Parlementaire*, 76.

pointed towards a national assembly and indeed a handful of Jansenist *parlementaires* began to invoke the name of the Estates-General.[114]

Yet the Parlement as an institution had not shifted its position so dramatically. A very small group of rabid Jansenists, perhaps persuaded of the significance of their words by their own notoriety, appeared intent on opposition whatever the issue.[115] But at the core of the court's argument with the crown was the traditional defence of its role as the guardian of political legality. The fierceness of its dispute with the *Grand Conseil* reflected the Parlement's fear of displacement from that key role. In the matter of *Unigenitus* it had pursued a consistent and justifiable policy in terms of its own legal history. It was not difficult by contrast to portray the crown's tergiversations as arbitrary and the bishops' attitude to the bull's opponents as despotic. However, although the Parlement's political stance had not changed, its arguments were inevitably couched in the most compelling language of the day. From the mid-century it started to develop an ambiguous vocabulary: 'nation', 'citizen', 'society'. Even words like 'men' and 'liberty' began to encompass the idea of individual rights.[116] Yet this tendency to suggest new meanings for old words lacked all precision. The Parlement was simply more assured in pushing its case because since Fleury's death in 1743 its adversary had become less formidable. It tasted success too, in September 1757, when the king agreed to suspend his proposed restrictions on *parlementaire* procedures, and allowed the court to interpret the 1756 declaration on *Unigenitus* in accordance with its Gallican tradition. The magistrates responded by adopting a less confrontational stance vis-à-vis the crown, not pushing to the limit every reported case of refusal of the sacraments.[117]

In financial matters too, the Parlement's opposition to government policy was relatively restrained and followed predictable lines. In 1749 a new universal income tax, the *vingtième*, was established. Although this imposition was to be levied in peacetime the Parlement made surprisingly few objections. However, when the Seven Years War broke out in 1756 a second *vingtième* was introduced and the first was extended for ten years after the end of the war. It was the indefinite

[114] Van Kley, *The Damiens Affair and the Unraveling of the Ancien Régime*, 194.
[115] Swann, *Politics and the Parlement of Paris under Louis XV*, 168–9.
[116] J.H. Shennan, 'The Political Vocabulary of the Parlement of Paris', 957–64; Jeffrey Merrick, 'Subjects and Citizens in the Remonstrances of the Parlement of Paris', 453–60.
[117] Van Kley, *The Damiens Affair and the Unraveling of the Ancien Régime*, 155–6.

nature of this taxation that the Parlement found unacceptable. The magistrates had long acknowledged the crown's need for additional revenue in exceptional circumstances, including times of war, but they rightly feared that such temporary measures could easily become permanent.[118] In 1760 an edict announcing a third *vingtième* was sent for registration in the Parlement. This provoked one magistrate to draw a dangerous analogy with the English parliament, which only voted supplies for a year at a time. Although the Parlement did not pursue this line of argument directly, it did request the king to limit his legislation to the year 1760. However, it did not push its opposition to the limit and the legislation was duly registered in its original form. Julian Swann makes the important point that had the Parlement been intent on waging an ideological war with the monarchy it would not have waived this classic opportunity to challenge the king's absolute authority.[119] Instead, it worked to persuade the government to set chronological limits to its tax demands. In 1767, for example, the controller-general of finance, L'Averdy, proposed an extension of four years to the second *vingtième* in the hope that the Parlement would accept three; its counter-proposal was two, which L'Averdy accepted. Significantly, it was only after the dissolution of the Parlement in 1771 that L'Averdy's successor, the *abbé* Terray, was able to make the first *vingtième* permanent and extend the second by a further ten years. That may have been an indication of the ultimately fatal incapacity of the *ancien régime* to provide for the needs of a modern state. Yet it also draws attention to the centrality of the Parlement's role in seeking to maintain the integrity of *ancien régime* government. Swann characterizes the situation admirably: '*Le Parlement n'empêcha jamais le gouvernement de percevoir ses impositions, mais il força au moins les ministres à justifier leurs actions. Il n'y avait aucune autre institution en France au dix-huitième siècle capable de remplir ce rôle, manifestement important et quelquefois constructif.*'[120]

Nevertheless, the decisive conflict leading to the Maupeou reforms of 1771 and the virtual dissolution of the Parlement did have a financial issue at its root. After the expulsion of the Jesuit order in 1764 the Jansenist magistrates no longer had a crusading role to play. As Van Kley observes, Jansenists having defined themselves in terms of

[118] Swann, *Politics and the Parlement of Paris under Louis XV*, 161.
[119] Julian Swann, 'Le parlement de Paris et la réforme financière', 333.
[120] Ibid., 346.

their opposition to the Jesuits had now defined themselves out of existence.[121] Yet one of their more seductive political ideas, that of the union of classes, remained to trouble the government.[122]

The Brittany Affair proper began (April 1765) with the suspension by the Parlement of Rennes of a royal declaration raising an additional two *sous* per *livre* in the province. The King's Council quashed the suspension and most of the Breton magistrates resigned on the grounds that the Council decision signalled '*la volonté de régner par la force*'.[123] Relations deteriorated rapidly thereafter. Six of the opposition leaders in the Rennes Parlement were arrested, including the *Procureur-Général*, La Chalotais, and accused of conspiracy, and the resignations of the remainder were accepted. A royal commission was set up to exercise justice until a new Parlement of Brittany was established.

Up to this point the Parlement of Paris had remained relatively aloof from this dispute. Although the court had given its support to the concept of the union of classes, which provided a justification for one parlement to support another, it remained jealous of its unique position as the court of peers, which set it apart from all the other parlements of France.[124] However, what the Parisian judges were now observing was the removal from office of virtually the whole membership of a parlement and the setting up of a royal commission to try the accused magistrates. Later the crown added to the Parlement's fury by evoking the trial of the Breton magistrates to the King's Council. The danger signals for judges in any of the sovereign courts were clear and in this instance 'the crown displayed signs of ruthlessness and contempt for legal forms that, for once, really did appear despotic'.[125]

Eventually, in December 1766, under severe financial pressure the king dropped the proceedings against La Chalotais and his colleagues. There were other examples, however, of the government's increasingly arbitrary response to *parlementaire* criticisms of its financial policies. In 1759 thirty members of the Parlement of Besançon were exiled to frontier fortresses for almost three years because they had opposed certain fiscal edicts that subverted the liberties

[121] Van Kley, *The Jansenists and the Expulsion of the Jesuits from France*, 228.

[122] Note too the continued high-profile role of Jansenist magistrates in apparently non-religious disputes like the Brittany Affair, Swann, *Politics and the Parlement of Paris under Louis XV*, 298, 308–11.

[123] Egret, *Louis XV et l'Opposition Parlementaire*, 161.

[124] David Hudson, 'The Parlementary Crisis of 1763', 108.

[125] Swann, *Politics and the Parlement of Paris under Louis XV*, 282.

of their province.[126] In 1763 all the members of the Parlement of Toulouse were put under house arrest for more than two months because of their unwillingness to register the legislation extending the second *vingtième*. In 1765 a number of magistrates in the Parlement of Pau resigned over a dispute with the First President on the subject of free speech. They were promptly replaced by more malleable judges and the number of judicial offices in the court was reduced by one third.[127] In this particular context it does appear that it was the crown rather than the Parlement that was threatening a radical break with the past, though its regular retreats from exposed positions indicate a pragmatic rather than an ideological approach.

This pragmatism reached its high point in the Maupeou reforms of 1771, which formed the final act of the Brittany Affair. William Doyle is surely correct in asserting that Maupeou had not planned any reform in advance.[128] His chief preoccupation was in ousting the duke de Choiseul in order to insinuate himself into the position of principal minister. Choiseul's foreign policy ambitions could not be realized without the granting of additional taxation, something that an embattled Parlement was certain to oppose. Doyle demonstrates how once again royal policy towards the Parlement was closely linked to factional disputes at the heart of government.[129] Although Maupeou's final draconian measures against the magistrates – his decision to deprive them of their offices and exile them to remote parts of the country – may have been forced upon him by the intransigence of the Parlement, there were recent precedents supporting his course of action. This was not, in other words, a watershed judgement but rather a dramatic extension of earlier policies.

Subsequently, in a propaganda war, the supporters and opponents of the Maupeou reforms fought to recruit public opinion to their point of view. In analysing these publications David Hudson detects an ideological struggle taking place, 'a dispute over what was the right form of organisation of the state, of where the supreme power was located'.[130] There were, undeniably,

[126] Julian Swann, 'Parlements and Political Crisis in France under Louis XV: the Besançon Affair', 803–28.

[127] Hudson, op. cit., 104–10; Egret, *Louis XV et l'Opposition Parlementaire*, 152–8.

[128] William Doyle, 'The Parlements of France and the Breakdown of the Old Regime', 416.

[129] Ibid., 417–22. For another, earlier example, see Swann, 'Parlement, Politics and the *Parti Janséniste*: the *Grand Conseil* Affair', 443.

[130] David Hudson, 'In Defence of Reform: French Government Propaganda during the Maupeou Crisis', 52.

significant changes introduced in 1771. The six local *conseils supérieurs*, set up in the Parlement's area of jurisdiction to judge most civil and criminal matters in the last resort, reduced the extent of the court's influence. More important, however, was the abolition of venal office in the Parlement, making it much easier for the king to remove his judges. On the other hand, the Parlement was not abolished but dramatically restructured. It retained its right of remonstrance, and when Maupeou suggested to the king that all the parlements should indeed be abolished, Louis refused on the grounds that such an action would appear despotic.[131]

That, indeed, was the basis of the propaganda campaigns waged by the two sides: was the king acting despotically by limiting the Parlement's legislative role or was he right to assert his own legislative sovereignty? There was little that was new in this debate, as Hudson readily admits, a fact that raises doubts as to whether it was genuinely ideological. Certainly the printed repetition of claims and counter-claims gave added weight to the contrasting arguments as did the uniquely strained relationship between the combatants. Yet the Parlement did not ever seriously aspire to become an English parliament, and Louis XV remained anxious to avoid the charge of despotism.[132] The problem remained that the government required more financial resources than it could traditionally justify. However, neither the king nor the Parlement was willing to accept the need for a fundamental reassessment of the old order and, paradoxically, this shared view both bound them together and set them at odds with each other. The true despotism of state necessity had yet to impose its irresistible logic; meanwhile, the petty despotism of feuding ministers was sure to provoke dissent.[133]

[131] Doyle, 'The Parlements of France and the Breakdown of the Old Regime', 426–7.

[132] Ibid., 436; Hudson, 'In Defence of Reform: French Government Propaganda during the Maupeou Crisis', 52–4. In his analysis of the *thèse royale* and the *thèse parlementaire* Durand Echeverria appears to support Hudson's view that a struggle between conflicting ideologies was taking place: *The Maupeou Revolution*, *passim*. However, his conclusion that the clash between the two produced a new synthesis leading to nineteenth-century libertarianism ignores another possibility, namely that it led to the despotism of the state. His observation that 'the new national sovereignty was more than an idea; it was at the same time a new sentiment of common nationality and of patriotism' (p. 74), certainly supports that alternative interpretation.

[133] The November 1771 edict which made the first *vingtième* perpetual and extended the second to 1781, might have formed the basis for radical government measures. Yet despite the fact that for 'the first time in years the government did not have to bargain over its financial policy', no effort was made to introduce fundamental reform. Doyle, 'The Parlements of France and the Breakdown of the Old Regime', 431.

Louis XV's death in May 1774 signalled the end of the Maupeou experiment. Although Louis XVI did not immediately recall the old Parlement, the pressure upon him to do so mounted rapidly and in August the chancellor was dismissed. In November 1774 the old Parlement's exiled members were recalled to the capital and their institution was formally restored. Doyle gives great weight to the importance of 'public opinion' in pushing the king towards this decision, though he also makes it clear that what public opinion amounted to was what the king and his ministers thought people believed to be important. Conversely, Hudson claims that the result of the propaganda war was a victory for Maupeou's supporters. On the evidence of the dramatic fall both in the number of pamphlets published between 1771 and 1774 and in the number of those arrested for selling them, as well as of the defeatist observations by some of those in the anti-Maupeou camp, Hudson concludes that 'by 1774 the public was indifferent, and there was no real demand for the recall of the old parlements'.[134] Bearing in mind the difficulties in measuring and defining 'public opinion', the two positions do not necessarily appear incompatible.[135] That view is reinforced by the evident lack of revolutionary fervour in the country. What was most sought after was a return to a more balanced and nuanced relationship between crown and Parlement, which was effective precisely because it stopped short of defining the limits of sovereignty. That very indecision, Madame d'Epinay observed acutely in 1772, '*fait partie de la constitution monarchique*'.[136]

The Parlement's conditional restoration – judicial strikes and mass resignations were prohibited – was followed by a decade of relative peace between the magistrates and the government. That situation changed in 1783 with the advent of Calonne as controller-general of finance. His appointment coincided with the conclusion of the American War of Independence, which finally bankrupted the French

[134] Ibid., 439; Hudson, 'In Defence of Reform: French Government Propaganda during the Maupeou Crisis', 76.

[135] See the important essay on this topic by Keith Michael Baker, 'Public Opinion as Political Invention', 167–99.

[136] Quoted in Doyle, 'The Parlements of France and the Breakdown of the Old Regime', 435.

state.[137] The size of the deficit transformed a chronic financial weakness into an acute crisis. The new controller-general was himself unaware in 1783 of the scale of the problem and we may assume that the Parlement was no better informed. Nevertheless, the court's remonstrances in December complained about the need for new financial expedients now that the war was over. It was still adhering to the unrealistic view that ordinary revenues should be sufficient for the government's peacetime needs. By the same token, however, the government surely needed in this critical situation to account for and justify its demands.[138] Again in 1787, in response to a proposal to extend the Stamp Tax to *parlementaires* the magistrates revealed their naiveté on the subject of government finance by expressing consternation at such a measure 'after five years of peace'. Their request on this occasion that the government's financial accounts be submitted to the court indicated as much a degree of rivalry with the Assembly of Notables, which had already received them, as any serious intention on their part to grapple with the overwhelming fiscal problems threatening to destroy the state.[139] In the last turbulent years of the Parlement's existence its official language became ever more extreme. There were echoes of Locke and Rousseau in its remonstrances, which appeared to adopt the standpoint of a public no longer made up of corporate groups but of individuals possessing inalienable rights and banded together in the equality of nationhood.[140] To protect the nation's prerogatives, especially in matters of taxation, the Parlement called for the summoning of the Estates-General. Though the court's fundamental position had not changed it did appear, finally, to glimpse, if not fully to comprehend, the momentous shift evolving at the centre of government, which would ultimately have to be faced. In referring to the French taxpayer in remonstrances of July 1787 it commented that 'those taxes which he pays to the king are a subvention which he owes only to the State . . . the Sovereign is merely the dispenser of such funds'. Here the idea was being expressed, in the words of Bailey Stone, 'that the monarch

[137] Between 1776 and 1786 the government borrowed 1,250,000,000 *livres*; normal state revenues stood at around 475,000,000 *livres* per annum. Emmanuel Le Roy Ladurie, *The Ancien Régime*, 495.

[138] Bailey Stone, *The Parlement of Paris*, 86.

[139] Bailey Stone, *The French Parlements and the Crisis of the Old Regime*, 85–7.

[140] Shennan, 'The Political Vocabulary of the Parlement of Paris', 964.

in France was unavoidably becoming little more than a distinguished servant of a dynamic and evolving master, the impersonal historic collectivity manifesting itself alternately as the "state" or as the "nation"'.[141]

The deception behind the Parlement's language was uncovered when it proposed on 25 September 1788 that the forthcoming Estates-General should be convoked and constituted according to the forms observed in 1614. Recently, the implications of that proposal have been re-examined in the broad context of the Parlement's support for the Gallican articles of 1682. These articles had justified the court's long battle against *Unigenitus* and encouraged its support for conciliar ideas of unanimity. Van Kley also points out that the magistrates' original proposal only applied to the convocation and composition of the Estates-General, the Parlement being anxious to prevent *intendants* and other government agents from exerting undue electoral influence. Only when the ministry itself raised the question of voting procedures did the court come down in favour of the traditional method by order rather than by individual; fearing that otherwise an increasingly despotic government would manipulate a tractable Third Estate and pursue a policy of 'divide and rule'.[142] This gloss upon the Parlement's fateful proposal does not in any way diminish the essential irrelevance of the court's position. It does, however, provide a further insight into why the Parlement acted as it did, in Mousnier's phrase consummating its political suicide,[143] and it supports Doyle's view that by this time the Parlement could do no more than act defensively against a government which did not wish to appear despotic but whose power nevertheless did seem irresistible.[144]

In its final months the Parlement held on to its vision of the natural order of things and to the terms of reference dictated by its own history. It is anachronistic to accuse its judges of an excessive regard

[141] Stone, *The French Parlements and the Crisis of the Old Regime*, 92–3.

[142] Dale Van Kley, 'The Estates-General as Ecumenical Council', 21–47.

[143] Mousnier, op. cit., II, 667.

[144] Doyle, 'The Parlements of France and the Breakdown of the Old Regime', 457–8, argues strongly that the Parlement's call for the summoning of the Estates-General was in recognition of its own inability to keep government policies in check any longer. Conversely, John Hardman, *French Politics 1774–1789*, 230, maintains that the court's call for the 'forms of 1614' was deliberately obstructive, indicative of its regret at having previously supported the summoning of the Estates-General.

for privilege and exclusiveness, or of a preoccupation with the *status quo*, for inequality was the dynamo of the *ancien régime*, and courts of law are inherently unlikely to breed revolutionaries. As from a craft drifting on the calm surface of water towards the precipice-edge, the Parlement's prospect appeared familiar and unchanging. Downstream, however, out of the tumult of the Revolution, a novel political order would shortly emerge. It would be based upon the ideology of patriotism, the unswerving commitment of all the citizens to the secular state, which itself would be the judge of their loyalty. There would be no place in this new world for the Parlement of Paris.

THE PARLEMENT OF PARIS

Introduction

Until the thirteenth century, the king, aided by his advisers, personally handled all aspects of French government. Moving about his realm from one royal residence to the next, he dealt with problems of justice, economy and administration as they arose. But as the monarchy became more powerful, the need for a more efficient centralized government became apparent and by the middle of the long reign of St Louis (Louis IX, 1226–70) the growing complexity of government had brought about substantial changes in the structure of the King's Court. Justice, for example, was no longer a simple matter of deciding the guilt or innocence of the accused; it was becoming a specialized field with its own forms of procedure, requiring expert knowledge. The king himself therefore was no longer equipped to dispense justice adequately. As a result, by the end of the thirteenth century a new organism had come into existence in France concerned with the administration of justice and called the Parlement. It was permanently installed in Paris in a royal residence which the king soon afterwards vacated. The present Palais de Justice in the French capital stands on the same site as the original home of the Parlement and, indeed, it is still possible to find there traces of that palace, dating from the early fourteenth century.

From its inception, then, the French Parlement was a judicial court, staffed by men learned in the law, whose duty was to dispense justice in the king's name and on his behalf. Like the English Parliament, however, it also played an outstanding public role in succeeding centuries and it is no exaggeration to assert that it is impossible fully to comprehend the role of the French monarchy before the revolution without taking into account the Parlement's political activities. But, unlike the English Parliament or the Spanish *Cortes*, the French institution was never a representative body. On the contrary, most of its members eventually succeeded in purchasing their offices and preserving them hereditarily in their families. The Parlement's influence in political affairs sprang from its judicial role, and in particular, though not exclusively, from its right to remonstrate. One of the duties of the Parlement was to record royal enactments in its registers. By means of this practice the king was able to publicize his orders and at the same time keep a record of his legislative acts. Though registration was a formality at first, in a short time a convention was established whereby the magistrates were permitted to point out to the ruler any objections that they had against legislation sent to the court. These objections might be that the legislation in question would injure the rights of individuals or groups, harm the king's own interests or clash with previous royal enactments already transcribed on to the Parlement's registers. The remonstrances were transmitted to the sovereign with whom the final decision lay.

Thus the political and judicial roles of this supreme court of appeal were of common origin, both dependent upon a concept of government in which the emphasis lay upon the king's obligation to rule his kingdom as its supreme judge. Throughout its history the Parlement's pre-eminent task was to enforce the law, not only in the interests of the sovereign, but in the interests of all those who could claim the law's support. As the monarchy became more powerful, the Parlement became the chief institutional opponent of royal arbitrariness and its attitude provoked a number of conflicts, of which the Fronde of 1648–9 is perhaps the best known and the most violent.

Though the Parlement's political role provides the most spectacular episodes in its history, its judicial contribution was also formidable. It drew together the various elements in the French legal heritage, canon, Roman and customary law, it built up a corpus of jurisprudence and it established a formal legal routine and procedure. All these achievements greatly contributed to the unity and stability of the country. Its history, therefore, is as much bound up with the development of the appeal, the procedure of *enquête*, the system of proofs, the use of judicial torture, as with its political battles.

In addition, because judicial institutions were also considered to be actively responsible for the preservation of law and order, the Parlement possessed extensive police powers which included the right to censor publications and theatrical performances, to supervise education and to exercise administrative authority over a wide variety of matters, especially in Paris, but also farther afield.

The Parlement's existence stretched from the days of St Louis to the Revolution. So great was its importance and so wide the variety of its activities that its most recent historian has claimed that its history constitutes little less than the history of France itself.[1] Yet, in pursuing this history, it is the essential unity of the Parlement's role, reflecting the judicial nature of French monarchic authority, which should be emphasized. With that proviso, it is possible – indeed, for the sake of clarity, it is preferable – to divide this study into two sections, one dealing with the structure, competence and personnel of the court of law and the other with that court's involvement in affairs of state.

[1] J.-F. Bluche, *Les Magistrats du Parlement de Paris*, 271

Book One

THE COURT OF LAW

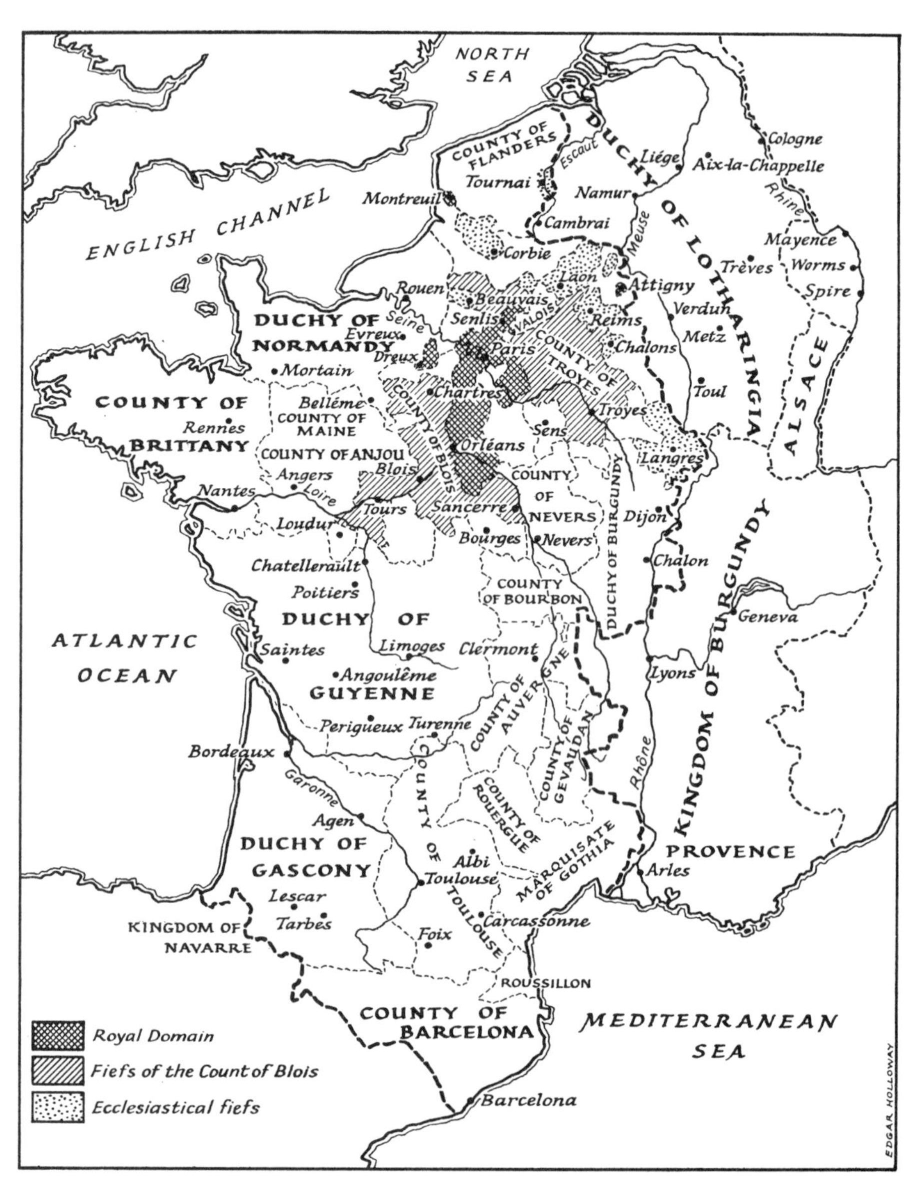

Map 1 – France at the beginning of the Eleventh century.

CHAPTER ONE

Structure and Organization

Historical background; origins of the Parlement, to 1345; the Parlement after 1345; the judicial routine; the chambers and their personnel; the *Gens du roi*; the chief clerk and the minor officers

---

After the break up of Charlemagne's empire, the forces of feudalism gripped western Europe, and great lords ruled as sovereigns in scores of fragmentary kingdoms. In the heart of what was to become the kingdom of France Hugh Capet and his successors began the slow process of re-establishing the authority of one man over a divided land. Their task was a formidable one. Originally, the domain lands over which they ruled directly as feudal lords were not extensive; they possessed territory in Picardy and Champagne, and land around and including Paris and Orléans. Surrounding them were powerful neighbours like the count of Flanders and the dukes of Aquitaine and Normandy. Seventy-nine years after Hugh Capet's election as king in 987, while the prestige of the royal house was at a low ebb, the duke of Normandy added England to his domains, thereby greatly increasing the problems of the French king and his successors. Yet the Capetians, for all their comparative territorial weakness, did possess advantages which enabled them ultimately to succeed. In the first place, they were the heirs of Charlemagne, and, as their consecration signified, the holders of a divinely bestowed office. Throughout the feudal period and beyond, this idea of divine appointment remained prominent and its effect was to add to the standing of the king, to place him apart from those who would otherwise have been his peers. This superiority was recognized in feudal terms, for he never swore fealty himself, though he was careful to receive homage from all his vassals. Thus, although he stood at the apex of the feudal system, the king derived his authority from royal as well as from merely feudal attributes and the power of the Capetian dynasty advanced along both royal and feudal lines.

The monarchy began to emerge as a strong force early in the twelfth century and Louis VI's success in curbing the terrorizing activities of unruly barons was the most striking proof of its growing prestige. Throughout that century additions were made to the royal domain, culminating in the achievement of Philip Augustus (1180–1223) who, in the years 1203–5, gained from King John of England the Angevin lands of Normandy, Maine, Anjou, Touraine, Poitou, Saintonge and Brittany. These acquisitions and preceding ones, all of them made strictly in accordance with feudal procedure, by the end of Philip's reign had given the French king a position of great prestige not only within his own kingdom but throughout western Europe. Such vast extension of the royal lands strengthened the king's claim to be considered the ruler of all France, and it was indeed during the twelfth century that the concept of France as a distinct entity with its own language first emerged and the first truly French literary masterpiece appeared, the *Chanson de Roland*. This development contributed in turn to the further consolidation of the royal house. Yet the king's chief strength remained the traditional regal qualities that distinguished him from his great vassals and of these qualities the most important was his right to dispense justice. On Hugh Capet's royal seal the figure of the king was depicted as a judge, not, as might have seemed more apposite, as a warrior. He himself stressed his responsibility to provide justice for all and to protect the rights of his subjects.[1] In support of their point of view, he and his successors maintained that the royal court was competent to judge disputes over the whole of the kingdom. In the early days of the dynasty bold claims like these could be ignored by powerful vassals, yet, significantly, they were never contradicted and ultimately, as Hugh Capet had foreseen, it was to be as the supreme judge, not as a conqueror, that the king of France would consolidate his kingdom.

The growing power and prestige of the crown was closely related to the king's increasing legislative activity. The first Capetian ordinances intended for application over the whole country date from the reign of Louis VII (1137–80) when the fortunes of the dynasty were beginning to improve, and their number steadily increased in the thirteenth century during the reigns of Louis IX and his successors.

In the Frankish kingdoms of the Merovingians and Carolingians the right to legislate had not been considered a necessary part of the royal prerogative; it was so considered with the Romans, but the concept was

[1] A. Luchaire, *Manuel des Institutions Françaises*, 461.

lost for much of the Middle Ages. In the thirteenth century the revival of the influence of Roman law contributed to the restoration of this royal attribute. Although it remained true, even during that century, that the king had to rely on the goodwill of his most powerful vassals for the implementation of his country-wide laws, the distinction between them and laws applying only to the royal domain had diminished appreciably since the reign of Philip Augustus. The increasingly centralized judicial authority which he wielded within the royal lands was particularly significant because that area already constituted a large part of the whole kingdom.

During his reign a new sort of royal official appeared, the bailiff.[1] Before his emergence, the royal lands were administered by *prévôts*, men who carried out military, financial and judicial tasks for the king in the various localities and who had succeeded, in the course of the tenth and eleventh centuries, in making their offices hereditary, a development militating against effective royal control. The office of bailiff figured prominently for the first time in the so-called 'testament' of 1190, an ordinance promulgated by Philip before he set off for the third crusade and intended to regulate the government of the country during his absence. A number of conclusions about the judicial role and importance of the new office may be drawn from this document. First of all, it is clear that the office was not being established at this date; in all the relevant clauses its prior existence is taken for granted. Its establishment, however, did not long precede Philip's reign. Next, clause seven of the testament, empowering the bailiff to dismiss the *prévôt* should he be found guilty of treason, murder or rape, demonstrates the superiority wielded by the new royal agent over the old. The king was attempting to reinforce his authority over scattered domains by a method that was to become traditional with aspiring European monarchs, namely, by employing officers who were entirely dependent upon himself for their position and therefore immune from the pressures of conflicting loyalties. The bailiff was also instructed to hold monthly assizes, so that the king's justice could be brought to all his subjects.

Two other clauses, likewise dealing with the means of dispensing royal justice, were rather more enigmatic. In the king's absence, the queen mother and the archbishop of Rheims, the king's uncle, were instructed to set aside one day every four months to pass judgment in Paris upon

[1] Y. Bongert, *Recherches sur les Cours Laïques*, 154–8; P. Viollet, *Histoire des Institutions Politiques*, III, 254–7.

suits brought to the capital from up and down the country. The bailiffs were also ordered to attend, to give accounts of their judicial stewardships during the preceding months.[1] Although the ordinance does not make it explicit, what was being indicated here was probably the elementary machinery by which appeals from the bailiffs' assizes were to be referred to the central authority of the king and his advisers for a final verdict.[2] The development of the appeal and its effect upon the king's position will be fully dealt with in a different context.[3] For the moment, the significance of these regulations should be seen in terms of the heightened centralization of royal authority by judicial means. The ordinance of 1190 marks an important milestone in this direction, certainly as far as the domain lands were concerned. Shortly afterwards, with the acquisition of the Angevin lands, the new system acquired a far wider application and as the thirteenth century progressed, the prestige of the King's Court, as the supreme court of justice, steadily grew.

Although the Capetians claimed the right to exercise justice personally, a claim based upon their succession from the Carolingian emperors, they had also to recognize the strong Germanic tradition of judgment by peers. Therefore, although the king did not sacrifice his right to dispense justice in person, it became more customary for him to judge with his court. The early history of the King's Court is obscure for the good reason that it had no sort of organization; neither its personnel nor the subject matter dealt with, or the meeting-place, was fixed. Feudal law demanded that a vassal should proffer advice to his lord if required to do so. Therefore the king was free to choose whichever of his vassals he wished, not necessarily the same ones on each occasion, taking care to select from among those who were faithful and not so powerful that they might refuse to obey the summons.

Besides the great barons, many of whom had been honoured by the king with domestic titles like butler, chamberlain or constable, prelates and less important officials of the royal household made up the membership of the royal court. They met wherever the king happened to be, for even after the emergence of Paris as the centre of the royal domains in the reign of Louis VI, the royal entourage did not at first lose its peripatetic character, and they concerned themselves equally with every aspect of government: administrative, financial and judicial. The authority

[1] F. A. Isambert (ed.), *Recueil des Anciennes Lois Françaises*, I, 177–82.
[2] F. Lot and R. Fawtier, *Histoire des Institutions Françaises*, II, 315.
[3] *See infra*, 56–8.

of the court over the whole kingdom remained tenuous so long as the king had not the power to enforce its verdicts. However, the aura of superiority that separated the monarch from his chief vassals also touched his court, enabling it to retain its prestige even when it was powerless to carry out its designs. The appeal of the barons of Aquitaine to the King's Court in 1202–3 and the subsequent successful implementation of its decision to deprive the king of England of his Angevin possessions, was a striking indication of the growing effectiveness of the French king's authority, exercised through his court.[1]

Before that date, however, changes had begun to take place in the structure of the *curia regis*. As the extent of the royal domains and the reputation of the ruler grew, the amount of business dealt with by the court increased correspondingly and also became more technical. This in turn led to a degree of specialization, particularly in judicial matters, that was observable from the time of Louis VII. The great lords, lay and ecclesiastic, had neither the time nor the inclination, or, in many cases, the capacity to deal with the complexities of written and oral evidence, the new methods of procedure that were ousting the unsatisfactory, though more straightforward judicial duel. The law, as it became more just, was becoming less intelligible to the non-specialist. In its judicial aspect, therefore, the court began to take on a dichotomous character: the great officers of the crown, the barons and prelates, continued to pronounce judgment, but the real work was increasingly undertaken by lesser members, mostly clerics, who had acquired the necessary technical legal knowledge. These men, called *magistri curiae*, formed a permanent commission, at work throughout the year and always in attendance on the king. The other members of the court tended to confine their appearances to the four great feast days of the year – Christmas, Easter, Pentecost and All Saints – when with full pomp and ceremony the decisions of the *curia regis* were made known. This was the state of affairs in 1226 when Louis IX, the future St Louis, ascended the throne.

The outstanding personal qualities of the new ruler enabled him to raise the prestige of the monarchy in France to heights previously unequalled and even to assume the role of arbiter in Europe. In many respects his long reign witnessed the consolidation of the gains achieved by Philip Augustus: certainly this was the case in the judicial domain. The king's justice, when it was administered by a man of such manifest

[1] Lot and Fawtier, op. cit., II, 297.

piety, became more widely sought after, and Louis IX answered the demand in part, in keeping with the tradition of his house, by exercising his right to judge in person. His friend, Joinville, has left a famous account of those *ad hoc* assemblies conducted by the king in the garden of his Parisian residence or under the legendary oak tree in the woods of Vincennes.[1] But at the same time, the number of plaintiffs claiming satisfaction from the *curia regis* multiplied and with the development of the judicial appeal also reaching significant proportions and producing an increasing volume of litigation, the organization of the King's Court underwent a radical change. In the course of this reign the Parlement began its independent existence.

The first surviving document to mention the word Parlement (*pallamentum*) in reference to the King's Court dates from the year 1239; 'the king travelled to Paris towards the feastday of St Michael, to hold a parlement'.[2] The word itself was not new; in France, as in England, it was used to describe a general discussion or conference and quite possibly it still retained this non-technical sense in 1239. However, within a short time, its meaning had been confined to an assembly of royal counsellors principally concerned with the administration of justice. Such assemblies were soon to crystallize into a form independent of the *curia regis*. The exact chronology of this metamorphosis is impossible to determine, for the king did not establish the Parlement by legislation. Its separation was an imperceptible process, and royal enactments that have survived from this early period demonstrate that the king did no more than regulate developments which had already taken place. An edict issued in 1253 on an appeal '*coram consiliariis domini regis Francie in pallamento Parisius*' might apply to the old arrangement or to the new. However, the appended list of judges makes it clear to what extent the legal aspects had come to dominate these sessions. On this particular occasion there were no great secular noblemen present; there were, however, five clerics, each with the title of *magister* or *maître*, signifying that they had obtained degrees in Roman and canon law, probably at one of the four universities of Orléans, Angers, Montpellier or Rheims. There were also five secular officials closely connected with the administration of justice, three bailiffs from Caen, Orléans and Etampes and the two *prévôts* of Paris. Even two of the three leading prelates present, the archbishop of Bourges and the bishop

[1] Joinville, *Histoire de Saint-Louis*, 184–5.
[2] C. V. Langlois, *Textes relatifs à l'histoire du Parlement*, 36.

of Evreux, had started their careers as *maîtres*.[1] Similar lists extant from the reign of St Louis tell the same story. It is possible to pick out the recurring names of his chief judicial advisers, clerics like Stephen de Montfort, the dean of St Aignan's Church at Orléans, and Eudes de Lorris, the dean of the cathedral at Angers; laymen like Geoffrey de la Chapelle and the celebrated jurist, Pierre de Fontaines, the bailiff of Vermandois.

Another indication of the increasing influence of the specialists and also of the growing complexity of judicial affairs is to be found in the appearance of *parlementaire* records, dating from 1254. These are the enigmatically named *Olim*, a title usually, though not entirely satisfactorily, explained as deriving from the opening word of the second book of this particular series. Of the seven original books, only four have survived and they contain pronouncements emanating from the judicial section of the *curia regis* between 1254 and 1319. Until 1298, the *Olim* consist only of brief résumés of decrees issued in response to both oral and written pleas. In the earlier period particularly, there are large gaps in the record. For the first official responsible for drawing up the *Olim*, Jean de Montluçon, did not begin his work until 1263 and his intention was not to provide a comprehensive register but to pick out what seemed to him the most important decrees contained on the *parlementaire* rolls, where the proceedings of each session were recorded. Although the first decrees in the *Olim* date from 1254, it is likely that rolls had been kept for some years before that date, the contents of which were not incorporated into Montluçon's selective record.[2] The appearance of these records, therefore, like other signs of the Parlement's imminent birth, raises almost as many queries as it solves. Although it confirms that in the reign of Louis IX the organization of the royal court was undergoing important changes, it does not give much indication of the new shape that was being formed. It was only in the following reign, that of Louis's son, Philip the Bold (1270–85), that its outline began to emerge.

In January 1278, Philip promulgated a series of regulations intended to govern the procedure of the Parlement. Though it is immediately clear from the first clause that this was not the earliest piece of legislation designed to that end, it is the first to have survived.[3] One of the significant facts to emerge from these regulations is that the Parlement apparently

[1] Ibid., 39–40.
[2] The *Olim* have been edited in four volumes by A. Beugnot; *see infra*, 75.
[3] P. Guilhiermoz, *Enquêtes et Procès*, Appendix IV, 600–10.

had ceased to accompany the king when he moved around his kingdom and had been permanently installed in Paris, in the royal palace on the Ile de la Cité. Clause eight, for example, regulating the manner in which plaintiffs were to leave the chamber after the hearing of their case – by the door into the garden – reveals that the king was thinking of his Parlement in topographical terms. In fact, between 1254 and 1302, only two of the sixty-nine sessions of the Parlement were held away from the king's Parisian residence.[1] The reference in this same clause to the *Chambre pour pledier* is the first allusion to the *Grand' Chambre*, the Parlement's central court, which for a long time retained its original title of chamber of Pleas. There every case began and there eventually it was concluded with the publication of a decree. However, while some causes could be decided immediately on the oral testimony of the opposing parties, the multiplication of appeals to the Parlement from subordinate jurisdictions and other suits involving the examination of witnesses and prolonged inquiries in the various regions where the disputes had originated, made it impossible in the majority of cases for a verdict to be reached at once.

The legislation of 1278 also alludes to the problem of who was to undertake these judicial inquiries in the provinces. This task, which had evidently been carried out in the past by members of the court, was to be taken over by new officials, the *auditeurs*. The king disliked the old arrangement because the number of judges available in the capital was thereby subject to drastic reduction. The *auditeurs* were, according to the regulation, to be not royal counsellors but local men, who were to be chosen by the bailiffs of each district and sent to the Parlement for it to make the final choice of two of them.[2] In fact, this particular regulation remained a dead letter, for the judges were unwilling to forgo the remuneration to be gained from this extra-mural duty, which, though imposing a strain upon the plaintiffs' purses, provided the judges with a very welcome supplement to the modest salary which they ordinarily received.

When the investigation was complete, the official findings were examined in the Parlement by members distinguished by the clumsy title of *regardeur-entendeurs*. These men, with 'certain other persons elected by the court', passed judgment in all cases involving written

[1] C. V. Langlois, 'Les Origines du Parlement de Paris', 103.

[2] Guilhiermoz, op. cit., 602; many commentators, including recent authorities like Lot and Fawtier, op. cit., II, 345, consider the *auditeurs* to be members of the court. However, the argument of Guilhiermoz, tending towards the opposite conclusion, seems more likely to be true.

evidence, unless the matter was considered too weighty or the parties concerned were too important, in which circumstance the decision was referred to the whole assembly, which was in any case responsible for producing the final decree. Despite a certain vagueness of language, it seems clear enough that even within the specialized court of the Parlement, additional specialization was already becoming necessary to deal with the influx of appeals and the mass of written evidence. Here in embryo was the future chamber of *Enquêtes*.

Finally, these regulations of 1278 also pointed a way to the establishment of the chamber of *Requêtes*, by stipulating that requests for justice should be considered in the Great Hall of the Palais – quite apart from the chamber of Pleas – by certain *maîtres* who would either refer them to the king if the petitioners were qualified to receive that favour or would send their decision to the bailiff who had jurisdiction over the area in which the matter had arisen. This delegation within the framework of the Parlement originated because every plaintiff had to have permission to cite the opposing party before a case could be brought to court. Thus each suit began with a request for the necessary authorization, and, as these requests became more numerous, the Parlement was forced, in the interests of efficiency, to depute at first two of its personnel to carry out this necessary preliminary.

Philip III's enactment of 1278 is of great significance, therefore, in indicating the lines along which the still inchoate court was evolving. For the first time it is possible to catch a glimpse of the Parlement's future organization, with its permanent chambers, the *Grand' Chambre*, the *Enquêtes* and the *Requêtes*. From this starting-point the gradual definition of these organs may be traced until the structure of the Parlement, in its completed form, is revealed.

Philip the Fair, who succeeded his father in 1285 and ruled until 1314, was the last great Capetian king, and his reign has been cited as the starting-point of the Parlement's independent history. Although he was responsible for a number of important ordinances relating to the court, in many respects he did no more than confirm established practice. His reign should not be allowed, therefore, to distract too much attention from the developments of preceding years. One small example illustrates the point. It has been asserted frequently that the Parlement became sedentary in Paris, after the ordinance of March 1303; yet, as already observed, it had moved from Paris only twice in the preceding half-century; in fact, it was again held out of the capital on more than one occasion after 1303.[1] What is true is that far more royal legislation throwing light upon the growth of the Parlement has survived from his reign than from the reigns of his father and grandfather, though here too a word of caution is necessary. Not all Philip's ordinances were effective, a fact which must be taken into account in any attempt at reconstructing the shape of the Parlement from these particular sources.

The first of these relevant ordinances dates from the year 1291.[2] It confirms the existence of two delegations, drawn from among the court's members, to take account of the *Enquêtes* and *Requêtes*. The distinction between those who carried out the inquiries – the *auditeurs* of 1278 – and those who passed judgment, was not repeated and this particular act gives no indication of how the task previously assigned to the *auditeurs* was to be fulfilled. However, another distinction, dimly perceived in 1278, was made more precise. A number of officials were appointed to examine the documents concerned with each investigation and then to draw up reports classifying the essential points, thereby simplifying the task of the judges. It was a measure of the complicated nature of the documents that these officers were to be allowed to take them away from the court to study in their own homes. However, the actual judging of the *Enquêtes* was to be carried out by two separate commissions, each composed of four counsellors, which were to meet every week, the first on Monday and Tuesday, the second on the following two days. The members of these commissions, each of whom was mentioned by name in the ordinance, were the successors of Philip the Bold's *regardeur-entendeurs*, while the men responsible for the preliminary reports are identifiable as the successors of those 'certain other persons elected by the court', who were mentioned in clause eighteen of the enactment of 1278; though it appears that the latter were not full members of the Parlement, since they were forbidden to enter the chamber of Pleas unless they were summoned. The ordinance of 1291 records a further stage in the development of a distinct chamber of *Enquêtes*; the eight counsellors nominated remained delegates of the court, but as a result of their special function, they acquired a greater corporate sense. As for the *Requêtes*, the king specified that three counsellors should be responsible for them, to sit, on every day that the Parlement was in session, in one corner of the great hall of the Palais, accessible to all would-be plaintiffs, surrounded by the ever-present noise and bustle of that tumultuous place. Like the judges in charge of

[1] *See supra*, 16.

[2] Langlois, *Textes*, 156–9.

enquêtes, those receiving *requêtes* were not yet members of a separate chamber.

The year of Philip the Fair's next regulative ordinance is traditionally fixed at 1296, though there is no positive proof that this date is accurate.[1] In this decree, the regulations governing the *enquêtes* took a new turn, presumably because the procedure envisaged in 1291 had not been successful. The basic problem, which had caused the commission of *enquêtes* to be established in the first place, remained that of contending with the rapidly increasing amount of litigation with which the king had to deal. The two small groups of counsellors established in 1291, intended to devote in all four days a week to judging cases involving the examination of documentary evidence, had turned out to be inadequate and they were not mentioned in this second ordinance. Instead, the king commanded that some weeks before the Parlement was convened – at this time two Parlements were supposed to be held each year – the members should assemble in Paris. After a proportion of them had been allotted special judicial tasks away from the capital, the remainder should occupy themselves with the task of working through the *enquêtes* and making their decisions before the next session began. The distinction made in 1278 between important and less important causes, was maintained. In the case of the former, although the judges could discuss the matters at issue, they could not arrive at a verdict; that had to be left to a plenary session. In more trivial cases, they could reach a decision, which had then to be communicated to, and agreed by, those members who had not been present before it was made public. At the close of each *parlementaire* session, the presidents of the court were to be made responsible for nominating those officials mentioned in earlier enactments, whose task was to facilitate the judging of *enquêtes* by extracting the significant matter from the documents concerned.

Previous legislation offers few details about these men, but this act of 1296 is a little more informative. It provided for the election, by the Parlement, of two of these officials, who would jointly sift through the mass of documents gathered in the course of the inquiries. They had to be clerics and reasonably scholarly. When dealing with matters of grave consequence, they had to co-opt at least one member of the Parlement to assist them, a fact which indicates that they themselves were still not judges, despite their onerous judicial responsibilities. Nor were those who actually carried out the investigation in the districts, the *auditeurs*, who

[1] Ibid., 161–7.

reappear in this decree, necessarily members of the court, though in fact many of them certainly were.

In attempting to provide more time for judging cases in which protracted local inquiries were involved, Philip the Fair introduced a novel procedure. But in other respects his second ordinance confirmed and consolidated developments of long standing. This was particularly the case with the *requêtes*, for from this time the chamber of *Requêtes* acquired a separate existence. The evidence is to be found in clause twenty-eight of this long enactment, ordaining that two clerics and two laymen assisted by two notaries should be appointed to hear requests. They were to have their own seal, which would be affixed to their own independent decisions. That was the significant point. In stipulating that matters which lay outside the competence of these counsellors should be dealt with by the judges in the chamber of Pleas, the king was underlining the distinction between the two groups.

The chamber of Pleas itself, or simply the Chamber, as it was more frequently called at this time, also received its share of attention. Because it constituted in itself the whole Parlement, at least until the secession of the chamber of *Requêtes*, legislation concerning it was of a more general nature than was the case with the *Enquêtes* and the *Requêtes*. The members of the Parlement were listed individually, barons, prelates, knights and clerics. A real attempt was made to define exactly who had the right to attend sessions of the Parlement, and just as this decree established the independence of the chamber of *Requêtes*, so it also demonstrated the final separation of the Parlement itself from the *curia regis*. That the two bodies were quite distinct is evident from the stipulation, contained in clause seven, that members of the King's Council should not judge in the Parlement unless they fell into one of a number of exceptional, precisely enumerated categories.

By the end of the thirteenth century, therefore, the basic shape of the law court was beginning to emerge, although there were to be many temporary aberrations in the future and several important new developments. However, the manner of judging cases requiring preliminary investigation remained a problem, for in that matter the provisions of 1296 were no more successful than earlier ones. The solution finally arrived at was the establishment of a separate chamber of *Enquêtes*, to function throughout the *parlementaire* session. The king recognized that the makeshift arrangements previously employed were inadequate to cope with the volume of work and he deputed nine counsellors, headed by two bishops, to work full-time at the *enquêtes*. The ordinance containing this list is undated, but cannot be earlier than 1307.[1] It contains, too, a list of the members of the chamber of Pleas, consisting of two prelates, two noblemen, eleven clerics and eleven laymen. This represented a fall in numbers from the minimum aggregate stipulated in 1296. However, French kings were never very successful in their efforts to control the membership of the Parlement; in fact, they were themselves frequently responsible for breaking their own enactments.

In seeking to define the Parlement's early structure, even in the broadest terms, due weight must also be given to the element of fluidity which remained characteristic of the court even at the time of Philip the Fair's death. While it had evolved its own rudimentary organization, in many respects it was still marked by the unregulated nature of its origin. Legislation affecting the Parlement had been essentially *ad hoc*, in that it was not concerned primarily with constituting a specific body, but with confirming established practices and attempting to solve new problems as they arose. It is not surprising, therefore, to find that what appear at a distance of more than six centuries to be clear-cut lines, upon closer scrutiny turn out to be extremely blurred. For a long time after the word Parlement had acquired its specialized connotation during the reign of St Louis, it referred not to a particular organization but to a type of assembly. Even as late as 1307, the king was legislating for *parlements*, not *the* Parlement. This distinction sums up all the instability of the early court and provides a salutary warning against equating the Parlement of Philip the Fair with the definitive institution of later periods.

One example of this instability may be found in the irregularity of *parlementaire* sessions. At first, while it was still an integral part of the *curia regis*, the Parlement had no routine for meeting. Generally there were three or four Parlements a year, commencing around the feasts of All Saints (1 November), the Purification of the Virgin Mary (2 February), Easter and Pentecost. These four assemblies tended to merge into each other and go on for half the year. Then in the reign of Philip the Bold the practice was introduced of holding two separate Parlements, at All Saints and Pentecost. This practice was followed, not entirely consistently, by Philip the Fair until 1291. Then war with England reduced the sessions to one a year. In his ordinance of 1296, Philip commanded that in time of war one Parlement should be held each year, commencing after the octave of All Saints and in peacetime there should be two, the second one to

[1] Ibid., 178–81.

commence after the celebration of Easter. Not until the reign of Philip V, the second son of Philip the Fair, were the sessions of the Parlement reduced to their final pattern of one a year, stretching from the beginning of November until some time in the following summer.

Nor was the personnel of the thirteenth- and early fourteenth-century Parlements as rigid as it later became. This applied not only to the non-legal element – the prelates and barons – whose attendance depended upon the importance of the cases to be judged, but also to the specialists. The long list included in the ordinance of 1296 of those dignitaries who were to retain their right to sit in the Parlement indicated that though the king may have been anxious to set an overall limit to the numbers, in the case of the former group, he was still willing to leave considerable room for variation. As for the legal experts, so long as the overriding concept of the Parlement was not institutional it was unlikely that a fixed personnel would have appeared necessary. Consequently, from the time of St Louis, the king drew up a fresh list of members each year, and while many names recurred year after year, there was no finality about the appointments. Even after the formation of the chambers of *Enquêtes* and *Requêtes*, the judges were not delegated permanently to a particular chamber. The presidents were permitted – by clause thirteen of the 1296 enactment – to allocate the judges to whatever section of the Parlement they thought fit.

In a list dating from 1313,[1] the names of those appointed by the king to judge the *enquêtes* of that year included Guillaume de Plaisien and Pierre de Blanon, both of whom had been judges in the chamber of Pleas in 1307, and in that same year the chancellor himself, Guillaume de Nogaret, who headed the clerical counsellors in the chamber of Pleas, was also nominated for a *parlementaire* commission sitting at Troyes in Champagne. In fact, by the beginning of the fourteenth century a yearly rota system had been established, not only for the chambers of the Parlement, but for other judicial commissions, too, whose members were drawn from among the royal judges. This was a step towards a more highly organized legal system, and even towards a more precisely defined personnel; nevertheless, the most striking aspect of the system remains its element of fluidity.

Yet, when that has been said, the importance of the period up to the death of Philip the Fair remains considerable in the history of the Parlement of Paris. Besides the growth of its various organs, there are a number of other developments which should be noted. It was necessary for the

[1] Ibid., 198.

Parlement to evolve some sort of hierarchy. There had to be somebody to pronounce the decrees, to lead off in the debates on cases heard in the chamber of Pleas and generally to regulate the court's activities. The first figure distinguishable in any of these respects from his fellows was Geoffrey de la Chapelle, who as far back as 1253 was deputed to pronounce a verdict reached by the judicial section of the *curia regis*. However, the most prominent of these early leading members was Renaut Barbou, the bailiff of Rouen. The regulations of 1278 empowered him to speak first and to direct the procedure of debate in the chamber of Pleas, and three years later, like Geoffrey de la Chapelle before him, he was given the task of formally pronouncing *parlementaire* decrees.[1]

By the time of Philip the Fair's enactment of 1296, the presidents had made their appearance. There were to be at least two of them present at every session of the Parlement, one prelate and one baron, out of a total list of six, three laymen and three clerics, whose duties included the supervision of the *rapporteurs*, the appointment of officials to carry out provincial investigations connected with the *enquêtes* and the distribution of duties among the judges themselves. Yet these men were neither the direct successors of Geoffrey de la Chapelle, nor the direct precursors of the First President and the presidents *à mortier* of later generations. In this, as in many other respects, this period reveals a characteristic lack of precision. Indeed, at the very time that these presidents were being appointed, Renaut Barbou was instructed to continue to pronounce the decrees and to direct the debates of the Parlement. In his absence a deputy, Jean de Montigni, was nominated to act on his behalf, and should both of them be absent, the presidents were empowered to name a third person temporarily to carry out their duties. This bifurcation was made necessary by the fact that, although the presidents, who were all important noblemen and clerics, were quite capable of supervising the ordinary running of the court, in matters of law they were forced to give place to the legal experts. It was the representatives of this group, men like Barbou and Geoffrey de la Chapelle, who were the true ancestors of the later presidential hierarchy.

Finally, the personnel of the Parlement was diminished about this time in two important respects. First of all, by the end of the thirteenth century, the bailiffs and seneschals – the latter being officials who performed duties similar to those of the bailiffs in the more recently acquired areas of the Midi – were excluded. Under St Louis and his son, bailiffs in particular

[1] Ibid., 226.

had figured prominently in the court. Renaut Barbou first came to the fore as the bailiff of Rouen, while Pierre de Fontaines, the bailiff of Vermandois, had been one of St Louis's closest legal advisers. The most notable exception was Philippe de Beaumanoir, the greatest jurist of the age, who succeeded Fontaines at Vermandois and who later became bailiff of Beauvaisis. He was never a member of the Parlement, though by virtue of his office he did attend those sessions in which matters relating to his own areas of jurisdiction were decided.

The influence of such men on the youthful court of law helped it greatly in the acquisition of legal expertise, but the benefits came to be outweighed by one clear disadvantage. In cases coming to the Parlement on appeal from the bailiwicks, the bailiff concerned was accustomed to assist the court in deciding on the validity of the appeal; in other words, he helped to pass judgment on his own verdict. The impartiality of the king's justice and the value of the appeal were endangered by the presence of these officials, and in 1291 Philip IV took the first step towards excluding them from the Parlement. In that year, they were forbidden to sit in the Parlement unless they were already members of the King's Council. In addition, even if bailiffs continued to sit in the Parlement as royal counsellors, they had to withdraw when they were themselves concerned in an action. Then in 1296 they were totally forbidden to sit as members, though the presidents could summon them for special reasons.

The other important absentee from the Parlement was the king himself. St Louis frequently presided over the judicial assemblies of his court, but by the time of Philip the Fair the king very rarely appeared, unless he wanted to bestow a mark of favour on an important plaintiff or was personally concerned in a particular issue. This did not mean that the dispensation of justice was taken out of the sovereign's hands. He remained the head of the Parlement, and if and when he chose to assume the ancient right of the Capetians to judge in person in his court, he was entitled to do so. In any case, whether he was present or not, the justice administered by the Parlement remained his justice, though Hugh Capet would no doubt have marvelled at its increasingly technical appearance. Incidentally, one result of the monarch's absence from the court was to produce a need for new officials who could take his place in regulating its activities, a contributory factor in the appearance of the presidents at the close of the thirteenth century.

Philip the Fair was succeeded by each of his three sons in turn, Louis X, Philip V and Charles IV, the last of the Capetian line. In all, their rule stretched over only thirteen years, of which the most significant in terms of the Parlement's development were those constituting the reign of Philip V (1316–22).[1] Charles the Fair was succeeded by a nephew of Philip the Fair, Philip, count of Valois, the founder of a new dynasty. His reign (1328–50) coincided with a disastrous time for France, culminating in his defeat by Edward III of England at Crécy in 1346 and the surrender of Calais to the English in the following year. Yet his tarnished reputation as a warrior was partly redeemed by his activity as a legislator. His great ordinance of March 1345, concerned with the organization of royal justice, was seen by later generations of *parlementaire* judges as the final contribution towards the permanent establishment of their court.[2] By that time, certainly, some of the fluidity of the earlier period had disappeared.

From 1318, for example, there was only one session of the Parlement each year, commencing on 12 November, the day following the feast of St Martin, and ending at an indeterminate date in the succeeding summer. It was considered fitting that the Parlement should assemble in the shadow of this feast day, on which one of the great missionaries to the Gauls was remembered, and until the end of the *ancien régime* this date was regularly adhered to, except when it fell on a Sunday, in which case the opening ceremonies were put off until the following day. Yet on the other hand the achievement of a stable membership was to take far longer, though as the Parlement acquired its own style and its own characteristics and the judges their *esprit de corps*, the need to define its personnel more closely became apparent. In June 1316, the king named twenty-nine members of the chamber of Pleas, yet by December of the same year the number had already risen to thirty-five. Three years later, an ordinance of December 1319 named only twenty-two judges, twelve laymen, eight clerics and two presidents, not including the chancellor and the abbot of Saint-Denis, whom Philip mentioned as *ex-officio* members. Finally in 1345, Philip VI of Valois nominated fifteen clerics, fifteen laymen and three presidents to constitute his chamber of Pleas. This number remained fairly constant, though not absolutely so; in particular, the number of presidents increased out of proportion to the number of counsellors. In 1715, for example, at the death of Louis XIV, there were still only thirty-three counsellors in the *Grand' Chambre* but there were nine presidents.

The growth in personnel of the *Enquêtes* and *Requêtes* cannot be traced

[1] The best account of the development of the Parlement in this reign is to be found in the work of P. Lehugeur, *Philippe le Long, Roi de France*, II, 143–213.

[2] *Ordonnances des Rois de France*, II, 219–28.

in quite so straightforward a fashion, for in their case, rising numbers led to multiplication of chambers so that by 1715 there were five chambers of *Enquêtes* and two of *Requêtes*. In some ways, though, there were signs during the first half of the fourteenth century that the *Enquêtes* in particular was acquiring a more positive identity. Originally, a distinction had been drawn between those who judged the *enquêtes* and those who prepared the written evidence for judgment, the *rapporteurs*. At Philip the Fair's death, the latter were still not members of the chamber of *Enquêtes*, but in a list of the Parlement's personnel for the year 1336 no distinction was made between them and the judges.[1] This coalescence was confirmed by the ordinance of 1345, which fixed the total complement of the *Enquêtes* at forty, without indicating any kind of discrimination.

Even more indicative of the chamber's increasing individuality was the appearance in the mid-1330s of a document, usually entitled, though not by its author, *Stilus Inquestarum* or 'Style of the chamber of *Enquêtes*'. It was written anonymously, though certainly by a member of the chamber who has been tentatively identified, and was intended to instruct newly appointed counsellors, especially in the art of reporting, but also in that of judging *enquêtes*. This document is the first indication from within the Parlement itself of a growing sense of distinctiveness. The *Stilus Inquestarum* must not be confused with the more celebrated *Stilus Parlamenti* of Guillaume du Breuil, which was composed at approximately the same time but was written by a barrister who practised before the Parlement, and was for the benefit of his professional colleagues. Yet it too illustrates the increasing rigidity of procedure in the court, though because of its particular point of view, its concern is only with the barristers' forum, the chamber of Pleas.[2]

As this hardening in routine progressed, the king also found it necessary to regulate the conduct of the judges themselves. In 1318 Philip V stipulated that, once members had taken their places, they were to occupy themselves solely with the business of the court and not hinder its dispatch by embarking upon private consultations within the chamber or outside it. In addition the judges were forbidden to fraternize with persons later to appear before them by eating or drinking with them or with their advocates. '*Trop grande familiarité*,' concludes the prohibition, '*engendra grand mal*'. This warning suggests that judges were being subjected to

[1] Guilhiermoz, op. cit., Appendix VI, 638–9.

[2] Guilhiermoz (op. cit., 181–234) has published the *Stilus Inquestarum*; the *Stilus Parlamenti* has been edited by F. Aubert.

heavy outside pressures, as did an earlier clause in the same enactment which forbade them to take any account of messages, private conversations and letters purporting to have a bearing on any case before the court. Two years later, in December 1320, Philip produced further rules to be observed by his judges. They were to assemble in their chamber when the first sung mass of the day began in the royal chapel of the Palais and there they were to remain until the angelus ringing in the same chapel proclaimed that it was noon. During those six hours they were forbidden to leave their places, save '*pour nécessité corporelle*'; they were to have no voice in matters which related to themselves or their friends, nor could they, without the president's permission, even give advice in court to friends or acquaintances. The penalty fixed for disobedience was the loss of a day's salary. Members of the chamber of *Enquêtes* had also to attend the Palais in the afternoons for the period between Easter and the feast of St Michael (29 September), and all the magistrates were instructed to remain in Paris whilst the court was in session.[1]

In 1345, Philip of Valois had some hard things to say about his judges, accusing them of failing, in a number of respects, to fulfil their offices satisfactorily. He criticized first the conduct of those members of the Parlement who went on commissions of inquiry into the provinces. As far back as 1278 the king had tried to prevent the judges from taking part in these investigations. In 1318 Philip V had forbidden the practice during the judicial term, and Philip VI renewed this prohibition. The commission had long been popular with the magistrates because of the financial rewards it offered. The ordinance of March 1345 makes it clear that the pursuit of these benefits had, in some cases at least, overtaken the disinterested pursuit of justice. So much is evident from the royal strictures against excessive demands for expenses which had impoverished plaintiffs and forced them to withdraw their suits. Another ruse, which had been brought to the king's attention and which he threatened to punish severely if the perpetrators were discovered, was the habit of some commissioners of beginning their inquiries very late each day and proceeding with the utmost dilatoriness thereafter, the object being to prolong the investigation and to extract thereby a greater sum in expenses from the unfortunate persons concerned.

The conduct of the judges within the Palais was also criticized in the same enactment. Evidently the bad habits attacked by Philip V had persisted, for the king reiterated the order of his predecessor, that during

[1] *Ordonnances*, I, 727–32.

sessions the counsellors were not to indulge in private discussions to the detriment of the Parlement's business. Quite clearly the king was not referring to occasional whispered consultations, but to a state of affairs bordering on chaos: the magistrates' preoccupation with a variety of private issues incapacitated them from dealing adequately with official business requiring urgent consideration. To make matters worse, they frequently arrived late and left early, and the king was at pains to point out the bad impression made upon parties awaiting judgment by the belated arrival of some of their judges, long after the sitting had commenced. Finally, the magistrates were reminded that what passed in their deliberations had to remain secret; only the decree containing their ultimate decision was to be made public. They were again warned against mingling out of court with those who were later to appear before them, or taking notice of any unofficial advice or communication about an issue that was *sub judice*.

Some, if not all of these regulations were ignored by the judges, a fact which indicates that, although the separate existence of the court with its three component chambers was an established fact by the middle of the fourteenth century, the Parlement had not yet acquired the dignity and formality normally associated with a court of law, which was the product not of royal legislation but of time and tradition. More serious than the mere lack of dignity was the danger of corruption, caused by both outside influences and by the inadequacies of the magistrates themselves. Tradition would help to eliminate that fault too.

Meanwhile the organization and procedure of the Parlement was slowly consolidated. Like all the *parlementaire* legislation of this early period, the regulations governing the conduct of the magistrates underlines the two contradictory aspects of the court's development. On the one hand they mark the tendency towards a more rigid routine, and on the other they demonstrate how little rigidity there yet was by the standard of later ages. However, in the long term it is not misleading to choose 1345 as the date by which the Parlement of Paris had been established as an homogeneous, permanent institution.[1]

Having examined in some detail the Parlement's early years, it becomes possible at this stage to substitute a broader, less strictly chronological inquiry into the structure and routine of the court as it became more rigid and formal with the passing of time. Not that increasing formality neces-

[1] E. Maugis, *Histoire du Parlement de Paris*, I, 1.

sarily prevented changes from taking place: the ceremonies marking the opening of each new session on 12 November, provide a case in point.

In the fourteenth and fifteenth centuries, this *séance de rentrée* was predominantly a grand ceremonial occasion, in which all the great dignitaries in the land participated, princes and prelates, leading noblemen and officers of the crown, headed by the chancellor of France, representing the king, who no longer presided in person. The ceremony began at 6 a.m. with the celebration of High Mass in honour of the Holy Ghost, sung in the Great Hall of the Palais de Justice. Then followed the chancellor's address to the magistrates, based on an apt scriptural quotation and intended to inspire his audience with zeal for the pursuit of justice. Thus, in 1413, for example, the chancellor Henri de Marle, chose as his theme St Paul's text, *Evigilate et nollite peccare*. The last stage of the proceedings was held partly in secret. At a private session, the chief clerk of the Parlement read out the ordinances governing the internal discipline and routine of the court, after which the doors were reopened, and the regulations affecting those attached to the court – barristers, solicitors, ushers – were similarly proclaimed.[1] Originally, while the concept of the Parlement was still that of an assembly existing for one year only, all its members were required on this occasion to renew their oaths, promising to act in accordance with the regulations enumerated by the chief clerk. However, by the reign of Charles V (1364–80), a new concept of the Parlement as a permanent institution had emerged. As a result of this change, the magistrates ceased to renew their oaths annually and instead swore obedience once only, when they were first installed as members of the court. Consequently, by the beginning of the sixteenth century, the character of the *séance de rentrée* had begun to change. Only the lesser officials were still required to repeat their oaths. The ushers were summoned first and in secret session listened to the relevant ordinances. There followed some observations from the First President about their responsibilities, after which each swore his pledge upon a copy of St John's Gospel. Next, in open court, came the turn of the barristers and solicitors, and finally once more *in camera* that of the king's representatives in the Parlement, the *Gens du roi*. These formalities eventually took up two days so that although the *séance de rentrée* still began ceremoniously with solemn High Mass, it went on to become a private disciplinary session of the court. [2]

[1] F. Aubert, *Histoire du Parlement de Paris à François Ier*, I, 177–9.
[2] Maugis, op. cit., I, 272.

After the opening ceremonies, the magistrates settled down to their daily routine. They were early risers, though they became slightly less so as the years passed. In the fourteenth century, they were expected to reach the Palais even during the winter by six o'clock, as the bells of the neighbouring churches announced the first mass of the day; from Easter until the end of the judicial year, they had to arrive even earlier. However, by July 1493, when Charles VIII promulgated his ordinance on the administration of justice, the magistrates had gained an hour's respite. In the winter months they were ordered to be present in their respective chambers not later than seven o'clock. But the penalty for unpunctuality confined to the loss of one day's salary in 1320, by 1493 included suspension from office.[1] Upon arrival, the magistrates changed into their formal costume in a cloakroom provided for the purpose, and then repaired to the Great Hall to hear mass, offered every morning that the Parlement was in session by a priest of one of the four mendicant orders. This obligation fulfilled, they retired to their chambers to begin the day's work.

In the reign of Philip V each daily session of the *Grand' Chambre* ended at midday, though as the amount and complexity of legal business increased, the official hours lengthened. By the mid-sixteenth century, the morning sessions ceased at eleven or even earlier, but from about 1360 afternoon sessions were held twice a week as well, usually on Tuesdays and Fridays. These additional assemblies ended at 5 p.m. until 1559 when, in the darkness of a December evening, a president of the court was assassinated as he left the Palais de Justice. After that incident the magistrates decided that between November and Easter it would be judicious to leave the Palais at 4 p.m., before the light failed.[2] By the eighteenth century, the timetable of the court's working day had grown far more complicated. The *Grand' Chambre* still held its afternoon sessions on Tuesdays and Fridays, but in the morning it met twice, first from seven to eight and then again for the *grande audience*, which lasted from nine to ten. The judges had also to fit in private sessions of *conseil*, to discuss cases which had been reserved for further consideration. The chambers of *Enquêtes* and *Requêtes* usually met on two days a week at hours never coinciding, at least in theory, with the sessions of the *Grand' Chambre*. When the Parlement became involved in extra-judicial activities,

[1] Isambert, op. cit., XI, 222–3.

[2] *See infra*, 207; Aubert, 'Recherches sur l'organisation du Parlement de Paris au XVIe siècle', 334.

however, these interlocking arrangements, which restricted the amount of time available for plenary sessions, were abandoned.[1]

The judicial routine was punctuated by an ever-increasing number of fixed holidays and by certain ceremonial events in which the Parlement had its role to play. Included under this second heading were such occasions as the entry into Paris of the king, the queen or the dauphin or a visiting sovereign, the birth, marriage or funeral of a member of the royal family, the funeral of an important public figure, a cardinal perhaps, or a great officer of the crown, and the funeral of any of the Parlement's own magistrates. In addition, there were the celebrations attending military victories, such as those of April 1495 to mark the entry of Charles VIII into Naples, or those held almost exactly seventeen years later to signal the victory of his successor, Louis XII, at Ravenna, the signing of peace treaties, the reception of foreign ambassadors, the public offering of prayers for the restoration to health of the king or queen. Then there were the recurring annual holidays: the great feasts of the Church calendar, Easter, Christmas, the Epiphany and Whitsuntide and a large number of lesser feast days, including those of the Virgin Mary and of the apostles and evangelists, those of St Louis, St Christopher, St Michael, Saint-Denis, St Catherine, St Nicholas, and many more besides. Sunday was never a working day. Over Christmas, work ceased in the Palais for four days; it ceased again for a fortnight over Easter and during the week following Whit Sunday. The summer recess remained variable for a long time because the date upon which the previous session ended was itself changed from year to year, though by the beginning of the eighteenth century it was always 7 September.

Even on normal working days, if the legal routine became dull and oppressive it was possible for the magistrates to escape for a while to the near-by *buvette* or refreshment room, where they could restore their spirits with food and drink and conversation. From time to time the lure of the *buvette* threatened to disorganize the administration of justice, as royal enactments, particularly those of the fifteenth century, indicate. The 1404 Parlement sought to solve the problem itself by limiting the amount to be spent per head on drinks in a single morning.[2] However, Charles VIII's ordinance of July 1493, with its strictures against the comings and goings of magistrates during sessions, suggests that the abuse still persisted. At that time there were two *buvettes*. By the eighteenth

[1] J.-F. Bluche, *Les Magistrats du Parlement de Paris*, 54–5.
[2] Aubert, *Le Parlement de Paris à Charles VII*, I, 157–8.

century there were eight, one attached to each chamber. Besides the coffee and the refreshing wines, which were so popular during the summer months, they dispensed a variety of foods, bread and butter, tongues, sausages, eggs, radishes. The *buvette du parlement*, which served the *Grand' Chambre*, was not simply a dining-hall: on more formal occasions it was used as a reception room for distinguished visitors. The Prince de Conti dined there in 1721, and there in 1768 the magistrates were presented to the King of Denmark.[1]

Although the number of chambers multiplied over the years, the basic divisions already distinguishable in the years before 1345 – the *Grand' Chambre*, the *Enquêtes* and the *Requêtes* – remained. However, the number of chambers dealing with *enquêtes* and *requêtes* increased, from one of each in the fourteenth century, to five and two, respectively, by the end of the sixteenth century. Despite these additions, the *Grand' Chambre* never relinquished its pre-eminent position. It had been the original chamber of Pleas, the heart of the early Parlement, and it continued to be the essential component around which the other chambers moved, fulfilling their complementary, yet subordinate roles. All the plenary sessions of the court, whether convened in the normal course of judicial business, or to mark some formal occasion, or to discuss extra-judicial matters, took place in the *Grand' Chambre*.

Such sessions might be held to examine royal legislation, to assist at the installation of new counsellors or to participate in the Parlement's most solemn assembly, the *lit de justice*, when the king presided in person and thus fleetingly restored the court to its ancient form. The counsellors who sat on the benches of this chamber only achieved their status after years of apprenticeship in the *Enquêtes*, being promoted according to their length of service when vacancies occurred. This procedure was followed from 1336 and periodic attempts to evade it always produced a lively response from the injured parties. The *Grand' Chambriers*, therefore, were usually the court's most sober and erudite judges; they were certainly its most experienced ones.

The total personnel of the *Grand' Chambre*, as has been observed, remained close to thirty from the reign of Philip of Valois and was still only thirty-seven in the last year of the Parlement's long existence. In the fourteenth and early fifteenth centuries, these offices were shared almost equally between laymen and clerics. However, in the second half

[1] Bluche, op. cit., Appendix 3, 392.

of the fifteenth century, in particular from the time of Charles VII's reorganization of the court after the triumphant conclusion of the Hundred Years War, the clerics began to yield ground to the laymen, a small shift symptomatic of a far wider and deeper change affecting the whole of Europe. In the great ordinance of April 1454, drawn up at Montils-les-Tours, one of the milestones in the Parlement's development, Charles VII did adhere to the stipulations of his predecessors, that in the *Grand' Chambre* there should be fifteen lay and fifteen clerical counsellors. But that balance was not long maintained.[1] By the reign of Louis XII (1498–1515) it had tilted in favour of the secular arm, and by 1715 less than a third of the *Grand' Chambriers* were clerics.

The presidents of the Parlement also sat in the *Grand' Chambre*. The most senior of them, the First President, was the chief of the court, at least in its day-to-day business, though the chancellor's presence on formal occasions indicated his overall headship. If the chancellor was absent, the First President took his place in such ceremonies as the election of counsellors and, eventually, at the *séance de rentrée*. He also presided over routine sessions both of the *Grand' Chambre* and of the whole Parlement. The early dichotomous aspect of the office disappeared as the First President came to acquire both the necessary legal and social accomplishments. He became a leading public figure, sometimes a chancellor in the making, and by the sixteenth century a permanent member, with his fellow presidents, of the King's Council. His office involved him in considerable expense. Every year he gave a lavish dinner for all the members of the Parlement on the evening following the opening of the new session. Presidential hospitality was extended to the greatest and consequently the most costly guests in the land. In 1600, Henry IV and his queen dined with one of the most celebrated of First Presidents, Achille de Harlay; in 1724, a rather less distinguished one, Potier de Novion, who had held the office for only a year, resigned because he found its social duties incompatible with his own parsimonious habits. In compensation, however, the First President was entitled to numerous gratifying privileges, from the right to a soft kneeler at the early morning mass in the Great Hall of the Palais to that of taking a prominent place on all public occasions. His formal dress also distinguished him from his colleagues within the court.[2]

Until the end of the fourteenth century the magistrates had not adopted

[1] Isambert, op. cit., IX, 204.

[2] Aubert, 'Recherches sur l'organisation du Parlement de Paris au XVIe siècle', 126–7.

a standard legal costume.[1] The presidents' earliest attire was directly traceable to that of the knights and barons who had frequented the King's Court in the days of St Louis. Over their plain tunic, long-sleeved and of ankle length, they wore a scarlet cape, ermine-lined; it was closed on the left side and open on the right, remindful of the fact that their predecessors were warriors, who passed judgment with swords on their left side. Similarly, the *mortier* or cap, by which the First President's colleagues the presidents *à mortier*, came to be distinguished, made its first appearance as an aristocratic fashion at St Louis's coronation in 1226. The earliest illustration of a plenary session of the Parlement[2] surviving from the year 1458 reveals that even at this comparatively late date there was not yet complete uniformity in dress. The presidents wore *mortiers* – and this black velvet cap had grown taller and more rounded by the fifteenth century – while the counsellors wore either flat black caps or rolled hoods attached to shoulder pieces. In other respects, their dress was similar to that of the presidents, with long outer tunics of different colours, pink or green or blue. The First President, however, was clearly identifiable by means of the horizontal bars of gold braid that decorated the shoulders of his cape.

The magistrates' official dress continued to alter for some time to come. In the late sixteenth century the variations were so great that the king, Henry IV, introduced legislation in 1602, clearly defining how the presidents and counsellors were to be dressed in the Parlement. Particular attention was given to the materials of which the costumes were to be made. Velvet, silk, satin and damask were not to be used; only plain cloth or serge was permitted. The costumes had to be in good condition, neither badly worn nor dirty, but, equally, they had not to be adorned by any trinkets or ornaments. For most of the seventeenth and eighteenth centuries, the official attire of presidents and counsellors alike remained almost unchanged. The First President's scarlet cape, decorated still at the shoulders, now by three rows of braid and three of miniver, was no longer open on the right side. Instead, there was a small slit at the front, almost covered by a furred collar-hood, surrounding the neck and the upper part of the chest. Across the left shoulder hung a broad band of material, scarlet and embellished with fur from November until Easter, black and plain from Easter until the end of the session. His *mortier* was

[1] Most of what follows is based upon W. N. Hargreaves-Mawdsley, *A History of Legal Dress in Europe*, 21–9.

[2] By Jean Fouquet, in the Munich edition of the works of Boccaccio.

still of black velvet, pyramid-shaped by the eighteenth century and decorated with two bands of gold lace. The other presidents were dressed in a similar manner, though lacking the more ornate *mortier* and the distinctive shoulder emblem of their chief. The secular counsellors of the Parlement wore scarlet, and the clerics violet, capes trimmed with fur, and both wore square black caps. During the eighteenth century, however, the *mortier* was no longer confined to the presidents of the court, being commonly in use as the insignia of the legal profession. In that century, too, as in the seventeenth, the magistrates' magnificent formal apparel was replaced for routine judicial sessions by the black gown and broad black hat that constituted the *petit habit.*[1]

The number of presidents in the Parlement increased fairly rapidly. By 1336 there were three, a fourth was appointed in the reign of King John (1350–64), and there were five of them by 1407. The total eventually reached nine, excluding the First President himself. The tendency, already observed among the counsellors, for the laymen to oust the clerics, was even more apparent with the presidents. Even in the fourteenth century, clerical presidents, like Arnold de Corbie and Firmin, a future chancellor and bishop of Paris, were rarely appointed, and from the reign of Francis I (1515–47), when the sale of office became widespread, that of president in the Parlement became the preserve of secular office-holders. In 1604 a royal edict allowed the transmission of offices to the holders' heirs, and after that date the great presidential families of the seventeenth and eighteenth centuries, Lamoignon and Maupeou and Molé, began to establish themselves. Access to the rank of president became extremely difficult for those without a family tradition of distinguished legal service. Of those men who held office between 1715 and 1771, only one, Charron de Menars, lacked such a background and he had the compensatory advantage of being the step-brother of the great Colbert.[2] Promotion within the presidential hierarchy was, theoretically, according to length of service, the Fifth President rising to Fourth and so on, but the practice was not followed invariably. The office of First President never became venal, the king thus remaining free to choose his own candidate, who was not necessarily the senior president.

The presidents and counsellors formed the permanent professional element in the *Grand' Chambre*, though there were also other individuals and groups with the right to take their places there. The first was the king,

[1] F. L. Ford, *Robe and Sword*, 56.
[2] J.-F. Bluche, *L'Origine des Magistrats, passim.*

who remained the unique source of justice in the kingdom. The chancellor, too, sat by right in the *Grand' Chambre*, as the sovereign's chief judicial officer and the court's titular head. Nor did the specialists ever entirely replace the non-professional group, whose right to a place in the court was a reminder of its original composition. As late as the fifteenth century great nobles still occasionally assisted at normal judicial sessions: some who died at Agincourt had also served the king as counsellors in his Parlement. This tradition was safeguarded by the continued right of privy counsellors and peers to sit in the *Grand' Chambre*.

The principle of judgment by equals was deeply ingrained in the French past, and though the Parlement was taken over increasingly by trained lawyers, the peers never relinquished their right to attend when one of their fellows was either the defendant or the plaintiff in a trial before the Parlement. Their attendance otherwise was gradually confined to ceremonial occasions. The number of peers seems at first to have been restricted to twelve, six laymen and six clerics. They were enumerated in 1275 as the dukes of Normandy, Burgundy and Aquitaine and the counts of Flanders, Toulouse and Champagne, laymen and the archbishop of Rheims, the bishops of Laon, Langres, Beauvais, Châlons-sur-Marne and Noyon, clerics.[1] A seventh spiritual peer, the archbishop of Paris, was named in 1690, while the number of lay peerages proliferated to such an extent after 1600 that by Louis XIV's death in 1715 there were fifty-five. In terms of power and influence these new peers were but polite counterfeits of their baronial predecessors, though one of them, the Duc de Saint-Simon, has acquired enduring reputation with his pen. In addition, the princes of the royal blood were members of the Parlement by right of birth and they, like the peers, sat in the *Grand' Chambre*.

Finally, among those who were entitled to a place in the *Grand' Chambre* were a group of honorary counsellors, either magistrates who had retired after many years of service, or distinguished figures in the legal world, *maîtres des requêtes*, whose office had been closely associated with the Parlement in its formative years, and certain *ex-officio* members, including the governor of Paris and the abbot of Cluny. However, most of these supernumerary members rarely attended the court; the daily business of the *Grand' Chambre* was the concern of its permanent personnel, the presidents and counsellors.

The *Grand' Chambre* remained unique and until Francis I's reign, there

[1] But cf. Lot and Fawtier, op. cit., II, 297 *n.* 1.

were only two chambers of *Enquêtes* and one of *Requêtes* in the Parlement. The original chamber of *Enquêtes* which took shape in the first half of the fourteenth century was kept very busy and its complement grew from eight in 1291 to forty in 1345. Although a second chamber of *Enquêtes* was not formally established until the ordinance of Montils-les-Tours in 1454, such a development was foreshadowed long before by Philip V, who in 1319 divided the chamber into two sections, to deal respectively with new inquiries and with those which had been pending for some time. Charles VII's famous ordinance went beyond this partial division by erecting two permanent and independent chambers, each fulfilling a similar role. They continued to meet in the same place for some time after 1454, but there is no doubt that by 1502 each had been allotted its own separate locale.[1] The sixteenth century brought a great increase in the number of magistrates in the Parlement; three additional chambers of *Enquêtes* came into existence during this time, making a total of five in all. The third and fourth chambers were established by Francis I in 1522 and 1543. The king's decision to multiply the number of his judges was no longer dictated solely by the overwhelming amount of judicial work to be done, though that motive remained valid. There was, however, another reason, a financial one, that was far more compulsive for a monarchy suffering from a chronic lack of funds. It was from the reign of Francis I that French kings began openly to create and sell offices in an attempt to refurbish the royal exchequer. Consequently the number of judges proliferated: besides the foundation of two new chambers of *Enquêtes*, each including twenty magistrates, Francis appointed two presidents and twelve counsellors to swell the personnel of the *Grand' Chambre*, and an additional president and three counsellors in the chamber of *Requêtes*. The introduction of venality into the Parlement produced profound changes, not least in its size.[2] Although its complement continued to fluctuate wildly after the death of Francis I, it never again fell close to the figure of one hundred, which earlier generations of magistrates, savouring a fanciful parallel with the Roman Senate, had claimed to be immutable.[3]

In 1568 Charles IX established the fifth – and as it was to prove – the last new chamber of *Enquêtes*. The motive was again financial. These five chambers continued to function for almost two hundred years, until 1756, when they were reduced to three. This was almost the last structural

[1] Aubert, *Histoire du Parlement de Paris à François Ier*, I, 26.
[2] *See infra*, 115–17.
[3] Maugis, op. cit., I, 143.

change in the court, save for the drastic measures of judicial reorganization undertaken in the years 1771–4 by the Chancellor Maupeou, measures which in effect abolished the Parlement altogether, but which did not long survive the accession of Louis XVI. Immediately prior to the edict of December 1756 the number of counsellors holding office in each of the five chambers of *Enquêtes* was thirty-two; by the outbreak of the Revolution there were about twenty-five in each chamber.[1]

Like the *Grand' Chambre*, the *Enquêtes* had their presidents, though the title is somewhat misleading, for these officials were not presidents *à mortier*, presidents of the court, but simply counsellors holding the commission of president within their own chambers. They appeared in the first half of the fourteenth century when the *Enquêtes* had acquired a personnel and a corporate feeling of its own. Originally they were simply the most senior counsellors; their title brought with it no other distinction of any sort. By the middle of the fifteenth century, however, these presidents were claiming precedence over all save the presidents *à mortier*, and by the sixteenth century they had achieved a higher salary than their colleagues and certain honorific distinctions. For a short period after 1704, the title of president was even recognized as a permanent office, only to be relegated again to the level of a commission in 1757. In exchange for their greater prestige, the presidents were required to assume more onerous responsibilities. They had to direct the internal business of their chamber in such matters as the appointment of commissioners to conduct the various inquiries, and they had also to fulfil certain judicial functions in the Parlement. In 1454 for example, Charles VII ordained that no legal decision of the Parlement would be valid unless at least one president from either the *Grand' Chambre* or the *Enquêtes* was present to pronounce it. Finally, the presidents of the *Enquêtes* had to see that in their own chambers the regulations of the court were observed and to that end Louis XII recommended, in the Ordinance of Blois (1499), that they should consult with the presidents of the *Grand' Chambre* at least once a month after dinner on Wednesdays.[2] The first two presidents to be positively identified, Jean de Huban and Foulques Bardoul, were in office in 1345. Both were clerics – Bardoul was a future bishop of Avranches – and the office remained the preserve of the spiritual order until 1413, when provision was made for the appointment of a lay president. The gradual triumph of secular authority within the Parlement was faithfully reflected

[1] H. Carré, *La fin des Parlements*, 318–21.
[2] Isambert, op. cit., IX, 235; XI, 341.

in the *Enquêtes*. There were three presidents in each chamber in 1715, two in 1789, and none of them was a cleric. It was a similar story with the counsellors: lists of the fourteenth and fifteenth centuries show a balance, but in the last Parlement, that of 1789, only eight clerics sat in the *Enquêtes*.

Lastly, it should be stressed that all the chambers of *Enquêtes* carried out the same judicial role, essentially that of judging cases in which written, not oral, evidence was concerned, and that, despite the discrepancy between the dates of their various foundations, none of them had precedence over the others. Magistrates seeking promotion to the *Grand' Chambre*, for example, derived their claim not from the particular chamber of *Enquêtes* to which they belonged, but from their own length of service.

There were never more than two chambers of *Requêtes* in the Parlement, and they too performed identical tasks and were of equal standing in the court. Although the *Requêtes* was formed originally to scrutinize petitions prior to the institution of a law suit, its jurisdiction, like that of the *Enquêtes*, was extended with the passing of time. In 1364 the magistrates in the *Requêtes* acquired the right to judge civil cases involving individuals holding letters of *Committimus*, a privilege which entitled the holders to eschew all inferior jurisdictions and appeal directly to the Parlement. Judgment of such cases became the chief preoccupation of the *Requêtes* in succeeding centuries. In the same year, Charles V attempted to stabilize the membership of the chamber, which until then had moved irregularly. From 1364 there were to be six magistrates in the *Requêtes*, including one president, normally the senior counsellor, whose title, like that of his colleagues in the *Enquêtes*, was held as a commission and did not give him the status of a president of the court. This number remained unchanged until 1454, when, following the ordinance of Montils-les-Tours, it rose to eight, five clerics and three laymen, one of whom had the title of president. By the advent of Francis I in 1515, it had dropped again to six, but from the sixteenth century, as offices in every branch of royal service multiplied, the number of places in the *Requêtes* likewise increased.[1] In 1580 Henry III founded a second chamber of *Requêtes*, with two presidents and eight counsellors. Both chambers endured with only a few numerical alterations until Maupeou's reforms. When Louis XVI recalled the Parlement, however, he only reinstated one chamber of *Requêtes*.

Historically, the *Requêtes* had always held a special and rather ambiguous

[1] *See supra*, 37.

place in the Parlement. Originally it had not formed part of the court and its members were considered as delegates commissioned by the Parlement to carry out a specific legal role. Even when that role had been enlarged and royal legislation had made it clear that the chamber was an intrinsic part of the court, the dichotomy persisted, and in the eighteenth century a member of the *Requêtes* still insisted that he held the office of counsellor in the Parlement and also a commission to serve in the *Requêtes*. If he resigned this commission he could take his place in the *Enquêtes*, and in due course, according to his years of service, he could aspire to the *Grand' Chambre*. In fact, few counsellors in the *Requêtes* followed that particular ascent; in the eighteenth century, at least, the *Grand' Chambriers* were usually recruited from among those who began their legal careers in the *Enquêtes*. That does not mean that a place in the *Requêtes* was considered inferior. Many magistrates moved directly from the *Requêtes* outside the court to the office of *maître des requêtes* which, in the middle of the eighteenth century, cost twice as much to purchase as a counsellor's office in the *Enquêtes*.[1] Nor was any distinction made between the presidents of the *Requêtes* and those of the *Enquêtes*; from 1704 to 1757 their offices were valued equally and on solemn occasions they all wore the purple robes and ermine capes that marked them out from their colleagues.

The *Grand' Chambre*, the *Enquêtes* and the *Requêtes*, these were the essential components of the court, its permanent chambers. There were, however, other chambers enjoying a periodic existence, whose personnel was drawn from one or other of these principal bodies. The most important of them was the *Tournelle*, the chamber in which criminal cases were judged. It was Francis I in 1515 who gave the *Tournelle* a separate identity, though of course the Parlement had always made provision for judging criminal matters. Initially the members of the *Grand' Chambre* had been responsible for both criminal and civil suits, but because of the custom preventing those in holy orders from pronouncing sentence of corporal punishment, only the lay counsellors, meeting in a separate room, carried out that obligation. For two centuries, therefore, a delegation of lay counsellors from the *Grand' Chambre* was responsible for criminal affairs and the small tower or *tournelle* in the Palais de Justice, in which these magistrates customarily met, furnished the delegation with a name. It sometimes happened that the pressure of work in the *Tournelle* so denuded the *Grand' Chambre* of counsellors that the business before that chamber had to be suspended. That was the case on two occasions in the

[1] Bluche, *Les Magistrats du Parlement de Paris*, 166.

summer of 1365. However, after the ordinance of 1454, which stipulated that a president and twelve counsellors from the *Grand' Chambre* should constitute the *Tournelle*, the criminal chamber in fact became a separate entity, continuously occupied during the sessions with its own work. This was the state of affairs which Francis I formally recognized. He ordained that two presidents and eight lay counsellors from the *Grand' Chambre* together with two lay counsellors from each of the *Enquêtes* should serve in the *Tournelle* on a rota system, the *Grand' Chambriers* for six months at a time, the members of the *Enquêtes* for three, so that all the lay counsellors of these chambers would take a turn in judging criminal cases. An eminent eighteenth-century magistrate, Joly de Fleury, defended this rotary system on the grounds that it prevented the judges' feelings of moderation and humanity from being dulled by the continual necessity of condemning men to die.[1] Each new chamber of *Enquêtes* provided two magistrates for the *Tournelle*, replacing them every three months, while the *Grand' Chambre* came to contribute its five most junior presidents *à mortier* for the whole judicial year, half of its lay personnel from November to Easter and the other half from Easter to the end of the session.[2]

The *Tournelle* did not deal with all criminal matters, however. Although Francis I did transfer to it, in 1540, criminal cases involving royal officials and members of the nobility, provided that they were not '*de bien grande et notable qualité*', in 1670 Louis XIV enumerated a long list of privileged persons, including both categories named by Francis, who had the right to insist on a trial before the *Grand' Chambre* in the first instance.[3] In fact, the prestige of that chamber persistently overshadowed the *Tournelle*. Before 1515, sentence of death could only be passed in the *Grand' Chambre* and trials leading to that verdict had to be transferred there. After 1515, despite royal edicts like that of 1540, the *Tournelle* tended to remain the criminal chamber for the unprivileged, whilst the privileged stood trial before a joint assembly of the *Grand' Chambre* and the *Tournelle*, from which the clerical members of the former were excused. At the lower end of the criminal scale, cases of *petit-criminel*-prosecutions involving fines, not physical punishment – went on appeal from inferior jurisdictions not to the *Tournelle* but to the *Enquêtes*.

Another delegation drawn from several chambers and functioning

[1] C.-J. de Ferrière, *Dictionnaire de Droit et de Pratique*, II, 420.

[2] Bluche, *Les Magistrats du Parlement de Paris*, 51; Bluche is amongst those historians who favour the opinion that the name of 'tournelle' derives from the rota system practised there.

[3] Isambert, op. cit., XII, 683; XVIII, 375–6.

periodically was the *Chambre des Vacations*. As its name suggests, this was a body called to provide justice during the long summer recess. The need to maintain a skeleton court during those months was recognized in the very early years of the Parlement, when the task was undertaken by members of the *Grand' Chambre* and from 1312 by the *Enquêtes*. The *Requêtes* also acted in this capacity in the course of the fourteenth century, and it was not until 1405 that a distinct *Chambre des Vacations*, with members drawn from the *Grand' Chambre* and the *Enquêtes*, was established. Its membership, however, continued to fluctuate. In 1531 Francis I stipulated that it should be composed of a president and twelve counsellors, but since the First President only asked for volunteers a few days before each session ended the number available altered from year to year. The duration of the chamber's sitting varied likewise. In the sixteenth century it usually met from mid-September until the beginning of the following judicial session, on 12 November, but later, when the length of the summer recess had become invariable, the *Vacations* sat from 9 September to 27 October. Its chief concern was with criminal cases, which by their nature often required immediate attention; by the beginning of the sixteenth century the *Vacations* had the power to pass the death sentence. In civil suits, however, in which the procedure was more leisurely, its authority was circumscribed: only in trivial affairs could it render a definitive verdict. In more serious cases its decisions had to be ratified when the Parlement reassembled.

There remains to be mentioned the *Chambre de la Marée*, whose history stretched from the fourteenth century to the eighteenth. Like the *Tournelle* and the *Vacations*, this very small body – in the eighteenth century it consisted of a president *à mortier* and the *Grand' Chambre*'s two senior counsellors – was a delegation appointed from a permanent chamber. Its duty was to try cases, civil and criminal, involving the traffic and sale of sea fish. Such a commission existed because the Church's laws of abstinence made fish a most valuable commodity.

Over five hundred years, although the structure of the Parlement became increasingly complex, the essential outline of its development remains plainly discernible. It is true that a closer examination of particular epochs would reveal other chambers appearing momentarily and vanishing again, fulfilling temporary needs or satisfying transient royal whims, like the civil *Tournelle* of Louis XIV and Louis XV, the *Chambre-mi-parti* of Henry III, the *Chambre Ardente* of Henry II. Nevertheless, though these *ad hoc* creations have their significance in the history of a reign or of a decade or of a single year, they have no place in the broad sweep of five centuries.

The Parlement's professional membership was not confined to the presidents and counsellors who held places in one or other of its permanent chambers. A very important group of magistrates had no such attachment. They were the representatives of the king's interests, the *Gens du roi.* The king's attendance at the Parlement became infrequent from the end of the thirteenth century; consequently when he was himself a party in a lawsuit, instead of appearing in person, he began to employ a legal representative or *procureur* to act on his behalf. At first he did this by choosing a lawyer who would certainly have other clients as well, only for the duration of a particular case. Yet early in the fourteenth century – certainly before 1323 – the king's interests came to require a permanent representative in the Parlement, who almost at once acquired the title of *Procureur-Général.* Besides representing the king in legal actions, this officer had also to see to the maintenance of public order. His office marked the highest expression of a concept which had its beginnings on a much more humble level. The bailiffs and seneschals were expected to defend the king's rights and to investigate crimes committed within their particular area of jurisdiction. This dual function proved impossible to sustain and so royal representatives, *Procureurs du roi*, were sent to assist them. These men were undoubtedly active by the reign of Philip the Bold and they are referred to in the earliest *parlementaire* records, the *Olim.*[1] They acted in the ordinary way as assistants to the bailiff, but also in a specific and novel capacity. If a crime or a tort was committed and no individual dared to prosecute the culprit, the *procureur* promoted a public action on the king's behalf. This was the origin of the office of public prosecutor, an institution which France bequeathed to Europe.[2] Such an office was bound to enormously increase the power and influence of the king, for it enabled him to take the initiative against powerful local interests and to be seen to be fulfilling the role of supreme judge which had been his in theory for so long. For this reason, the royal *procureurs* were very unpopular figures with powerful barons, who, for a short time after the death of Philip the Fair in 1314, succeeded in curbing their influence. But this was only a temporary set-back, coinciding in fact with the permanent establishment of the office of *Procureur-Général* in the

[1] A. Beugnot (ed.), *Les Olim*, II, 112.

[2] E. Glasson, *Histoire du Droit*, VI, 630.

Parlement. So overwhelmed was this new official with business that in 1351 he was allowed to co-opt two assistants, provided that he paid them out of his own pocket.

Not only did he need help with a mass of material, he also required expert aid in pleading his suit, for his chief task was to conduct the investigation preceding the court hearing. Therefore, he relied upon a barrister to present his case in the Parlement. The royal barristers – the *avocats du roi* – appeared in the bailiwicks around 1300, several decades after the *procureurs*, and from about 1330 there were two regularly employed in the Parlement. In 1375 their office was formally recognized and from the beginning of the following century they acquired the title of *Avocats-Généraux*. Originally, one was a cleric, dealing with civil cases, the other a layman, dealing with criminal affairs, but in the second half of the sixteenth century, this distinction disappeared and the two officials performed exactly similar functions. The *Procureur-Général*, on the other hand, had always been responsible for both civil and criminal matters. His office remained unique, but by the eighteenth century the number of *Avocats-Généraux* had risen to three. These four officials were known collectively as the *Gens du roi*, or metonymically, as the *Parquet*, a title derived from their customary place on the floor of the *Grand' Chambre*.

Fundamentally, their duties remained what they had always been – to protect the rights of the king and his domain and to preserve public order. However, with the extension and consolidation of royal authority their mandate widened correspondingly and with it the prestige of their office. The *Parquet* became a sure ladder for promotion to high legal positions. One of the most eminent jurists of the eighteenth century, Henri d'Aguesseau, was successively *Avocat-* and *Procureur-Général* and finally chancellor. Nor was this sort of progress a relatively late development. Guillaume de Dormans, who became chancellor in 1372 had likewise begun his career as an *Avocat du roi* in the Parlement. In fact, the king's representatives, like the presidents *à mortier*, came to occupy an important role in the State outside the confines of the Palais de Justice: by the middle of the sixteenth century they were *ex-officio* members of the King's Council. Within the *Parquet*, the *Procureur-Général* never lost his initial preeminence, although in 1554 Henry II introduced equal salaries for all the *Gens du roi*. Indeed, before that date the greater renown surrounding the barristers' role had allowed the senior *Avocat* to acquire a ceremonial precedence over the *Procureur-Général*. But the powers and prerogatives of the latter enabled him to remain the *Parquet*'s effective head. Because they were his particular representatives, the king was anxious to control the appointment of the *Gens du roi*. During the fifteenth century, however, the Parlement did succeed on occasion in electing its own candidates, though the practice of *parlementaire* election to any office in the court died out during the following century. With the introduction of venality most offices again passed out of the crown's control, but those of the *Gens du roi*, like that of the First President, remained royal appointments.[1]

Besides the magistrates who constituted the Parlement proper, there were a host of lesser officials, barristers, solicitors, clerks, ushers, notaries, who worked closely with the court and formed part of the *parlementaire* world. Before reviewing in brief the work of these subordinates in the Parlement, one other official of major importance remains to be considered, the *greffier* or chief clerk of the court, whose primary task was to draw up its judicial record and to preserve its official documents. As is the case with so many other aspects of the Parlement's early history, it is difficult to trace accurately the appearance of this official and to define his role, especially in the thirteenth century. Jean de Montluçon is generally held to be the first man appointed to keep a record of the court's activities, though he was certainly not known as the *greffier*, a title in general use only from the fifteenth century. Nor were the early keepers of records confined to that task: they were judges, too, at least on occasion. Montluçon's name appears among a list of judges summoned by the king in 1273, and even Pierre de Bourges, the last of the three men responsible for the *Olim* records, was still performing judicial tasks in the early fourteenth century, though by that time the volume of written evidence was large enough to require full-time attention.[2]

The number of *greffiers* increased over the years; by the eighteenth century there were seven of them. However, the *greffier* in charge of all civil matters remained the most important. He was a full member of the Parlement, sharing the magistrate's privileges and prestige. He had precedence over the *Gens du roi* within the court, and outside, on ceremonial occasions, he walked at the Parlement's head. So important a personage was he that counsellors sometimes resigned their position to become *greffier*, a unique reversal of the usual procedure. In the eighteenth century two members of the great *robe* family of Gilbert de Voisins

[1] Ibid., 338–44.

[2] Langlois, *Textes*, 86–7; A. Grün, *Actes du Parlement de Paris* (ed. E. Boutaric), I, LXXVII.

successively held the post from 1717 until 1771, and their predecessor, Dongeois, who was also their relative, was one of the richest men in the Parlement. The other *greffiers*, though not such impressive figures, were not of negligible importance either. In particular, the *greffier* who was responsible for criminal records, whose office can also be traced back to the thirteenth century, was an important official, and in 1691 Louis XIV decreed that the office should henceforth bring noble status to its holder.

Perhaps the most famous of the Parlement's chief clerks was Nicholas de Baye, who exercised the office of civil *greffier* from 1400 to 1416. Born into a servile family, he gained his freedom, entered the Church and graduated as a lawyer. When he died in 1419 after nineteen years of high judicial office he left a valuable library of classical and Christian authors, Aristotle and Cicero, Virgil and Ovid, Augustine, Jerome and Aquinas, and a *Journal* of his own times. His term of office was troubled, now by the extreme winter of 1408 when the ink congealed on his pen as he wrote and the frozen Seine became the main street of Paris, now by the war between Burgundians and Armagnacs and the arrival of Charles VI with his armed supporters to stay in the Palais and threaten the safety of his, Nicholas's, precious registers.[1] He complained that he was inadequately paid and certainly he lacked the opulence of some of his successors, but he possessed all their authority. He was in close and constant touch with the king and the chancellor; he drew up and expedited letters to the Holy See, to prelates, to towns; he signed commissions entrusted to members of the court and drew up letters instituting new counsellors. He was present at all the public and formal assemblies of the Parlement. Thus may his office be described as '*la pièce maîtresse de toute la machine parlementaire*'.[2] All the chief clerks were assisted by notaries, from whose ranks they were themselves frequently recruited.

The concept of a professional counsellor putting his client's case was well known in Roman law, and with the revival of Roman law studies in the thirteenth century it reappeared, notably in the ecclesiastical courts' procedure.[3] Barristers were working in the Parlement from a very early date; Philip the Bold saw fit to publish an ordinance in 1274 prescribing the oath to be sworn each year by the *avocats*, according to which they promised to plead only in support of just cases, and regulating their salary. The ordinance of 1345 – a milestone in so many aspects of the court's

[1] Nicholas de Baye, *Journal*, I, 213–17, 339–40.

[2] Lot and Fawtier, op. cit., II, 402.

[3] The most comprehensive work on the barristers for the period up to 1600 is that of R. Delachenal, *Histoire des Avocats au Parlement de Paris, 1300–1600*.

evolution – completed the task of organizing the barristers into a permanent corps with its own rules and customs. Inclusion in the Parlement's list of accredited *avocats* depended on a number of qualifications, professional and otherwise. The professional requirement was a degree in laws, though for some time this meant only canon law since the university of Paris did not provide instruction in civil law. For the rest, they had to give evidence of their catholicism and their personal worthiness and they had to be at least seventeen years of age. Having qualified, they could plead before any court within the Parlement's jurisdiction. They wore magisterial dress, took part in the Parlement's public ceremonies and gained the right of *committimus*. Above all, they became a part, however subordinate, of the Parlement itself and thereby acquired a not inconsiderable status, though conversely their conduct in the Palais was subjected to the stern discipline of the court.

A number of these men, like Dubreuil, the author of the *Stilus curie Parlamenti*, and Barbier, the chronicler of Louis XV, acquired enduring reputations. Many, again like Dubreuil, made a great deal of money, some by carrying out his dictum that it was not the justice of the dispute that mattered but the wealth of the client; others by acting permanently for a great lord or for an abbey, a town or university, thus ensuring for themselves a fixed annual salary and usually additional offerings too. Such positions of course went only to men whose reputation had already aroused the interest of these rich and influential clients. The remainder made themselves available in the Parlement, but their number had grown so considerable by the sixteenth century that briefs were no longer easily obtained.[1] In the early history of the Parlement magistrates were frequently recruited from the barristers' ranks; indeed, between 1350 and 1400 this *métier* provided four chancellors and six presidents of the Parlement. In the eighteenth century, on the contrary, though many judges had *avocats* as forebears and had served an apprenticeship at the bar themselves, the social gulf between the two professions was such that 'the attitude of sovereign courts judges towards the *avocats* seems generally to have been at best one of condescension and at worst one of contempt'.[2]

The *procureurs* or solicitors in the Parlement occupied the same status as the barristers: they shared the same privileges, were subject to the same discipline, swore a similar oath each year. Like the barristers they too

[1] There were fifty *Avocats* in the *Parlement* in 1340, about 500 by the mid-sixteenth century; Lot and Fawtier, op. cit., II, 397–8.

[2] Ford, op. cit., 55.

relied for employment either on wealthy clients, whom they contracted to serve permanently, or less affluent litigants, who engaged them at the Palais de Justice for a specific case. Both the solicitors and barristers belonged to the confraternity of St Nicholas, a society founded in 1342 with the approval of Philip V, which, besides providing for the spiritual needs of its members, also organized a system of assistance from funds collected in annual subscriptions for those of its members who had fallen on hard days.[1] The barristers and solicitors were assisted by clerks who though not members of the Parlement were closely associated with the Palais de Justice, or the *Basoche* (Basilica), as they called it. These clerks of the *Basoche*, an ill-disciplined, turbulent crowd of young men usually recruited from among unsuccessful law students, acquired notoriety through their unruly conduct, but through their theatrical productions in the Palais during the fourteenth, fifteenth and sixteenth centuries, in turn approved and condemned by the Parlement, they acquired, too, a place in French literary history. Their farces and morality plays provided the only comic element in the theatre before the French Renaissance.

There were also a number of notaries serving in the Palais whose legal expertise was valuable to the Parlement in matters of routine judicial administration, as for example in the drawing up of inventories and other technical documents.

Finally, in the long line of *parlementaire* officials came the *huissiers* or ushers, who kept order within the confines of the court and also performed certain police duties, the collecting of fines, the enforcement of *parlementaire* decrees, the seizure of recalcitrant debtors or wanted men.[2] These duties made them unpopular in some quarters and they were no doubt grateful for the protection, including the right of *committimus*, which the court extended to them. The ushers were also responsible for the heating and lighting of the Palais and for the upkeep of its furniture and furnishings. By 1345 their number had reached twelve and the comprehensive *parlementaire* ordinance of that year introduced a rota system, by which the ushers worked in two groups of six, alternating every two months. In the eighteenth century, there were twenty-five, headed by the first usher, who had particular duties to perform, like that of summoning the parties when their case was about to be heard, and in 1691 Louis XIV endowed this office with noble status.

All these men played their various parts in the hectic life of the Palais

[1] Aubert, *Histoire du Parlement de Paris à François Ier*, I, 205–28.
[2] *Ibid.*, 249–60.

de Justice and in the daily routine of the Parlement of Paris. In the years after St Louis's death, that court, which had first emerged in his lifetime, became the most important permanent institution below the monarchy in the French state. Its role was many-sided: not only judicial, but administrative and political too. All its members, from the First President himself to the humblest usher, gained great prestige from their association with the court and all were imbued with the *esprit de corps* that membership of any select and privileged organization habitually inspires. That spirit helped generations of magistrates to preserve a deep respect for their court's judicial traditions, and it is with the Parlement as a court of justice that the next chapter will be concerned.

CHAPTER TWO

The Parlement and the Law

The sources of French law; changes in legal procedure before the Parlement's appearance; civil procedure in the Parlement; criminal procedure in the Parlement; the records of the Parlement; the Parlement and rival jurisdictions

---

The development of French law was complicated by the diversity of its sources. By the end of the tenth century or the beginning of the eleventh, the Carolingian capitularies had been forgotten, and customary law was becoming the dominant legal force in the country. Customary law was always territorial, never personal. It was derived neither from Roman, Germanic nor Carolingian precepts, but was entirely pragmatic, fulfilling particular needs at a particular time. It was based on vague oral traditions and changed from one district to another, according to the slope of a mountainside or the course of a stream; it remained valid only so long as it commanded universal acceptance within the locality.[1] Because these customs were so variable and ill-defined, they had to be pronounced as valid by a judge before they could be invoked in evidence. The king himself sometimes intervened to distinguish between good customs and bad: in 1081 Henry I suppressed an unjust custom in Orléans, and from the reign of Louis VII, royal confirmation of customary law became frequent. In the thirteenth century, St Louis was especially active in this direction, and royal judges were frequently called upon to establish the law. They could do so in a number of ways: by claiming personal knowledge of the custom, having previously applied it, by seeking advice either from individuals or from groups likely to be able to offer a fair and reasonable opinion; finally, by setting up an inquiry and by interrogating witnesses.

In the thirteenth century a great deal of written evidence appeared to support the oral traditions. Indeed, long before that time rare examples existed of customary law set out in writing in town charters: a tenth-

[1] J. Declareuil, *Histoire Générale du Droit Français*, 830–1; G. Ducoudray, *Les Origines du Parlement de Paris*, 712.

century custom of Strasbourg, for example, and an eleventh century one of Grammont.[1] These were certainly exceptional, though in the following century such charters had already become numerous. One of the most celebrated was that granted to Lorris by Louis VII in 1155 and subsequently confirmed by Philip Augustus.[2] It became a model for scores of other localities anxious to obtain the same freedom and privileges. The custom of Beaumont in the Ardennes, granted in 1182 by Guillaume de Champagne, the archbishop of Rheims, was scarcely less famous: it too inspired many imitations, especially in north-eastern France. However, it was in the thirteenth century that the impact of written law began to be decisive. By that time, royal intervention in customary law usually took the form of a written declaration establishing what customs were to apply in a particular area; in this manner, in 1246 Louis IX established the customs of the nobility of Anjou and Maine.[3] But more important sources of written law were the *coutumiers*, works of professional jurists, who, aided by the gradual integration of local custom, itself brought about by the growth of the king's judicial prestige and inspired by the example of canon and Roman law, attempted to write down the customary law of areas as wide as Normandy, Anjou and the Orléannais. The first to appear was the *Très Ancien Coutumier de Normandie*, part of which dates from about 1200. This was followed in the middle of the century by a much larger and more important volume, the *Grand Coutumier de Normandie*, one of the most remarkable juridical works of the Middle Ages;[4] its influence may be detected still in certain Norman localities.[5] The *Conseil à un Ami*, whose theme was the customs of Vermandois, was the work of the bailiff Pierre de Fontaines. The anonymous *Livre de Jostice et de Plet* from Orléans appeared a little later and shortly before the so-called *Établissements de Saint-Louis*. The latter, written about 1270, is misnamed, for it consists chiefly of two anonymous *coutumiers*, one referring to the Orléannais, the other to Touraine and Anjou; it is not, as the title suggests, an official royal document. However, none of these *coutumiers* bears comparison with that written around 1280 by Philippe de Beaumanoir, the *Coutumes de Clermont en Beauvaisis*, incomparably the greatest legal work of the century and the only one touched with genius. Beaumanoir was no mere compositor of contemporary forensic practice.

[1] P. Viollet, *Précis de l'Histoire du Droit Français*, 115.
[2] M. Prou, 'Les coutumes de Lorris et leur propagation aux XIIe et XIIIe siècles', 303–20.
[3] F. Olivier-Martin, *Histoire du Droit Français*, 114.
[4] Declareuil, op cit., 861.
[5] Olivier-Martin, op. cit., 116.

Like another profound legal thinker of a later age, Montesquieu, he was not content with understanding and interpreting the letter of the law; his examination of the customs of the small county of Clermont was at the same time a study in comparative law and an analysis of underlying legal principles.

Beaumanoir's work was the supreme example but by no means the last of this *genre*. Late in the fourteenth century, Jean Boutillier produced his *Somme Rurale*, a work less concerned with a specific region – Boutillier, like Pierre de Fontaines and Beaumanoir himself, had been bailiff of Vermandois – than with an overall synthesis of regional custom. At about the same time the so-called *Grand Coutumier de France*, a composite work containing royal ordinances, rules of *parlementaire* procedure and the custom of Paris, was given its final form by another bailiff, this time from Evreux, Jacques d'Ableiges. Yet these diverse collections and commentaries, concerned as they were with only that part of the country in which the author was interested, only emphasized the lack of an official, authenticated and coherent set of customs which was certainly necessary if litigation was to become a less prolonged and expensive procedure. In the fifteenth century, the consolidation of the king's position as the victorious leader of a relatively united country, enabled him to take the lead in this direction. In his ordinance of Montils-les-Tours, Charles VII ordained that the customs of the kingdom should be drawn up in writing, approved by his legal advisers in the Parlement or in the *Grand Conseil* and finally confirmed by the king himself. The customs collected in this manner would then be enforced as law in the particular area from which they came.[1]

This royal initiative had few immediate repercussions; it was not until the very end of the century that further progress was made. In 1497, Charles VIII published an ordinance altering the procedure by which definitive customary laws were to be arrived at. Henceforth, a royal judge in the area concerned, after consultation with his colleagues and important local figures, was to draw up a tentative list of customs. Representatives of the three estates were then summoned to meet in the chief centre of the locality, to debate the contents of the draft. A majority of each estate's representatives had to approve the proposals before they were promulgated in the king's name.[2] Most of the written customary laws proclaimed

[1] Isambert, op. cit., IX, 252–3.

[2] Points remaining in dispute were subsequently settled by the Parlement of whichever region was involved; A. Esmein, *Cours élémentaire d'Histoire du Droit Français*, 750.

in this way appeared in the short period covering the reigns of Louis XII (1498–1515) and Francis I (1515–47), though the custom of Paris was not officially set down until 1570. Not infrequently the first composition proved to be defective and a revised version was needed. Thus the custom of Paris was rewritten in 1580, that of Orléans in 1583.

The final stage in the pre-revolutionary development of custom belongs to the legal commentators of the sixteenth to the eighteenth centuries. Once customary law had been written down it became possible to examine and criticize it systematically and from 1679 it took its place beside Roman and canon law in the curricula of French universities. Detailed study revealed diverging legal patterns in various regions and the vision of a uniform code of customary law engrossed the minds of a succession of eminent jurists. The first of them was Charles du Moulin (1500–66), a barrister in the Parlement whose incisive commentaries on the custom of Paris provoked that custom's revision in 1580. He envisaged a single code, separately ratified by all the towns in France and then promulgated by royal command. His enthusiasm for the idea blinded him to the impossibility of effecting such a formidable compromise by one simple process. The other famous names among sixteenth-century jurists are those of Guy Coquille (1523–1603) and Antoine Loisel (1536–1617). Both were concerned with the idea of unifying customary law and both published works seeking to identify the principles upon which all such law should be based so that ultimately a single law code might emerge. The same ideal was pursued during the seventeenth and eighteenth centuries, notably by two distinguished magistrates, Guillaume de Lamoignon, a First President of the Parlement under Louis XIV and a member of a famous *robe* family, and Henri-François d'Aguesseau (1668–1751), chancellor for more than thirty years, the most renowned lawyer of his time. However, it was not until 1804 that the desire expressed by Louis XI in the fifteenth century for '*une seule coutume*' was finally realized. Napoleon's Civil Code drew its inspiration in part from the revolutionary doctrines of 1789, but it was also the fulfilment of the long, slow process by which customary law had been first written down, and then sifted and unified.[1]

Roman law provided the second element in the development of the French legal system. Before the collapse of the Roman Empire in the west, Roman legislation had ceased to penetrate into Gaul and consequently for a long time afterwards that part of the country which retained Roman legal ideas depended not upon the law of Justinian but upon the

[1] Viollet, *Précis de l'Histoire du Droit Français*, 173 et seq.

Theodosian Code of 439 and especially upon its abridgement drawn up in 506, the so-called Breviary of Alaric. Then at the end of the eleventh century in Italy, the great revival of Roman law studies began. In the law school of Bologna, Irnerius and his disciples subjected Justinian's rediscovered texts to detailed interpretative analysis and both the texts and the new teaching method found their way across the Alps to Montpellier, where the first law school outside Italy was founded about 1160. In the course of the thirteenth century the teaching of Roman law spread as far north as the University of Orléans.

This expansion was viewed with misgivings by the French kings, for Roman law was represented by its teachers as the law of the German emperors, and as such it could constitute a political threat. Consequently, in 1219 Philip Augustus obtained a decretal from the pope, forbidding Roman law to be taught in the university of Paris. The wording of this papal command assumed the division of the country into the two areas of Roman – or civil – and customary law, which was to persist until the Revolution.[1] This division was an over-simplification, however, as the irregularity of the dividing line might suggest. From the west coast the border ran along the northern edge of Saintonge, Périgord and Limousin, dropped sharply to split the Auvergne between the two laws, and rose steeply again to round the Mâconnais and end above Lake Geneva. The land to the south of this line was the domain of Roman law. However, there were enclaves of civil law to the north of the line, the largest being the province of Alsace, and in the south the hold of Roman law was not strong enough to prevent towns like Arles and Montpellier, Toulouse, Avignon and Marseilles from drawing up their own customary codes in the course of the thirteenth century.[2]

In addition, the *coutumiers* which began to appear at the same time were markedly influenced by Roman law. Pierre de Fontaine's work on Vermandois, the *Livre de Jostice et de Plet*, and the *Établissements de Saint-Louis* all contained texts from Justinian's Code and Digest, and attempted crudely and unsuccessfully to marry the two forms of law, a task accomplished at last by Philippe de Beaumanoir. In later *coutumiers* there was less concern with the problem of reconciling the two forms, for a gradual fusion was taking place. In the traditional *pays de coutumes*, however, Roman law never obtained undisputed precedence, partly because of the increasing tendency for customary law to be written down

[1] Olivier-Martin. op. cit., 122.
[2] Viollet, *Précis de l'Histoire du Droit Français*, 118.

and therefore preserved. Nevertheless, Loyseau was one jurist who believed that in the absence of adequate guidance from custom, Roman law should be consulted, though both Du Moulin and Coquille maintained that in such circumstances the custom either of neighbouring areas or of Paris should be examined first and Roman law invoked only as a last resort.[1]

In analysing the sources of French law, a third important element, canon law, must be included. The body of doctrine, which in the sixteenth century became known as the *Corpus Juris Canonici*, consisted of five distinct parts. Its bases were the Scriptures, interpreted in the light of tradition, and conciliar and papal decrees. Though not surprisingly, since Christianity had originated in the Roman empire, the influence of Roman law was also considerable. The first part of the *Corpus* was the so-called Decretal of Gratien (*c.* 1150), the work of an Italian monk, containing a collection of texts with critical commentaries upon them. This was followed by the Decretals of Gregory IX, drawn up at that pope's command in 1234 and including papal decrees of the preceding half-century, a period of great legislative activity. The third part of the *Corpus* was the *Liber Sextus* of Boniface VIII (1298), which was intended to bring the collection of papal decrees up to date. After the Council of Vienna in 1311, Clement V promulgated its canons and some of his own decrees, in a collection known as the *Clementines* and this collection became the penultimate section of the *Corpus Juris Canonici*; the final part, the *Extravagantes*, containing a number of pronouncements by Pope John XXII, was only edited at the beginning of the sixteenth century.[2]

All these elements contributed to the final pattern of French law. Canon law provided the starting-point for judicial pronouncements on marriage, in secular as in ecclesiastical courts, the validity of the institution itself, its indissolubility, the equality of the partners. The condemnation of usury also sprang from the teaching of canon law and its rules were applied in a variety of other matters, including disputes over benefices and wills and crimes against the Catholic religion. Finally, it exercised a considerable influence in the development of legal procedure. Roman law left its mark particularly in the sphere of criminal law, for, despite the contrary influence of canon law with its emphasis upon the need for reparation by pilgrimage or public penance, the French penal laws became

[1] Esmein, op. cit., 723.

[2] Olivier-Martin, op. cit., 122–5; E. Glasson, 'Les sources de la procédure civile française', 413–23.

increasingly brutal. In the civil sector, Roman law gradually ousted custom from the field of contract. In this long, slow process of synthesis, the Parlement from its origin was deeply involved.

The growth in royal prestige and the accompanying centralization of justice clearly observable from the reign of Philip Augustus partly explains the Parlement's emergence in the thirteenth century. However, this purely political explanation conceals another equally important contributory factor – the profound changes in legal procedure, culminating in the establishment of the judicial appeal, which were also taking place. This development likewise dates from the time of Philip Augustus, when the *curia regis* in its judicial capacity began to formulate a more sophisticated procedure. The impetus for this change was provided by the renaissance in Roman law studies and by the foundation of a body of canon law. Both these disciplines encouraged the systematic and critical examination of sources, so that from being simply an *ad hoc* guide to specific problems, the law became a science worthy of study in its own right. One result of this new emphasis upon order and definition has been indicated already: the flurry of thirteenth century *coutumiers* written by jurists trained in Roman and canon law. Another result was that these same jurists became increasingly dissatisfied with the rudimentary procedure followed in secular courts and in particular with the irrational means of testing the sworn oaths either of the principals or of the witnesses, by ordeal or by duel.[1]

The judgment by ordeal was rare after the mid-twelfth century, though it did persist into the thirteenth. There were three forms of ordeal: by hot iron (*judicium ferri candentis*), by boiling water (*judicium aquae calidae*) and by cold water (*judicium aquae frigidae*). In the first two cases, the hand of the person submitting to the proof was made to grasp the iron or was plunged into the water, and if after three days the burns were not beginning to heal, he was presumed guilty of perjury. In the third case, the victim was thrown into a trough of cold water with his hands and feet bound. If he sank his cause was assured, though not his survival, on the principle that only a guilty man, rejected by the water, would float to the surface. All these methods of checking the truth of the evidence depended on the belief that God would give a sign of his displeasure if a false oath had been sworn and consequently the Church invested the ordeal with much religious solemnity. Before it began, the candidate attended mass and received Holy Communion. He was accompanied to

[1] Bongert, *op. cit.*, 201-3.

the preordained place by a priest, who played an important role in the grim proceedings.[1] The Church was less willing to give her blessing to another method of obtaining proof, the judicial duel, which involved the shedding of blood, and from the time of Louis VII French kings also proscribed this procedure. Nevertheless, the habit was not easily broken. Duels persisted into the thirteenth century, though by then they were invariably fought not by the persons concerned but by their champions. They were founded on the same principle as the ordeal, namely that through their outcome God would indicate where the truth lay.[2]

In the light of developments in Roman and canon law studies, such procedures seemed crude and unconvincing. From the end of the twelfth century the King's Court increasingly substituted the *inquisitio* or *enquête*, a procedure borrowed directly from canon law, by which the conflicting parties in civil cases each had the right to summon witnesses to give their sworn evidence before the judge, who would then decide on the basis of what he had heard. The emphasis upon oral testimony is important. When St Louis sought to have the system of *enquête* adopted throughout the royal domain, he was by no means proclaiming the superiority of written law. Indeed, if evidence was written down, it was only to record what was said in order to assist the judges and to prevent the parties from disputing statements previously made.[3]

At the same time, the amount of written material employed in civil cases was bound to increase under the *enquête* procedure. The judges could not be expected to remember all that had been said on both sides, and where a court covered a wide area of jurisdiction, like the *curia regis*, the distances involved made it difficult for witnesses to attend in person. On both counts, written testimony provided a solution. Therefore despite the continued emphasis upon its oral character, French civil procedure, as it developed, was forced to give a prominent place too to written evidence. That fact was responsible for a serious deficiency in the legal system. As we shall see, the attempt to combine oral and written procedure produced a time-consuming legal mechanism so that justice was dispensed extremely slowly, and the backlog of suits mounted steadily. By the middle of the fourteenth century the Parlement was overwhelmed with business, a state of affairs which persisted down to the eighteenth century.[4] However, before examining this procedure in detail, it is necessary to note

[1] Esmein, op. cit., 97–8.
[2] Bongert, op. cit., 228 et seq.
[3] P. Guilhiermoz, 'De la persistance du caractère oral', 22–3.
[4] Ibid., 42 et seq.

one other extremely significant legal development in the years immediately preceding the emergence of the Parlement, that of the appeal.

The concept of the appeal from an inferior to a superior jurisdiction and ultimately to the emperor existed in Roman law, and through the agency of ecclesiastical courts it was passed down to the Capetians. The revival of Roman and canon law undoubtedly stimulated the use of the appeal, though it is not clear when the practice was established in the royal domain. Beaumanoir described the appeal from the *prévôt* to the bailiff and from the bailiff to the king, but the procedure may have been in existence for at least a century before he wrote.[1] What was significant about this development was the fact that royal agents were now judging on appeal cases tried in the first instance before seignorial courts, and in that way the king's justice was reaching out beyond the boundaries of the royal domain.[2] That was the effect, not the cause, of the growth in royal prestige. However, expansion of the judicial role of the *curia regis* brought about by the use of the appeal was in turn a cause of the Parlement's institution. Both the *enquête* and the appeal were to become normal aspects of *parlementaire* procedure and by that means would be ultimately accepted throughout the kingdom.[3]

Every plaintiff seeking to bring a civil action before the Parlement, whether on appeal or in the first instance, had to present a formal written request to the king. This document was examined by the chamber of *Requêtes*, which, so long as the request was in order, then provided the necessary authorization to proceed in the form of *lettres de justice*, stamped with the royal seal. Next, the plaintiff cited his adversary to appear before the Parlement. The citation was delivered by a sergeant,[4] at first orally, but from the fourteenth century, in writing; and it contained also the date assigned for the first appearance in the Parlement. This date had to coincide with the period already set aside in the following session of the Parlement for cases from the bailiwick in which the defendant lived. In addition, sufficient time had to be allowed – a minimum of a week – for the accused to make the journey to Paris. If the defendant could not be found, the sergeant was permitted to leave the writ with his relatives or neighbours. Until the beginning of the fifteenth century in cases of

[1] Philippe de Beaumanoir, *Coutumes de Beauvaisis*, II, 399–400.

[2] Lot and Fawtier, op. cit., II, 321; M. Fournier, *Histoire du Droit d'Appel*, 231–2.

[3] The judicial duel persisted for a long time and traces of it may be found as late as the reign of Charles VI (1380–1422); Lot and Fawtier, op. cit., II, 320.

[4] A corps of law-enforcement officers based on Paris. The title was also used by the ushers of the *Chambres des Requêtes*.

appeal the sergeant had to summon both the judge who had passed the original verdict and the opposing party. Finally, having done his duty, he was required to draw up a report that might subsequently be employed to confirm the legality of the writ which he had served.[1] In practice, however, the sergeant could not always carry out his task efficiently because he could not always write. As late as 1667 Louis XIV ordered all such unqualified men to resign their office within three months.[2]

The paucity of qualified sergeants reflected the hazardous nature of the post. The nobility in particular had long shown their resentment against this intruder by murdering or mutilating him, or in one instance by making him eat the writ that he had brought to serve.[3] Royal legislation sought in vain to protect him from such treatment. By the ordinance of Moulins of 1566 sergeants were permitted to call for assistance from the local inhabitants and any attempt to interfere with them in the execution of their duty was punishable by death.[4] That these measures did not solve the problem was demonstrated a hundred years later, when in 1667 Louis XIV made provision for the sergeants to avoid having to make dangerous journeys to isolated country manor houses. The fact that the bearer of the Parlement's writ ran such risks suggests that it was one thing to deliver the writ and another to get the defendant before the court.

Apart from the defiance of powerful subjects, there were also a number of legitimate means of disobeying the summons. If the accused or any close relative was seriously ill, if the birth of his child was imminent, if he himself or a relative was due to be married, if communications between his home and Paris had been severed by flood or storm, by the collapse of a bridge or the approach of an enemy, if he were in prison or had lost his reason, he had a claim to be excused attendance. He then had to swear before the Parlement that his plea was valid, or if he could not attend in person, someone close to him had to testify in his stead. If his excuse was considered genuine and sufficient, the date of his appearance in court was postponed. If he was found to be malingering, the case was awarded to the plaintiff. This system remained operative until the seventeenth century, by which time representation by a solicitor had become obligatory, thereby rendering such a procedure irrelevant.[5]

[1] Aubert, *Histoire du Parlement de Paris à François Ier*, II, 26-39.
[2] Isambert, op. cit., XVIII, 108.
[3] Glasson, 'Les sources de la procédure civile française', 487.
[4] Isambert, op. cit., XIV, 198.
[5] Aubert, *Histoire du Parlement de Paris à Françios Ier*, II, 39–42; Glasson, 'Les sources de la procédure civile Française', 446–8.

The final preliminary stage in the legal process was the presentation when, on the day stipulated in the writ of summons, the plaintiff and the defendant appeared before a clerk of the Parlement whose task was to list the cases from each bailiwick and to settle the order in which they would be heard. In time the procedure was modified, and from the seventeenth century the solicitors of the two parties simply notified the chief clerk of their clients' names.[1] At last, the case was ready to be heard and at the appointed time the two adversaries entered the *Grand' Chambre.*[2]

At this point the gradual superimposition of written procedure upon the old oral practice may be clearly seen. Originally, the plaintiff – or his barrister – began by stating what he sought from the suit and why he believed that it should be settled in his favour, trying at the same time to provide supporting proof for his claim. In reply, the defendant rejected the plaintiff's case, alleging his own point of view, and often raising objections which had to be settled before the case could proceed further. Such delaying tactics might include the claim that the defendant was only acting on behalf of a superior; that he had not had sufficient time in which to prepare his case; that he required to see the land or property in dispute to be sure of the correct identification; that the plaintiff was not competent to prosecute, or that the procedure up to that point had not been entirely at one with the law. This preliminary hearing in the fourteenth century took the form of an oral debate before the *Grand' Chambre.* It was likely to last for a long time, particularly if the defendant was adept at invoking the various methods of retarding the proceedings or if – as was often the case – his counsel's methods and speeches were unusually prolix.[3]

Over a period amounting perhaps to several years, the employment of a purely oral procedure made it extremely difficult for the judges and the barristers to follow the threads of an argument and the use of documentary evidence was bound to increase. Already in the thirteenth century the practice of drawing up articles had been accepted by Beaumanoir.[4] These documents, composed by the barristers representing each party, stated the facts that each hoped to prove; they repeated in writing the oral pleas with which the hearing had begun. However, the articles could only be written down after the oral debate had ended and if the court decided that it required further clarification before passing judgment.

[1] Glasson, 'Les sources de la procédure civile Française', 488.
[2] Guilhiermoz, *Enquêtes et Procès*, 3 et seq.
[3] Aubert, *Histoire du Parlement de Paris à François Ier*, II, 55 et seq.
[4] Beaumanoir, op. cit., II, 132–3.

The procedure governing the preliminary part of a civil trial was modified in the course of the fifteenth and sixteenth centuries. Originally, writs did not always specify the reason for the plaintiff's action and therefore the defendant had sometimes to wait until the case came to court before he heard the charge; in consequence he could not prepare his defence adequately without a delay. It was to prevent this delay that in 1446 Charles VII ordered that writs should invariably state the object of complaint so that the defendant could come to court prepared to answer the charge. This development precipitated another: if the defendant could prepare his case in advance, why should not the plaintiff also know beforehand what line the defence intended to take? Gradually, the oral debate came to be preceded by an exchange of documents between the legal representatives of the two protagonists. First, the plaintiff's solicitor handed over an account of the prosecution's case, at the same time depositing in the registry of the Parlement any written evidence intended to support it. The defendant's solicitor in turn communicated his client's denial and surrendered his documentary proof. The written exchanges did not end there, however, for the prosecution could reply to the defence's statement and the defence could counter the prosecution's response. In 1667 Louis XIV sought with some success to eliminate these time-wasting and expensive refinements, whilst preserving the essential exchange of written statements.[1] The whole procedure was evolved for the benefit of the parties; the court itself had still to await the oral pleas for its enlightenment.

When the oral debate had ended, a number of possibilities were open to the judges. They could pass judgment at once, if they felt sufficiently well apprised of the issues involved, or, and this was a far more likely course, they could postpone their verdict until they had discussed the case further in private. If judgment was deferred it might be simply to allow the court more time for deliberation or it might be that the complexity of the case made it necessary for the parties to set out in writing, in the form of articles, the arguments which they had already propounded orally. However, it was unusual for the case to end at that stage. Most frequently the allegations made and denied by the contending parties could not be substantiated without further investigation, often involving the interrogation of witnesses. In such instances, the court made an order *en faits contraires*, the necessary preliminary to an inquiry or *enquête*. However, with the further slowing down of judicial business caused by

[1] Guilhiermoz, 'De la persistance du caractère oral', 54–6.

the protracted nature of the inquiry judges became more and more unwilling to invoke this procedure. Instead they increasingly preferred to issue an order *en droit*, which required only further scrutiny of written evidence in private session, without recourse to the *enquête*. The ordinance of Moulins supported this tendency and the ordinance of 1667 which further attenuated the *enquête* procedure and abolished altogether the order *en faits contraires*, substituting the order *à verifier*, confirmed the superiority of the *en droit* procedure. However, until the sixteenth century the *enquête* procedure remained predominant. This procedure too began with the drawing up of articles stating the facts which each side hoped to prove in the subsequent inquiry.[1]

The next move was for the presidents on behalf of the Parlement to appoint commissioners to carry out the investigation. These commissioners were not necessarily members of the court. If the parties so requested, local men of good reputation could be chosen. The most favoured arrangement, however, from the middle of the fourteenth century was the appointment of two commissioners, the principal one being a magistrate and his assistant a local man. If the inquiry was pursued according to that procedure the subordinate only took up his duties when his *parlementaire* colleague arrived in the district from Paris. The latter brought with him a letter of authorization carrying the royal seal and stipulating the commissioners' precise terms of reference. Usually he left the capital in July or August when the court was not in session, accompanied by a clerk and pack-horses loaded with parchment on which the commissioners' findings would be written down, and sacks in which that information would be sealed. As the magistrates with their entourage passed through one of the great gates of Paris, they often faced the prospect of a week or more upon the road. However, the expenses of the journey were paid for by the parties and, as we have seen, few magistrates did not welcome the opportunity provided by the commission for making a little extra money.[2]

When the commissioners reached their destination, the plaintiff and the defendant were summoned before them to hand over their copies of the commission, the writ ordering them to appear, sealed copies of the articles and if they were represented by solicitors, warrants of attorney. All these documents were read by the commissioners who then deposited them in

[1] Guilhiermoz, *Enquêtes et Procès*, 47 et seq.; Ducoudray, op. cit., 446–59; and Aubert, *Histoire du Parlement de Paris à François Ier*, II, 79 et seq., all give detailed accounts of the inquiry procedure in action.

[2] *See supra*, 16.

the sack brought for the purpose and noted their deposition in their official report which already contained the texts of the letter of commission and of the writ of summons. At this stage further delays were to be expected. One side or the other might object to the form of the summons or to the way in which it was served, to the opposing solicitor's authorization, to the commissioners' interpretation of their terms of reference, even to the commissioners themselves. The manner in which the commissioners dealt with these complaints depended upon the nature of their authority. Until the end of the fourteenth century they were appointed either as judges or as investigators. If their mandate gave them authority to judge, the dissatisfied party could demand an immediate decision upon his grievance and if he failed to obtain it, he could appeal to the Parlement. However, if the commissioners were empowered to act only as simple investigators, they first required the complaint to be written down and after assessing its gravity, they acted accordingly. In the case of a serious objection they stopped the proceedings and referred the matter back to the Parlement for judgment. When the objection was less weighty, they did not suspend the inquiry but did note it in their report and preserved it with the other documents in their voluminous sack, and reserved for the Parlement the final decision on its merits. Before the end of the fourteenth century, commissioners were almost always appointed as investigators, not as judges.

After disposing of the various objections raised by the parties, the commissioners originally administered oaths to the plaintiff and to the defendant by which each attested to the veracity of his articles and swore to answer truthfully when questioned about those of his adversary. However, this practice died out early in the fourteenth century and the commissioners thereafter proceeded directly to the central business of the inquiry, the examination of witnesses. The witnesses were chosen by the parties and served with subpoenas issued on the authority of the commissioners. If they failed to appear at the time and place specified, they could be brought by force, though if they did attend, their expenses were paid by the party in whose cause they were summoned to testify. They were first of all required to swear to speak the truth about the particular article on which they were to give evidence. No more than ten witnesses could be called to support any article, though before the fourteenth century this rule was not always rigorously applied. The commissioners interrogated the witnesses one by one, writing down their answers and the details of their name, place of residence, age, status, the date upon which the evidence was given and the article or articles concerned. When the deposition was complete it was read out to the witness in order that he could check its accuracy and have any mistakes corrected.

The list of people disqualified from acting as witnesses was large: all women (until the fifteenth century), servants, relatives or close friends of one of the parties, drunkards, professional soldiers, minors and known enemies of one of the litigants. Of course, if any witness failed to observe the correct procedure before the commissioners his evidence also was invalidated. The parties usually produced written evidence in support of their case, as well as the oral testimony of witnesses. These letters, memoranda, deeds, writs or whatever they might be, were added to the contents of the commissioners' sack and their receipt was indicated in the official report.

At the conclusion of the inquiry, the commissioners informed the litigants of the date on which their case would be judged before the Parlement. Then they closed the sack containing all the documentary evidence, attached to it a notice proclaiming to the court that they had carried out the inquiry according to the terms of their commission, and finally sealed it in the presence of both parties. The sack was either dispatched to Paris in advance of the commissioners, or was brought back with them for the final stages of the suit.

Very frequently the final part of the trial began with further delays and prevarications.[1] One of the parties, or both, might ask that the inquiry should be extended because he had more witnesses to summon, or that it should be annulled because of some irregularity in the procedure. The *Grand' Chambre* debated and pronounced upon the various objections. If they were dismissed or if no objections were raised by either party, the relevant sack of documents was dispatched from the chief clerk's office to one of the chambers of *Enquêtes*. There the presidents of the chamber concerned were responsible for nominating a counsellor to act as *rapporteur*. His duty was to sift the documentary evidence, to assess in writing which articles had been proved and which remained doubtful, and finally, in the light of this detailed scrutiny, to estimate what the correct verdict should be. He was then ready to lead the final discussion on the suit which would take place in private among the judges of his own chamber. At that session, the *rapporteur* took his colleagues through the case article by article; he gave them his opinion upon the value of the

[1] Aubert, *Histoire du Parlement de Paris à François Ier*, II, 114 et seq.

testimony offered by the witnesses, supporting his view with quotations from the various depositions; and he provided them with any further information if it was required. He had to do all this without indicating directly what his own decision had been. When he had finished speaking, the senior president took the opinions of the judges, and originally, with the exception of the presidents themselves, the *rapporteur* spoke last.

However, from the sixteenth century the practice changed, and though the order of speaking tended increasingly to depend upon the president's whim, the *rapporteur*, as the judge best equipped to give an opinion, habitually spoke first. He was also entitled to intervene if any of his colleagues made a factual error in arriving at their verdict. When the majority opinion had been ascertained, the *rapporteur* drew up the judgment or *arrêt* of the court, not a simple task since the *arrêt* had to be as succinct as possible, yet at the same time containing details of the evidence which the judges considered important. For a long time it was written in a form of dog-Latin reasonably intelligible to Frenchmen, whether they knew Latin or not; from 1539, however, French became the official language of the courts. When the chamber had approved the draft of the *arrêt* it was sealed and handed over to the chief clerk's office, whence it passed to the *Grand' Chambre* to be formally pronounced. The senior chamber remained, therefore, the ultimate judge, '*le moteur et le régulateur du parlement*'.[1]

Although in the course of time the chambers of *Enquêtes* did acquire powers of judging civil and criminal matters both in the first instance and upon appeal, in the last resort their decisions always required the corroboration of the *Grand' Chambre*. A similar situation existed with regard to the chambers of *Requêtes*. They too acquired the authority to judge certain cases in the first instance. Such cases were either pleaded orally by the court's barristers or were judged on written evidence. In either instance, an appeal from the verdict of the *Requêtes* was cognizable in the *Grand' Chambre*. Thus the *arrêt* had legal force only when it had been solemnly read out at a public audience of the whole Parlement by a president *à mortier* or, following the royal ordinance of 1536, by the chief clerk. But what had once been a great ceremony taking place on each of the four vigils of Christmas, Easter, Pentecost and All Saints, was transformed by the vast increase in *parlementaire* business into a routine fortnightly event. The *arrêts* drawn up in the preceding two weeks were

[1] Esmein, op. cit., 388.

published on alternate Saturdays, and in 1667 Louis XIV decreed that the publication of decrees should no longer be treated as a ceremonial occasion.

It should be emphasized again that the *enquête* did not remain the dominant feature of civil procedure, because it aggravated the slow and cumbersome nature of the whole legal process. It was the persistence of the oral tradition in that process side by side with the written element which was the root of the trouble. Royal ordinances continually sought to abbreviate the procedure, but because for the most part they did not touch this basic problem, they had only a limited effect. However, in the sixteenth and seventeenth centuries, two reforms were carried out which did have a lasting effect upon the judicial system. One of them, the reduction of the number of documents exchanged between the parties before the first hearing, has already been mentioned.[1] The second was more important. By the ordinance of Moulins in the reign of Charles IX, written evidence was finally given precedence over oral testimony, while Louis XIV's important ordinance upon the reform of justice in 1667 strictly limited the latter and in fact reversed the procedure according to which written evidence had always depended upon a prior court appearance. Henceforth, if one of the litigants wanted to call upon oral testimony he had to submit his reasons to the court in writing. His adversary could object, also in writing; the question was then debated in court and judgment given for or against. Thus the extreme dilatoriness of the old *enquête* system was at least mitigated, though it would be a mistake to imagine that judicial procedure was a brisk affair thereafter. The Abbé de Saint-Pierre was still complaining bitterly in the eighteenth century about the delays and high expenses involved in seeking legal redress.[2]

The execution of the Parlement's decisions frequently provoked further delays. The losing party was officially notified of the court's verdict and allowed a certain time, which he could usually have extended without difficulty, in which to carry out its findings. If these were ignored, the Parlement empowered its agents to enforce its decisions. These agents were the sergeants, the same officials who were also responsible for delivering writs at the beginning of the legal process. That task was not without its problems and neither was this second duty of persuading the recalcitrant parties to conform. The sergeants had power to confiscate

[1] *See supra*, 61.

[2] Guilhiermoz, 'De la persistance du caractère oral', 52.

property and even sell it by public auction, and as a last resort they could arrest and imprison the most stubborn offenders.[1]

Criminal procedure differed widely from the pattern of civil actions.[2] In cases requiring the intervention of the Parlement in the first instance the court's chief agent was the *Procureur-Général*, who from the beginning of the fourteenth century acted as public prosecutor on the king's behalf. He could denounce a suspect to the court upon his own authority or he could act jointly with a private individual who sought legal redress through his intercession. After Louis XIV's great criminal ordinance of 1670,[3] the *Procureur-Général* became the sole plaintiff; the private prosecutor could ask only for damages. Once the *Procureur* had obtained *lettres de justice* and made his denunciation, it was the task of the *Grand' Chambre* or of the *Tournelle* to appoint a commission to inquire into whether or not the evidence justified further proceedings. This examination was conducted in private; the various witnesses were seen separately and their signed depositions entrusted under conditions of the utmost secrecy to the chief clerk of the court. The commissioners' findings were handed on to the *Procureur-Général*, who gave his second opinion upon the matter in the light of the fresh evidence gathered during the inquiry. If he recommended that the prosecution should proceed, the court issued a writ. This could be one of two kinds, a personal summons or a warrant for arrest. As in civil cases, the former was delivered directly to the party concerned unless he was known to be likely to resist it, in which case a public proclamation was deemed sufficient. The order for arrest was issued only when very serious crimes were involved.

When the accused person appeared to answer his summons, he was questioned immediately by a judge nominated to examine his case. The rules governing this first interrogation were heavily weighted against the suspect. The absolute secrecy of the proceedings was maintained. He was allowed no defending counsel and kept in ignorance of the charge against him and of the evidence collected in the preliminary investigation. The questions asked and the answers given were all written down. If the accused admitted the charge a transcript of his confession was sent with other details of the interrogation to the *Procureur-Général*. Provided that the offence did not warrant capital or even corporal

[1] Aubert, *Histoire du Parlement de Paris à François Ier*, II, 136 *et seq.*

[2] Much of this section is based upon A. Esmein, *A History of Continental Criminal Procedure*, *passim.*

[3] Isambert, op cit., XVIII, 371 et seq.

punishment of some sort, the trial was almost at an end. The defendant could at last ask for a copy of the charges laid against him and was allowed, also in writing, to plead any extenuating circumstances. It then only remained for the *Tournelle* or the *Grand' Chambre* to pass judgment.

However, if the crime was a serious one and the accused persisted in denying his guilt, the trial was greatly prolonged. Before 1539, the year of Francis I's ordinance of Villers-Cotterets, the accused was permitted at this point to plead his innocence before the assembled chamber of judges, and to demand bail or acquittal. After 1539 he lost that right, and instead, the *Procureur-Général* proceeded at once to present, in writing, the case for the prosecution.[1] He usually demanded that the trial should continue according to the 'extraordinary' procedure. The euphemistic terms 'ordinary' and 'extraordinary' when applied to French criminal procedure concealed its most brutal aspect, the use of torture. Roman law had permitted torture as a means of obtaining proof when a strong supposition of guilt already existed, though in general it was only employed against the least considered classes of society. Its use declined in the feudal period and none of the great thirteenth century *coutumiers* discussed its role in criminal procedure. Yet the principle survived and, as early as 1254, St Louis was legislating about the details of its application. By the fourteenth century its use was widespread, and the king himself, through the agency of his *Procureur*, was taking the lead in its development.

Towards the end of that century, when Jean Boutillier wrote his *Somme Rurale*, the legal distinction between the two forms of criminal trial was becoming clear. Briefly, it was as follows: the 'ordinary' procedure was conducted in public, with provision made for the defence of the accused and without recourse to torture. According to the 'extraordinary' form, all these conditions were reversed: the trial proceeded clandestinely, the accused lost the right adequately to defend himself and the use of torture was permitted. This form did not become commonplace suddenly. For a long time the 'extraordinary' procedure remained exceptional, but as the judges found that they could not obtain sufficient proof from testimony, they yielded increasingly to the temptation to exact confessions through torture.

To appreciate fully why resort to torture should become prevalent, it is necessary to understand the rules of evidence which governed the

[1] Ibid., XII, 630.

judges' verdicts. In feudal procedure, those rules were often irrational or crude, the judicial duel, for example, or the presumption that an escaped prisoner had, in escaping, acknowledged his guilt. However, as the study and application of the law became more systematic, such rules were abandoned in the search for more exact and convincing methods of obtaining proof. One effect of this shift was that presumption of guilt ceased to be sufficient evidence for conviction; more compelling, irrefutable proof was required. By the seventeenth century three types of proof had become firmly established. The first was proof by testimony. For this form to be considered unassailable, there had to be at least two witnesses in support of each fact; they had to be genuine witnesses, reporting what they had seen and not what they had heard; they had to be disinterested observers, neither related to the accused nor biased for any reason for or against him. The second form was written proof, which might be produced at trials for such offences as treason or heresy. To constitute complete proof, the documentary evidence had to contain unequivocally criminal statements and be of indisputable authenticity. Even the testimony of handwriting experts was not always considered enough to ensure a document's genuineness. The third and last method of obtaining complete proof was by presumption, if the circumstantial evidence was sufficiently weighty and if the facts from which the inferences were drawn had been themselves incontrovertibly established. Even a voluntary confession made at the first investigation did not constitute sufficient evidence for complete proof. However, such a confession, if joined to other evidence of an inconclusive kind – the testimony of one witness, for example, instead of two – was deemed a sufficient proof of guilt.

Yet frequently, it was not possible to obtain either complete proof or a voluntary confession, although enough evidence existed to convince the judges of the defendant's guilt. In these cases, if the crime was a serious one, recourse could then be had to torture, as a means of extracting a confession which would, when added to the incomplete evidence available, provide the requisite proof. In cases which did not involve capital punishment, complete proof of the sort outlined above, was not always considered essential.

If the *Procureur-Général*'s appeal for the 'extraordinary' procedure was allowed, the witnesses already interviewed in the preliminary hearing were again summoned and asked to confirm on oath the validity of their earlier depositions. Having done so, they were then confronted separately and in secret by the defendant, who now, for the first time, was given the opportunity of countering the accusations made against him. He could object to the witnesses themselves and to the facts contained in their depositions, which were read out by the judge in charge of the interrogation. He could also put forward his own defence, seeking to prove his innocence through an alibi, for example, or to justify his action, perhaps on the grounds of self-defence or of insanity. However, after 1670, when the last major revision of criminal procedure of the *ancien régime* was undertaken, it was made even more difficult for the prisoner to defend himself effectively at this stage. All that was said at the various confrontations was written down and handed over, with the rest of the documentary evidence, to the *Procureur-Général.* He might require an investigation of the defendant's counter-claims; or he might recommend the application of torture if the proofs remained inadequate, or he might call for a verdict on the evidence already collected. His written report was sealed and put aside until all the judges of the chamber concerned – the *Tournelle* or the *Grand' Chambre* – had debated the case.

With the conclusion of the confrontations the role of the examining judge was at an end. The evidence was handed on from the *Procureur-Général* to another judge, whose task was to act as *rapporteur*; like his counterpart in civil matters, his task was to sift and analyse the documents, elucidate the case before the assembled bench and offer his own considered judgment upon it. If the judges ruled that the accused should be tortured – 'put to the question', as another euphemism had it – he was informed of the sentence by the *rapporteur*, who interrogated him once more before the torture began, and again after it had ended.[1] The torture could be more or less severe according to the powers of resistance exhibited by the victim; if he withstood it without confessing he could not be condemned to death, though he might still suffer corporal or afflictive punishment if the case against him was a strong one. Sentence in that case might be to perpetual or temporary banishment – not from the kingdom, but from the area of jurisdiction in which the victim lived – to the galleys either for life or for a term; to torture as a direct punishment; to the lash or to the *amende honorable*, a degrading public exhibition of guilt, whereby the victim, guarded by the public executioner, was forced to kneel in a

[1] Some indication of the techniques employed in the 'extraordinary' procedure may be obtained from R. Archel, *Crimes et Châtiments au XVIIIe siècle; see also* Esmein, *A History of Continental Criminal Procedure*, 137–9.

prominent place, dressed only in a long shirt with a rope around his neck and a lighted candle in his hand.[1]

If the accused confessed under duress and was condemned to death, he could then be subjected to further torture before execution to force him to disclose the identity of his accomplices. This preliminary torture was abolished on the eve of the Revolution in 1788, while the use of judicial torture to extract a confession had been forbidden eight years earlier. In fact these practices had already become obsolescent in the Parlement during the preceding decades.

Finally, if the defendant could not be convicted, one of three sentences remained. He could be acquitted altogether; he could be 'put out of court', a less complete absolution, which carried the implication of unproven guilt; he could be provisionally acquitted, whilst further inquiries were made with a view to obtaining more evidence. Whatever verdict the judges reached, they reached it collectively, although the opinions of the *Procureur-Général* and of the *rapporteur* were particularly influential.

The above procedure refers to criminal cases brought before the Parlement in the first instance. A word ought also to be said about cases reaching the court on appeal. The defendant could appeal not only against the final verdict, but also against all the interlocutory judgments pronounced against him during his trial, and he was able in some circumstances to plead orally before the judges. Yet, even on such occasions, the procedure did not allow real argument; the accused was simply interrogated about his objections to the sentence but was not given the opportunity to state his case fully. In cases of appeal, whether oral or conducted solely in writing, the opinion of the *rapporteur* was frequently decisive. Finally, the *Procureur-Général* could also appeal *a minima* if he considered the sentence to be an inadequate punishment for the crime.

In the middle of the eighteenth century the great political philosopher Montesquieu wrote that 'political liberty consists in security . . . Therefore the citizen's liberty chiefly depends upon the excellence of the criminal law'.[2] This comment was by no means intended to justify the extremes of brutality which characterized much of criminal procedure, yet it does

[1] Prison sentences as a punishment were fairly rare, though it was possible nevertheless to spend a good deal of time there both before trial to prevent flight, and afterwards, if fines had not been paid: F. Aubert, 'Le Parlement et les Prisonniers', 101–14; M. Marion, *Dictionnaire des Institutions*, 456–8; for a more recent, modified view, *see* R. Grand, 'La Prison et la Notion d'Emprisonnement dans l'ancien droit', 58–87.

[2] Montesquieu, *De l'Esprit des Lois*, Bk XII, Chapter II, 197.

provide the clue to its justification. Nobody doubted that the prime task of government was the maintenance of law and order, and it was widely believed that that duty could not be carried out without recourse to the deterrent principle. The savagery of the punishment was considered an important means of preventing crime. Thus one of the recommendations submitted by a counsellor of state preparatory to the drawing up of the criminal ordinance of 1670 noted: 'Impunity for crime is the greatest of all disorders met with in the administration of justice and it springs from the favourable and lax interpretation put by the judges from time to time upon the Ordinances which have been issued on this matter.' Whatever truth there may have been in this criticism, there is no doubt that the 1670 Ordinance not only confirmed but extended the harshness of the procedure and tipped the scales even further against the accused. In the words of La Bruyère, one of the few figures in seventeenth-century France to oppose the underlying principles of the ordinance,

> Torture is a wonderful invention and may be counted upon to ruin an innocent person with a weak constitution and exonerate a guilty person born robust . . . I might almost say in regard to myself, 'I will not be a thief, or a murderer'; but to say, 'I shall not some day be punished as such', would be to speak very boldly.[1]

La Bruyère's lonely voice was not the first to be raised in criticism of this sort. A legal commentator of the previous century, Pierre Ayrault, had already attacked some of the developments of the system: its secrecy and the overwhelming advantage given to the prosecution. Yet, until the end of the seventeenth century such criticisms were exceptional and support for the existing system could still be found in the last years of the *ancien régime*. Thus, Muyart de Vouglans, a criminal law writer of the 1760s, claimed:

> It may . . . be confidently asserted that for a single example of an innocent person who has yielded to the violence of the torture for a century, a thousand others can be cited to prove that, without the aid of this proceeding, the majority of atrocious crimes . . . would have remained unpunished and this impunity would have engendered disadvantages much more dangerous than those of torture by making a multitude of people the innocent victims of these wily rascals.

[1] Both cited by Esmein, *A History of Continental Criminal Procedure*, 192, 352.

However, when this defence of torture appeared, it represented only a minority opinion; the ideals of Ayrault and of La Bruyère, aided by the powerful advocacy of their successors, had gained widespread support. The first of these advocates was a forceful magistrate, Augustin Nicolas, the president of the Parlement of Dijon, who launched a trenchant attack upon the system of judicial torture only twelve years after it had been officially approved in the ordinance of 1670. His estimate of its effects was markedly different from Vouglans's later assessment. He wrote:

> Do sufficient reasons exist for dismembering a man alive and exposing ourselves to the chance of finding him innocent, and at the most setting him at liberty, however criminal he may be, if he has the good fortune to possess a charm or a constitution to endure these torments, or to top the injustice by adding a final punishment to an innocent person who confesses himself guilty under compulsion, to the first martyrdoms which we have already made him suffer? Does not this happen every day?[1]

It would be difficult to put the argument against judicial torture in a more persuasive and convincing form. However, it was not until the eighteenth century, through the writings of three great publicists, Montesquieu, Voltaire and Beccaria, that such arguments became generally respectable.

In *De l'Esprit des Lois*, Montesquieu denied the validity of the deterrent theory of punishment – 'At present, cases of desertion are very frequent; the death penalty has been invoked against deserters, but desertion has not been reduced'[2] – and went on to denounce the use of torture and the inadequate opportunities given to the accused to defend himself. Shortly after the appearance of *De l'Esprit des Lois*, the marquis of Beccaria published his *Essay on Crimes and Punishments*, a work originally written in Italian but available from 1766 in a French translation with annotations contributed by Voltaire, which was shortly afterwards translated into English. Beccaria was much more concerned with detail than Montesquieu had been. His condemnation of secret trials, of torture, 'this pretended test of truth, worthy only of a cannibal'; of secret accusations, 'a manifest abuse . . . consecrated by custom in many nations, where from the weakness of the government, they are necessary', was spirited, compelling and

[1] Ibid., 169–74, 373.
[2] Montesquieu, op. cit., Bk VI, Chapter XII, 91.

influential.[1] Voltaire was delighted with it, as his additions to the text reveal. Voltaire himself was perhaps the most important figure of all in shaping public opinion in these matters: his enormous prestige and reputation, his prolific literary output, his personal involvement in several *causes célèbres* like the Calas affair, which enabled him to demonstrate publicly the enormous capacity for brutality and injustice which was built into the criminal procedure, all these factors made him the leading advocate of a reform which would be ushered in shortly after his death with the coming of the French Revolution.[2]

The harshness of the 'extraordinary' procedure, the secrecy, the overwhelming disadvantage at which the defendant found himself, these were the abuses of the system against which the reformers chiefly levelled their attacks. Yet, ironically, they all sprang from a first principle which was in itself entirely admirable, namely, that conviction must depend upon certainty of proof. In England, the guilt or innocence of an accused person depended upon how twelve non-expert jurors assessed the available evidence given orally in open court. Their verdict was not reached mechanically according to an inflexible and demanding set of rules; it was a judgment based only on moral certainty. In France, on the contrary, the system of legal proofs left the judge no freedom of choice; he had to pronounce according to whether the accused was guilty or not guilty in the light of the regulations. This system frequently produced a situation in which the judge, despite possessing sufficient proof to be morally sure of the defendant's guilt, was nevertheless unable to convict. Consequently, the 'extraordinary' procedure was evolved to compensate for the impracticality of the system and to ensure that the deterrent principle would not be sacrificed. Because the essential problem was that of deciding whether the necessary proofs had been established or not, the way in which the defendant was treated was considered to be of secondary importance.

The various series of registers which constitute the official record of the court together form a vast and at first sight complicated and confusing collection of documents.[3] They become more intelligible, however, when examined in the light of the procedures outlined above. The Parlement was not the first French institution to preserve written records. The dukes

[1] C. Beccaria, *An Essay on Crimes and Punishments*, Chapters XV and XVI, 53–69.

[2] *See*, for example, Edna Nixon, *Voltaire and the Calas Affair*.

[3] The best study of these records is to be found in A. Grün's introduction to the *Actes du Parlement de Paris* (ed. Boutaric), I, i–ccxcvi; *see also* Ducoudray, op. cit., 262–84.

of Normandy had adopted the practice in their Exchequer – or judicial court – towards the close of the twelfth century, and when that province was incorporated into the French kingdom in the reign of Philip Augustus, and royal legists went to Caen and Rouen to hold sessions of the Exchequer, they came to appreciate the advantages of not having to rely upon memory, as was still customary in the *curia regis*. A more immediate precedent was provided by the king's chancery, where the practice had been established of writing down those judicial decisions of the *curia regis* which referred to the king's rights or domain.[1]

Mention has already been made of the oldest surviving records of the Parlement, the four books of the *Olim*, covering the period between 1254 and 1319, and drawn up by three successive scribes, Jean de Montluçon, Nicholas de Chartres and Pierre de Bourges.[2] The contents of the four volumes are divided into two sections, dealing with *enquêtes* and with *arrêts*. In a sense, the distinction is misleading, since both sections are only concerned with the final decree. In that dealing with *enquêtes* there is no mention of the witnesses' testimony, simply the court's decision. Montluçon indicated the context by writing at the head of each entry, *Inquesta facta* and at the end *probatum est* or *nihil probatum est*, formulae which later became variable. The second section, of judgments, contains decrees or summaries of decrees, pronounced after trials which did not require the procedure of *enquête*. Until Pierre de Bourges took over the registers they consisted mostly of *résumés* with little additional information. From the beginning of the fourteenth century they become much more informative; each decree is dated and copied out in full and even the name of the *rapporteur* is added. No separate register existed before 1312 for criminal records, and until that time the *Olim* included criminal as well as civil decisions, besides orders sent out to the bailiwicks and ordinances and letters from the king. It is unique amongst the court's records, for it alone is made up of texts copied from the great rolls upon which the Parlement's official decisions had been originally written. All subsequent registers contain the official acts themselves and therefore supersede the rolls.

Next came the *Jugés*, civil registers following on immediately after the *Olim*, containing, like them, decrees referring to trials conducted both with and without the procedure of *enquête*. In 1334, an attempt was made

[1] Langlois, 'Les Origines du Parlement de Paris', 92; L. Perrichet, *La Grande Chancellerie de France*, 272–3.

[2] *See supra*, 15.

to distinguish between the two when a separate register was opened for *arrêts*, decrees pronounced after oral pleadings only. However, a further complication now arose, for it became difficult to distinguish between those decrees which had been pronounced at the end of the public hearing and those only agreed upon after subsequent private deliberation, often necessary to allow a more intensive study of the documentary evidence.

All the Parlement's final decrees, in fact, were drawn up either in open court, after the pleas had been heard, or after private discussion at sessions of the *Conseil*, as such meetings were called. In the *Conseil* the judges reached their verdict upon all causes which, for one reason or another, had been referred for further scrutiny, including those which had been examined by *enquête*. Their decisions upon this last category – the *jugés*, strictly speaking, although the registers of that name contained additional material as well – were not liable to confusion. But between 1334 and 1364 it is very difficult to distinguish between decrees pronounced in audience and those pronounced after further discussion – though not involving an *enquête* – in the *Conseil*. Royal ordinances and letters, which also figured originally in the *jugés*, were separated in 1337 and 1342 respectively, though these new divisions were not strictly adhered to, and the *jugés* continued to include examples of each. Altogether, the *jugés* numbered 1,462 registers dated from 1319 to 1779.

The separate *Conseil* registers stretch from 1364 to 1776, and they, like the *jugés*, contain much additional material, as well as the decrees decided in council. Until the middle of the seventeenth century, the record of the Parlement's political deliberations is to be found in the *Conseil* registers, besides matters concerning the reception of new members, and royal ordinances affecting the salary, status or function of any member of the Parlement. There are 3,309 registers in all, a vast collection reflecting the significant amount of judicial business that was decided upon appeal; all those cases that had been judged in the first instance in lower tribunals upon written evidence were judged on appeal in council by one of the chambers of *Enquêtes*, and appeals that were pleaded orally in the *Grand' Chambre* might very well be reserved for further consideration too. This collection also illustrates the essential unity of the Parlement in the *Grand' Chambre*, for whether the *Conseil* decisions were reached by members of that chamber or by members of the *Enquêtes* or *Requêtes*, they were all entered without distinction in the same registers. By the same token, all decrees issued on cases pleaded orally are to be found in the *Plaidories* registers, irrespective of the chamber in which the case was originally heard.

The *Plaidories* date from 1364 to 1773, being sub-divided from 1372 until 1571 into separate registers for morning and afternoon sessions. At first the morning sessions were considered more important but gradually that distinction disappeared and with it the separation of the records. The *Plaidories* also contain ordinances published at the end of each *parlementaire* term relating to the next session and dealing with such matters as the dates upon which appeals from the various bailiwicks within the Parlement's jurisdiction would be considered by the court.

There is in addition a separate register for ordinances covering the period 1337 to 1785, though not all royal ordinances were sent to the Parlement for registration. Those that were had to be copied out accurately and without abbreviation, for the Parlement's record then constituted the authoritative version. However, careless transcriptions were by no means infrequent and in the eighteenth century the chief clerk was no longer even required to indicate, as he had done formerly, that he had compared the court's copy with the original for mistakes.

The last important civil registers are those of the *Conseil Secret*, which only begin in 1636 and end in 1786. There is nothing clandestine about these records, as their title might misleadingly suggest. They contain accounts of *lits de justice*, of deliberations upon political affairs, of the examination and verification of ordinances and other royal legislative acts sent to the court, with copies of remonstrances presented to the king and his replies, details of internal discipline and ceremonial – the reception of new counsellors, for example – together with matters relating to other sovereign courts and to inferior tribunals under the Parlement's jurisdiction. All these affairs were the concern of the whole court, meeting in plenary session. Finally, there are the criminal registers, beginning in 1312 and ending in 1784. The collected judgments of the *Grand' Chambre*, the *Tournelle* and the *Enquêtes* fill 906 volumes.

These seven collections form the bulk of the Parlement's official records, and all of them are to some extent duplicated by the minutes, the original rough drafts from which the official records were transcribed. There was always a time-lag between the act and its transcription into the registers; hence none of the latter is complete to 1790, the last year of the Parlement's existence, though the minutes for these remaining years have been preserved. In fact, many of the court's earlier minutes were destroyed in two fires which devastated the Palais de Justice in 1618 and 1776. Nevertheless, a formidable collection remains, housed in the Archives Nationales, some 10,500 volumes, an estimated 5,000,000 judicial decisions, the desiccated and summary history of five and a half centuries.

In the eighteenth century the Parlement's area of jurisdiction covered about one third of the country. Originally it had covered the whole kingdom, but with the extension of royal authority other sovereign courts had been set up in the newly acquired provinces, while the Parlement of Paris retained judicial control over that part of France which had at first constituted the king's domain. Thus, the Ile de France and Picardy, Champagne and Brie, Touraine and the Orléannais, Anjou and Maine, the Auvergne, Saintonge and Poitou all fell under the court's jurisdiction, as well as Dunkirk and parts of Burgundy. Within this area the Parlement was the supreme judge under the king of all matters which had not been specifically reserved by royal ordinance for other sovereign courts: the *Cour des Aides*, the *Chambre des Comptes* or the *Cour des Monnaies*. It judged in the first instance all matters concerning the king's person, rights and domain, including litigation on the subject of the *régale* – the king's right to administer vacant bishoprics and draw revenue from them; disputes involving princes of the Blood and the great officers of the crown; suits brought by privileged persons holding royal letters of *committimus*; crimes committed by noblemen, clerics, or judicial officers. However, the Parlement's chief judicial role was as a court of appeal to pronounce a final verdict upon cases which had been settled in the first instance in inferior tribunals. No appeal was permitted from the Parlement's judgment, though the king could quash it if sufficient grounds existed. He could do so because he remained the unique source of justice in the French state, never relinquishing his right to intervene personally in judicial affairs. It was because the Parlement judged on the king's behalf and with his authority that its competence ultimately became all-embracing and its decisions final.[1]

However, it had not always been so. In the feudal period sovereign justice had been exercised in the localities by seigneurs in accordance with customary law. Yet with the growth of the royal domain and of royal prestige, the king's justice began to undermine that of the great lords. In addition, because the nature of the king's authority had always been superior to that of his vassals, certain cases in which the king's person or his rights were involved, whether they originated in the royal domain or not, had to be brought directly before his courts. Such cases were at

[1] Olivier-Martin, *op. cit.*, 537–8.

first few in number and included *lèse-majesté*, the forgery of the royal seal and the debasement of the royal coinage. These *cas royaux* multiplied as the king tightened his hold upon the kingdom. They came to include all instances of private war, of usury, of highway robbery, all matters pertaining to ennoblement or legitimization, to trade or to the peace of the realm. The *cas royaux* were all judged in the first instance in the bailiwicks and on appeal by the Parlement.

The extension of the king's judicial authority by no means eliminated the seignorial courts which retained a wide variety of cases within their competence until 1789. Nevertheless, by the seventeenth century royal officials were supervising them closely and long before that time the principle of the appeal had been established, emphasizing the uniqueness of the king's authority and the judicial dependence of these tribunals upon the royal court. The importance of seignorial justice was further diminished by the growth of the theory of *prévention*. Royal lawyers argued that since the king was the source of all justice in the state, the seigneurs' right to administer it could only be delegated from the monarch. Thus the king, through his officers, began to intervene if judgments were not given expeditiously in the seignorial courts. The parties themselves were also encouraged to appeal to royal tribunals if they did not receive prompt justice.[1]

The Parlement had other formidable rivals within its area of jurisdiction, royal courts possessing sovereign powers of their own. One of the most important of them was the *Chambre des Comptes*, which, like the Parlement, stemmed from the *curia regis* and was empowered to judge in the last instance matters relating to the king's finances. Its jurisdiction was important enough and vague enough to provoke frequent quarrels with the Parlement, dating back to the early fourteenth century.[2] Successive rulers sought to extinguish the antagonism by appointing commissioners from each court to decide jointly upon controversial issues or by withdrawing such matters from the jurisdiction of both bodies and reserving them for judgment in the *Grand Conseil*. With some success the Parlement sought to establish a right of appeal from the *Chambre des Comptes*, though in cases incontrovertibly within its competence the latter retained its sovereign authority until the end of the *ancien régime*.

To a lesser extent, the *Cour des Aides*, another sovereign court based upon Paris, also offered a source of friction for the Parlement. This court

[1] Ibid., 513–18.

[2] Aubert, *Histoire de Parlement de Paris à François Ier*, I, 281–4.

was less ancient than the Parlement or the *Chambre des Comptes* and of different origin, having been instituted by the Estates-General in 1355 to supervise the payment of subsidies voted to the crown in that year. It was soon taken over by the king, however, and incorporated into the machinery of royal government. Its judicial task was to decide on appeal suits involving the payment of certain long-established taxes like the *taille* and the *gabelle*. The Parlement's disputes with the *Cour des Aides* were neither prolonged nor serious, partly because its origins made it a less formidable rival, partly because its jurisdiction was more narrowly based.[1]

More amicable still were the relations between the Parlement and the *Cour des Monnaies*, whose authority was clearly defined and limited to cases arising out of the counterfeiting or devaluation of the currency. These four sovereign courts all met under a single roof in the Palais de Justice in Paris. A fifth, perhaps the Parlement's chief rival, the *Grand Conseil*, was located some distance away, close to the Louvre. This court had acquired a distinct identity in 1497 when it was separated from the King's Council. Its competence was extremely vague; it was frequently called upon by the king to judge cases in which the Parlement had either shown signs of partiality or become involved in a jurisdictional dispute with another sovereign court. Because the *Grand Conseil* was used in this way to limit the Parlement's authority and because its jurisdiction extended over the whole kingdom, including those areas under the jurisdiction of provincial Parlements, it was frequently the object of bitter attack, not least in the last decades of the eighteenth century when the Parlement variously condemned it as supernumerary, parasitic, irrelevant and harmful to the country's judicial system.[2]

The existence of all these sovereign courts emphasizes a point of great importance about the French monarchic system, namely that the king remained the unique source of justice, delegating his judicial power to one court or another. He could also exercise it through his council. From the sixteenth century onwards the *Conseil du Roi* was increasingly subdivided; under Louis XIV a whole series of councils existed, some containing the same personnel but meeting under different titles: the *conseil d'en haut*, the *conseil des dépêches*, the *conseil royal des finances*, the *conseil privé*. All these branches of the King's Council wielded judicial powers which could be used to overrule decisions of the Parlement. In addition the king could delegate his judicial authority in specific matters

[1] Marion, op. cit., 156–7.
[2] Ibid., 265–6; Ford, op. cit., 39–41.

to his officials – something he frequently did for his *intendants* in the course of the seventeenth and eighteenth centuries.[1] Consequently, the Parlement's judicial freedom of action was limited more by royal authority than by the authority of seignorial courts, a fact which caused a great deal of friction between the king and his court. There was yet one other power to challenge the Parlement within its own domain, the Church.[2]

The boundary between secular and spiritual jurisdiction had long been in contention. In the thirteenth century the Church tribunals, the *officialités*, were able to judge a variety of cases not connected with purely spiritual or ecclesiastical affairs. They took over from the lay courts those cases concerning land or property in which the Church claimed ownership; cases involving feudal obligations when the Church was a party; crimes of violence if committed in a church or convent; cases involving contracts between laymen if one or other of them had undertaken by oath to respect his obligation; and the habit of taking an oath before the *officialité* as a means of confirming contracts was practised increasingly in the first half of the thirteenth century. In addition, the Church courts had complete control over cases involving heresy, sorcery, widows and illegitimate children, marriage, Church regulations and disputes between clerics. Slowly the Parlement succeeded in regaining lost jurisdictional ground for the king at the expense of the Church. In 1377, it forbade *officialités* to take cognizance of possessory or property disputes even if the defending party was a cleric, and it gradually added to the list of offences which were not covered by privilege of clergy. Grave crimes, like treason and forgery, were among the first to be excluded and then all serious criminal offences. With the passing of time, the lay courts, having repulsed the incursions of the *officialités*, themselves took the offensive. The Parlement began to assert its authority in questions relating to benefices, to heresy, to blasphemy; and bishops who resisted its intervention were heavily fined and even imprisoned.

The most protracted struggle between the secular and spiritual authorities concerned the cognizance of suits arising out of marriages and wills, a dispute beginning in the fourteenth century and lasting into the seventeenth, with the advantage falling increasingly to the Parlement. From the fourteenth century, cases which were not primarily concerned with the validity or nullity of marriages, but were nevertheless closely connected

[1] Olivier-Martin, op. cit., 435 et seq.

[2] Lot and Fawtier, op. cit., II, 448-59; Aubert, *Histoire du Parlement de Paris à François Ier*, I, 321 et seq; Olivier-Martin, op. cit., 479-83.

with the institution – questions of legitimacy, adultery, separation – were settled in the Parlement; indeed, its right to register dispensations and articles of marriage gave it an indirect control over questions of validity too. It also controlled the amount payable to the clergy in fees for baptisms, marriages and burials and it acquired cognizance over all cases involving the welfare of widows and their children. In the matter of wills, the Church retained its rights in theory, but in practice more and more disputes were taken before lay tribunals, and eventually the Parlement became the ultimate arbiter in this legal sphere as in almost every other. In fact, the Parlement intervened with increasing regularity in the day-to-day activities of the clergy: in disputes between *curés* and their parishioners, their bishops and their patrons; between bishops and cathedral chapters, between bishops and monasteries; between secular and regular clergy. In the fifteenth century it acquired the right to judge disputed episcopal and abbatial elections.

This supremacy of the lay court over the spiritual was crowned by the formulation of the appeal *comme d'abus*, first employed at the end of the fifteenth century. This was a legal process by which the *Procureur-Général*, or a private individual, could complain directly to the Parlement against an ecclesiastical judge who was considered to have exceeded his powers, trespassed on secular jurisdiction or contravened the liberties of the Gallican Church. By this means the Parlement gained the right to act as arbiter between lay and spiritual jurisdictions, thereby subordinating the Church's judicial authority in France to that of the king. The appeal played a particularly significant role in defence of the Gallican Liberties, a complex and prolonged issue which is best understood in terms of the Parlement's political activities.

The Parlement originally claimed jurisdiction over the whole kingdom but as time passed a number of provincial courts with sovereign powers within their own areas were established.[1] Their appearance was the result of the expansion of the royal domain, causing a great increase in the Parlement's judicial work and making the expedition of justice even more difficult. Besides, the king wished to respect long-established judicial traditions which existed in some of the newly acquired lands. Before indicating where and when these provincial Parlements were set up, mention should be made of the *Grands Jours*, a hybrid institution composed of magistrates from the Parlement of Paris but located in the provinces. The most regularly constituted of the *Grands Jours* was that

[1] Lot and Fawtier, op. cit., II, 469 et seq; Ford, op. cit., 38.

held at Troyes in Champagne, a province which came under the control of the French king when Philip the Fair married the heiress, Jeanne, in 1284. The king inherited the judicial court of the counts of Champagne and staffed it with members of his own Parlement. When Champagne was finally incorporated into the kingdom of France in 1360, the Parlement of Paris became the sovereign court of appeal for the province, but the *Grands Jours* continued into the early fifteenth century. They were subsequently revived on several occasions, the last time in 1583 to deal with the disorders created by the Wars of Religion.

In fact, the need to restore law and order or to assert the king's authority in a rebellious area or one not yet accustomed to accepting royal supremacy, was the most frequent cause of the appearance from time to time of other *Grands Jours*. Those held in 1454 at Poitiers, and in 1456 and 1459 at Bordeaux, were intended to restore the judicial machinery disrupted in the Hundred Years War; those held at Moulins in 1534 were to impress the newly acquired area of the Bourbonnais; those of Clermont in 1665, which were also the last in which the Parlement of Paris was concerned, followed the civil wars of the Fronde. All these *Grands Jours* were assizes conducted by delegates from the Parlement of Paris, usually held during the summer vacation and with no permanent existence.

The provincial Parlements, the first of which was the Parlement of Toulouse, were in quite a different category. At the beginning of the thirteenth century the south of France from the Rhone to the Garonne was ruled by the count of Toulouse, who continued to dispense justice through his own court until 1271 when Philip the Bold extended his royal jurisdiction into the Midi. For a time, two methods were employed by French kings to dispense justice in the south: a special chamber was established in the Parlement of Paris, the *auditoire du droit écrit* – since the influence of Roman law was predominant in the Midi – and *parlementaire* delegations were sent from Paris to Toulouse. Eventually, in 1443 Charles VII established a second Parlement, to sit at Toulouse, independently of the Parlement of Paris, with supreme jurisdiction over the Midi and administering the written law of the area. The next provincial Parlement to be established was at Grenoble in Dauphiné. In 1456 Charles VII confirmed that the ancient sovereign court of Dauphiné would henceforth become a royal Parlement. Shortly afterwards, in 1467, the area of Guyenne and Gascony, which immediately after its reconquest from the English had been placed under the jurisdiction first of the Parlement of Paris, then of the Parlement of Toulouse, acquired its own Parlement at

Bordeaux. Next came the Parlement of Burgundy, which sat at Dijon and was established in 1476 by Louis XI shortly before the death of the last duke of Burgundy, Charles the Bold.

The Exchequer of Normandy was of ancient origin and it remained a sovereign court after the province's absorption into France. However, the influence of the Parlement of Paris increasingly restricted the Exchequer's independence and was partly responsible for its decline as an effective organ of justice. In 1499 Louis XII reconstituted the Exchequer, making it entirely independent of Paris; from the reign of his successor, Francis I, it became known as the Parlement of Rouen. The Parlement of Aix in Provence was set up in 1501, nineteen years after that province had been inherited by Louis XI, to replace the existing judicial organization of the counts of Provence. The Parlement of Brittany was eventually constituted in 1553 after a long period of resistance from this most separatist inclined province. Further Parlements were established during the seventeenth century at Pau for Navarre in 1620, at Metz for the Three Bishoprics in 1633, at Besançon for Franche-Comté in 1674 and at Douai for French Flanders, Hainault and Cambrésis in 1686. Three supreme councils, which were Parlements in all but name, were also set up at Arras for Artois in 1530, at Colmar for Alsace in 1657 and at Perpignan for Roussillon in 1660. Finally a Parlement was established at Nancy for Lorraine in 1775.

The relations between the Parlement of Paris and its provincial counterparts varied from time to time and from court to court. The creation of other sovereign jurisdictions was certainly a blow to the pride of the magistrates in the Parlement of Paris; they resented too the division of the king's judicial authority and it was true that although he could delegate that authority to as many institutions as he pleased, the resulting judicial disunity did conflict to some extent with the idea of the indivisibility of royal justice, an idea upon which the development of monarchical power in France had been largely based. Until the seventeenth century, the Parlement's hostility was reserved particularly for the Parlements of Bordeaux, Burgundy and Brittany. It considered that all these institutions served areas in which the spirit of separatism and independence remained strong and in which, therefore, the centralizing influence of the Parlement of Paris was especially necessary.

However, parallel with this spirit of animosity the theory of the unity of all the Parlements in one class also developed. It was first enunciated in 1560 by the chancellor, Michel de l'Hôpital, who argued: 'If the king could exercise his supreme judicial authority through a single Parlement, he would do so. The different Parlements are only divisions of the royal Parlement.'[1] For a long time the Parlement of Paris refused to countenance the idea, but by the second half of the eighteenth century its attitude had changed. In 1755, it even quoted l'Hôpital's own words in upholding the theory to the king, Louis XV.[2] Ironically, its altered point of view was based upon its contention that royal justice was indivisible, a claim which previously had made it oppose the establishment of provincial Parlements altogether. However, it remained unassailably the most important Parlement, not only because of its seniority and the size of its area of jurisdiction; certain cases – like those concerning the king's right of *régale* – continued to be settled in Paris irrespective of their place of origin; certain privileged individuals holding royal letters of *committimus* under the great seal could take their disputes directly to the Parlement of Paris; and only on its benches could the princes and peers sit as counsellors by virtue of their title.

The Parlement was of course far more than the chief court of law in the land; before 1789, powers of justice, administration and police were not separated, and the Parlement had important responsibilities in the latter two spheres as well as in the former. In addition it was a great political institution. All these facets, however, require separate examination. In the sphere of justice alone, it is possible to detect in the Parlement all the weaknesses of pre-revolutionary French law: the excessive length of trials and the consequent high costs for the parties; the unjust brutality of the criminal procedure; the mechanical but by no means infallible system of proofs, the difficulty of enforcing legal decisions. Yet the Parlement's contribution to the maintenance of law and order and to the stability of the country under the crown was immense. The seventeenth century jurist Loyseau wrote that France, like Italy and Germany, would have been a divided country had it not been for the Parlement.[3] Largely through its agency French kings were able to unite their piecemeal inheritance into a single kingdom.

[1] Cited in Maugis, op. cit., I, 418.
[2] R. Bickart, *Les Parlements et la Notion de Souveraineté Nationale*, 152; *see infra*, 311.
[3] Lot and Fawtier, op. cit., II, 508.

CHAPTER THREE

The Parlement in Paris

Administration and police; the Palais de Justice

Before 1789 it was widely accepted in France that all judicial institutions should possess police powers in order to enforce their own legal decisions, to take action against suspected persons, and in general to preserve law and order. In the Parlement of Paris, the chief police officer was the *Procureur-Général*, whose orders were carried out by the ushers or by sergeants acting under his command. Through their agency wanted men were constrained and brought to trial.

There was another aspect, however, of the Parlement's power of police besides the right to arrest lawbreakers: that of issuing regulations which covered omissions in the law or which interpreted how a law should be understood. It exercised this right by means of *arrêts de règlement*.[1] These decrees could be annulled by the King's Council, if the sovereign considered them to be misconceived; otherwise they had permanent and universal application. They were of two sorts. There were those issued after judgment in suits in which novel implications had been raised, about which the Parlement felt the need to give a ruling. Almost always this sort of *arrêt* was concerned with narrow points of law or procedure, with how appeals were to be organized, for example, or how bailiffs were to act in cases of mortmain, or with what rights the king possessed over the sale of wood from royal forests or the holding of fairs, or with countless similar jurisprudential matters. In one sphere in particular, that of customary law, the Parlement frequently intervened with such decrees to define, suppress or amend traditional practices.

Other *arrêts de règlement*, however, were more broadly based, concerned not with legal technicalities but with administrative rules governing a wide variety of subjects, the maintenance of public order, the regulation of commercial transactions, the supervision of trade guilds. It was this second sort of decree which helped to make the Parlement a powerful

[1] Lot and Fawtier, op. cit., II, 440.

force outside the purely judicial sphere and especially within the confines of Paris itself. French kings were perfectly willing to tolerate this kind of action by the Parlement – at least until the appearance of the *intendants* – for it was considered a legitimate function, but they never allowed the court to claim the right to take innovatory measures without the tacit consent of the monarch. That would have been to deprive the prince of his essential role of governing the state. Nevertheless, occasions did arise when, for one reason or another, the king was unable to take necessary and urgent decisions and then, by means of *arrêts de règlement*, the Parlement did intervene in his stead to safeguard law and order in the kingdom. During the madness of Charles VI, the captivity of Francis I after Pavia and the civil wars of religion, the Parlement took the initiative. Although such occasions were rare, they are indicative of the high place held by the Parlement in the administrative hierarchy of the state.

Usually, however, its administrative role was performed on a less spectacular level; in particular, it was concerned with Parisian matters. The magistrates were responsible for the cleanliness and the upkeep of the public highways, of public monuments and fountains, of bridges, of the quays along the river's edge.[1] From the end of the fifteenth century, judges were nominated to visit different areas of the city to ascertain whether householders were keeping the space in front of their houses clean, whether the street cleaners were doing their job properly, and whether the residents were paying their share of the tax instituted in 1506 to cover the cost of keeping the roads in a clean condition. In fact, contributions were usually in arrears and the state of the capital's roads remained unsatisfactory. In 1547 the Parlement threatened with hanging those road makers who continued to ignore its hygiene regulations; almost a hundred years later, in the last years of Louis XIII's reign, one observer described the streets of Paris as more squalid than ever, impossible to walk along without high boots, which the judges themselves were forced to wear on their way to the Palais.[2] In the fourteenth and fifteenth centuries, animals contributed greatly to the filth of the streets: in 1377 butchers were commanded to prevent their beasts from wandering away and to kill them with care, lest the blood and offal should foul the street in front of their stalls; in 1400 the Parlement was alarmed at the number of hogs roaming freely through the city and orders were issued for their removal.

[1] Aubert, *Le Parlement de Paris à Charles VII*, II, 67–8.
[2] E. Boutaric (ed.), *Actes du Parlement de Paris*, I, Preface, lxx.

Besides the hygiene of the streets, the magistrates were also concerned with their freedom from obstruction. They insisted upon free circulation for carriages and pedestrians, opposing the construction of new buildings or the setting up of traders' stalls which hindered the traffic or shut out the light. In 1508 the court ordered a number of houses to be rebuilt, all to a uniform design, and in 1533 it forbade the building of houses with sections jutting out into the road. It also assessed the amount to be spent on road repairs and decided who was to pay.[1]

The Parlement had obligations too, in the matters of provisioning the capital. It was particularly concerned with the task of ensuring a constant supply of bread, moderately priced and of reasonable quality, a task involving it in numerous quarrels with millers and bakers. Sometimes the flour was bad, sometimes the bread was underweight, sometimes the price was disproportionate to the cost of corn. The punishments meted out for this sort of deception varied. On occasion it was both humiliating and apposite, as in 1420 when Guillaume le Vavasseur was commanded to plead for mercy in the *Grand' Chambre*, then to make public reparation before Notre Dame, and finally at his own expense to distribute a stipulated quantity of bread among the principal hospitals of the city. At other times the court imposed more peremptory punishments, as in 1476 when it imprisoned a number of bakers for false declarations about the price of corn.[2]

The provision of bread was only one aspect of the problem of feeding Paris; the Parlement had similar difficulties with butchers, fishmongers, tripe sellers and purveyors of salt. Fish was brought to Paris from the Channel ports, a journey which took merchants over great noble and ecclesiastical estates, whose proprietors demanded a share of the catch as a toll. Without royal protection there was a possibility that Paris would suffer a permanent dearth of fish. Thus the *Chambre de la Marée* was established to counteract this danger and to deal with all disputes arising out of the sale of fish.[3] As in the case of bread, the Parlement fixed the maximum price of fish and kept a watch upon its quality. On occasion it even went so far as to ordain what those people under its jurisdiction should not eat or drink; in 1272 the Normans were forbidden to make beer, because of the high cost of grain, and in 1565 Parisians were forbidden to eat lamb.

[1] Ibid., lxiv.

[2] Aubert, *Le Parlement de Paris à Charles VII*, II, 75; Aubert, *Histoire du Parlement de Paris à François Ier*, I, 305.

[3] *See supra*, 42.

Finally, it was the Parlement's responsibility to provide the city with wood for fuel in the winter, to regulate its sale and its price. Thus, in 1419 it authorized the cutting of wood from the forests of Vincennes and Saint-Cloud, though in 1473 the court had to remind one of its bailiffs that no trees in the royal forests could be felled without its permission. Ironically, the magistrates themselves often had a good deal of difficulty in persuading the particular official in Paris who was in charge of supplying wood to give them enough to heat the Palais.[1]

Much of the Parlement's authority in Paris came from its influence in municipal affairs. In 1499 one of the bridges linking the Ile de la Cité with the right bank collapsed into the Seine, with its houses and their occupants. The Parlement at once imprisoned the mayor and a number of local officials, and having instituted an inquiry into the disaster, temporarily took over the running of the municipal administration. From that time forward, the court exercised a permanent supervisory role, and the mayor himself, elected by Parisians – though later the election became a formality to disguise royal nomination – but under no direct obligation to the court, came to accept a position of subordination to the Parlement. At other moments of crisis the court once more took charge of the city's administration. This happened in 1512, for example, when Paris was threatened by the English army, and again thirteen years later when the king was a captive of the emperor. It happened during times of plague and pestilence as well as natural disaster. The Parlement also supervised municipal elections and it kept a close watch upon the city's finances, frequently inspecting its accounts, and upon the state investments or *rentes*, for which the mayor of Paris was responsible. Twice in one year, 1718, he was summoned before the assembled chambers to give an account of the state of these funds.

All the powers possessed by the Parlement in Paris applied equally in other towns within its jurisdiction, though normally – and this was equally true of the capital – day to day municipal business was controlled by municipal officials. The Parlement only intervened if the matter was serious or if an arbiter was required. When it did decide to act, it had a number of agents at its disposal to enforce its decrees, in particular its own ushers and the sergeants attached to the *châtelet*, the tribunal of the *prévôt* of Paris, whose police functions were gradually taken over by the civil lieutenant, himself replaced in 1667 by the lieutenant-general

[1] Aubert, *Le Parlement de Paris à Charles VII*, II, 77.

of police. Outside Paris the bailiffs and their representatives fulfilled a similar role.[1]

The need to preserve law and order enabled the Parlement to intervene in a number of other aspects of Parisian life. It was charged with regulating the conduct of Jews residing in the capital; indeed, the activities of all foreigners were closely scrutinized by a generally suspicious court. In 1651 it demanded that the king should dismiss Mazarin, claiming that no foreigner, even if naturalized, could sit in the King's Council. It made the same assertion against the Scots financier, John Law, in 1718. The magistrates sought in a number of ways to curb the frequent outbreaks of lawlessness, sometimes by forbidding duelling or the carrying of weapons, sometimes by admonishing the lieutenant and his officers of the *châtelet*, sometimes by the imposition of a curfew. Often the trouble was caused by marauding soldiers and the magistrates were then responsible for taking steps to discipline the troops and to prevent further pillaging and robbery. In 1524 they went so far as to condone the killing of such adventurers if done as an act of reprisal.[2]

The Parlement was aware, however, that the darkness of Parisian streets at night offered the greatest encouragement to crime, and its decree of 1658, that lights should be erected at the corner of every street to shine between ten o'clock in the evening and four o'clock on the following morning, did much to dissipate the darkness and to discourage the criminal. It kept a close watch too upon the poor, organizing collections for their relief and assisting their children to obtain work. It should be added, however, that the magistrates' attitude in this matter was not uniformly charitable; on some occasions the needy found themselves in the galleys.[3] Prostitution, vagrancy and public spectacles, whether banquets, festivals or theatrical performances, were all the subject of *parlementaire* regulations. In the case of the latter, the magistrates not only authorized or prohibited the entertainment itself, but even settled the prices of admission and the dates of performance. Their censures were not easily ignored: in 1571 and 1588 they prevented a troupe of Italian actors from performing in public or private, despite the fact that on

[1] Ibid., II, 69–72; although the *châtelet* was only on the level of a *prévôté*, it was an extremely important tribunal, first because it was immediately subordinate to the Parlement since there was no bailiwick in the region of the capital, and secondly because the law of Paris tended to be applied over a far wider area; *see* Marion, op. cit., 88–90; Lot and Fawtier, op. cit., II, 372–85.

[2] Boutaric, op. cit., I, Preface, i.

[3] Ibid., lxxviii.

each occasion the invitation to appear in Paris had come from the king himself.[1]

Under the banner of public order the Parlement also supervised prisons, hospitals and trade guilds. From the fifteenth century it nominated jailers, provided the prisoners with priests to say mass on Sundays and Holy Days and instructed a number of counsellors to visit the prisons four times a year to assess the prisoners' conditions and to discover whether any of them needed medical care. It took over the administration of the hospitals in the sixteenth century. Originally, this task had been solely a clerical responsibility usually resting with a bishop or with a cathedral chapter, but in that century lay control became general. The ordinance of Blois (1579) specifically excluded clerics from the administration of hospital funds. In Paris the Parlement had intervened earlier: in 1497 it was asked to arbitrate in a dispute between the master of the hospital, known as the Hôtel-Dieu, and the chapter of Notre Dame, which was responsible for its administration. A number of disputes followed this initial litigation until the Parlement stepped in to control the Hôtel-Dieu through the municipal council, which had inherited the chapter's authority. In 1751, the Parlement was involved in a bitter struggle with the archbishop of Paris to maintain its right of administration over Parisian hospitals.

The Parlement's regulations of guilds involved the control of wages and working hours, the supervision of all trades and professions – it was the Parlement which forbade a barber, whose patient had died whilst being bled, to continue his occupation – and the arbitration of disputes between different guilds, or between the same guilds in different towns. Sometimes it was called upon to settle disputes between workers and employers, as in sixteenth-century Lyons when a dispute broke out over terms of apprenticeship, between printers and their employees. Similarly, on a wider scale, the Parlement intervened in commercial disputes involving foreign merchants, in 1409 in a dispute between merchants from Holland and Zealand and the aldermen of Abbeville, in 1412 between Spanish merchants and traders from La Rochelle.[2]

Education, and particularly university education, also slipped from the jurisdiction of the spiritual authorities to that of the court during the fifteenth century. In 1446 Charles VII confirmed that all suits involving the University as a body should be carried directly before the Parlement.

[1] Ibid., lxxiii–lxxiv.
[2] Aubert, *Le Parlement de Paris à Charles VII*, II, 99–108.

This was a valuable privilege, for the Parlement, jealous of its authority, had already proved to be a tribunal immune to the pressures of the most powerful in judging disputes in which the University was concerned. An impressive example of this inflexibility may be found in the trial of Charles de Savoisy, chamberlain to King Charles VI. In 1404 the University walked in solemn procession to the church of St Catherine-des-Ecoliers to join in prayers for the cessation of war between England and France. On the way it encountered some of Savoisy's retainers leading their horses to drink at the river's edge. One of them blocked the procession and a scuffle developed. Being informed of what was happening, the chamberlain sent armed men who attacked and wounded a number of the students. All Savoisy's influence with the king could not save him from the consequences: the Parlement decreed that his house in the rue Antoine should be demolished and the site converted into a public square at his expense. Its contents were to pass into the possession of St Catherine's church. In addition, he was to contribute large sums towards the foundation of a chapel to which the University would have the right of nominating the incumbents, towards the expense of the trial and in compensation for the injuries inflicted upon the students by his retainers. Finally, again at his own expense, he was ordered to seek out the assailants and hand them over for trial. It was a savage sentence. Savoisy was particularly mortified by the cruel decision to destroy his magnificent home, and his friends sought in vain to persuade the king to save it. It was pulled down, though later rebuilt when Savoisy and the University made their peace.[1]

Sometimes, however, feuds within the University itself caused the Parlement more trouble than outside agencies.[2] In the sixteenth century the election of the rector was a frequent cause of disturbance. The rector, the head of the University, was elected annually, as were his subordinate officials, and on many occasions the neighbourhood of the church of St Julien-le-Pauvre, where the installation ceremony was conducted, was the scene of student riots and demonstrations. In 1525 and again in 1536 two candidates, each supported by their armed followers, claimed electoral victory, and on both occasions the Parlement intervened to appoint a third person. In 1545 the court took the precaution of appointing ushers to keep order during the election, since one of the candidates was known to be using bribery, corruption and intimidation in his efforts to enrol supporters. The coming of the Reformation to France and the civil wars

[1] Ibid., 89–92.

[2] Maugis, op. cit., II, Appendix II, 352, et seq.

of religion added to the number and violence of the disputes. In 1563 two Calvinists took over the rectorship of the University of Orléans and immediately altered the format of the master's degree to make it conform with their religious opinions. Five years later a similar Huguenot appointment at Poitiers produced such violence that parents withdrew their children *en masse*. In Paris in 1566 the rector refused to resign at the end of his year of office; in 1571, on the other hand, one of his successors sought in his own interests to bring forward the date of election.

It was the Parlement's task to settle all these matters. It had other duties too, in relation to the universities. It fixed the times of lectures and the dates and method of examinations, it gave permission to teach and approved what was taught, it laid down minimum periods of study and named the examination fees to be paid. It introduced a variety of regulations to deal with irregular and dishonest practices among students and teachers alike; it sought to prevent professors from selling their chairs, refusing to perform their statutory two lectures a day and awarding degrees in return for financial favours; and to prevent students from cheating at examinations, acting in a disorderly fashion, visiting taverns and gambling houses, dressing *à la mode*, or using the excuse of Holy Days to miss innumerable lectures. However, the results of the Parlement's efforts were disappointing; in 1737, the rector of the University of Bourges boasted that in one year alone he had conferred over five hundred degrees upon candidates who had studied neither in that town nor in any other. The Universities of Paris and Orléans were those with which the Parlement was most frequently concerned, but through its bailiffs it could and did intervene in the administration of all the universities within its area of jurisdiction.

Below university level, the court also possessed important responsibilities in college administration, and its intervention here was often of a remarkably detailed nature. It prescribed the order and duration of courses and the division of instruction into the various years of the scholar's career. In 1543, for example, it insisted that pupils at the Collège de Navarre in Paris who had a knowledge of elementary grammar should be segregated from their fellows who had not. It also dismissed schoolmasters at will and closely supervised their conduct. In the same school in 1576 a pupil was violently beaten by his tutor; the Parlement fined the latter and sentenced him to a year's imprisonment, and shortly afterwards, because of similar brutalities by other teachers, it completely revised the school regulations.

Closely linked with its supervisory role in education was the Parlement's function as a censor.[1] Because advances in printing coincided with the coming of the Reformation, it was in the area of religious polemics that censorship was first introduced. In 1521 Francis I made the faculty of Theology in the University of Paris responsible for approving the contents of volumes treating religious subjects. In 1624 this obligation was limited to four royal censors, at first appointed from within the faculty but later chosen from outside as well. By 1789 their number had risen to one hundred and seventy-eight. From the very beginning, however, the University sought the assistance and support of the Parlement. The magistrates had already become involved in printing and publishing matters as a result of the practice of authors and publishers of applying to the court for protection against exploitation by other publishers. From the Parlement they received a guarantee of their sole right to profit from the book or books concerned. Consequently, when in 1521, alarmed at the number of controversial religious tracts emanating from Germany, the University appealed to the Parlement for help, the magistrates found no great difference between their novel task of forbidding books to be printed and their established practice of authorizing their publication on behalf of particular beneficiaries.

From that time the Parlement's authority in this sphere grew. In 1523 it ordered the seizure of all works by Martin Luther which were being offered for sale in and around Paris, and in the same year issued general regulations aimed at all suspect religious volumes. From 1525 French translations of the Bible could not appear without the court's sanction, and in 1526 Francis I, who had been at odds with the Parlement over its censoring role, finally ordained that no book on a religious topic could receive the University's *imprimatur* unless it had also been approved by the Parlement. A little later, in 1535, royal letters-patent decreed that the Parlement should draw up a list of twenty-four approved printers, who would have the monopoly of their trade but who would have to practice it in Paris under the court's inquisitorial eye. In 1540, the Parlement issued a further list, this time of books which it was prohibited to print, sell, read or pass on, including Erasmus's *Enchiridion Militis Christiani* and Melanchthon's *De Corrigendis Studiis*.

Other volumes subsequently added to this *parlementaire* index included Calvin's *Institutes*. That work first appeared in France in 1542 and it provoked an increase in the severity of the Parlement's censorship. Having

[1] Ibid., Appendix I, 310 et seq.

heard the *Procureur-Général*'s report on the *Institutes*, the court ordered that all proscribed books, including this one by Calvin, should be brought to the chief clerk of the Parlement within twenty-four hours of the publication of the court's order under pain of hanging. Booksellers were forbidden to sell unauthorized volumes, while printers were required to work only in approved premises and to affix their own mark to each book that they produced.

However, the magistrates' attempt to eliminate the traffic in heretical works was unsuccessful, no doubt partly because of that perverse human trait, which, in spite of penalties, causes us to find what is forbidden infinitely more attractive than that which is simply ignored. The penalties were certainly fearsome. In 1547 a bookseller from Mâcon was condemned to make an *amende honorable*, the books found in his shop being burnt in his presence. Next, he was flogged in every part of the town where the public was accustomed to gather, and finally sent to serve in the galleys for life. As a caveat, the Parlement ordained that if at any time he tried to escape, he should be hanged forthwith, without further legal process. In the same year, a similar offence caused another bookseller to be tortured, flogged on three separate occasions and banished for ever from the kingdom. Nevertheless, by the end of the century the Parlement had accepted the fact that its harsh policy had failed. Henceforth, its attitude became a little less repressive, its supervision less suffocatingly paternal.

The spheres in which the Parlement exercised the power of censorship grew with the passing of time. Already in the sixteenth century, by forbidding the publication or sale of almanacs and books of astrology, unless previously approved by the faculties of medicine and theology, the magistrates were acting against a form of secular, pseudo-medical literature. Indeed, it was into the field of secular writing that their censorial activities were increasingly to be channelled. In particular, novel political works came under the Parlement's ban. In 1582 it condemned two books of Rabelais's *Pantagruel*, and in the later years of the century a number of other, less famous, works, but it was in the eighteenth century that the Parlement was most active in this direction. Then, its roll of condemned books included most of the best-known works of the French Enlightenment: Voltaire's *Lettres Philosophiques* and his *Dictionnaire Philosophique*, Holbach's *Le Système de la Nature*, Rousseau's *Emile* and *Le Contrat Social*, and a score of other volumes besides.

The attitude of the Parlement has been much criticized on the grounds that it was unenlightened and reactionary. However, it must be remembered that it was not the business of the court to adopt or reject contemporary attitudes; its essential task, on the king's behalf, was to maintain the law and to prevent attacks upon the established order. Like all judicial institutions it drew its inspiration from precedent, thereby providing the king's government with a continuity and a tradition of the utmost importance. Nor was its attitude to innovation always hostile: it reacted favourably to the new learning of the sixteenth century and supported the establishment in the universities of teachers of Greek and Hebrew, mathematics and history.

The Parlement exercised one other administrative duty, not concerned with the enforcement of commercial, municipal, police or educational regulations, but with supervising the administration and conduct of other royal officials. In the fourteenth and fifteenth centuries, despite royal objections, the Parlement acquired the right to nominate its own judicial subordinates – bailiffs, and seneschals, the *prévôt* of Paris, even minor officials like the sergeants and solicitors who were attached to the bailiwicks. The bailiffs and seneschals had to present themselves before the *Grand' Chambre* to have their letters of nomination registered, to take their oaths and to be formally inducted into their office. Often the ceremony would begin with a speech from the *Procureur-Général* reminding the novices of their obligations: the need to choose honest lieutenants and to pay them justly, to reside permanently within their area of jurisdiction, to refuse bribes. Finally, the First President warned them that if they failed in any of their obligations, they would be answerable to the Parlement. By the sixteenth century, the court had lost the right to name these officials itself for the offices were becoming venal and hereditary, but the ceremony was still performed and the court's supervision was no less real.

Of those royal officials whose duties were not directly the concern of the Parlement, the most junior amongst them were not expected to attend; it sufficed for them to take their oaths before the bailiff, but an impressive collection of important royal functionaries did make an appearance. They included members of the King's Council, the constable, the high admiral, the marshals, the colonel-general of infantry, the royal governors in the provinces, and in Paris, the mayor and aldermen and the officers of the *prévôt*. The ceremony was exactly the same for these officials as for the bailiffs and it was not intended to be a simple formality. Although the Parlement could scarcely challenge the right of great nobles like Anne de Montmorency, whom Henry II appointed Constable in 1547, it could and did order inquiries into the lives, morals, abilities and religious beliefs of less distinguished candidates before their reception.[1]

In the seventeenth century two rival institutions reduced the volume of administrative matters dealt with by the Parlement. In 1667 the office of lieutenant-general of police was established with wide-ranging powers. This officer was given responsibility for the city's security, for the cleaning and lighting of its streets, for the provisioning of its citizens, for the regulating of its guilds, for the supervision of its prisons, bookshops, hospitals, markets, taverns and brothels. The establishment of the office marked the beginning of a regular police force.[2] The second institution was that of the *intendants,* whose functions, though still far from clear, certainly overlapped those of the lieutenant-general to some extent. Besides their chief concern, which was with the collection of the *taille,* the *intendants* were occupied with problems arising out of famine or the spread of contagious disease: the supervision of markets, the procuring of adequate supplies of grain, the setting up of state workshops, at which the poor could gain employment, the distribution of money, the organization of alms. They were also involved in the suppression of local disturbances and in the surveillance of Huguenots. Before the repeal of the edict of Nantes in 1685, they were responsible for enforcing the anti-Protestant measures then in force; afterwards, they had to keep a close watch upon those converts whose zeal was suspect, to pursue Protestant pastors and to distribute confiscated Protestant goods to various hospitals and charitable institutions. They were also obliged to see that the funds raised by *rentes* remained at an adequate level.[3] Between them, the lieutenant-general of police and the *intendants* made considerable inroads into the Parlement's administrative preserves.

Since this administrative role was mainly exercised in the capital, the Parisian populace was very conscious of the court's prestige and authority. This awareness was further heightened by the fact that the surroundings in which the Parlement functioned, the Palais de Justice, provided both a daily meeting-place for Parisians and a suitably solemn and impressive setting for the court's deliberations.

• • • • •

[1] Aubert, *Histoire du Parlement de Paris à François Ier,* I, 290 et seq.

[2] Marion, op. cit., 441-2; G. Pagès, *Les Institutions Monarchiques*, 106-14; a more detailed study of the new office is to be found in P. Clément, *La Police sous Louis XIV.*

[3] Pagès, op. cit., 121-2; M. Bordes, 'Les Intendants de Louis XV,' 57; the work of C. Godard, *Les Pouvoirs des Intendants sous Louis XIV,* is an older, more detailed, but not altogether reliable account.

During the nineteenth century, archaeologists digging on the site of the ancient Palais de Justice unearthed coins dating from the reigns of Augustus Caesar, Trajan and Hadrian. Their discovery increased the probability that at least since the time of the Roman occupation some sort of building had stood there.[1] Situated in the cradle of Paris on the western side of the Ile de la Cité, guarded all around by the river Seine, it was almost certainly a fortified citadel built to guard the infant settlement against marauding Germanic tribesmen. Later, the Merovingians constructed a palace on the same site, which was subsequently restored by Hugh Capet's son, Robert II (996–1031); in the following century, Louis VI introduced drastic alterations, tempering its martial character with the foundation of a chapel dedicated to St Nicholas. From this time forward, the history of the Palais, obscure for so long, gathers life and detail.

The Capetian palace was by no means a spacious dwelling: when the English king Henry II stayed there in 1158, his host and hostess, Louis VII and his queen, had to lodge near by in the cloister of Notre Dame, and in 1201 Philip Augustus moved out in favour of another English visitor, King John.[2] At this time, it was still Paris's principal fortress – though shortly to be replaced by the Louvre – yet evidently it was not altogether invulnerable. In the spring of 1207 Philip Augustus was once again forced to leave the Palais, this time by the rising flood waters of the river. Nor was it the most salubrious of residences; the stench outside the royal apartments, caused by the mud and the refuse churned up by the wheels of passing carriages, persuaded the king of the advantages of paved streets around his palace. Within its walls was a garden, which afforded St Louis great pleasure and in which, in December 1259, he received the homage of King Henry III of England. From 1234 a gardener was regularly employed at the Palais. It was long believed that St Louis was responsible for extensive alterations in the structure of the building, but no evidence survives to support that tradition. He was, however, responsible for the erection of the contiguous Sainte-Chapelle, the church which served first as a royal chapel, and later, when the king bequeathed his palace to the Parlement and to the other sovereign courts, as a place of worship for the magistrates. This ethereal masterpiece of Gothic art, consecrated on Low Sunday, 1248, has outlasted both king and Parlement.

It is possible to reconstruct the outline of the Palais as it existed at the

[1] E. Boutaric, 'Recherches archéologiques sur le Palais de Justice de Paris', 3, *n.* i.
[2] J. Guerout, 'Le Palais de la Cité à Paris', I, 151.

death of St Louis's son, Philip the Bold (1285), on the eve of the drastic reconstruction at the hands of Philip the Fair.[1] Its boundaries were still those of a thousand years before, set in the shape of an irregular quadrilateral. Over the years, the Seine had been pushed back to the west, and facing the river at the north-western angle of the Palais stood the Great Tower or keep, where the king's treasure was housed. Almost opposite, on the eastern boundary of the building, was the entrance, leading from the rue de la Vieille Draperie, which followed the line of an earlier Roman road, opening into a wide courtyard. From the south-eastern corner of this courtyard a passage led away from the Palais to the Sainte-Chapelle and to the royal archives, the *Trésor des Chartes*, where the king kept his rapidly expanding collection of documentary records. Opposite the entrance, along the western side of the courtyard, ran the mercer's gallery, which led from the king's apartments to the Sainte-Chapelle. The king's dining-hall was situated on the northern side of the courtyard, and it was in this chamber that the first sessions of the Parlement were held. By 1278, however, an adjoining room had already been set aside for the hearing of law suits, and the *Salle du Roi* became the ante-chamber in which the parties awaited their summons to appear. Above it were the royal sleeping apartments, where the king held private council sessions.

In 1299 the first signs appear of the very considerable structural alterations which were to transform the Palais during the reign of Philip the Fair. An order dated May of that year commanded the royal treasurers, now transferred to the Louvre, to pay one Jacques Luce 1,500 livres to be distributed among the workmen at the Palais, and accounts drawn up in the following years by the same man fill in the details of what was being done.[2] The king apparently had three objects in mind, to extend the royal residence itself, to modernize the old building and to reshape it so that his principal administrative, financial and judicial officers could be installed conveniently around him. He had inherited a conglomeration of buildings widely disparate in style, ranging from the refined grandeur of St Louis's Sainte-Chapelle to the massive, sturdy simplicity of the great tower, the one remaining relic of the palace of Robert the Pious. His reconstruction recognized the fact that the Palais was no longer primarily a fortress; in its altered form it looked forward to the Renaissance *châteaux*. For the first time, the king's private apartments were clearly separated from that part of the building in which judicial and administrative matters were

[1] Ibid., 174–82.
[2] Ibid., II, 28–9.

attended to.[1] Access to the Palais was still by the door leading from the rue de la Vieille Draperie, which continued to be the principal entrance until the fire of 1776.

The courtyard beyond also remained structurally unaltered until that date, though over the years its appearance changed as well as its name. It became the Cour du Mai following the introduction of a brief ceremony held in that month every year, when clerks of the Palais planted a single hawthorn bush in the courtyard, to the sound of cymbals, trumpets and hautboys. Its character changed too, when, like many other parts of the Palais, it was invaded by merchants with their stalls and became the crowded setting for frenzied trading and bargaining. After the fire of 1776, it was decided to enlarge the Cour du Mai, and to build an impressive façade containing a grandiose entrance. Three architects were employed to produce a new design and a tax was levied on the people of Paris to help to pay for the expensive project. However, much of the ornamental gilt of which the new structure was mainly composed was destroyed during the Revolution and only restored in 1875.

From the time of Philip the Fair, a flight of stairs at the opposite end of the courtyard from the entrance led to the mercer's gallery. At its head two doors, separated by a pillar in which was set a statue of the king, barred the way. The gallery beyond led to the private royal apartments. The reconstruction of the Palais was not complete when Philip IV died in 1314 – it was not considered finished until 1324 – and the apartments were not immediately available for use by his successor, Louis X, whose wife gave birth to a son in 1316 in the Louvre. The principal royal chamber in the renovated Palais was at first the green room, its name derived from the predominant colour of the tapestries which embellished its walls. Towards the middle of the fourteenth century, however, its status declined; it became a mere ante-chamber, though a splendid one, adorned with fleurs-de-lis and the royal arms of France. The chief apartment now was the *chambre de bois d'Irlande*, a room sumptuously panelled on walls and ceiling with the costly wood after which it was named. It was situated above the green room, close to the roof, and from its high window the king looked out across the gardens of his palace to where the Seine flowed westward, past the Louvre and beyond the boundary of his still compact capital. He had been driven to this new retreat by the noise and bustle which succeeded the partial conversion of a private residence into a court of law.

[1] Ibid., 64–8.

A host of judges and functionaries, plaintiffs and petitioners, barristers, solicitors and sightseers thronged the narrow confines of the Palais, soon to be followed by hawkers and street-traders, who saw the possibilities of this new market. They first established their stalls along the eighty-foot length of the mercers' gallery, whence they swarmed like ants into every corner of the building. In 1406 they were granted the use of a kitchen off the gallery, which became the headquarters of their confraternity. In the sixteenth century especially, their number multiplied: haberdashers, seamstresses, booksellers, hatters, cutlers, sellers of ribbons and mirrors, purses and plumes, dolls and beads and pictures; jewellers, toymakers, lacemakers, clockmakers, all proclaiming their wares, struggled to attract the attention of the crowd milling around their stalls in the courtyard and along the ill-lit passages. Most of them were women, the most attractive and comely in Paris, according to one traveller who visited the Palais in 1664. This particular visitor, an Italian called Sebastian Locatelli, left the following advice, no doubt written with the wisdom of experience:

> One ought not to go to the Palais carrying money, for the young women quickly recognize ingenuousness; they plead with you, take your hand and will not desist until you have bought something. It is far better to go without money, to be cajoled and enjoy the pleasure of seeing so many beautiful things, without it costing a penny.[2]

An earlier visitor, who also succumbed to the flattery and persuasiveness of the stall-holders, commented that to leave the Palais without buying anything, in spite of the cajolery and charms of these women, implied either a lack of feeling or of money.[2] An eighteenth-century observer, Sebastian Mercier, found the scene unchanged; the tradeswomen, their hair prettily decorated with ribbons, were still the cynosure of every judicial eye.[3]

In the wake of the traders came the gossip-mongers, the sensation-seekers, the prostitutes and the unemployed. In addition, a group of parasites attached themselves to the Parlement itself: out-of-work clerks who acted as guides to newly arrived plaintiffs or as interpreters for those whose dialect they understood; out-of-work barristers, like the extra-

[1] H. Stein, *Le Palais de Justice*, 60, 194–5; Ducoudray, op. cit., 15.
[2] Stein, op. cit., 29.
[3] Bluche, *Les Magistrats du Parlement de Paris*, 276.

ordinary La Barre who came every day to the Palais in the early years of Louis XV's majority, without ever obtaining a brief.[1] Finally there were representatives of high society, for the Palais became a fashionable place in which to shop and to discuss the latest scandal. Lords and ladies of the court mingled with the crowds, and on occasion, as in 1534 when the duchess of Orléans was espied there, so did princes and princesses of the blood royal. The Palais presented a veritable cross-section of Parisian society. Throughout the day its walls reverberated with the cacophony produced by so many throats. Rumours flew and died, like sparks from a fire; altercations erupted and were submerged again in the general chorus; the shrill voices of innumerable street-traders shared a ceaseless litany. Other sounds besides the human voice were sometimes heard: the ringing of the tocsin, not always as an alarm, but perhaps to announce the birth of a dauphin; the peal of bells which signalled the beginning of a new *parlementaire* session; the trumpet blast preceding the publication of a royal ordinance or, on ceremonial occasions, heralding the arrival of the princes. These dramatic and unusual sounds raised the day-to-day tumult to an even higher pitch.

A similar effect was produced when the Parlement was engaged in controversial political matters. Then, the excitement became feverish and the mob swirled around the court's chambers, hungry for a glimpse of the principal actors or for a snippet of sensational news, either acclaiming or deriding the magistrates as they arrived and departed, according to the dictates of its extremely variable temper. In 1720, when the magistrates were exiled for their opposition to government policy, the crowds around the Palais watched their departure without emotion, yet twelve years later, upon their return from another exile imposed in very similar circumstances, their reception was rapturous enough to cause the Parlement's leading protagonist, the Abbé Pucelle, to hide his face, and his embarrassment, behind a large handkerchief.[2]

But these were extraordinary occasions. It was the court's judicial visage which visitors to the Palais most frequently observed; in the shape of the ushers, who policed the area in which the Parlement sat – an unenviable task punctuated by the arrest and summary imprisonment of over-enthusiastic spectators – summoned the parties when their case was due to be heard and supervised the ceremonial burning in the Cour du Mai of books proscribed by the court; in the shape of solicitors and bar-

[1] Ibid., 276–7.
[2] E. J. F. Barbier, *Journal*, II, 366.

risters interrogating their clients amid the jostling crowds or of condemned prisoners under escort, beginning the short, final journey to the place of execution. It was a paradox that the seething, febrile world of the Palais should be dominated by an institution as essentially unemotional and impassive as a court of law.

The king did not remain in residence for very long after Philip the Fair's reorganization. His withdrawal to new quarters within the Palais proved an unsatisfactory solution, for the tumult pursued him even there, and around 1360 Charles V abandoned this traditional royal residence altogether. Henceforth, it became the Palais de Justice and there the Parlement was king. However, the sovereign returned to the Palais on numerous festive occasions. In 1378 a royal reception was held there for the emperor, Charles IV, which included an elaborate and realistic theatrical representation of the capture of Jerusalem (1099) by Godfrey de Bouillon, the French hero of the First Crusade. In 1399 the Byzantine emperor, Manuel Palaeologus, was entertained at the Palais and in 1540 Francis I arranged a magnificent feast in honour of his old antagonist, the emperor Charles V. Such state occasions sometimes disorganized the judicial routine or left the ushers with the task of repairing the harm caused by convivial and exuberant guests. The feast held in 1558 to celebrate the marriage of King Henry II's daughter to the duke of Lorraine caused so much damage to the Parlement's official chambers that the court was forced to take up temporary residence in another part of the Palais. It suffered in this way because, ever since the days of Philip the Fair, its chambers had been considered to be the real heart of the Palais and it was natural, therefore, that such receptions should be held there.[1]

Of these chambers the most renowned was the Great Hall, built between 1301 and 1313 along the northern edge of the Cour du Mai, on the site of the former dining-hall.[2] It was the central feature of Philip's reconstruction. The main entrance was through the mercers' gallery to a staircase narrower than that giving access from the courtyard, though otherwise similar, leading up to an imposing Gothic door. Above the door, a trefoiled tympanum was encased in an arch whose outline was broken by ornamental moulding. To the left stood a statue of the Virgin and Child. Inside, the first impression was of spaciousness. The hall was over seventy-five yards long and almost thirty yards wide. It was divided

[1] Boutaric, 'Recherches Archéologiques sur le Palais de Justice de Paris', 54–8; Stein, op. cit., 38 et seq.

[2] There are a number of illustrations of the Great Hall and of other parts of the Palais in E. Fournier, 'Le Palais de Justice et le Pont-Neuf', I, 1–68.

lengthwise by eight pillars, which supported the double-vaulted gilded ceiling and turned the long room into two distinct halves. The ceiling was further reinforced by thirty-four horizontal beams, equally spaced, spanning the distance between the walls and the central column. The floor was a chessboard of black and white marble. The windows stretched along the upper third of the north and south walls; like all the windows of the Palais, they consisted of rectangular panels, mostly of clear glass, but bordered with colour and emblazoned with the arms of France. A series of statues of French kings, coloured in blue and gold, formed the chief decorative feature of the hall. Each of them was perched high on one of the pillars along the walls or along the central columns, some five or six yards above the ground. In 1618, when the Great Hall was destroyed by fire, there were fifty-eight statues beginning with the mythical fifth-century frankish ruler Pharamond and ending with one of Henry III, all so tightly clustered that no space could be found for one of Henry IV. Indeed, the superstitiously minded were inclined to view the fire as a divine, albeit drastic solution to an apparently insuperable problem of accommodation.[1] The series commenced with ten statues on the south side of the central pillars, moving chronologically from west to east, from Pharamond to an early Merovingian king, Dagobert I (d. 639). Ten more statues on the northern side of the pillars returning from east to west, almost concluded the Merovingian dynasty. The nineteen statues ranging from east to west along the north wall included Childeric III, the last of the Merovingians, all the Carolingians, and Hugh Capet and his successors down to Louis VIII, the son of Philip Augustus. The remaining statues were placed along the opposite wall, from west to east, beginning with St Louis and ending with the last Valois king, Henry III. The earliest statues dated from Philip the Fair's reign and came from the workshop of the royal painter, Evrard d'Orléans. Beside each statue was an inscription giving the name, dates and affiliations of the ruler.

Closely rivalling this royal display in fame was the immense banqueting table, composed of nine separate pieces of black marble, which stood in the south-west corner of the hall. The light reflected through the stained glass in the windows shone on its dark polished surface and added lustre to the gleaming plaques provided by Philip the Fair for its adornment. It too was destroyed in the fire of 1618. The walls were painted in various hues and from the mid-fourteenth century were decorated with animal skins, of which the most celebrated was that of a serpent – possibly a

[1] Guerout, op. cit., II, 132.

crocodile – traditionally identified as a trophy brought back from the Crusades by Godfrey de Bouillon. Under the third arch of the central column, seen from the eastern end, stood a golden stag carved in wood and gilded in 1364 by the brush of Jean d'Orléans; some time later it was replaced by a similar statue in bronze and in 1550, when a new door to the *Grand' Chambre* was constructed in the wall opposite, that too was replaced by the figure of a lion couchant, erected above the new entrance to symbolize the submission of even the most powerful figures in the land to the king's justice.

At the eastern end of the hall stood an altar dedicated to St Nicholas. Before 1340 mass was said regularly at a portable table but after that date Philip VI allowed this particular area to be reserved permanently for the purpose. In 1361, upon his return from captivity in England, John the Good ordained that every member of the Parlement, from the First President to the most junior usher, should have the right to hear mass there. Thus, the court's daily routine began henceforth with a corporate act of worship in the Great Hall. The cost of maintaining this oratory was met from two sources: in 1369 a judge of the Parlement, one Evain Dol, was assassinated by his wife's lover at her instigation, and in reparation the accomplices were ordered to endow the new shrine; and this income was further supplemented by a tax levied on all magistrates, solicitors and barristers at the time of their investiture.[1]

Until the second half of the fourteenth century at least, a series of high seats was ranged along the walls of the *Grande Salle* to accommodate the king's notaries and other forensic experts who, while not being members of the court, were closely associated with royal justice. In addition, the magistrates of the chamber of *Requêtes* held their sessions in one corner of the hall until about 1360. The solicitors and barristers accredited to the Parlement also set up their benches there, to be surrounded by the ubiquitous traders and the strident multitude who together gave the world of the Palais its characteristic atmosphere. There were three large fireplaces, two of them situated in the long north wall, from which the vast room could be heated, and a number of entrances. Besides the ceremonial door at the west end, another door near the marble table led to the royal apartments, and the entrance to the *Grand' Chambre*, constructed in 1550, was situated in the north wall. Until that door was built there was no direct communication between the two rooms. Instead, it was necessary to pass through a round tower at the north-eastern angle of the Great

[1] Delachenal, op. cit., 27–8; Guerout, op. cit., II, 141.

Hall, along what was virtually a passageway guarded by a door at each end. The intervening space was called the ushers' bar, for it was from the door opening into the hall that the ushers summoned the parties and read out official communications.[1]

The *Grand' Chambre* was scarcely less famous than the Great Hall itself. The original chamber of Pleas was demolished in 1302 and its successor completed in 1314, though it was as a result of its renovation under Louis XII that it became specially renowned. The entrance from the ushers' bar opened into the south-east corner of the chamber and from that angle the eye was attracted diagonally across the room to the opposite corner where the royal throne was situated. There the king presided in person over his Parlement when he held a *lit de justice*. The royal dais was draped with fine blue cloth and covered with cushions and pillows, all sewn with golden fleurs-de-lis. A canopy was spread above it. Below the level of the dais, along the north and west walls were the high benches, occupied on state occasions by the princes and peers and left vacant during normal judicial sessions. Those on the left of the royal throne were reserved for clerics, those on the right for laymen. They too were cushioned and decorated with lilies. Below them were the plain seats from which the judges carried out their routine judicial tasks. All this section of the *Grand' Chambre* was separated from the rest of the chamber by a barrier which cut the long room into two almost equal halves. The low seats were arranged around three sides of this inner square, and on the remaining south side, beyond the barrier, benches were set aside for the parties and their barristers. Access to the inner court was through a locked entrance directly opposite the *lit de justice*; each president and counsellor was provided with his own key. After 1550 the other half of the *Grand' Chambre* was invariably filled by members of the public, for few suits involving oral pleading were heard *in camera*, and the doors separating the Great Hall from the chamber of Pleas were usually open. Two ushers were always on duty to regulate the conduct of the audience.

The dominating feature of the whole room was an altarpiece depicting the crucifixion, fixed to the north wall on the left of the royal throne. It was first mentioned in 1405 in the chief usher's report of his spending for that year: 'To Jean Virelay, illuminator, living in Paris . . . for having delivered a picture on wood . . . which has been placed in the *Grand' Chambre* of the *Parlement*'.[2] It is probable that this painting was a replace-

[1] Guerout, op. cit., II, 132 et seq; Stein, op. cit., 21–7.

[2] Boutaric, 'Recherches Archéologiques sur le Palais de Justice de Paris', 39–40.

ment for an earlier one on the same subject. The walls of the *Grand' Chambre* were decorated with tapestries which were removed once a year for dusting and repairing; the floor was tiled and covered with matting in the winter and freshly cut grass in the summer. There was one large fireplace, equipped with enormous andirons, situated in the west wall beyond the high benches. The six principal windows, three in each of the long east and west walls, were guarded with shutters. Before 1550, when the communicating door with the Great Hall was constructed, an additional window existed in the wall between the two rooms through which the chief usher read out royal orders and the closing dates of *parlementaire* sessions.[1]

The *Grand' Chambre* acquired its reputation for magnificence, however, as a result of its renovation during the reign of Louis XII, which transformed it into a glittering, gilt-laden room; it became known as the Palais's 'golden chamber'. Its walls were hung with blue velvet embroidered with yellow lilies and the same material decorated the *lit de justice* and all its benches and desks. But it was the ceiling which had undergone the most spectacular metamorphosis. The original timber had been covered with a new ceiling of oak, whose series of pointed arches, each dropping into finely carved pendants, bore striking testimony to the flamboyant eccentricity of the late-Gothic style. Although its glory had faded by the seventeenth century, this was essentially the room described in such detail by Saint-Simon in his memoirs.[2] Of course there had been alterations in one hundred and fifty years: besides the new door to the Great Hall two boxes had been built out from the walls at the end of the high benches, one adjacent to the fireplace, the other to the entrance of the *buvette* whither the counsellors repaired for refreshments. From these twin vantage-points on ceremonial occasions foreign ambassadors and other distinguished visitors could watch the proceedings. The inner square of the *Grand' Chambre* was no longer inaccessible except through a locked door, though head-high barriers still divided the chamber and prevented unauthorized entry to the court-room proper. Finally, the mural dominating the room from its position on the north wall was not the one which Virelay had presented in 1405. The subject, the crucifixion, was the same, but four new figures had been added to those of the Virgin and the apostle John, at the foot of the cross: Solomon and St Denis stood on the right-hand side, John the Baptist and St Louis on the left, and in the background

[1] Guerout, op. cit., II, 145 et seq.

[2] Saint-Simon, *Mémoires*, xxv, 294 et seq.

views of Paris and of the Palais de Justice were depicted. The painter remains unknown, though his picture, the last of the series which the *Grand' Chambre* possessed, has survived.[1]

The topographical details of the Parlement's lesser chambers and offices are more difficult to establish, chiefly because of the court's expansion and the rebuilding which took place during five hundred years. However, certain locales are identifiable. Close together, along the northern perimeter of the Palais, stood, and indeed still stand, two tiled towers, the *tour de césar* and the *tour d'argent*, relics of Philip the Fair's reconstruction. Sessions of the *Tournelle* were held in the former, which also served as the king's robing-room when he visited the Parlement, although there was no direct access from there to the *Grand' Chambre*. Nearby was the criminal registry, one of the rooms destroyed in the fire of 1618. The records themselves survived because they were stored elsewhere in the attics of the Palais. The chief clerk originally had his office in the *tour d'argent*, but his collection of records proliferated to such an extent that they filled all the adjacent galleries; in the seventeenth century his office and his records were transferred to a more spacious site. The original chamber of *Enquêtes* was also burnt down in 1618 and there are only fragmentary clues as to its appearance: its windows were of the same pattern as those of the other rooms, its walls were panelled and hung with tapestries and it boasted a number of miniatures painted by Virelay.

Though these were the features of the Palais about which most has been written, it must be remembered that there was much more to be seen in this rambling building: the *conciergerie*, the jail to which offenders arrested within the area of the Palais itself were consigned, whose chief officer, nominated by the court, was the *concierge*; the Parlement's later chambers of *Enquêtes* and *Requêtes*; the private apartments of the First President and the *Gens du roi*; the accommodation set aside for the *Chambre des Comptes* and the other sovereign courts; the Montgomery tower, the ancient keep in which illustrious prisoners were confined; the clock tower dating from the mid-fourteenth century which became the public timepiece of Paris.

During its long history the building was structurally altered on a number of occasions and was frequently in need of serious repair. Each year the chief usher was authorized to spend a certain proportion of the money received in fines upon new fabric, though this grant only covered minor maintenance. In 1400 a number of presidents and counsellors made

[1] Guerout, op. cit., III, 22–3.

urgent representations to the king to repair the Palais, particularly the *Tournelle* whose floor was on the point of collapse. In 1406 the benches and doors of the *Grand' Chambre* had to be replaced, the new benches being lined with leather. Two years later the walls were threatened and in 1416–17 the building required further major repairs: the criminal registry was redesigned, the chamber of *Enquêtes* was repainted, the door of the *Tournelle* was renewed. In 1497 the floor of the Great Hall needed attention and in 1525 it was decided that its ceiling and fireplaces were unsafe. In 1549 the floor of the *Grand' Chambre* was also considered to be dangerous. In 1562 it was discovered that rain was leaking into all the rooms of the Palais.[1] But the most dangerous enemy, inflicting the most serious damage, was fire. There was an outbreak in 1557 begun by thieves in the chief clerk's office. Shortly afterwards a fire in the *Grand' Chambre* forced the magistrates to move for a fortnight to another room, while the outbreak in 1776 caused so much damage that the Cour du Mai and the whole façade of the Palais had to be redesigned. But it was the fire of March 1618 which had the most disastrous results.[2] The first warning was sounded at 2.30 in the morning by a sentry on duty in the palace garden. A strong wind was blowing and by the time he had roused the jailer the roof of the Great Hall was alight. At 5 a.m. it collapsed and the most famous room in the Palais, with its marble table, its royal statues and its bronze lion, was gutted by the flames. The fire swept into the chambers of *Requêtes*, the first chamber of *Enquêtes* and the ushers' bar, destroying them all. The construction of a new hall began almost immediately and work on the other rooms followed within twenty years of the calamity; yet with the disappearance of the historic hall the character of the Palais was permanently changed, its grandeur permanently diminished.

This, then, was the setting in which the Parlement functioned, splendid yet dilapidated, solemn yet irreverent, exalted in the midst of vulgarity. It has been argued that it was an unreal world in which the magistrates acquired a false view of their own importance.[3] But in Paris the Parlement was only less important than the king and was much more concerned than he with the citizens' day to day affairs. For most Parisians the Palais de Justice was far more the centre of the world than the Palais Royal. It follows, too, that the magistrates who made up this august body should attract to themselves as individuals some of its enormous prestige.

[1] Stein, op. cit., 10–14.
[2] Ibid., 50–4.
[3] Bluche, *Les Magistrats du Parlement de Paris*, 296.

CHAPTER FOUR

The Members of the Parlement

Recruitment; the magistrates' social status; the distinctiveness of *parlementaire* society; the sources of magisterial wealth; conclusion

---

During the five hundred years of the Parlement's existence, its members always occupied a leading place in society; the nature of their responsibilities made that fact inevitable. Originally, the king's counsellors had been great barons and prelates, and indeed the Parlement never altogether lost its ancient lineage: thus it remained the sole tribunal before which cases involving peers could be decided and the only one upon whose benches peers and royal princes sat by right.[1]

From the very beginning of the court's history, however, a growing number of qualified counsellors, the *magistri*, who were experts in the law, sat among the traditional royal advisers. These new men did not at first come from a particular social background. Some were clerics, others members of the lesser nobility, others again of non-noble origin. Until the middle of the fifteenth century the majority of these *magistri* were clerics – monks, archdeacons and, more rarely, bishops – but from that time onwards, laymen predominated. They were recruited increasingly from a non-noble background. In 1340, twenty-five out of twenty-nine counsellors in the *Grand' Chambre* were members of the lesser nobility; nineteen years later only one in five could claim that status, and by the beginning of the fifteenth century their appearance was exceptional.[2] However, they did not disappear altogether from the *parlementaire* scene. In the eighteenth century representatives of a number of knightly families, Berthelot, Mesmes, d'Argouges, La Bourdonnaye, Lefebvre de Laubrière, all held office in the court; indeed, Jean Antoine de Mesmes was its First President from 1712 to 1723.

Nevertheless, from the fifteenth century, magisterial rank in the Parle-

[1] *See supra*, 85.
[2] Lot and Fawtier, op. cit., 356–60.

ment was usually bestowed upon men of more humble origin, whose families had gained success in the law, or in administration, commerce or finance. The genealogies of some of the most famous magisterial families typify the general pattern. The fortunes of the Briçonnets – first represented by a counsellor in 1470 – were established by a mayor of Tours; the Lamoignons, who achieved *parlementaire* status in the mid-sixteenth century, made their way as secretaries to the Ducs de Nevers; the Séguiers, who first provided a member of the court in 1569, rose to prominence as tax collectors; the Aligres were descended from a chief clerk in the service of Louis XI, the Potier de Novions from a mayor of Paris, the Molés from a merchant draper, the Joly de Fleurys from a barrister in the Parlement of Dijon.[1]

The rate of social ascent varied greatly from family to family. The Chauvelins were represented by a barrister in the late fifteenth century, but only reached the Parlement in the mid-seventeenth century; the Bèze family, already prominent merchants in Nevers in the fifteenth century, had to wait until 1714 for an office in the *Enquêtes*. On the other hand, a very eminent *parlementaire* family, the Longueils, had as its first magistrate, in 1380, the son of a Dieppe merchant; Nicolas Soullet, received in the fifth chamber of *Enquêtes* in 1697, was the grandson of a successful Parisian draper. Gabriel Nègre, received in 1714, was the son of a solicitor in the court. Yet, however long or short the time taken to acquire membership of the Parlement, once that aim had been achieved there was a tendency at every stage of the court's history to retain that membership in the family, a tendency, in other words, towards the formation of an hereditary magisterial class.

There are examples of this development in the fourteenth century: Simon de Bucy, First President of the Parlement from 1345 to 1357, was followed into the court by his two sons, Simon and Regnault, both of them clerics, and by his son-in-law, Guillaume Morhier. Henri de Marle became a president *à mortier* in 1394, and was still in that post in 1400 when his brother became a counsellor. The president's son and two grandsons served in the Parlement and both the latter were linked by marriage with other legal families. One was a son-in-law of Adam de Cambrai, a counsellor in 1412 and a future First President, whose own son also became a counsellor in 1474. The other was the son of Anne du Drac, herself a member of another well-established legal dynasty. The family networks

[1] Details of these and other magisterial genealogies may be found in Bluche, *L'Origine des Magistrats*, *passim*.

became much more complex in the fifteenth century. One reason for that was that the clerics and the lesser nobility declined in number, and more opportunities were created for the new dynasties to establish themselves. Guillaume de Corbie, the grandson of a former First President and chancellor, acquired a seat in the court in 1446. Two of his sons followed him into the Parlement in 1484 and 1486 and he himself married into the Longueil family, the most firmly rooted of all *parlementaire* dynasties in the fifteenth century. The first Longueil representative in the Parlement died in 1431, but long before then, in 1418 and 1421, his two sons had also become members of the court. In 1461 a grandson and in 1500 a great-grandson maintained the family tradition. The Longueils were closely allied by marriage not only with the Corbies but also with the Marles and the Morvillers; in 1418 the latter were able to boast a First President.

It is notable that it was especially the senior posts in the Parlement which were becoming family property. The lists of presidents *à mortier* appointed during the reigns of Charles VII, Louis XI and Charles VIII reveal that half of them had relatives who had served or were still serving in the Parlement.[1] In the sixteenth century, however, the pattern was extended to include all offices in the court, partly because of the great increase in the number available, but chiefly because of Francis I's decision to sell offices publicly as a means of acquiring money for his depleted treasury.

The practice was not novel, though to appreciate how it applied to offices in the Parlement it is necessary to understand how magistrates were appointed in the first place. Originally the king, after consultation with his chancellor and other advisers in his entourage, nominated the members of his Parlement before each session began. This discretionary method accorded well with the sovereign's right to choose whoever he wished to give him counsel, but it became less satisfactory as the Parlement strove to become a permanent institution with its own regulations, procedure and tradition. Equally, however, the king would not approve a method of appointment which would enable the Parlement to become independent as well as permanent. Consequently, a compromise was tried in 1343, when Philip VI adopted a system of presentation according to which, at the conclusion of each session, a special commission composed of the chancellor and a number of presidents and counsellors drew up a list of members to sit during the following judicial year. The king had then to

[1] Maugis (op. cit., III, *passim*) has provided an invaluable record of the Parlement's personnel for the period from 1345 to 1610.

confirm the list. This confirmation soon became a formality, carried out at the beginning of each reign, and the lists themselves simply enumerated the Parlement's permanent staff. In addition, the king began to allow the court to recruit its own personnel: in 1366 Charles V permitted the election of presidents by vote of the members, and his son, Charles VI, extended that privilege to all offices if – as was usually the case – more than one suitable candidate presented himself. However, the sovereign maintained, and on occasion, exercised his right to appoint candidates of his own choice; it was still unthinkable that the Parlement should claim immunity from royal control.[1]

Hence, after 1418 when the successful Anglo–Burgundian alliance drove the French king from his capital and two Parlements were established, one in Paris under English control, the other at Poitiers, loyal to Charles VII, in neither capital was it considered a revolutionary step that the privilege of election should be withdrawn. The members of the Parlement in Paris were nominated by the duke of Burgundy or the king of England until 1426, when the new regime was sufficiently secure to allow the return of a limited electoral procedure. At Poitiers too, Charles VII kept a tight control over the recruitment of his magistrates: when he established new offices he nominated the candidates directly, and when he had to fill vacant places he permitted only a perfunctory election. After his triumphant return to Paris in 1436, when the two courts became one again, the king continued to supervise the membership. At first he contented himself with vetoing elections by the Parlement when he disapproved of the successful candidate. Later, he once more nominated his own candidates without recourse to the court's opinions. Then, in an ordinance of 1446, he officially re-introduced the electoral procedure, permitting the magistrates to choose the candidate whom they considered to be the most worthy, though nobody doubted that the king's tacit approval remained essential. In fact, Charles VII often took active steps to influence the election, especially in the case of presidents, by letting the magistrates know his own preference before voting took place. Towards the end of his reign a new convention was established, by which the Parlement proposed three candidates to fill any one vacancy and the king made his choice from them.

In 1465 Charles's successor, Louis XI, confirmed this practice, but this was a misleading and empty gesture at the beginning of a reign which has recently been called one of the most melancholy pages in the annals of

[1] Ducoudray, op. cit., 143–5.

the court.[1] In practice, Louis XI totally eschewed the electoral procedure; for the fifteen years of his reign for which exact figures have been established, every new counsellor taking his seat in the Parlement did so as a result of direct royal appointment. Charles VIII reversed the arbitrary policy of his father by restoring the court's right to elect three candidates from amongst whom the king made the final choice, though he, too, intervened increasingly in favour of his own nominees. Louis XII began his reign by confirming the list of members submitted to him. The magistrates made their oaths of allegiance to the new sovereign, but this time the *parlementaire* session, which had been in progress when these events occurred, continued without a break. This was the Parlement's most determined move yet in its efforts to persuade the king of its permanent nature and to protect itself against the arbitrariness of individual rulers. In comparison with Louis XI and with Francis I who succeeded him, Louis XII's attitude towards the court seemed far from authoritarian, yet the statistics indicate that the principle of royal nomination continued to vie with that of election. Of appointments made to the office of counsellor during the reign, thirty-two were preceded by an election, twenty-seven were imposed by the king's command.[2]

At the accession of Francis I, therefore, although the Parlement had become a corporate institution with clearly defined functions and attributes, it still did not control the recruitment of its own members. However that is only half the story: the question of how offices came to be vacant is also a problem closely connected with the growth of heredity and venality, which needs to be examined if that growth is to be fully comprehended. Death was the most obvious cause of vacancy, and promotion to a post incompatible with service in the Parlement was also common. There were other causes, however, one of which became especially prevalent from the early years of the fifteenth century: resignation. A counsellor might decide, for some perfectly honourable reason, to resign his office, and having previously secured the king's consent, he would announce his intention to his colleagues and suggest the name of his successor. The Parlement undertook an inquiry to ensure that the resignation was voluntary and in keeping with the regulations and that the proposed successor was worthy and capable to succeed. If its findings were satisfactory on all counts, the candidate was accepted without a vote.

[1] Lot and Fawtier, op. cit., II, 351.
[2] Maugis, op. cit., I, 125.

It thus becomes clear that the absence of an election did not necessarily imply an arbitrary royal nomination. Although evidence for such nominations is plentiful, the fact that magistrates too could name their own successors certainly introduces another element into the situation. Although the king's consent remained indispensable, this procedure did, to some extent, offset thoroughly capricious appointments and allowed the principle of hereditary succession to make some progress in the Parlement. Resignations became more numerous as the fifteenth century progressed. Under Charles VIII, thirty-two out of the thirty-five appointments not preceded by a vote were made in this way.[1] Among the magistrates the procedure was beginning to compete for popularity with that of election. As more and more of them acquired office by that means, fewer felt the need to support the old system, which in any case had never offered the opportunity of hereditary permanence. Resignation did not have to be in favour of a successor, however; it could be made directly to the king. When that happened, the king exercised the right to name the successor.

The growth in the number of resignations brought with it the abuse of *survivance*, which was to become an accepted part of office-holding under the *ancien régime*. This was the practice of resigning in favour of a close relative, son, son-in-law, nephew or brother, while at the same time obtaining a dispensation from the king to continue to hold the office jointly until eventually it passed into the possession of the survivor.[2] This procedure was evolved to preserve the office within the family, even if sudden death intervened – as it frequently did as a result of plague or epidemic. Its appearance was another indication of the growing importance of the hereditary principle among the magistrates. Its persistence, however, was due to the fact that French kings found a way of making it profitable, and at this point the whole question of venality, as it affected the Parlement, becomes germane.[3]

A sort of venality had already appeared by the second half of the fourteenth century, when the king began to distribute signed but unsealed letters of provision to offices in the Parlement, which could then be produced whenever a vacancy occurred. The letters were given out on the recommendation of princes and other influential figures in the royal

[1] Ibid., 111.

[2] R. Mousnier, *La Vénalité des Offices*, 15.

[3] A useful introduction to the problem of venality is to be found in G. Pagès, 'La Vénalité des Offices dans l'Ancienne France', 477–95; the classic study, however, is that of R. Mousnier, *La Vénalité des Offices sous Henri IV et Louis XIII*.

circle, who expected the recipients to express their gratitude in financial terms. In the fifteenth century, venality began to appear in the resignation procedure: a sum of money paid to the king could ensure the succession of a particular candidate. Nevertheless, although the sale of subordinate judicial offices had flourished since the fourteenth century, until the sixteenth century the Parlement as a body remained antagonistic to the practice of venality within its own ranks. When a magistrate resigned, the ensuing inquiry sought to establish whether or not there had been any financial arrangement between the retiring member and his proposed successor.[1] Yet the fact that such an inquiry should be deemed necessary was itself an indication of the prevalence of the abuse.

Despite the Parlement's strictures, by the beginning of the sixteenth century, in the reign of Louis XII, venality was becoming a feature of office, not only in the bailiwicks and *prévôtés*, but in the sovereign courts themselves. The magistrates' collective hostility was based in part upon their own professional *amour-propre*: if wealth became the most important qualification for office, judicial standards would certainly be jeopardized. Another reason existed, however, for their opposition and that was the threat apparently posed by venality to the principle of heredity, a principle which had made great strides in the course of the fourteenth and fifteenth centuries. The prospect of profit could encourage the king to insist upon his right of nomination at the expense of the electoral and resignation procedures, in order to appoint the candidate who could pay most. In fact, in the sixteenth century venality became the necessary ally of heredity because the magistrates were forced to accept the king's terms and to pay for the right to retain their offices within their own families.

Francis I made venality a coherent system of government. The customary financial plight of the French crown was exacerbated by his Italian adventures, and in 1521 he created new offices of presidents and counsellors in the Parlement, distributing them in exchange for payment. To the court's remonstrances he replied baldly that he needed the money, and if the Parlement could not suggest other means of obtaining it, it would have to accept his method. In the following year, the king chose to reimburse two rich merchants who had made him a substantial loan by giving them counsellors' seats in the Parlement. These instances involved the creation of new offices, and Francis erected over fifty during his reign, but he also took advantage of existing malpractices concerning resignation and *survivance*. When he gave a magistrate permission to

[1] Maugis, op. cit., I, 114.

resign, he also extracted from the beneficiary a tax amounting to a proportion – usually a tenth or a twelfth – of the office's estimated value. Francis also authorized the retiring magistrate to accept money from his successor. In addition, he stipulated that if the resigning party died within forty days of the agreement, his office would revert to the king, who could then draw its full cash value in the resale and not simply the proportion which he would otherwise have received.

This was not an attempt on the king's part to restrict the growth of hereditary office, but rather a method of obtaining a higher price. Similar guile was employed in dealing with *survivances*. In 1541 the king acknowledged that many of the most important offices in the state were held with the privilege of *survivance* in favour of children or other relatives, mostly young men. He announced his intention of abolishing the practice except in those cases where money had been paid to the crown; he was promptly inundated with offers of huge sums from office-holders who were not in that category.[1] Succeeding Valois kings all followed the example of Francis I by employing these methods to raise additional revenues. The effect was greatly to increase the hereditary tendency in the Parlement. By the second half of the fifteenth century the provision of office was normally looked upon as a life-long endowment – unless the office-holder chose to resign or was guilty of some grave defect in the execution of his functions, in which case the king could declare his office forfeit – but office-holders remained uneasy in the face of sporadic royal assaults upon this principle.

The coming of venality, however, tended to strengthen the magistrates' hold upon their office, for the king was disinclined to remove office-holders who had ministered to his financial needs. Also, if offices were considered to be hereditary, their value would rise and that would be to the king's advantage. For their part, the magistrates, having invested in what was virtually a piece of property, were naturally more anxious than ever that it should remain in the family. Hence, in the course of the sixteenth century, the hereditary pattern which had been more apparent earlier among the presidents, enveloped the whole court. Of course, there were many new magisterial families established in the sixteenth century, when the court's personnel was almost doubled, but it does seem that the fears of their fifteenth-century predecessors about the effect of venality upon heredity were groundless; in the first twenty years of Francis I's reign, from 1515 to 1535, at least one third of the new counsellors

[1] Mousnier, op. cit., 20 et seq.

came from families which had previously provided members of the Parlement.[1] The origins of the new families were not different from those of the old: the Charlets were originally merchants and municipal office-holders in Poitiers; the fortunes of the celebrated family of Lefèvre d'Ormesson originated with a solicitor in the Parlement, and that of the equally renowned Lefèvre de Caumartin de Boissy with a royal treasurer in Picardy; the Larchers were descended from a Parisian fish merchant.[2]

The hereditary principle was given its final support in 1604 with a declaration of Henry IV according office-holders the right to transmit their office to their heirs, without the forty-day reservation, if they paid an annual sum to the crown equal to one sixtieth of the office's value. This was the *paulette* tax, named after its instigator, a royal secretary called Charles Paulet. A recent analysis of the eighteenth-century personnel of the Parlement indicates how far this long-term hereditary process had gone. Between 1715 and 1771 members of 590 families sat in the court. Of these families, 212 were represented by two or more magistrates and 150 others were established legal dynasties. One family dominated all others: the Le Peletiers contributed eight representatives, including a First President, three presidents *à mortier* and a president of the second chamber of *Enquêtes*. Almost as impressive was the Lamoignon record, with five presidents *à mortier* and five counsellors. In this period too, the last representative of the ancient family of Longueil, which claimed six presidents *à mortier* between 1418 and 1716, took his place.

As had happened previously, marriage alliances widened and consolidated family interests. The Gilbert de Voisins, who in the eighteenth century provided the Parlement with two presidents *à mortier*, an *Avocat-Général* and two counsellors, were directly related to sixteen families with representatives in the court between 1715 and 1771. Some of these families were themselves allied with others, the Lamoignons with the Catinats, the Maupeous and the Potier de Novions; the d'Aguesseaus with the Talons, the Le Brets and the Lefèvre d'Ormessons; the Larchers with the Fortias, the Parents with the Voyer d'Argensons. Altogether, the Gilbert de Voisins were connected either by marriage or by indirect alliance with seventy-one *parlementaire* families. This was an exceptional case, but there were numerous examples of similar, though less extensive family trees.

[1] Maugis, op. cit., III, 159–76.

[2] Bluche, *L'Origine des Magistrats*, 124–5, 240, 258–9.

The hereditary process had produced a solidarity among the magistrates which was by no means solely based on direct kinship.[1]

Nevertheless, despite this general tendency towards hereditary office in the Parlement, a contrary proviso must be added: the court never became a wholly closed caste limited to a handful of magisterial families. The above-quoted statistics also reveal that even in the eighteenth century 228 counsellors were new men, representing their families in the Parlement for the first time. Of course, a number of them had relatives who had already occupied high legal office, as *maîtres des requêtes* or as members of provincial Parlements or of the other sovereign courts, but far more had no such impressive lineage. Their origins were the traditional ones: many were the descendants of solicitors, barristers, clerks or notaries. The celebrated Abbé Pucelle was the son of a barrister and the grandson and great-grandson of solicitors. Some were the sons of financiers, like Bernard de Rieux, whose father was the prodigiously wealthy banker Samuel Bernard; others reached *parlementaire* rank from either an administrative or a commercial background. There is evidence that at the very end of the *ancien régime* the number of new men was actually increasing and that at least one new magistrate out of every four was not a member of one of the traditional legal dynasties.[2] These are important facts, for it has been argued that the Parlement's political behaviour in the eighteenth century was affected by an increasing spirit of exclusiveness.[3] Yet although the hereditary tendency in the court's structure was certainly maintained during the final decades of the Parlement's existence, there is nothing to suggest that it developed to such an extent as to change the magistrates' traditional outlook.

However, a broader change in the magistrates' social attitudes during the eighteenth century is also predicated by those who support this particular point of view, and it may be worth while, therefore, at this stage to examine the extent to which the social status of the Parlement's members altered with the passing of time. It has already been noted that from the beginning, membership of the court conferred great prestige upon its members. For the Parlement was the highest tribunal in the land, frequently called upon to pass judgment upon the disputes of the social *élite* and it was inconceivable that the magistrates should not themselves acquire a lofty status through the exercise of their professional duties.

[1] Bluche, *Les Magistrats du Parlement de Paris*, 121–30.

[2] Carré, *La Fin des Parlements*, 312–22.

[3] *See*, for example, Ford, op. cit., 250; G. Lefebvre, *The Coming of the French Revolution* (trans. R. R. Palmer), 29–30.

In one of the late fourteenth century *coutumiers*, the *Somme Rurale*, it was asserted that the profession of barrister conferred a dignity equivalent to that bestowed by knighthood. If that were true for members of the bar, it was certainly true too for members of the Parlement. However, nobility depended upon the will of the king and the fact that a man became a member of the King's Court did not at that time make him *ipso facto* a nobleman; he had still to be ennobled by the monarch.

Many of the early magistrates were clerics, the possessors of ecclesiastical fiefs, and the equal in dignity and prestige of the secular nobility. They were able to take their place in the Parlement without any feelings of social inadequacy. However, the situation was not very different for the non-noble laymen who had studied and qualified in the law. The nineteenth-century French historian Fustel de Coulanges, has emphasized the high standing enjoyed by the lawyers:

> The society of the Middle Ages held these men in great respect; the profession of the law was considered as honourable as that of arms. As soon as a member of the middle class made his name as a lawyer, it was considered just and natural that he should be made a nobleman.[1]

The *magistri* therefore had sufficient professional prestige to enable them to sit beside great clerical and secular dignitaries, and indeed, to pass judgment upon them. In the early lists of counsellors contained in the *Olim* records, the names of the *magistri* are mixed indiscriminately with those of bishops and barons and knights.[2] Nevertheless, the status of the lay magistrates was frequently confirmed by the bestowal of royal letters of nobility, a practice which can be traced back to the reign of Philip the Bold. Not all non-noble magistrates were thus honoured, but most of them did acquire a fief, albeit a very small one, and with it they acquired the reputation if not the strict legal title of nobility.

With the growth of heredity in the court, however, there developed an intermediate stage in the process of ennoblement. In his famous regulation of 1600, regarding the *taille*, Henry IV ordained that nobody should include himself in the ranks of the nobility if he was not descended from a father and grandfather who had served in certain honourable offices which were capable of initiating that rank.[3] This somewhat vague prohibition was explained more precisely in the works of contemporary legal

[1] Cited by Ducoudray, op. cit., 132.
[2] *See*, for example, Beugnot, op. cit., IV, 1051, 1053, 1314.
[3] Isambert, op. cit., XV, 234.

commentators like Charles Loyseau, who maintained that counsellors in the Parlement were invested with personal nobility by virtue of their office – the acceptance of a traditional point of view – but that the achievement of hereditary nobility came only in the third generation of successive occupancy of one of these 'certain honourable offices', of which a counsellorship in the Parlement was undoubtedly one. This was the celebrated formula *patre et avo consulibus*, which French lawyers borrowed from Roman law and fitted into French jurisprudence. Loyseau further defined the service requirement for each generation as twenty years or death whilst in office, a rule which was generally accepted and was quoted with approval by Louis XIV in an edict of 1704.[1]

However, in 1644 all the members of the Parlement – presidents, counsellors, *Gens du roi*, even the chief clerk – were exempted from the formula of *patre et avo consulibus*; they achieved full nobility transmissible to their heirs upon their reception into office in the court. Subsequent legislation was contradictory but by 1715 nobody doubted that the magistrates of the Parlement, by law as well as by function and status, were true members of the second estate.[2]

Their noble rank entitled them to certain privileges.[3] They were exempt from paying the *taille*, the most onerous of taxes; they were not subject to the *corvée*, the obligation to provide public labour for a number of days each year; nor were they obliged to serve in the militia or to quarter royal troops. In addition, they enjoyed freedom from the *gabelle* or salt tax. In the judicial sphere, every nobleman had the right to have cases in which he was involved tried in the first instance at no less than bailiwick level. Finally, he enjoyed certain honorific rights in any public gathering at which he was present, whether it was a large formal assembly or simply the congregation of his local village church. His nobility bestowed upon him, therefore, real advantages and great social prestige.

However, the magistrate in the Parlement of Paris possessed additional privileges over and above those of the nobility in general. As a royal counsellor, he enjoyed the right of *committimus* which enabled him to carry personal litigation directly to the King's Council. He also enjoyed additional financial immunities, including exemption from a wide variety of feudal dues, which were paid by the rest of the noble class. Thus the argument has been put forward that in the course of the eighteenth century

[1] Ford, op. cit., 62.
[2] Ibid., 59.
[3] But *see infra*, 132–3.

the magistrates, as the most exclusive and privileged representatives of a privileged class, tended increasingly to identify themselves with that noble class and to take the initiative in the struggle to retain its privileges. The points in favour of this argument are impressive.

Certainly, by the eighteenth century the members of the Parlement were in many ways indistinguishable from the non-robe nobility. A high percentage of them had acquired baronies, counties or marquisates; almost all were landed property-holders. The possession of land was considered the surest means of preserving a family tradition or of masking too recent humble origins. During the Parlement's long vacations, its members put aside their magisterial robes and returned to their estates, there to become local seigneurs, preoccupied with all the problems which habitually concerned the landed nobility. Most of them were unwilling to leave the business of administering their estates entirely to their stewards, but took an active part themselves whenever judicial duties allowed. Like the majority of landowners, they were anxious that the boundaries of their estates should be indisputably defined and they were constantly on the look out for additional land. As a result, they were regularly involved in disputes, arbitration, purchases and exchanges.

In the course of the eighteenth century, they took part with the nobility in general in the so-called 'feudal reaction', seeking to acquire grazing land long held in common, and to revive and enforce obsolescent seignorial rights.[1] Their motives were mixed: some desperately needed to increase their income, others sought to apply standards of good husbandry, others again were content to follow the example set by their neighbours. In any event, the result was not always detrimental to the local peasantry for the magistrates, as landed aristocrats, imbibed not only an interest in exploiting their estates but also a sense of patronage towards the rural community. Many obtained royal permission to establish fairs and markets in their localities. These certainly provided additional revenue for the seigneur but they also brought greater prosperity to the whole area. In 1735, Delpech de Méréville obtained for Angeville, situated on the road between Paris and Orléans, the right to hold four fairs every year and two market days every week.[2]

Indeed, the majority of Parisian magistrates seemed successful in establishing excellent personal relationships with their rural dependants.

[1] G. Lefebvre, *La Révolution Aristocratique*, 52–5.

[2] Bluche, *Les Magistrats du Parlement de Paris*, 186 et seq. Much of the material in the following pages is derived from the same extremely valuable source; similar studies for earlier centuries have not so far appeared.

Invariably, eighteenth-century *parlementaire* wills contained legacies intended to relieve the indigence of the poorest families on the lord's estates. Bequests were set aside for the sick and for dowries for impoverished young women. Sometimes the legacies were in kind: Chauvelin, the Keeper of the Seals (died 1762), who regularly had bread distributed to the poor of his marquisate of Groisbois, requested in his will that the practice should be continued for a year after his death. Some magistrates left money to found hospices run by the sisters of charity or bequeathed generous sums to existing institutions – hospices or hospitals – close to their estates.

More important in the establishment of amicable relations was the fact that most of them did not confine their charity to posthumous acts, but behaved with the same sense of responsibility during their lifetime. Their most enlightened contribution was in the field of primary education. They founded schools for boys and girls, they set aside funds for the appointment of teachers, they bestowed property and money, as gifts or legacies, upon needy educational institutions. When the wife of President d'Aligre made her first visit to her husband's parish church at La Rivière in 1742, her reception, with gunshots and drumrolls, was tumultuous enough to reduce her pet dog to a state of abject terror, and though such a spontaneous popular demonstration was exceptional, it was not uncharacteristic of the general regard in which these magisterial seigneurs were held.

The country houses in which the magistrates resided for a part of every year were symbols of high social rank, and consequently much care was lavished upon their selection. It was considered a great advantage to possess an ancient *château*, like that of the Doublet de Persans at Saint-Germaine-Beaupré, which dated from the thirteenth century. A *château* with distinguished connections was equally desirable: the Le Peletier family acquired Saint-Fargeau, whose previous owners had included the Grande Mademoiselle. Most impressive of all, however, were the ancient family seats, like that of the Longueils at Maisons, with a record of continuous occupation stretching over centuries. Another such country establishment was that of the Lamoignon family at Basville. Their first humble residence had been bought there in 1559; then, in 1625 when the family fortunes were rising, a new *château* was built; a generation later, it was set in a spacious, formal park. Succeeding generations added further embellishments and took great pride in the fact that their splendid home was a family achievement.

The great *parlementaire* houses normally included a chapel and often a theatre. They were sumptuously and tastefully decorated and furnished, and were frequently surrounded by expensively planned gardens arranged *à l'anglaise* or in imitation of Versailles. There were, of course, gradations of magnificence between them; less wealthy magistrates had to be content with small and unimpressive establishments. However, for the most part these magisterial residences were the homes of prosperous noblemen, unselfconsciously reflecting their owners' high social standing.

During their periodic visits to the country the magistrates enjoyed a full social life. Entertaining on a large scale was prevalent; even among the less affluent courtesy visits from and to the neighbouring nobility were considered *de rigeur*. Card-playing, especially piquet, was an acceptable diversion, but even more favoured was the practice of putting on theatrical performances. Bernard de Boulainvilliers, the grandson of Samuel Bernard, staged Marivaux's *Le Jeu de l'Amour et du Hazard* with the celebrated Madame de Genlis as Lisette, while at Basville, shortly before the Revolution, some of the most famous *robe* names – Lamoignon, d'Aguesseau, Pasquier – appeared together in the cast of *Le Barbier de Séville*. Finally, hunting was another relaxation which appealed to the magistrates, not least because it was the traditional sport of the landed nobility. In their leisured pastimes, therefore, as in every other facet of their rural lives, the magistrates of the Parlement fitted perfectly into the noble pattern.

However, Paris remained the heart of the magistrates' world and there, too, they lived in style. Almost all of them owned town residences or land in the city.[1] They employed at least a cook, a coachman, one or two maids and sometimes a nurse or a tutor. Although many of their *hôtels* have now disappeared, they were solid enough in their day and even the smallest of them represented a considerable investment. There were also scores of town houses which in magnificence rivalled the establishments of the most considerable families in the land. Counsellor Titon's house in the Saint-Antoine district of Paris was considered splendid enough to be lent to the Turkish ambassador in 1742; Hénault's, in the rue Saint-Honoré, with its garden of shrubs and orange trees, could stand comparison with the most palatial residences in the capital. The *hôtels* of a number of families, including the Amelots, the Joly de Fleurys, the Longueil de Maisons, the Lambert de Thorignys and the Molés, were all considered important examples of French architecture. One of the most impressive of the magisterial houses was the Hôtel Lamoignon in the Marais district, a

[1] Ford, op. cit., 156.

former home of Diane de France, the illegitimate daughter of Henry II, whose initials, with those of the Lamoignons, were inscribed upon its walls.

Yet, there can be no argument about which of the magisterial dwellings was the most spectacular of all: that honour went to the official residence of the First President, situated within the confines of the Palais, and dating from 1607 when Achille de Harlay was the First President. The first set of apartments after the main entrance hall comprised a large wainscotted ante-chamber, a multi-mirrored room giving direct access to the gardens, a study with panelled walls and inlaid floor, a fourth room with mantles, mirrors and fireplace to match those in the other chambers and a dressing-room which completed the set. The First President's private apartments also opened off the ground floor. An oval ante-room led to the first chamber, a room of half panelled walls with a marble hearth and table and a portrait of Louis XII above the fireplace. The three succeeding rooms were similar, save that in the eighteenth century the portraits were of Louis XIV and Louis XV. Beyond them ran a gallery, fitted from one end to the other with cupboards and furnished with marble tables, serving as the president's library. Along its walls were arrayed portraits of every First President. A small room at one end, also fitted with cupboards, was reserved for rare books and *objets d'art*. There were scores of other rooms besides, of varying size and magnificence, quarters for the large domestic staff, and outside, no fewer than seven stables which could accommodate forty-five horses.

The furniture and accoutrements of these great houses matched the elegance and luxury of their setting. Hénault's drawing-room was dominated by a Bohemian crystal silver chandelier; around the walls eight mirrors were hung, reflecting shelves lined with Dresden china, green marble tables and furniture draped in crimson damask. His dining-room contained twenty-eight chairs, ten armchairs and a sofa, and curtains of pure white linen offset the deep red of the furnishings. The clerical counsellor Louis de Salaberry slept in a richly carpeted bedroom, with walls hung with family portraits, curtains of crimson taffeta and furniture of satinwood. His drawing-room was decorated with tapestries, china and expensive trifles and furnished with armchairs covered in chintz or damask. Counsellor Pierre Chaillon had nine tapestries adorning the walls of his *salon*; pieces of Delft were arrayed as ornaments along his mantelshelf; chairs and a sofa, the latter with a green taffeta covering matching the curtains, were arranged around the room, together with a marble-topped table, a display cabinet containing china, a satin covered screen and a rosewood chest of drawers.

Such samples of elegant living were not confined to a handful of judges. The most celebrated Parisian cabinet-makers of the eighteenth century counted magistrates among their most valued clients. One of the best of them, Pierre Migeon, carried out commissions for the chancellors D'Aguesseau and Blancmesnil and for Counsellor Claude Glucq. The equally famous Lazare Duvaux was employed by a host of *robe* families – Ogier, Lamoignon, Portail, Molé, Gilbert de Voisins – among others, to provide articles of beauty for the embellishment of their *hôtels*. Ogier bought china from Sèvres and Vincennes, Lamoignon lacquer work and crystal chandeliers, Molé Bohemian crystal and china. The existence of especially prized possessions may be elicited from *parlementaire* wills. Thus Counsellor Genoud mentioned his marble tables and tapestries, Fagon his painting of the Nativity by Veronese, Gon d'Argenlieu his painting by Le Sueur of the Transfiguration, La Grange his paintings of the Holy Family by Raphael and of the Virgin and Child by Corregio. Bequests of paintings were quite common and sometimes very impressive. Crozat de Tugny possessed a Tintoretto, a Poussin, a Watteau and paintings by Rembrandt, Le Brun, Le Sueur and Gelée. Chauvelin, the former Keeper of the Seals, left two paintings by Philippe de Champaigne, two by Watteau and a Vermeer. Even more spectacular was the collection of Lalive de Jully, the son of Madame de l'Epinay, the erstwhile confidante of Rousseau, which included works by Rubens, Van Dyke, Rembrandt, Poussin, Gelée, Boucher, Chardin, Greuze, as well as sculptures by Pigalle and Falconet. Not only paintings and sculptures, but antique cameos, Etruscan vases, engravings, pendulum clocks, bronzes and alabasters, all added lustre to the magistrates' homes.

It followed naturally from this domestic background that the magistrates, as a group, would seek to act socially in the most aristocratic fashion. Some of the tiros were evidently over-anxious to establish their reputation in society. One eighteenth-century observer noted, 'A young magistrate fears nothing so much as to be known for what he really is. He talks horses, theatre, women, racing, battles. He blushes to admit a knowledge of his profession.' [1]

Dandies were sufficiently numerous in the Parlement to be portrayed in contemporary literature – not usually in a very flattering light. But all the magistrates were preoccupied with their appearance and with their dress;

[1] J. McManners, 'France', *The European Nobility in the Eighteenth Century*, 27.

the Abbé de Salaberry, who was by no means a dandy, bought six new wigs each year. They were limited in regard to dress by long-established regulations, which they were not altogether able to evade. Nevertheless, when the working day was over, they appeared in the livery of the *noblesse d'épée*, and the evidence suggests that they were by no means inadequate when a matter of honour caused them to draw their swords.

Although it was mainly the youthful magistrates who loved to play the fop, the counsellors as a whole enjoyed the pleasures and the company of the high non-*robe* aristocracy. They were carried about Paris in their own carriages drawn by their own horses, they gave banquets on a grand scale, they gambled likewise, they flocked regularly to the theatre. They interested themselves in the arts and in the contemporary literary scene. President de Maisons was a friend of Voltaire, Lalive de Jully and Le Mercier de la Rivière friends of Diderot, the Abbé de Saint-Non a friend of Rousseau. A few magistrates succeeded in entering the literary and scientific academies: Malesherbes was a member of the academies of Sciences and of *Belles Lettres*, as well as the Académie Française. Two First Presidents, Mesmes and Portail, the chancellor D'Aguesseau and half a dozen other counsellors achieved membership of the latter and a similarly small group was admitted to membership of the academies of science, painting or inscriptions. On a less official level, in the literary salons of the capital, the magistrates also played a role. There, President Hénault, lover of the Duchesse du Maine and of Madame du Deffand and patron of Madame de Lespinasse, was the undisputed king. This literary lion held the stage at Madame Geoffrin's and at Madame de Lambert's; all the considerable figures in the literary and artistic world found their way to his bountiful table. Indeed, this most cultured and urbane figure had access to the very highest circles: in the bedroom of his magnificent residence in the rue Saint-Honoré hung three paintings, executed and signed by Queen Maria Lesczinska herself.

Members of the Parlement themselves employed the most sought-after artists to paint their portraits. Mesmes commissioned Philippe de Champaigne, Doublet de Persan commissioned Louis Vigée and the D'Aguesseau family employed both Tournières and Madame Le Brun. Liaisons between the magistrates and the court aristocracy were extensive and went back to their common educational background.

Most of the magistrates were educated by the Jesuits or by the Oratorians. The largely classical education provided by both these orders was substantially the same and was shared alike by *robe* and non-*robe* aristocracy. There was a difference in approach, however, caused by the fact that the Oratorians had become deeply involved in the theological controversy of Jansenism, which, by its emphasis upon austerity and self-denial, appealed far more to the magisterial background than to that of the court nobility. Consequently, some magistrates preferred to have their sons educated at the Oratorian colleges of Beauvais or Juilly, where the outlook, though not the curriculum, was less in keeping with the noble tradition. Yet, even at Juilly old attitudes were changing in the course of the eighteenth century, as more and more non-*robe* nobles passed through its gates to study beside future magistrates with names like Chauvelin and Séguier, Boutin and Davy de la Fautrière.

However, only a quarter of the magistrates were educated in Oratorian colleges; most of the rest attended the great Jesuit College of Louis-le-Grand in the rue Saint-Jacques, opposite the Sorbonne. The tone of this institution was aristocratic: its pupils wore swords and were instructed in the virtues of nobility, its syllabus encouraged an interest in rhetoric and in the theatre. After school, the students were instructed in the art of dancing; some attended finishing courses like that provided by the *Académie du Roi pour l'éducation des jeunes gentilhommes*, where they practised horse-riding and fencing; some completed their education with a European grand tour, on the English model. It is not surprising that the close contacts between these future magistrates and their erstwhile student colleagues should be maintained. Madame Dupin, an illegitimate daughter of Samuel Bernard – and the great-grandmother of Georges Sand – kept a list of the visitors who regularly called upon her, a list in which *parlementaire* names like Portail, Feydeau, Moreau and Potier de Novion were interspersed with those of the Princesse de Rohan, the Marquise de Broglie, the Duchesse de Boufflers. More intimate friendships also existed, like those between the Abbé Menguy and the Prince de Conti, between René de Maupeou, the father of the chancellor, and Marshal Saxe, between Lefebvre d'Amécourt and the Prince de Soubise.

It was only to be expected, therefore, that marriage alliances between magisterial families and ancient or influential court families would be arranged. Thus the Lamoignons were related to the Caumonts, the Aligres to the Boulainvilliers, the Bérulles to the Latour du Pins, the D'Aguesseaus to the Noailles. Some of the most ancient and illustrious houses of the French nobility were united with the *robe*, the La Trémoïlles, the Montmorencys, whose pedigree went back to 955, the Crussol d'Uzès, the Beauvilliers, the Clermont-Tonnerres, the Rochechouarts, the Rohan-Chabots, and perhaps the most ancient of all, the La Rochefoucaulds. The Montmorencys were directly related to eight *parlementaire* families, the Béthune-Sullys to five, the Rochechouarts and the Choiseuls to four, the La Rochefoucaulds to three, and a considerable number to one or two.

Such relationships and such a way of life suggested that few doors were likely to remain closed to members of the Parlement. They certainly acquired complete equality with their military cousins, the *noblesse d'épée*. In the eighteenth century, there was no doubt that *robe* and sword were simply alternative professions on exactly the same social footing. Montesquieu wrote to his son, 'You may belong to the robe or the sword . . . the choice is yours.'[1] A two-way movement took place between the army and the magistracy. The most distinguished recruit from the latter to the former was President Maupeou, the chancellor's son, who resigned his office to take up a colonel's commission, while Louis Séguier, who fought at Malplaquet, entered the Parlement eight years later, and Michel de Ferrand, who lost a leg at Fontenoy, became a counsellor in 1755. In addition, many of the magistrates were the sons of military men, who had chosen not to follow their father's career, but the equally honourable one of the *robe*, while others, whose family tradition was in the law, made their reputations in the army. Even more indicative, however, of the magistrates' status not only *vis-à-vis* the sword, but at the very apex of society, were the honours to which they were admitted. Many *robe* families boasted knights of the Order of St Louis despite the order's military bias; indeed, a former counsellor, Robert Rossignol, became its Grand Cross, secretary-general and chief clerk. Only the most eminent representatives of the Parlement, like the Lamoignons, could aspire to the *cordon bleu* of the order of the Holy Spirit, but the honours of Saint-Lazare and Mount Carmel were less difficult to acquire. A far greater honour than these two, and one well within the magistrates' grasp, was membership of the order of Malta, requiring in theory a minimum qualification of sixteen generations of nobility, but obtainable in practice with proof of about one hundred years of unimpeachable nobility; over fifty *parlementaire* families were represented by knights of the order.[2] More than thirty families also achieved the signal honour of having their marriage contracts signed by the king and the event duly publicized in the *Gazette de France*. Others succeeded in placing their children as royal pages, side by side

[1] Cited by Bluche, *Les Magistrats du Parlement de Paris*, 305.

[2] Further details of these various orders may be found in Marion, op. cit., 409–12.

with the sons of the court nobility. Finally, the supreme accolade – the honours of the court, enabling the men to ride in royal carriages and the ladies to be formally presented to the king and queen – was accorded to thirty-nine *parlementaire* families in the course of the eighteenth century.

All these factors seem to support the view that in the last decades of the court's existence its members achieved complete unity with the second estate. Yet, there are contrary arguments to be examined. First of all, though, it is important to bear in mind the fact that the magistrates' situation in the eighteenth century had not been arrived at suddenly; in that sense it was neither novel nor remarkable. Because their prominent public role had always given them high social standing, when the practice of selling offices was introduced, those who bought them frequently had the support of considerable wealth, which also enabled them to buy at least some of the appurtenances of nobility. In any case, as we have already seen, the mere performance of *parlementaire* duties traditionally implied the status of personal nobility. Therefore, much that has been observed about the magistrates' attitudes and their way of life in the eighteenth century may also be detected in preceding generations. In the sixteenth century, Lippomano, the Venetian ambassador in Paris, observed that the town houses of the members of the Parlement were amongst the most elegant in the capital.[1] Nor were their seignorial estates a novelty. The Longueil home at Maisons was established in 1390; in the fifteenth and sixteenth centuries, most of the lay estates situated immediately to the south-west of the capital belonged to the magistrates and certainly all the leading robe dynasties had been firmly settled in their country manor-houses long before 1700 – the Lamoignons at Basville from 1559, the Potier de Novions at Groslay from the end of the fifteenth century, the Aligres at La Rivière from the end of the sixteenth, the Chauvelins at Grisenoy from the mid-seventeenth century. Pride in their inheritance, a desire to improve their property for future generations, and a sense of responsibility towards their tenants and servants were felt as keenly by sixteenth- and seventeenth- as by eighteenth-century magisterial landed families.

Similarly, with regard to marriage alliances, the eighteenth century only witnessed the climax of a tendency which had been present in society for a long time. At the beginning of the seventeenth century it was common to find two members of the same family holding office, one in the magistracy, the other in the army and they were frequently related by marriage

[1] Bluche, *Les Magistrats du Parlement de Paris*, 180.

to a wide range of *robe* and non-*robe* families, bourgeois and noble. Here is one example: when Adrien de Canonville, lord of Grosménil, married a daughter of Raoul Bretel, a president in the Parlement of Rouen in 1629, his relatives included the hereditary governor of Boulogne, who was also a *cordon bleu*, the archbishop of Paris, the Duc de Retz, who was a peer; the General of the Royal Galleys, two counsellors in the Parlement of Rouen, two presidents *à mortier* in the Parlement of Paris – Potier de Gesvres and Potier de Novion – and two counsellors in the same Parlement, a *Maître des requêtes* who was also a counsellor of state, the bishop-count of Beauvais, a spiritual peer; and the governor of the province of Maine, who was a captain in the royal bodyguard and a *cordon bleu*.[1] Such examples could be multiplied, and they merit particular attention, for as long as feudal relationships governed society, family connections, the basic social links, imposed obligations to protect or to serve, however distant the relation, however far removed in status. Thus, although families like the La Rochefoucaulds and the Montmorencys were still beyond the reach of the magistrates, some of the latter were already firmly linked with very distinguished representatives of the second estate, long before the eighteenth century began. Even the problem of the eighteenth-century fop who seemed intent on disguising his real identity was far from new. In 1623, a contemporary described the young men who appeared in the mornings at the Palais in the sombre robes of their office, but who emerged in the afternoons dressed as seigneurs in cloaks of amaranthine velvet with matching breeches, white satin doublets and the inevitable swords at their waists.[2] This phenomenon went back beyond the seventeenth century: in the court's own registers for the 1570s there were a series of complaints about the velvet worn by some counsellors, and the general unsuitability of some of the young magistrates' attire.[3] For some long time, magistrates had been acting and living like noblemen.

The special significance attributed to their status in eighteenth-century society diminishes, therefore, when viewed in the light of their earlier role. Of course, the evidence already adduced demonstrates conclusively that the magistrates had not only succeeded in entrenching themselves resolutely in the sweet pastures of the second estate; they had also scaled the highest social peaks, though in so doing they had to cling to very narrow footholds: the *cordon bleu* remained almost out of reach and

[1] Mousnier, op. cit., 537–8.
[2] Bluche, *Les Magistrats du Parlement de Paris*, 363.
[3] Maugis, op. cit., I, 365.

although thirty-nine *parlementaire* families acquired the honours of the court in the eighteenth century, a further 551 families remained excluded. Yet, such reservations are little more than hair-splitting and do not alter the fact that legally and demonstrably the magistrates of the Parlement of Paris were full members of the second estate. On the other hand, solid grounds still remain for arguing that the magistrates never lost their own identity within the noble class, and were therefore never wholly absorbed by it. The chief support for such an argument is the fact that in the last resort the magistrates did not depend on their noble rank to give them privilege and status, but upon their membership of the Parlement.

The fiscal privileges of the nobility, for example, were also extended quite separately to the magistrates. The burdensome tax of the *taille* was levied originally by seigneurs upon their tenants, or by the ecclesiastical authorities upon clerics as well as by the king. Before the fifteenth century the magistrates were not absolutely discharged from the obligation of paying it, though they were either exempted altogether – as in the case of the first mention of the tax in the court's registers, in August 1381, when royal letters were sent to the Parlement excusing its clerical members from a levy carried out by the bishop of Paris on the pope's behalf – or they were allowed to indicate that their donation on a particular occasion did not imply a permanent obligation, as in 1404, when the magistrates contributed to a tax designed to strengthen the king's hand against Henry IV of England. In 1439 the ordinance of Orléans made the *taille* a permanent and strictly royal method of taxation, and shortly afterwards in the reign of Louis XI the presidents and counsellors were granted immunity from it.

In addition, from 1398 the magistrates were permanently exempted from the levy of *aides*, taxes on the sale of wine produced on their estates. Subsequently the same privilege was extended to include the sale of corn, wood, hay and cattle, and they were also excused payment of tolls and other exactions which could reduce their returns. Under Louis XI came the first indications that the magistrates were to be excluded from the salt tax, a privilege confirmed by Charles VIII and Louis XII. In 1520 Francis I guaranteed 'to all presidents, counsellors and to their widows the right to purchase salt for domestic use without *gabelle* . . . paying only the merchant's price'.[1] A less direct but no less valuable fiscal privilege was the magistrates' exemption from accommodating the royal suite or having their property requisitioned by the army, a privilege guaranteed by the

[1] Ibid., 495–6.

mid-sixteenth century but generally acknowledged by sovereigns for over a hundred years before. Nor had they themselves to join the army, or perform fief-service, known as *ban et arrière-ban*. This duty, still imposed upon the non-*robe* nobility as late as 1689, required them to perform military service for periods of up to three months within France and forty days beyond her frontiers; failure to appear or to send a suitably equipped substitute was punishable with a fine. At the beginning of the fifteenth century the magistrates' exemption was an act of grace, periodically renewed until the reign of Louis XI, when it was firmly and formally established. From that time until the end of the seventeenth century, when the *ban* fell into disuse, this privilege profited a growing number of magistrates who had bought fiefs and were living nobly. Finally, the obligation of the *corvée* was waived for all the members of the Parlement as royal office-holders. Thus without their noble status the magistrates could still claim, through membership of their court, rather more than equal financial or equivalent advantages.

In addition, service in the Parlement required legal training, inculcating a professional, erudite tradition which remained formidable even to the end of the court's existence and of which the non-*robe* nobility knew nothing. Records survive of more than a hundred and sixty eighteenth-century *parlementaire* libraries.[1] Some of them, those belonging to the Chauvelins, the Joly de Fleurys, the D'Aguesseaus and the Lamoignons, had a European reputation, and scholars came to Paris to examine rare manuscripts in their collections. D'Aguesseau possessed such a large library that when he resigned from the office of chancellor in 1750 he was allowed to stay in the chancellor's residence until his death, to avoid the enormous task of moving his collection. The works of these libraries may be divided into five broad classifications: theology, jurisprudence, arts and science, literature and history. Books on theology were less frequently found as the century progressed and the great Jansenist against Jesuit controversy died away. In any case, they were almost always in a minority, except in the libraries of clerical counsellors or ardent Jansenists. Jansen's *Augustinus*, the spiritual letters of Saint-Cyran, Pascal's *Pensées* and the works of Quesnel and Nicole figured prominently, but so did non-Jansenist works, the writings of Bossuet, lives of the saints, histories of the papacy and works on Gallicanism.

As with theology, so with jurisprudence, there was a sharp decline in the magistrates' interest in the decade before the Revolution. Unlike

[1] Bluche, *Les Magistrats du Parlement de Paris*, 290–6.

theology, however, jurisprudence remained for most of the century one of the major sections in most *parlementaire* libraries. Books on customary law were more frequently found than those on Roman law, while those on foreign law, with the exception of the works of Grotius, were very rare indeed. Pithou's volume on the rights and liberties of the Gallican Church appeared in most libraries, as did the work of a distinguished seventeenth-century barrister, Omer Talon, on the king's authority in the administration of the Church. Other recurring works included collections of royal ordinances, of *parlementaire* decrees, of provincial *coutumiers*, of celebrated trials.

Under the heading of arts and science could be found numerous copies of the works of the natural scientists Buffon, Réamur and Pluche. Books on algebra, arithmetic and geometry were also common; much rarer were books on chemistry and electricity. Treatises on art and architecture, Rousseau's *Lettres sur la Musique*, occasionally even the scores of works by Lully and Rameau completed this section, which made up about fifteen per cent of the magistrates' collections.

Works on literature, however, constituted on average about a quarter of the total and grew in popularity as interest in theology declined. Greek authors, usually in Latin or French translations, were especially prominent, Homer, Demosthenes, Plato, Aristophanes, Pindar. Roman authors were most frequently represented by Virgil, Ovid, Cicero and Horace. The works of Dante and Montaigne were well represented, as was *The Prince* of Machiavelli. The names of Corneille, La Fontaine, Molière and Racine recurred even more regularly than those of Fénelon and Descartes, and among near-contemporaries, Voltaire and Marivaux, Montesquieu and Bayle, Locke and Rousseau all had their devotees, while two famous heroines, *Manon Lescaut* and *Pamela* more than held their own against more weighty rivals.

Finally came the historical books, which remained throughout the eighteenth century by far the most popular *genre*. They included works by Thucydides, Herodotus, Tacitus and Boulainvilliers, with a number of geographical books and accounts of voyages of exploration. These *parlementaire* libraries represented a broadly based culture, slanted none the less towards the magistrates' professional interests and presenting a tradition of erudition at the same time superior to and different from that of the non-*robe* aristocracy.[1] This was true in the eighteenth

[1] Ford (op. cit., 220–1) also emphasizes the divisive influence of education upon the *robe* and non-*robe* aristocracy during the first half of the eighteenth century.

century, even though it was beyond doubt that professional standards then were less stringent than formerly and that the *métier* of magistrate was taken less seriously by its young recruits than in earlier decades.[1]

The procedure by which young men entered the court amply demonstrates the declining standards. Having made the necessary arrangements with an office-holder and secured the rights to a vacant office in the Parlement, the prospective magistrate then had to obtain letters of provision from the chancellor, which were rarely refused. A number of conditions still remained to be fulfilled, in theory at least. If the office was a clerical one, the candidate had to be in Holy Orders; whether he sought a clerical or a lay office he had to prove that he had no relatives who were at that moment members of the Parlement; he was not allowed to take office as a counsellor before the age of twenty-five, or as a president before the age of forty. However, it was relatively simple in the eighteenth century to obtain royal dispensations from all these conditions. In particular, dispensation from the age qualification became very frequent, causing great alarm among discerning magistrates. In 1698 D'Aguesseau remarked that youths were becoming judges several years before they reached manhood. The average age of entry of counsellors into the court during the second half of the seventeenth century was over twenty-six years; in 1715 it had fallen to under twenty-three. It varied very little for the remainder of the eighteenth century, though for the decade 1726–35, it even dropped below twenty-two.

The same pattern was true of presidential appointments. In theory, candidates were not only expected to be at least forty years of age, they were also required to have served as counsellors for ten years. Nevertheless, one of the Lamoignon family became a president *à mortier* in 1730 at the age of seventeen, a Potier de Novion, a Molé and a Le Peletier at twenty-one, a Maupeou at twenty-three. Although efforts were made to minimize the bad effects of such recruitment by refusing to allow these juveniles the right to opine for a number of years after their reception, further dispensations eliminated even that safeguard. As a result, the element of levity and frivolity in the Parlement became more pronounced. In 1742 the *Grand' Chambrier* Thomé exhorted the young men of the court to behave with a little more sobriety and dignity, and in the same year several erring young counsellors were made to resign their offices – a most unusual occurrence. In the words of D'Aguesseau, the prestige of

[1] Bluche, *Les Magistrats du Parlement de Paris*, 55–62.

the Parlement suffered from the reckless impatience of a number of ambitious fathers.

A further condition of *parlementaire* office was that the aspirant should be a graduate in laws and a member of the bar. It followed from the practice of granting age dispensations that a number of candidates would have insufficient time to fulfil these requirements adequately. The minimum age for registration in a university faculty of law was sixteen, but this rule too was subject to dispensation. Nor did the courses themselves, even if undertaken at the correct age, offer a serious intellectual training. The standards at provincial universities, notably at Rheims, were extremely low and susceptible to various abuses; the situation was not much better at the Sorbonne. Unless further dispensations were obtained, students were required to work three years for their master's degree: the first year was dominated by the study of Roman law, the second by Roman and canon law studies, the two years together constituting the bachelor's degree course, and the third year by the study of French law, the latter dating only from 1679 and including customs and ordinances, civil and criminal procedure, feudal and commercial law. Despite this formidable-sounding curriculum, however, it was possible for students who were so minded to absent themselves from most of the classes and still to survive the far from onerous examinations. As to their training at the bar, it had become excessively brief by the eighteenth century. All prospective counsellors, in addition, had to convince the Parlement of their jurisprudential ability, but not surprisingly the examination was not unduly searching. A date was nominated by the First President, on which each candidate had to present himself before a general assembly of the court, meeting in secret, there to explain, in Latin, the significance of a particular law which he had drawn by lot some days before and to answer questions. By the eighteenth century the inquisition was such a formality that the admission ceremony was usually arranged to take place later on the same day.

Nevertheless, there is a danger of exaggerating the decline in the magistrates' professional standards towards the end of the court's life. During the crisis years of Charles VI's reign and in the reign of his successor, Charles VII, standards were very low indeed. It was not until 1499, under Louis XII, that the practice of examining prospective members of the court before their admission became a formal regulation, though admittedly it was a practice of long standing. Even then dispensations were envisaged both for those whose qualifications were already well known, which was sensible enough, but also for persons of social distinction, which offered no guarantee for the maintenance of high judicial standards.[1] In the reign of Louis XII's predecessor, Charles VIII, the magistrates deputed by the court to scrutinize candidates' qualifications paid sufficient attention to their age to suggest that abuses in that sphere were already a problem. In Francis I's reign, the Parlement paid great attention to its examination of aspirants, as its only method of countering the king's penchant for creating new offices. The examination did not differ very much in substance from its eighteenth-century form, though it was enforced far more strictly: failure was not uncommon and was followed by temporary or indefinite postponement of the candidate's application.

Yet the old problems remained: both in 1524 and 1525 the *Gens du roi* requested the Parlement not to accept such youthful members, but rather middle-aged men of learning and quality. They added that inexperienced counsellors who were accepted should take the trouble to learn what was required of them.[2] There were other instances too in the same reign which demonstrated that the severity of the examination was sometimes reduced to accommodate the sons or sons-in-law of resigning magistrates. Upon his accession in 1547 Henry II fixed the minimum age for admission to the Parlement at thirty. He limited dispensations from its examination to those candidates who were already members of another Parlement and stipulated that no friends or relatives of the candidate should take any part in the examination. However, with the growth of venality and heredity in the court, these royal reforms were not as enthusiastically received as they would have been even fifty years earlier, and in 1553 the king lowered the minimum age to twenty-five.

The behaviour of the young counsellors in the late sixteenth century was not very different from that which caused D'Aguesseau concern a hundred and fifty years later: mention has already been made of their fondness for fashionable attire, and to this may be added their liking for feasting within the Palais on such a scale that in 1568 it was necessary to control the sale of food and wine at the *buvettes*.[3] Under Henry IV the age of new recruits sometimes dropped as low as twenty-one and the established rules forbidding relatives to hold office at the same time were also waived.[4]

[1] Maugis, op. cit., I, 125–6.
[2] Ibid., 181.
[3] Ibid., 366.
[4] Ibid., II, 214–15.

It is clear, therefore, that threats to the judges' professional standards existed long before the eighteenth century, though with the triumph of venality and the growth in the number of hereditary offices they became progressively more serious. On the other hand, it would be a mistake to assume that the magistrates' formal training was the sole, or even the chief factor in forming their professional outlook. Their family background became increasingly important as offices became family property. D'Aguesseau believed that the future magistrate should be accustomed from an early age to admire the austere magisterial virtues of his forefathers, and most of his contemporaries did in fact receive their early training within the family. From father to son, from father-in-law to son-in-law, the traditions of the Parlement were instilled into successive generations and material mementoes – family portraits, books and manuscripts – were carefully preserved and handed on to each succeeding heir. The solidarity of this family tradition was reinforced by the fact that even in the eighteenth century, when marriages with representatives of the *noblesse de race* were becoming more common, one magistrate in two still married into a *robe* family. This tradition, together with the magistrates' professional education, shaped their basic outlook which clearly distinguished them from the non-*robe* nobility.

A third important formative influence came later, in their day-to-day judicial work inside the Palais. It was impossible to dispense justice for long at the highest level without being impressed by the awesome authority of the court and by the age and continuity of its judicial tradition, without being caught up in its procedures and rituals. Once again, D'Aguesseau expressed his feelings with some apprehension.

> Everything surrounding the magistrate [he wrote in 1706] conspires to beguile him . . . the magnificence of the purple in which he is attired, the honours paid to his dignity, the majestic silence of his tribunal; the respect, the reverential dread with which the litigant faces the judge; the supreme authority and the irrevocable nature of the judgments that come from his lips; all these things seem to lift him above the level of ordinary men.[1]

The *esprit de corps* thus engendered was further strengthened by the tumultuous atmosphere of the Palais, where the Parlement was sovereign, and by the high place accorded to the court on public occasions, proces-

[1] Cited by Bluche, *Les Magistrats du Parlement de Paris*, 270.

sions, *te deums*, royal marriages and funerals. Perhaps the best example of the Parlement's corporate self-esteem was provided by the famous bloodless battle of precedence known as the *affaire du bonnet*, in which the presidents successfully challenged the peers in a struggle lasting from the mid-seventeenth century well into the years of Louis XV's majority. By establishing his right to address the peers without doffing his official cap or *bonnet*, though he did remove it when addressing his fellow-presidents, the First President struck a major blow for his company's prestige at the expense of extremely distinguished representatives of the non-*robe* aristocracy.[1] Finally, its corporate spirit was greatly fortified by its political traditions, which are momentous enough to require separate examination.

Family traditions, therefore, professional tuition, the judge's function and his place of work, his specialized erudition, in a word his multifarious links with the institution of which he was a member, all set the magistrate apart from his noble cousins. His prestige and his privileges, even his noble status, were guaranteed by membership of the Parlement, and in many instances derived solely from it. There were of course wide social and financial divisions within the court in the eighteenth, as in preceding centuries: on the one hand, the Longueils and the Voyer d'Argensons, the Mesmes and the d'Argouges, houses of ancient lineage and nobility; on the other, Lefebvre de Saint-Hilaire, a notary's son, or Anselme d'Outremont, appointed counsellor in 1766, though his family had been ennobled only seven years earlier; on the one hand the opulence of Hénault and of Bernard de Rieux, on the other the comparative indigence of Nigon de Berty. Yet, despite such variations, all these men, all these families, whatever their social standing, whether or not they were supported by great wealth, whether sprung from a line of presidents *à mortier* or from a peasant grandfather, derived from their membership of the Parlement a unity of outlook and a spirit far deeper rooted than the ties which they shared with the nobility as a whole. That fact is of paramount importance in any consideration of the magistrates' conduct and motives in the declining years of the *ancien régime*.

Traditionally, members of the Parlement were believed to be wealthy, and indeed their high social standing was not easily maintained without considerable financial resources. For his capitation tax of 1695, Louis XIV assessed all the presidents *à mortier* in the third category and all the counsellors in the eighth, but in fact there was no uniformity of wealth within

[1] The development of this astonishing dispute is traced by A. Grellet-Dumazeau, *L'Affaire du Bonnet, passim.*

the court. There were a number of magistrates whose capital was over a million *livres*: Hénault had three million, while Bernard de Rieux inherited almost seven million from his father, Samuel Bernard. The fortune of the Longueil de Maisons in the eighteenth century approached three million *livres*, that of the Molés was twice as much, the Chancellor d'Aguesseau left over one million *livres*. These were very rich men by any standards; indeed, those who possessed only half as much, 500,000 *livres* or more, were extremely wealthy except in comparison with these millionaires. They included such families as the Lefèvre d'Ormessons, the Amelots and the Potier de Novions. Lower down the scale came those who possessed less than 400,000 *livres*, who could not afford to live quite as extravagantly as their wealthier colleagues: included in this group in the eighteenth century was one of the most famous and ancient *robe* dynasties, the Séguiers. Finally came the poorest counsellors who could afford few extravagant gestures with which to prop up their dignity.[1]

Nevertheless, the overall impression was one of affluence and had been so at least since the sixteenth century when one commentator noted that judicial office-holders were rich beyond measure.[2] Indeed, before offices became venal, their status was such as to attract ambitious men of means. Afterwards, of course, offices acquired the additional attraction of becoming a valuable form of investment. However, few men entered the Parlement to make their fortune. Although the rewards were not inconsiderable, the investment was by no means gilt-edged. Usually, the fortune was acquired first and membership of the court added the social distinction which wealth on its own account could not command.

An examination of the origins of the eighteenth-century magistrates' fortunes demonstrates the point. Almost all the very rich men inherited wealth either directly from extremely opulent financiers or from a series of well-calculated marriage alliances. Chaumont de la Millière was the son of Antoine Chaumont, a financier who had made a fortune out of the wreck of John Law's notorious system. President Hénault was the son of a tax-farmer general; President de Tugny inherited six and a half million *livres* from his father, the banker Crozat. Marriage alliances also helped indirectly to boost *robe* fortunes. Members of the Molé and Lamoignon families married a daughter and grand-daughter respectively of Samuel Bernard, the former bringing a dowry of 1,200,000 *livres* and subsequently inheriting almost seven million *livres*. Counsellor Montullé married a

[1] Bluche, *Les Magistrats du Parlement de Paris*, 150–2.
[2] Mousnier, op. cit., 54–5.

tax-farmer's daughter with a dowry of 400,000 *livres* and a member of the Joly de Fleury family married a financier's daughter who was heiress to nearly 600,000 *livres*. By no means all the wealthy magisterial families depended upon such transfusions of non-*robe* capital, although many of the richest ones did. Some profited from marriage between rich *robe* dynasties and thus inherited the carefully accumulated wealth of generations of frugal *parlementaire* forefathers; none of them was founded solely upon a lifetime's service in the Parlement.[1]

Remuneration in the shape of salary was never satisfactory; French kings were consistently parsimonious in their dealings with the court. When it was first permanently established, the judges' salary came from the litigants, though from the end of the thirteenth century the king paid it himself. At the end of Philip the Fair's reign it was fixed at five *sous* a day for clerics, ten *sous* for laymen and it did not change for almost a hundred and fifty years, until the beginning of the reign of Louis XI. It was payable not every day, but only on those days when the Parlement was in session. In the first half of the fifteenth century when money values were fluctuating and the political future was uncertain, such wages represented little more than subsistence payments to a number of needy counsellors.[2] Nor were they regularly and promptly paid. In 1438 the magistrates complained that they were owed eighteen months' salary, and on occasions in 1440, 1441 and 1442 they refused to carry out their judicial duties as a protest against such treatment.[3]

In 1454, Charles VII agreed for the first time to pay the magistrates for their service at the *après-diner* sessions which had been instituted in 1360. He also contributed funds for such requirements as the purchase of wood, paper and parchment and for stocking the *buvette*. Until this time, the magistrates had been using their own money for these purposes, usually being reimbursed very belatedly by the king. Their financial situation did improve a little, therefore, in 1454, though the salary for the *après-diner* sessions soon fell into arrears. A further improvement came in the reign of Louis XI: the *après-diner* salary was regularly paid, expenses for magistrates appointed to serve on judicial commissions were increased and the payment of salaries reverted to the monthly basis originally laid down in Philip V's regulation of 1321. However, the situation quickly deteriorated again, and in 1494 the court once more complained to the

[1] Bluche, *Les Magistrats du Parlement de Paris*, 143–8.

[2] Maugis, op. cit., I, 445–6.

[3] Aubert, *Histoire du Parlement de Paris à François Ier*, I, 102.

king, Charles VIII, about arrears of salary. In 1525, when a serious famine underlined their difficulties, the magistrates insisted that irregular payment was preventing a number of counsellors from living in the manner required by their position, and four years later they revived the threat of judicial strikes if their arrears were not paid off. Again in 1561, a *parlementaire* deputation stoutly maintained before Catherine de Medici that justice was not a gratuitous service, yet by the end of the following year payments were fifteen months in arrears. Under Henry III conditions deteriorated further as the arrears mounted, and the Parlement threatened once more to withhold its services.[1]

With the coming of venality, the nature of *parlementaire* wages changed, becoming in theory the interest payable upon the original capital invested in the office. However, though the method of assessment altered, the complaints continued. Now they were concerned not only with the arrears but with the government's frequent manipulations of the interest rate upon which their returns were supposed to be based. In addition, the inflationary movement in prices in general and in the price of office in particular quickly diminished the value of the annual sum originally fixed to an insignificant level. In 1597 the annual return from lay counsellors' offices in the Parlement was fixed at 500 *livres* and represented about four and a half per cent of the offices' current value; by 1617 it represented only 0·74 per cent. In accordance with a melancholy tradition, the money was seldom available on time and was frequently inadequate: in 1595 and again in 1597 there was not enough to pay all the counsellors in the court. In 1618 a deputation of magistrates reminded Louis XIII of the modest wages that they received; twelve years later they were complaining again of the hardship caused by the inadequacy of their salary.[2] The complaints recurred in the eighteenth century also, and in 1717 a royal declaration was issued, promising more regular payment in the future. By that time, however, the amount payable represented a very small return and only a tiny fraction of the magistrates' total income. Most of them had other considerable assets to rely upon. But in earlier periods, in the fifteenth century, for example, the urgency and intensity of the frequent requests for relief was a fair indication of the real privation which some, at least, of the magistrates were suffering.[3]

The magistrates received subsidiary payments in the form of *épices*.

[1] Maugis, op. cit., I, 446 et seq.
[2] Mousnier, op. cit., 425–6.
[3] Ford, op. cit., 152.

Originally, these had been simple presents in kind given by grateful clients to solicitors and barristers, often wine, cheese or fish. The practice was then extended to the judges themselves, becoming an accepted emolument of the *rapporteurs*. When money began to replace offerings in kind, the court became alarmed lest the *épices* should prove to be a temptation to corruption. Strict regulations were therefore drawn up in 1437 forbidding the magistrates to accept gifts until after the publication of the judgments with which they had been concerned.[1] The practice survived, however, and became formally established, chiefly because salaries were so small and were paid with such irregularity. By the eighteenth century, the custom had been established of pooling the *épices* and dividing the profits once a year between the *rapporteurs* and the judges. The amount to be made from this source, therefore, depended upon how much judicial work each magistrate was willing to undertake. Added to their salaries and to other casual sources of income – derived from service in the criminal chamber and in the *Chambre des Vacations* – the *épices* could provide the magistrates with a reasonable income, but never with a really substantial one. It has been estimated that in the mid-eighteenth century, if a magistrate worked conscientiously at his *métier*, he could earn annually the equivalent of about five per cent of the value of his office – not an extraordinary return for his investment, especially since it depended upon his own hard work.[2]

If the income derived from offices in the Parlement was only modest, the value of the offices themselves fluctuated dramatically during the seventeenth and eighteenth centuries. In 1597 it was possible to obtain a counsellor's office for 10,000 *livres*; in 1600 it cost 21,000 *livres*, in 1606, 36,000, in 1614, 55,000 and in 1635, 120,000 *livres*. By 1700 the price had dropped slightly to 100,000 *livres*; it then wavered around that level or just below until the beginning of Louis XV's majority, when it suffered a rapid decline. In 1732 an office cost only 40,000 *livres*, by 1751 it was down to 34,000, though in 1771 it climbed to 50,000 once more, the price which is also quoted as the value of an office at the end of the *ancien régime*.[3]

It is far easier to trace these fluctuations than to explain them. First of all, the rapid rise in prices: opponents of the *paulette* attributed it to that measure which made offices more attractive as investments because they could be permanently retained in the family, and that fact itself gave them

[1] Maugis, op. cit., I, 451; Ducoudray, op. cit., 167–71.

[2] Bluche, *Les Magistrats du Parlement de Paris*, 172.

[3] Mousnier, op. cit., 336; Bluche, *Les Magistrats du Parlement de Paris*, 167; Carré, op. cit., 7.

an added scarcity value. Against that explanation, it may be reasonably argued that signs of rapidly spiralling prices already existed before the *paulette* edict was published at the end of 1604, even if that measure did subsequently aggravate the tendency. Another explanation involves the general inflationary situation which existed at the time: as everything became more expensive, the office-holder selling his office was forced to ask more for it to preserve his own standard of living. However, the price of offices apparently rose far more spectacularly than did the price of wheat in Paris during the same period. Between 1615 and 1640 the latter increased by a little over twenty per cent, while the former had more than doubled.[1] The comparison is very limited and it would be over-optimistic to expect an exact correlation even if the general rise in prices was the required explanation.

In fact, a number of circumstances probably played a part besides those already mentioned. One was the desire to reach high political office via the Parlement at a time when the opportunities were beginning to burgeon. Another was the royal habit of extracting forced loans from office-holders, the operation being euphemistically called the granting of higher salaries. The additional salaries represented the interest to be drawn from a lump sum which the office-holders were forced to hand over to the government. Thus the value of the offices was raised by the additional amount subsequently levied from its holders.[2] Finally, with the end of the civil wars and the firm revival of the king's authority, his chief court also regained its prestige and importance, and under Henry IV became an attractive investment again, both socially and economically.

The decline in prices that followed in the eighteenth century is even more difficult to explain, especially since it occurred at a time when the Parlement's political authority and reputation was far higher than it had been under Louis XIV. The offices of president *à mortier* suffered less than counsellors': Chauvelin sold his in 1746 for over half a million *livres* and in the same year Portail tried to sell his to Bernard de Boulainvilliers for 800,000 *livres*.[3] However, the grandson of Samuel Bernard was not considered eligible to enter the exclusive ranks of the *mortier*. As regards counsellors' offices, it has been suggested that rich members of the middle class were tempted to invest in the increasingly attractive alternatives of industry and commerce and again, that the growing hereditary tendency

[1] Mousnier, op. cit., 339–43.
[2] Ibid., 371 et seq.
[3] Bluche, *Les Magistrats du Parlement de Paris*, 168.

in the court was making it more difficult for newcomers to gain access.[1] However, the evidence for the end of the eighteenth century suggests that the difficulties were diminishing;[2] in any case, that argument could be used equally to account for rising prices. Nor does it seem likely that the social attractions of *parlementaire* status were any less alluring for rich men than they had been in the preceding century.

The fall in prices cannot be dismissed as an illusion, yet it is equally necessary to avoid exaggerating the decline. There was a general fall in prices – particularly in land prices – between 1675 and 1725; indeed, it has been estimated that the cost of land dropped by forty-five per cent during that time. Offices were the equivalent of land; they could be bartered, sold, leased or bequeathed by their owners, and the reduction in the value of offices was one symptom of this deflationary movement.[3] In addition, the deterioration in the relationship between the government and the court during the eighteenth century no doubt contributed to the diminishing worth of *parlementaire* offices, but perhaps most of all it was the decline in royal prestige which cast doubts upon the value of offices in the king's chief sovereign court.[4]

Finally, there were a number of other expenses which office-holders in the Parlement were forced to meet. Upon receiving office, they usually had to pay a tax to the king called the *marc d'or*, established in 1575.[5] In 1656 the tax was doubled, becoming the equivalent of one-sixtieth of the office's value. It was also levied in return for dispensations of age, study and kinship. There were other incidental costs, too, and the total initial outlay, according to the eighteenth-century barrister and diarist, Barbier, mounted to about 8,000 *livres* above the cost of the office itself.[6] In the eighteenth century it included a reversion tax which was less onerous than the *paulette*, the tax formerly levied as a guarantee of the hereditary nature of the office, from which the magistrates were by this time exempt. The existence of these obligations underlines the fact that the chief lure of *parlementaire* office lay not in the profits but in the dignity that it conferred.

Many magistrates had a variety of other sources of revenue besides their office. Their town houses in Paris, with the contents, represented a

[1] Ford, op. cit., 148–9.
[2] *See supra*, 119.
[3] Ford, op. cit., 150–1.
[4] *See infra*, Bk II, Chapter IX, *passim*.
[5] Mousnier, op. cit., 366–8.
[6] Barbier, op. cit., V, 78.

considerable capital outlay – over eleven per cent of the total assets of President Longueil de Maisons, over thirty-three per cent of those of his rich contemporary, Hénault. In addition, they made money by renting their properties whilst they themselves were out of Paris during the judicial vacations. Some magistrates also owned property in other towns, like the Abbé Pucelle, who had a house at Nogent-sur-Marne; others, like the chancellor's brother, D'Aguesseau de Valjouan, speculated profitably in Parisian land and property. Their wealth was invested, too, in varying degrees in their estates. Olivier de Sénazon possessed land worth more than four million *livres* in Normandy, Dauphiné, Burgundy and the Ile de France, though the Gaudart family owned an estate worth only 32,000 *livres*. Between these extremes of value and between geographical limits ranging from Normandy to Provence, all the landed magistrates drew some profit from their rural possessions, either by improving the yield of their estates or by leasing parts of them to tenant farmers.[1]

There was another important source of magisterial wealth, however, which has not so far been mentioned and which dominated the fortune of many presidents and counsellors: the state investments known as *rentes*, which were a favourite source of income ever since their introduction under Francis I. Any reduction or threat of reduction in the interest rate paid by the government on these securities was always certain to arouse the indignation of the Parlement. That happened in 1638, and again in 1720 and once more in 1761.[2] Some magistrates invested so heavily in *rentes* that they had to employ secretaries to administer their investments for them, and in the eighteenth century about two-thirds of them owed an important part of their wealth to this source.

Finally, there were a number of other subsidiary sources of income of which the magistrates could avail themselves from time to time. They might be asked to sit on a commission, like the *Chambre de Justice* of 1716–17. They might be in receipt of pensions from the king. Indeed, the First President, the presidents *à mortier*, the *Gens du roi*, the dean, or senior lay member of the Parlement, the senior clerical counsellor from the *Grand' Chambre* and the dean of the lay counsellors of the *Enquêtes*, all received *ex-officio* allowances, and from time to time individual counsellors were also granted pensions. Members of the royal family extended their patronage, too, to the magistrates, in return for help in the administration of their affairs. Inadequate salary payments tempted the magis-

[1] Bluche, *Les Magistrats du Parlement de Paris*, 175–80.
[2] Ibid., 212–13.

trates to offer their services more widely, to the detriment of their official duties, and in 1583 Henry III sought to confine their extra-mural services to the queen and to the princes of the royal blood. Of course, this source of income was limited to a few magistrates. On the other hand, all of them were well qualified to act as executors and in that capacity they received handsome presents from wealthy clients in the form of jewellery, tapestries and paintings. The clerical counsellors in the Parlement also drew their prebends or benefices, without the obligation of residence, and a number of them also drew revenue from abbeys held *in commendam*.[1] All these additional sources of income, as well as the privileges and immunities that membership of the Parlement bestowed, must be taken into account in any consideration of magisterial wealth.

It is difficult enough to generalize about a body of men as unequal in wealth and origin as the magistrates, even within the context of a limited span of time. It is almost impossible to do so for a period of five hundred years. Yet, one or two basic generalizations are justified. Although some representatives of the *robe* made large fortunes, served in great offices of state and reached the highest social rank, whilst others acquired little beyond the reputation of their office, though some had more professional learning, aptitude and zeal for their task than others, all of them, presidents and counsellors, clerics and laymen, nobles and non-nobles, were men of the law; their world was the Palais and their primary obligation was to dispense royal justice. Their attitudes were moulded primarily by the institution in which they served, and those attitudes remained remarkably consistent for five centuries. The eighteenth-century magistrates made no break with the past, neither by developing into a narrowly exclusive caste, nor by taking over the leadership of the second estate. They maintained traditional social patterns, accepted traditional judicial obligations and, until the last years of the *ancien régime,* retained their traditional political relationship with the crown. The true significance of their role lay in the totality of judgments, which over hundreds of years emanated from their court. Together, they represented the triumph of royal authority over conflicting customary law, over the law of feudal and church courts, over lawlessness itself.

French kings had never ceased to assert that their authority was based upon the right to dispense justice, and, in the absence of a written constitution, the registers of the Parlement provided the best support both

[1] Ibid., 216–21.

for the supremacy of the king over his realm and of the law over the king. All his advisers, members of his Parlement, from the legists of St Louis's time, men like Pierre de Fontaines, to ill-fated magistrates of Louis XVI's reign, like Malesherbes, the most celebrated representative of the great house of Lamoignon who died on the scaffold in 1794, all were united by the common obligation of defining, enforcing and preserving the king's law, a duty which implied nothing less than the preservation of the French state itself. It was not surprising, therefore, that the magistrates should add to their judicial authority very extensive political powers as well.

Book Two

THE POLITICAL INSTITUTION

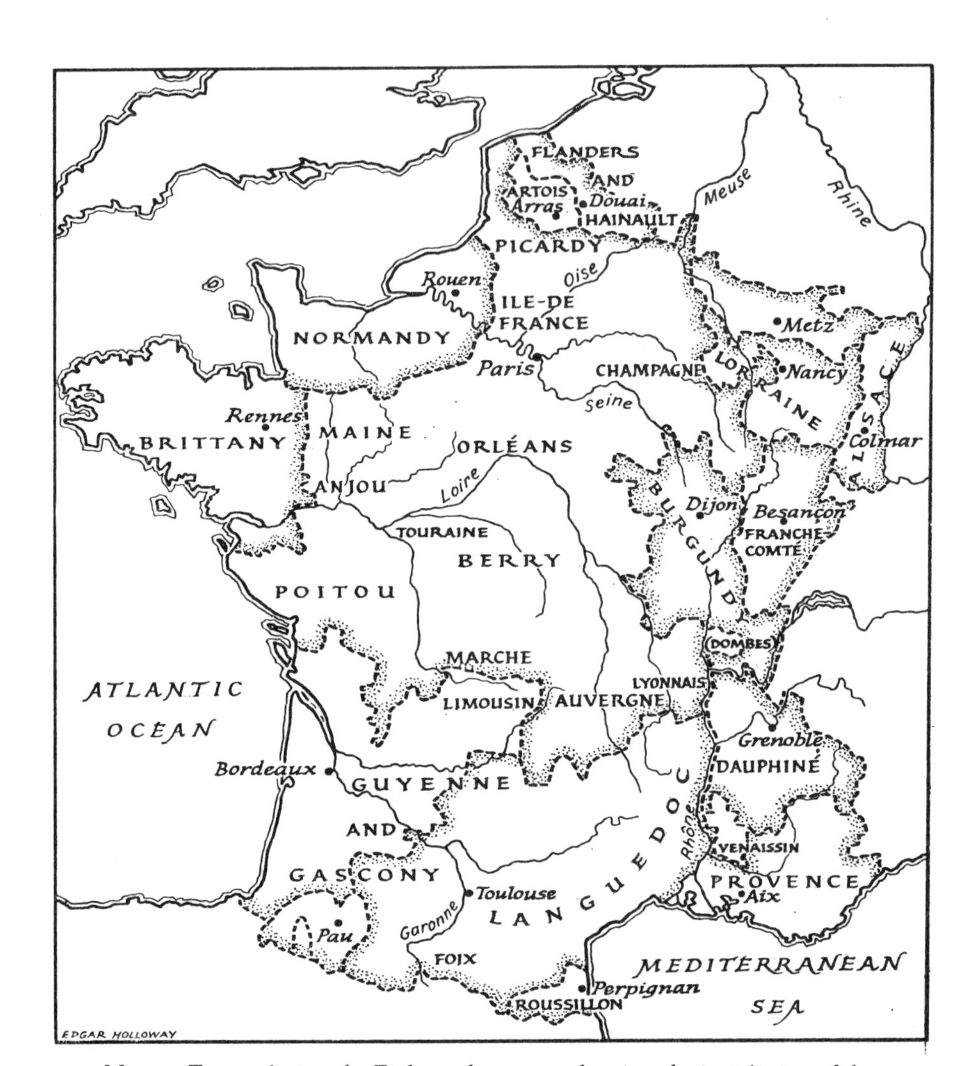

Map 2 – France during the Eighteenth century showing the jurisdiction of the Parlements and the *Conseils Souverains*.

CHAPTER FIVE

The Medieval Parlement

The nature of royal authority; the Parlement's part in state affairs; the doctrine of Gallicanism; the Pragmatic Sanction and the concordat of 1461; the changing relationship between king and Parlement

---

Though requirements of clarity may justify the separate treatment of the Parlement's judicial, political and administrative functions, there is nevertheless a danger of such an approach producing a serious misinterpretation of the nature of French monarchy. There was no division in fact; the king's political and administrative responsibilities – and therefore those of the Parlement likewise – were intelligible only within the context of his judicial authority. Hugh Capet's seal, it will be recalled, depicted the king as a judge, and the Capetians' concept of the monarchy's essential characteristic was passed down to their Bourbon successors. In the seventeenth century the king remained the great justiciar; it was his judicial role which entitled him to exercise executive power. The king judged affairs of state, even those involving relations with foreign countries, just as he judged between individuals. His prime obligation was to be the state's chief judge: both the fullness of his authority and its limitations flowed from that basic fact.[1]

Even before the coming of the Capetians, writers on the Carolingian monarchy had supported this view. Shortly after Charlemagne's death in the ninth century, Jonas, bishop of Orléans, composed a treatise, *De Institutione Regia*, whose ideas faithfully reflected informed contemporary opinion about the nature and attributes of kingship. Justice, piety and compassion were for Jonas the chief virtues which a king should practice, and of these three, justice was pre-eminent. Properly exercised royal justice provided a safeguard against oppression and crime, the chief support for the Church in the kingdom and the best guarantee against tyranny. Yet in enforcing his authority, Jonas admonished the king to

[1] R. Mousnier, 'L'Evolution des Institutions Monarchiques', 65.

respect existing laws, especially canon law, and also the local customs which regulated conduct in the various parts of his kingdom.[1] These views were repeated without modification in the tenth and eleventh centuries, not only in the writings of episcopal observers like Ivo of Chartres, but in royal charters, too, like that of Hugh Capet himself, in which the king insisted: '*Nostrae sublimitas pietatis non aliter recto stare valet ordine nisi . . . ac justa priorum sectando mentaliter decreta regum*'.

From the time of Philip I's consecration in 1059, French kings swore at their coronation to maintain the laws.[2] In the twelfth century John of Salisbury reiterated the principle of the rulers' subjection to the divine law, the natural law and the laws of the kingdom, claiming that respect for the law alone distinguished the legitimate prince from the tyrant, an opinion strongly supported five centuries later by Bishop Bossuet.[3] The thirteenth-century legists took up the same position. The author of the *Livre de Jostice et de Plet* asserted that the law was above princes and not vice versa, while Beaumanoir maintained that the ruler always had to act in accordance with what was just and with what was customary. Not long after the composition of the *Coutumes de Beauvaisis*, King Philip V, in an ordinance of 1318, expressed his adherence to the same principle: 'when we received our kingdom from God, our desire was and is to maintain the just bases upon which it is established and to govern in accordance with the good customs which prevailed in the time of Saint Louis'. Later in the same century, Charles V went to the trouble of having his coronation oath copied out in the *Livre du Sacre des rois de France*, which he kept close at hand in his library in the Louvre.[4]

French kingship, therefore, was regarded as an essentially judicial function, requiring the monarch to respect the laws and customs, secular and ecclesiastical, which he had inherited and to legislate, if legislation were necessary, in conformity with accepted ideas of justice. The background against which this concept must be viewed was a religious one: the king was God's lieutenant on earth, *le roi très chrétien*, whose chief task was to establish in his kingdom a regime which would reflect divine justice, however imperfectly. Many centuries before Louis XIV's reign, generally considered to mark the apogee of divine-right monarchy, that

[1] A. Lemaire, *Les Lois Fondamentales*, 1 et seq; R. W. and A. J. Carlyle, *A History of Medieval Political Theory in the West*, I, 225–6.

[2] Luchaire, *Manuel des Institutions Françaises*, 457–62.

[3] Carlyle, op. cit., III, 138; Bossuet, *Politique tirée de l'Ecriture Sainte*, Bk VIII, 432.

[4] Lemaire, op. cit., 38; Beaumanoir, *Coutumes de Beauvaisis*, II, 264–5; G. Dupont-Ferrier, 'La Formation de l'Unité Française', 108.

idea had been embedded in the French mind. Jonas of Orléans asserted unequivocally that royal authority had its source in God, and indeed it is not unreasonable to maintain that all the elements necessary for the evolution of divine-right kingship were already present in the first half of the ninth century.[1]

In fact, the quasi-spiritual character of the monarchy may be traced back to that period in a very particular way. Louis the Pious, Charlemagne's son, was the first Frankish ruler to be anointed at his crowning with sacred oils. Henceforward the coronation became a religious ceremony, investing the new ruler with unique authority. Though great feudal vassals like the dukes of Normandy and Aquitaine might imitate at Rouen or Limoges the ceremony of the royal crowning at Rheims, they never dared to include the unction in their versions. The Capetians inherited from their Carolingian predecessors the peculiar prestige attached to the coronation and very quickly added to that prestige the claim of miraculous power. Hugh Capet's son, Robert the Pious, was believed by his contemporaries to possess the gift of curing all ailments. The power was transmitted by heredity, though from the reign of Robert's grandson, Philip I, it was considered to apply only to the very widespread disease of scrofula. The thaumaturgic gift further underlined the religious basis of the French monarchy; not until the eighteenth century did scepticism eat away this particular prop of kingship.[2]

The authority of the king grew along with the complexities of government, requiring him frequently to take the initiative, and the problem therefore arose of how he should reconcile his legislative power with the authority of existing laws. The king was the ultimate source of power in the state – nobody denied that – and if the laws were inadequate or no longer just, he could and, indeed, should amend or repeal them. In so doing, he would be implementing his prime task of ruling in accordance with just laws. However, there were certain tenets which came to be considered as basic elements in the French state, to be ignored only at the cost of abrogating its characteristic constitution. Under no circumstances therefore should the king repeal these fundamental laws and any attempt to do so would signal his departure from the ranks of legitimate rulers. If the theory of divine support for his authority helps to explain the king's

[1] Lot and Fawtier, op. cit., II, 11.

[2] M. Bloch (*Les Rois Thaumaturges*, 27–86) provides the classic account of the origins of this royal therapy; J. de Pange ((*Le Roi très Chrétien*) offers some interesting reflections upon the enduring alliance between the French king and the spiritual order.

obligation to act justly, the fundamental laws emphasize his obligation to act legally.[1]

These fundamental laws required France to be ruled by a Catholic monarch, who derived his claim to the throne from being the eldest male relative in the direct line of descent; they further required that the kingdom should not be inherited by illegitimate heirs, or by foreign princes, that the king should have sovereign authority within his kingdom, and that he should not under any circumstances alienate any part of his royal domain. In a word, all these basic constitutional rules sought to support and maintain the integrity of the kingdom. They also added to the monarch's own aura of legitimacy, provided that he continued to respect them.

The law of hereditary succession was the most striking example of that fact. The order of succession was uncertainly established under the early Capetians. Hugh Capet's son, Robert, was crowned in his father's lifetime; Robert's eldest surviving son, Henry, was similarly crowned in 1026, five years before his father's death, and Henry's successors, his son Philip I, his grandson Louis VI and his great-grandson Louis VII, all associated their eldest sons with the throne during their own lifetimes. The practice ceased in the reign of Louis VII's son, Philip Augustus, an indication that the Capetian line was by then wholly accepted and the order of succession clearly established. The good fortune of the dynasty in producing male heirs continued with Louis VIII, Louis IX, Philip III and Philip IV, but with the death in 1316 of Philip the Fair's eldest son, Louis X, leaving only a daughter in direct line of descent, a new problem presented itself. However, his widow was pregnant and a period of regency intervened until the child was born. It was a boy, John I, but he only survived four days. The question had still to be decided, therefore, whether a king's daughter could inherit the throne. In February 1317, in a solemn assembly made up of prelates, barons and representatives of the capital, with the advice of the doctors of law from the Sorbonne, it was decided that the dead infant's uncle, Philip, should be crowned king. When Philip V died in 1322 he too left only a daughter, and consequently his younger brother Charles inherited the crown. He met no difficulties, for the precedent established six years earlier had been accepted without demur. Charles IV also died without a male heir in 1328, and since he had no brothers to succeed him, the question of female

[1] Lemaire (op. cit., *passim*) surveys the concept of fundamental law in France from the ninth to the eighteenth centuries.

hereditary rights again arose. It took a different form on this occasion, however.

There were now three claimants, two grandsons of Philip III, Philip of Valois and Philip of Evreux, and Edward III of England, the son of Philip the Fair's daughter Isabel. If a woman, though incapable of succeeding herself to the throne, could transmit her rights to her son, then the rightness of King Edward's claim was irrefutable. Once more an assembly of notables, guided by the opinion of the University of Paris, took counsel and decided that the right to the French throne could not be passed on through a woman and that therefore Philip of Valois, the representative of the elder line of descent from Philip III, was the rightful king. Henceforward, until Louis XVI died on the scaffold in 1794, the crown continued to be handed down to the eldest male heir, so long as his claim was not derived through a woman.

The decisions, both of 1317 and 1328, were prompted in part by political considerations – a queen's position was always likely to be less secure than a king's and Edward's chances would certainly have been better had he not been king of England – but they were essentially judicial verdicts. The choice was not made under duress from any quarter nor was it unlimited; the question to be settled was the nature of the law governing the succession. A precedent had to be established one way or the other and once the decision had been made it was never subsequently invalidated. The arguments in support of the decision may be briefly stated. In 1317 France had been ruled for almost 350 years by male representatives of the Capetian dynasty. Brothers had always taken precedence over sisters; custom, therefore, could be adduced to support the exclusion of royal princesses from the throne. In addition, kings were consecrated at their coronation, a ceremony that was akin to ordination, and no woman could be ordained. When the first decision had been taken in 1317, what followed in 1328 was logical enough. It was argued then that since Edward III's mother had no right herself to the throne, she could not possibly convey any claim to her son, an argument supported by certain contemporary customary laws. Thus the French law of succession was settled and successive monarchs in assuming their crown tacitly acknowledged that they were the creatures of the law.[1]

The French king, therefore, was the servant of what was just and of what was legal – the latter was expected to mirror the former – and

[1] Ibid., 42–5; de Pange, op. cit., 395–6; Lehugeur, *Philippe le Long, Roi de France*, I, 84–92; J. Le Patourel, 'Edward III and the Kingdom of France', 173–5.

traditionally he was not expected to carry out his responsibilities unaided, but to seek advice before taking any important decision. Ninth-century commentators maintained the necessity of royal consultation and deliberation with the great lay and spiritual lords and with the chief officers of the crown before such decisions were reached. This tradition was upheld by the Capetians and their successors. The coronation ceremony itself contained a simulacrum of the great vassals' assent to the new king's assumption of authority in the formal acclaim called for from the assembled dignitaries by the archbishop of Rheims, a custom that persisted until the end of the *ancien régime*. The early Capetian assemblies, about which very little is known, were certainly assemblies of great vassals summoned by the rulers to give advice on and support for royal policies. A contemporary of St Louis noted that the kings held regular assemblies at which a great number of counsellors, barons and prelates were present, and where, after due reflection, ordinances necessary for the kingdom's well-being were drawn up. Philip the Bold summoned an assembly in 1284 before undertaking a war against the king of Aragon, and Philip the Fair did likewise in 1302 to gain support for his opposition to the pope, Boniface VIII. Out of these gatherings were to grow the Estates-General and the assemblies of Notables.[1]

However, such large, formal and increasingly extraordinary assemblies did not provide the most convenient source of counsel for the sovereign. Consequently, from the twelfth century onwards he came to rely upon a smaller body of advisers, dominated by professional, paid counsellors, usually legists, who were always available to give opinions on a variety of matters, financial, judicial or administrative. It was from this inner council that the Parlement emerged.

It was to be expected that members of the Parlement would play their part in state affairs. They stood very close to the throne and, as royal counsellors, they inherited the traditional obligation to proffer advice to the king. In fact, their particular function made their advice especially relevant. So long as the king's essential role was that of supreme judge and decisions of state continued to be judicial in character, the opinions of his chief magistrates upon political matters would remain a valuable and entirely legitimate source of counsel for him. Besides, the Parlement was also the peers' and princes' tribunal, so that it did truly represent

[1] Lemaire, op. cit., 12–13, 40; Luchaire, op. cit., 459; E. Perrot, *Les Institutions Publiques et Privées de l'Ancienne France*, 454.

all those persons who traditionally advised the king. As a result, from an early date, magistrates of the Parlement were concerned with politics.

In 1312, the count of Namur submitted his dispute with Charles of Valois, the brother of King Philip IV, for adjudication by the Parlement; in 1342 the duke of Lorraine and his brother-in-law did likewise. In 1402 a deputation of Spanish knights asked the court to publish the treaty of alliance signed between the kings of Castile and Portugal, a striking indication of the Parlement's prestige and authority. Charles V habitually consulted his court before signing treaties: in 1368, by insisting that the Parlement had competence to hear appeals from Aquitaine, he precipitated the reopening of war with England, convinced that not to have done so would have been a denial of his coronation oath and his role of sovereign judge. The Parlement's opinion was sought again in 1417, about the pretensions of Sigismund, king of the Romans, to exact fealty from Dauphiné. Charles VII received its advice about how best to negotiate with the rebel princes, and after the king's death it continued to be informed of the negotiations between the English, the dauphin and the duke of Burgundy. Louis XI was careful to have his treaties registered in the Parlement, a procedure followed by Louis XII with the registration in 1502 of the Treaty of Cambrai.

Individual magistrates were also employed as ambassadors or secret envoys. In 1438 Guillaume le Tur was sent to Dauphiné, in 1444 President Rabateau was chosen by Charles VII to invite Metz to recognize him as king, in 1478 Counsellor Pichon was included in an embassy to treat with Maximilian of Austria, while four years later a dozen magistrates helped to negotiate the treaty of Arras with Burgundy, which itself contained a clause stipulating that the treaty should be freely verified by the Parlement.[1]

The magistrates invariably tried to intervene when the alienation of royal rights or of parts of the royal domain were at stake. In 1370 they objected to the privileges granted by Charles V to the duke of Anjou. For two years, 1442–4, they resisted royal letters which handed over part of the domain to the Constable de Richemont, and for more than a year, in 1472–3, they sought to prevent Louis XI from giving land in Poitou to Philippe de Commines in return for his services to the king. On a less serious level, in 1418 the *Avocat-Général* protested vehemently against

[1] Aubert, *Histoire du Parlement de Paris à François Ier*, I, 346 et seq; Aubert, *Le Parlement de Paris à Charles VII*, II, 189–90; Maugis, op. cit., I, 519–20.

the decision to hand over to the monks of Saint-Denis the royal rents payable upon sixteen stalls in the butchers' market in Paris. That sort of complaint was frequently addressed to Louis XI, who took little notice of his court, but opposition to more drastic alienations sometimes forced the magistrates to add reservations of their own to safeguard the king's position. They did so in 1513, for example, when registering the gift of the county of Etampes to Queen Anne of Brittany and her heirs, by ruling that since it formed part of the royal domain the county should remain indivisible and inheritance should be strictly in order of primogeniture. Again, when Louis XII bestowed upon her for life the benefits accruing from the duchy of Nemours, the Parlement insisted that the king should not alienate his judicial rights there.[1]

Finally, two judgments pronounced by the court towards the end of the Hundred Years War illustrate very clearly how apparently trivial judicial verdicts could yet encompass broad political considerations. In April 1436 French troops drove the English out of Paris, and early in the following year the Parlement was called upon to resolve a case involving a French girl and an English soldier. The two were engaged to be married, and the girl, despite her parents' opposition, remained determined to follow her fiancé. The Parlement instructed her parents, under pain of a fine, to prevent such a flight. Shortly afterwards it received a written request from the soldier, asking for permission to marry and to take his bride away with him. The Parlement refused whilst hostilities between England and France continued. Its verdict was not based upon any legal impediment or irregularity, but simply upon the fact that the two parties were representatives of countries at war.

Similarly, in 1436, shortly before the liberation of the capital, another young Parisienne had married an Italian merchant who was closely allied with the English and who followed them to Rouen after the evacuation of Paris. His wife joined him there at his request. Subsequently all their possessions in Paris were confiscated. The wife's mother succeeded eventually in having the matter raised before the Parlement, but to her argument that her daughter was simply obeying the dictates of canon law by joining her husband, the *Procureur-Général* replied that the public interest came first and that by joining her husband and the English she had been guilty of the crime of *lèse-majesté*. She had further aggravated the situation by bearing a number of children, thereby adding to the ranks of

[1] Aubert, *Histoire du Parlement de Paris à François Ier*, I, 353 *et seq*; Maugis, op. cit., I, 676–80; Kervyn de Lettenhove (ed.), *Lettres de Philippe de Commines*, I, 92–102.

the prospective enemies of the king of France. The Parlement agreed with the *Procureur-Général*.

By these two judgments the court decided in effect that it was no longer possible for Frenchmen to remain neutral in the struggle with England; nationality was henceforth considered sufficient in itself to involve everybody. On other occasions the magistrates accepted the implications of their verdicts by admonishing merchants who traded with the enemy, and peasants and townsmen who protested against the performance of military obligations. The political overtones of these judgments were indeed far more striking than the simple judicial fact that they deprived one young Parisian woman of her possessions and another of a husband.[1]

All these examples furnish evidence of the court's involvement, by its very nature, in affairs of state, and in the course of time a novel procedure grew up which took account of that fact and enabled the Parlement to proffer advice on a wide range of royal proposals. The procedure centred upon the court's practice of publishing and registering royal letters and ordinances. This ceremony was held in public in the *Grand' Chambre*, where all the magistrates gathered to hear new enactments solemnly read out. After the readings, the various royal pronouncements were transcribed on to the Parlement's register. The practice served a double purpose, that of providing publicity for the letters and ordinances, as well as an authenticated and permanent record of all royal legislation. It began soon after the Parlement had acquired a separate identity, as early registers reveal: 'Given at Paris in our parlement in the year of grace 1325, in the month of March . . . read and published in the parlement and to the assembled chamber.'[2] The formula varied slightly in succeeding decades, though the key words, '*lecta et publicata*', recurred regularly.

However, the practice of publishing royal enactments in this way soon ceased to be a simple formality. In March 1302, the king instructed his bailiffs, seneschals and *prévôts* not to execute royal orders if the king had been persuaded to issue acts contrary to the law, or if they found any other good reason for not enforcing them, until they had explained the difficulties to the king. There was nothing remarkable about this decision. The monarch's judicial officers were experts who could be expected to

[1] A. Bossuat, 'L'Idée de Nation', 54–61; for a glimpse of the Parlement's many-sided role during this war, *see* P. C. Timbal, *La Guerre de Cent Ans vue à travers les registres du Parlement, passim.*

[2] Maugis, op. cit., I, 522–3.

detect legal contradictions or a lack of equity; they were also royal counsellors who were obliged to give the king the benefit of their professional advice. This advice was all-important if the king was to fulfil his essential duty of ruling in accordance with just laws. It would have been remarkable, however, if the Parlement had not shared this right of questioning royal enactments. As royal counsellors, the magistrates stood closer to the throne than the bailiffs and as a court of law the Parlement had pre-eminence over every other royal jurisdiction in the country. It would have been absurd if officers of lesser jurisdictions, but not the magistrates themselves, could have questioned the wisdom or legality of the king's decisions, especially since the practice of publishing and registering his enactments in the Parlement was intended to provide an official, authenticated version. However, no regulation exists which formally bestowed upon the Parlement the right granted in 1302 to the bailiffs, seneschals and *prévôts*.

Nevertheless, the king did issue a number of ordinances during the first half of the fourteenth century, referring explicitly to the Parlement, ordering it not to execute either royal letters of grace granted in favour of individuals or orders involving the setting aside of existing decrees, if in so doing the course of justice would be harmed. It is true that these ordinances applied even more specifically than that of 1302 to administrative decisions and not to royal legislation in general, but in the fourteenth century the distinction was not clear enough to prevent the magistrates scrutinizing all royal enactments sent to the court.[1]

From the middle of the century the formula of registration began to alter. On important matters consultation between the Parlement and the *Grand Conseil* sometimes took place, and in 1366 after one royal ordinance had been examined in such an assembly it was registered with the phrase, '*Visa, lecta ET CORRECTA** *per dominos Magni Consilli et Parlamenti regii ad hoc deputati*'. In 1376 another royal ordinance was published and registered with reservations inserted by the *Procureur-Général*, with the court's approval, to protect the rights of the king.[2]

Out of this habit of scrutinizing royal acts and seeking to modify them arose the procedure of remonstrance. At first the Parlement made informal, verbal complaints to the king about aspects of his legislation which it considered to be ill-judged. But during the reign of the weak-minded

[1] Esmein, *Cours élémentaire d'Histoire du Droit Français*, 531.
* Author's capitals.
[2] Maugis, op. cit., I, 523.

Charles VI, when the court's importance in state affairs was greatly enhanced, its remonstrances became a recognized, though ill-defined part of *parlementaire* procedure. Of course, the king was not always willing to fall in with the magistrates' objections and change his acts, nor could he allow them to dictate legislation to him by their refusal to register enactments of which they disapproved. Consequently, in 1392 the practice was established of issuing royal *lettres de jussion*, if the Parlement still refused registration after hearing the king's reply to its complaints. These letters ordered immediate and unqualified registration, a fact that was usually signified in the register by the phrase, '*Lecta et publicata de expresso mandato domini regis*'. If the Parlement remained recalcitrant in the face of *lettres de jussion*, the king came himself to the court to hold a *lit de justice*, a ceremony appearing for the first time early in the fifteenth century, at which the king personally supervised the registration of the contentious letter or ordinance in question.[1] In this way he preserved his sovereign authority, while the procedure of remonstrance preserved his counsellors' right to advise and gave formal recognition to the Parlement's important political role. Both procedures arose quite naturally out of the French monarchical tradition.

When Charles V died in 1380 his successor, Charles VI, was only twelve years old and authority in the state fell chiefly into the hands of his uncle, Philip the Bold, duke of Burgundy. Since Charles's mental state made it impossible for him ever to govern the country adequately, even after reaching his majority, Philip became the virtual ruler of the kingdom.[2] Thus the weakness of the monarchy opened the way for a struggle for political control in which Burgundy's chief rival was the king's younger brother, Louis, duke of Orléans. The animosity between the two protagonists remained muted until 1401, when in Burgundy's absence, Orléans persuaded the king to intervene on his behalf in opposition to Burgundy's policy towards the papacy. An armed confrontation was narrowly avoided and an unenthusiastic reconciliation was arranged. Before it took place, however, Burgundy wrote to the Parlement, protesting at the interference which had taken place during his absence and the way in which affairs had been conducted and appealing for the court's support in protecting the king's domain and property. The magistrates' reply, that in so far as such matters concerned them, they were always

[1] Esmein, *Cours élémentaire d'Histoire du Droit Français*, 532–3; Isambert, op. cit., VI, 703.

[2] The history of Charles VI's madness is thoroughly examined by G. Dodu, *Les Valois*, 74–102, a volume concerned with the monarchs' personalities rather than with the history of their reigns.

willing to deliberate, advise and do everything within their power to preserve the honour and appurtenances of the king, was extremely circumspect.[1] What was significant, however, was Burgundy's decision to appeal to the Parlement at all. Its prestige had begun to grow from the very beginning of the reign, when on several occasions it had formed the nucleus of great political assemblies of princes, barons, prelates and magistrates. With the eclipse of the king's personal authority that of his Parlement, judging in his stead, grew more apparent and Philip of Burgundy's letter suggested that he certainly appreciated the court's political importance.

In 1404 Philip the Bold died and was succeeded as duke by his son, John the Fearless. The antagonism between the houses of Burgundy and Orléans grew more intense. In August 1405 Orléans protested to the Parlement against the actions of his cousin. In the same month Burgundy also passed on to the court a memorandum written by him to the king, designed to point out the damage inflicted upon the crown and the kingdom by the policies of Orléans, and later in the year he communicated a second document defending his own actions against Orléans's allegations. Caught between two powerful factions on the brink of civil war, the Parlement, not surprisingly, was unwilling to take the initiative which was being proffered to it by both sides.[2]

Towards the end of 1407 Orléans was assassinated by hirelings of the duke of Burgundy and an already perilous situation became desperate. At the ceremonial opening of the new *parlementaire* year in November 1408, the chancellor warned the magistrates that their court constituted the sole remaining source of justice in the kingdom.[3] It was by no means beyond reproach itself: a great many counsellors were creatures of one or other of the great princes and an increasing number of magistrates were undertaking special missions outside the court, which slowed down the judicial procedure. Besides, the enthusiasm of even the most zealous magistrates was being constantly worn away by the frequency of royal evocations.[4] Nevertheless, with the outbreak of civil war in 1411, signalling the breakdown of royal power, the Parlement did appear to be the only source of legitimate authority in the country. In 1412 it finally gained the courage to make a stand. After a deliberation in the court on 20 January of that year, the magistrates decided to complain to the king

[1] L. Douët-d'Arcq (ed.), *Pièces Inédites*, I, 212–15.
[2] Nicholas de Baye, *Journal*, I, 139–41.
[3] Ibid., 245–6.
[4] J. d'Avout, *La Querelle des Armagnacs et des Bourguignons*, 114–15.

that appeals which should have been cognizable in the Parlement were not in fact reaching it, and they claimed the right of free access to the sovereign when the cause of justice was at stake. Their action was in fact the first formal assertion of the right of remonstrance,[1] and although their intervention was purely judicial in character, it was also a potent appeal for the return of political stability. A few months later, a delegation from the Parlement, headed by the First President, helped to negotiate the peace of Auxerre between the dukes of Burgundy and Berry. In April 1413 the dauphin consulted the court on the subject of military precautions against a possible English invasion; and in the same year it acceded to the request of the citizens of Paris temporarily to suspend its session of pleadings to concentrate on securing a general peace; though earlier in the year it had refused to join with representatives of the city and of the University in undertaking the reform of certain aspects of government, chiefly financial.[2] Its refusal to take that sort of initiative clearly demonstrated the distinction made by the Parlement between intervention as his sovereign and chief court in support of the king's position, and independent political action taken without his authority.

The Parlement saw itself as the support, not the rival, of the monarchy. In 1415 it drew the king's attention once more to the state of misery to which war had reduced the kingdom and suggested remedies upon the lines of earlier royal ordinances. But no remonstrances could mend, nor could the conflict between Armagnacs and Burgundians match, the disaster with which the year ended, when several thousand French nobles fell before the English bowmen on the muddy field of Agincourt.

In 1417, the Parlement was asked for advice on how extra funds could be secured to help combat the English threat. In the spring of 1419 it decided on its own initiative to ask the king and the duke of Burgundy to enter into negotiations with the dauphin, the future Charles VII, with a view to healing the divisions of the kingdom, and in the summer one of its members, President Rapiout argued forcefully and successfully against the conclusion of an agreement with King Henry V of England, which would have given the latter certain territorial acquisitions in France, on the grounds that Henry had no claim to French lands, which remained in the inalienable possession of the rightful kings of France.[3]

This opinion reflected the Parlement's role as guardian of the law, as

[1] Douët-d'Arcq, op. cit., I, 347; Maugis, op. cit., I, 526.
[2] Douët-d'Arcq, op. cit., I, 354–8; 362–5.
[3] Ibid., 387–8; Clément de Fauquembergue, *Journal*, I, 287–8; D'Avout, op. cit., 289–90.

upholder of the legalistic concept of French kingship, yet shortly afterwards it betrayed that role by adhering to the treaty of Troyes, ratified in May 1420 between Charles VI and Henry V, by which the dauphin was disinherited from the French throne and replaced by the king of England and his successors. Not all Frenchmen were scandalized by this flagrant denial of the law of succession: any chance of a permanent settlement after years of war seemed worthy of consideration, and the personality of Henry V offered the promise of a more effective rule than did that of his ousted rival, the dauphin. Nevertheless, the treaty of Troyes went directly against established custom. The right of succession from father to son had a tradition stretching back over four centuries, while almost a century before the treaty was signed it had been affirmed that women could neither succeed to the throne nor transmit rights to their sons. Therefore, because the treaty sought to reverse that decision it was illegal, and no other possible benefits accruing from it could alter that basic fact.[1]

The Parlement was especially culpable in accepting and registering the treaty without demur. More than any other body or group of individuals in the state it had the obligation of pointing out to the king the illegality of what was contemplated. By failing to do so, it undermined the prestige and authority of the monarchy and compromised its own position as the champion of the king's justice. Indeed, its credit had seriously diminished since 1418, when John the Fearless, having gained control of the capital, took measures to ensure that a large number of his supporters joined the ranks of the magistrates. Under the pressure of political circumstances the Parlement lost its integrity, much of its expertise and therefore its reputation. A second Parlement, loyal to Charles VII, containing a number of magistrates who had formerly sat in the Parlement in Paris, was established at Poitiers in 1418, and from then until 1436 the court bore a dichotomous aspect. With the triumph of Charles VII and his return to the capital, the two courts were merged[2]. However, the Parlement's prestige had suffered greatly from this division and the victory of the legitimate sovereign, though it heightened the reputation of the monarchy, only underlined the heinousness of the Parlement's action in supporting the treaty of Troyes. It was not until the middle of the century with the great reforming ordinance of Montils-les-Tours that the court regained its former reputation.

During the second half of the century, the procedure of registration

[1] The treaty is printed in E. Cosneau, *Les Grands Traités de la Guerre de Cent Ans*, 102–15.

[2] E. Perroy, *La Guerre de Cent Ans*, 228–30; Maugis, op. cit., I, 24–61.

and remonstrance was finally settled. Until then, remonstrances especially had lacked formal definition. The king's practice had often been to seek the opinion of a commission of presidents and counsellors in advance of issuing legislation, or of associating certain magistrates with the actual composition of the enactments, thus assuring himself of the court's approval when the time came for registration. Very different was the procedure that eventually emerged, by which royal proposals were discussed in detail by the assembled court, without prior collaboration with the king or his advisers. A comparison between two ordinances, both of them introducing judicial reform, one dated October 1446 and the other July 1493, illustrates the different procedures.

The preamble of the first ordinance declared that in order to remedy the vices which had crept into the administration of justice and to recall the dictates of earlier ordinances, a number of presidents and counsellors had suggested certain reforms, which were duly set out in writing and sent to the king. He examined their recommendations with his council, found them helpful and accepted them. They were subsequently incorporated into the royal ordinance and accepted for registration without further discussion.

In 1493, however, it was the king who took the initiative, sending to the Parlement an ordinance of which it had no knowledge in advance. The magistrates discussed the ordinance at a plenary session, modified and amended the text and reserved the right to make further alterations if they deemed them necessary in the light of experience. The king, Charles VIII, acquiesced in this procedure and did so again in April 1499 when the Parlement discussed a second ordinance concerned with judicial reform. On this occasion the court appointed commissioners to examine certain articles in greater detail, inserted amendments, corrected faults and careless phrasing in the text, and registered the ordinance on condition that no further faults came to light subsequently.

The procedure of registration and remonstrance which was made precise during the reign of Louis XI was as follows: when a royal project was presented to the court for registration, according to its importance one or two *rapporteurs* were nominated to examine it. When it came up for discussion before the assembled chambers, the *Gens du roi* gave their opinion first, followed immediately by the *rapporteurs* and then by the other magistrates in order of seniority. According to the majority opinion the First President then pronounced in favour of registration or of remonstrances. If the verdict favoured the former, there followed the solemn publication of the act at the request of and in the presence of the *Gens du roi*, whose express consent was contained in the official formula of registration, '*audite et requirente procuratore generali*'. This phrase was considered to be a guarantee of the king's determination to support the law concerned and an insurance against royal vacillation. If, on the other hand, the court decided to remonstrate, it had then to decide further whether its remonstrances would be written or verbal. If the former, a commission of magistrates was nominated to draw them up and then submit them for approval at a plenary session of the Parlement. Next a deputation was nominated to present the remonstrances to the king; then came the royal reply and the debate upon it, which might lead to immediate registration or to further remonstrances repeated five or six times, with a *lettre de jussion* or a *lit de justice* finally procuring registration on the king's terms.[1]

Such procedures raise the question of whether the king's relationship with his court was changing, and changing to his disadvantage. Before that matter can be considered, however, it is necessary to examine another aspect of the Parlement's relations with the crown before 1515 which has not so far been mentioned and which is important enough to deserve separate consideration: the problem of the Gallican liberties.

The doctrine of Gallicanism grew out of the disputes between Pope Boniface VIII and Philip the Fair, though conditions favouring its birth had long been present in Capetian France. Hugh Capet acquired the throne with the help of the clergy, and both he and his immediate successors depended upon bishops and abbots not only to act as counsellors and administrators but also to provide financial assistance. In return, the kings defended the property and privileges of the Church against feudal incursions. As the monarch gained in authority his relationship with the Church changed: from being its protector he became its tutor. He intervened regularly in the appointment of prelates, nominating them himself, bestowing the right of nomination upon favourites, or even selling it. The eleventh-century Investiture Contest, however, though it had far less effect on the French than on the German and Italian churches, led to a modification of this royal privilege, with the restoration of the principle of self-governing election by chapters for all major benefices. Nevertheless, the king retained the right to draw revenue from vacant benefices, and although he ceased to control elections directly, no election could

[1] Maugis, op. cit., I, 538–44.

take place without his permission, the successful candidate had still to obtain royal approval and to take an oath of fidelity to the king and no metropolitan could proceed with the ceremony of consecration without royal authorization.

Consequently, the king's role remained very important and certainly as far as the candidate was concerned, he was bound to feel beholden to the sovereign for his appointment. This position began to change from the middle of the thirteenth century when the popes progressively claimed the right of appointment to more and more French benefices, a development which reached its climax during the period of the Avignon papacy. However, the long era of close co-operation between king and clergy in France remained a powerful tradition, speedily invoked when the dispute between king and pope flared up. Another aspect of the same tradition, not even broken by papal intervention, permitted the king to summon and preside over the prelates of his kingdom, in order to discuss questions concerning the Church in France, notably in its relations with Rome. In addition, he remained concerned with a great many details of diocesan administration, with all matters concerning the protection, acquisition or alienation of church land or property. Finally, the close bonds between the sovereign and the French clergy were further tightened by the religious character with which the former was invested at his coronation, and particularly by the oath pronounced by all French kings since the consecration of the Carolingian Louis II, in 877, which committed them to preserve the canonical privileges of the Church in France. These privileges consisted of diverse immunities and franchises granted on different occasions by the monarchy and also of the right of self-government according to the ancient canons of the Church. This last privilege which the king swore to maintain ran counter to the papal policy of intervention in local church affairs, and, like the other customary links between the king and his clergy, it tended to unite them in one camp in opposition to Rome.[1]

The great struggle between Philip the Fair and Boniface VIII began in February 1296 with the publication of the papal bull, *Clericis Laicos*, excommunicating any secular ruler who taxed the clergy without the permission of the Holy See. Philip's response was to publish two ordinances, one forbidding money under any form to be taken out of the

[1] V. Martin, *Les Origines du Gallicanisme*, is the standard work on the subject; a useful summary and critique of this work is provided by A. Fliche, 'Les Origines du Gallicanisme', 145–58.

kingdom without royal consent, the other forbidding foreigners – including papal legates – to remain in the country. By these acts the king cut off the supply and the means of transport of French money to the papal treasury in the form of various taxes. In the following year, Boniface, who badly needed the money and who had received no support from the French hierarchy, gave way and abrogated the bull so far as France was concerned. The quarrel was resumed in December 1301 with the publication of two more bulls, *Salvator Mundi*, which in effect reimposed the doctrine of *Clericis Laicos*, and the famous bull, *Ausculta, Fili*, in which Boniface claimed not only spiritual but also temporal sovereignty over all christendom.

They were followed in the next year by perhaps the most celebrated manifesto of the Middle Ages in support of the doctrine of papal supremacy, the bull *Unam Sanctam*. The conclusion reached by Boniface in this document was as follows: 'We declare, assert, define and pronounce that it is absolutely necessary for salvation that every human being should be subordinate to the Roman pontiff.'[1] Faced with Philip's decision, with the support of the French clergy, to appeal from the pope's pronouncements to a general council of the Church, Boniface not only excommunicated the king, but at the same time declared him incapable of exercising the power of sovereign jurisdiction – of acting as king, in other words – and declared his subjects freed from their duty of obedience to their ruler. The affair ended with the pope's brief capture by Philip's mercenaries and his death shortly after his release. His successors retracted the anathema hurled by Boniface against his arch-enemy and recognized Philip's contention that the papacy had no temporal authority over the French king, and no right to interfere in the government of the kingdom.

In the years that followed, a number of writings appeared in support of the king's position *vis-à-vis* the pope; they included the *Songe du Vergier*, a semi-official publication emanating from the immediate entourage of Charles V, which reiterated the fundamental claim established by Philip's victory, that the king, unlike the emperor, being neither approved nor crowned by the pope, was in no respect his temporal subject.[2]

The decisive period came, however, at the very end of the century, provoked by the continuing scandal of the Great Schism. In 1394 the

[1] Martin, op. cit., I, 190.

[2] This document, with an introduction by J. L. Brunet, is printed in *Traitez des Droits et Libertez de l'Eglise Gallicane*, II.

cardinals who supported the Avignon papacy elected Benedict XIII as successor to Clement VII, and it seemed to influential French clerics, whose allegiance was also to Avignon, that drastic measures would have to be taken to mend the cleavage in the Church, which had already persisted for sixteen years. In 1395 an assembly of the French Church, summoned by Charles VI, voted in favour of the resignation of both popes so that an agreed pontiff could heal the rift. Benedict was uncompromising in his refusal to contemplate such a course. The doctors of the Sorbonne then advised Charles VI that, in view of the pope's attitude, it was impossible to envisage an end to the schism, unless pressure was brought to bear by the king, and they suggested that the pope should no longer be allowed to appoint to benefices in France nor draw the substantial revenues attached to the right of nomination. If that was done, they argued, Benedict would not be able to exert such influence over the French clergy nor pay his retainers to remain loyal.[1]

The justification for such a course was to be found in the customary electoral procedure for major benefices and the system of appointment by a clerical officer, a bishop or abbot, with the agreement of the patron for minor benefices, which had preceded papal intervention, constituting a part of those ancient liberties that every French king swore to preserve. After a meeting between representatives of the king and of his council and the leading prelates of the country, an ordinance was published in July 1398, by which Charles VI proclaimed that he, his clergy and his people had withdrawn their obedience from Benedict XIII and would pay no revenues to the pope at Avignon. Furthermore, he decreed that all benefices in France should be filled in accordance with the ancient tradition. This withdrawal of obedience lasted for five years, until May 1403, but even after the country's submission, Benedict's attitude did nothing to alleviate the hostility that had grown up between himself and the French hierarchy.

Another general council of the French Church was summoned in 1406. Its decisions were incorporated into two royal ordinances published in February 1407. The first of them confirmed the council's resolution that

> the archbishops, etc. . . . declare and determine that the Church of France . . . must be recalled to its ancient observance by which it must be regulated in the future. As the statutes of the general councils and

[1] C. E. Du Boulay, *Historia Universitatis Parisiensis*, IV, 752–3. The university was particularly active politically at this time and this work provides much useful information.

the decrees of the Holy Fathers ordain, prelates must be chosen by election by chapters, convents and colleges.[1]

Similarly, it was ordained that the nomination to minor benefices had to be made by the usual officer with the consent of the legitimate patron. Charles pledged royal support in the future for the maintenance of these ancient liberties and ordered his Parlement to ensure that his enactment remained inviolable and that the elections and appointments were conducted without interference. The second ordinance forbade any financial exactions arising out of the pope's intervention in beneficial affairs to be paid to the Holy See by the French clergy. Both documents were registered in the Parlement. The French king and his clergy thus combined to claim limited independence from the papacy, on the grounds of a tradition of ecclesiastical self-government and of royal guardianship: the birth of Gallicanism had been formally announced.

Shortly after this date the Parlement was to take a more positive role in formulating official French policy *vis-à-vis* the Holy See, but already for a hundred years previously it had been pursuing a judicial role which underlined royal influence and authority over the Church in France and thereby greatly facilitated the events of 1398 and 1407. From the beginning of the fourteenth century, in the reign of Philip the Fair, members of the French clergy, abbots, priors and *curés*, began to bring their beneficial disputes with other clerics before the Parlement. At first they based their appeal upon the royal safeguard, a privilege by which the king guaranteed redress to those who held it, if physical violence was committed against their persons (by that time the safeguard was included among the *cas royaux*, matters specifically reserved for the royal courts).[2] The Parlement's task in such circumstances was simply to decide whether the safeguard had been broken, a duty that could frequently be accomplished without much difficulty. In 1330, for example, one unfortunate prior was dragged out of his church by his feet and his surplice torn from his back and burnt. In 1338 an archdeacon from Dinan was forcibly removed from his archidiaconal chair, the symbol of his authority, and stood helpless while it was broken into pieces. The Parlement punished the defendants severely with heavy fines.[3] Nevertheless, it did not at first concern itself with further disputes, which sometimes arose in the course of such

[1] Martin, op. cit., I, 325.
[2] *See supra*, 78–9.
[3] G. Mollat, 'Les Origines du Gallicanisme Parlementaire', 93.

cases, either about the legality of the plaintiff's right of possession or about the fact of his possession; these were matters for the ecclesiastical judges.

Yet, from 1340 or thereabouts, the Parlement did begin to encroach further upon spiritual preserves, when it began to allow that the clergy could have seisin of ecclesiastical property. The concept of seisin, which was common to all western Europe, concerned the fact of possession as opposed to legitimate ownership, and it introduced another legal channel through which clerical litigants could reach the royal courts: the appeal *en cas de saisine et nouvelleté*. This process came to entitle those who had been evicted or threatened with eviction from their benefices to invoke the king's justice in support of their possessory claims. It was enlarged to include the holding of benefices on the grounds that the king could always intervene to prevent the eruption of violence in his kingdom, and also, because their holders enjoyed certain purely temporal advantages. Thus the Parlement extended its jurisdiction over the fact of possession. That still did not make it competent, however, to pass judgment on the quite separate matter of whether possession was legitimately held.[1]

These incursions of royal authority into the sphere of ecclesiastical jurisdiction were not only prompted by the king's determination to strengthen his own position at the head of the state. Members of the clergy who were appealing more regularly to the royal courts were themselves responsible to some extent. By the second quarter of the fourteenth century the professional standards of the Parlement were high and its law, logically and systematically deduced from existing custom, was set down in its official records. Its decisions, therefore, had an aura of consistency and permanence. From the concluding years covered by the *Olim* registers the magistrates had assumed the practice of writing into the court's records increasingly complete accounts of the legal arguments behind every decision and of collecting *résumés* of important judgments, including the names of the parties concerned, the session in which the judgment had been given, the matter in dispute and the point of law upon which the issue was decided. Precedent, in other words, was beginning to play a highly important role.[2]

For many clerics the rational and scientific nature of the Parlement's jurisprudence made the court an attractive alternative to the ecclesiastical tribunals. Its procedure was also more speedy and less complicated and,

[1] Ibid., 91–2; F. Cheyette, 'La Justice et le Pouvoir Royal', 382–4.
[2] A. Sergène, 'Le Précédent Judiciaire', *passim*.

besides, a favourable verdict meant the protection of a royal officer, who provided far greater security than the spiritual courts could offer: since most suits began with acts of violence against the person or with the destruction of property, that was an important consideration. Thus without in any way seeking to restrict the activities of the ecclesiastical courts, but simply by offering a more efficient alternative, the king underlined his traditionally close relationship with the Church in France, setting these problems of disputed benefices into the framework of the king's law.

Nor was his judicial influence confined to beneficial matters. The growth in the importance of precedence in the Parlement's jurisprudence greatly increased the scope as well as the number of cases brought before the court by members of the clergy. The first case involving the citation of precedents was in 1355, when one cleric complained that several other clerics had violated his seisin of a certain priory: his counsel maintained that the Parlement had the right to judge the dispute, because it had judged numerous similar actions previously, and he proceeded to quote them. This development enabled clerical plaintiffs to bring a variety of disputes before the court if they could relate a single precedent to their particular problem.[1] In addition, the Parlement's decision to extend the concept of seisin to clerical possessions itself justified intervention in many matters besides the possession of benefices though that fact was not recognized for some time. Seisin referred to the possession of rights as well as property, but while the holding of benefices had a clearly temporal aspect, many other clerical rights seemed purely spiritual, and therefore outside the purview of *parlementaire* action.

In 1374 a case arose which brought this difficulty to the fore. The bishop of Châlons-sur-Marne ordered a procession to be held in his diocese on a particular day. He nailed up his instructions for the occasion on the usual diocesan notice board, the door of the cathedral church. The cathedral chapter tore down the notice, ordered a procession on their own account, and nailed their instructions on the door of the episcopal court. Both sides complained to the Parlement that the seisin of each had been violated. The question arose, therefore, of whether the rights at issue in this matter were spiritual or temporal, and initially the court declined to give a ruling. Then, in 1381, the bishop of Beauvais, who was also the chancellor of France, appealed *en cas de saisine et nouvelleté* against his cathedral chapter, alleging that the monks had trespassed upon his ecclesiastical jurisdiction.

[1] Cheyette, op. cit., 386–7; Sergène, op. cit., 370.

He claimed that the Parlement had cognizance of the matter on the grounds of a number of precedents, including the dispute between the bishop of Châlons and his chapter, which should have been judged, so he maintained, by the King's Court. This time, after examining the precedents, the Parlement accepted the chancellor's plea and in so doing established that the possession of spiritual rights was temporal in character – the emphasis being upon the holding of rights rather than upon their nature – and was therefore cognizable in a secular court.

Thus the appeal *en nouvelleté* opened the door to a host of clerical plaintiffs, who sought to have a wide range of disputes settled in the Parlement. By the end of the fourteenth century the court was concerned with all cases involving ecclesiastical rights, privileges, exemptions and immunities, save those which directly concerned the faith and the administration of the sacraments, and plaintiffs who had sued before it included cardinals, archbishops, even the patriarch of Antioch, and a multitude of bishops, abbots and lesser clergy. Long before the withdrawal of obedience from Benedict XIII and the publication of the royal ordinances of 1407, the Parlement, aided by the concepts of seisin and of judicial precedent, had been asserting the king's authority over spiritual matters. It did not intervene indiscriminately, however, but strictly according to the concept of seisin, in defence of the existing rights and liberties of French churches and clerics. Since its *raison d'être* was to protect and maintain the law, the Parlement was only concerned with acting in a manner consistent with its own juridical principles, and therefore its jurisdiction was limited by the very rights and liberties which it fought to maintain. The court defended this position on many subsequent occasions, even against the wishes of the king himself; already in the fourteenth century, indeed, it showed itself to be relatively free of bias in applying this rule to cases involving royal intervention in the provision of benefices.

The alliance between the court and the clergy did more than settle a number of isolated ecclesiastical disputes; it provided a judicial basis for the idea that the king had the obligation to uphold the established liberties of the French Church, the idea which was uppermost in the minds of French prelates in 1398 and 1407.[1] It was to be expected, therefore, that the Parlement would register the royal ordinances of 1407 with a clear conscience, and it was not surprising that shortly afterwards it should take a further initiative of its own.

In October 1413 the king requested his court to give its opinions on

[1] Cheyette, op. cit., 388–94.

how the Gallican liberties could be maintained, and the continuing excessive influence of the Pope in France curbed. On 10 November the Parlement drew up its report, in which it advocated that the electoral procedure for appointments to benefices, as laid down in the royal ordinance of 1407, should be rigidly observed, and that to prevent money from leaving the country in the form of various papal exactions a committee of twelve experts should be appointed to study what steps ought to be taken. Meanwhile, the export of gold or silver should be prohibited under pain of confiscation of goods and of temporalty, and the necessary police arrangements made at frontier posts and ports.[1] However, these resolutions remained without effect because of the manœuvres of the papal legate in France, the intermittent madness of Charles VI and the summoning of an ecumenical council in Constance.

The Parlement returned to this theme four years later, in November 1417, when in six articles it declared that it was lawful and expedient for the king to preserve in perpetuity the ancient liberties of the French Church, which provided for the election of candidates to major benefices and required that those who exercised the right of advowson in respect of minor benefices should appoint worthy candidates; that the king should at once prohibit the payment of any taxes to the Holy See arising out of the holding of benefices; that letters should be drawn up and published to the effect that the French representatives at Constance had no authority to consent to any decision reached at the council which could prejudice the Gallican liberties; that the Parlement had no wish to advise the king against a moderate contribution by the Church in France to the needs of the papacy; that when the ancient beneficial regime had been fully restored, the king should take measures to ensure that suitable candidates, especially graduates in theology, were available to fill vacancies; that candidates who had been granted benefices since the accession of Pope John XXIII (1410) should be allowed to hold them, without prejudice to the Gallican liberties.[2]

At almost precisely the time that the Parlement was drawing up these recommendations, a new pope, Martin V, was elected at the council of Constance. The reaction of the French government to this news was cautious, and final recognition of the new pope was withheld until the circumstances of his election could be precisely ascertained. The University of Paris, however, at once appealed to him on the subject of vacant

[1] Martin, op. cit., II, 188.
[2] Ibid., 204.

benefices. The Parlement reacted vigorously on the king's behalf. The *Avocat-Général* read out the text of the famous ordinances of 1407, alleged that no external power could be allowed to challenge either directly or by implication the temporal decrees of the French sovereign in so far as they concerned the government of his realm, and accused the ring-leaders of the University's appeal of high treason. The court supported him and a number of leading members of the University were arrested and imprisoned.[1] Thus, after some tergiversations in the years immediately following 1407 when the self-interest of the Parlement's clerical members inclined them to ignore the newly restored liberties – in 1409 they appealed to the pope in exactly the same way as the University was to do later – first by its pronouncements in 1413 and 1417 and then by its harsh treatment of the University's representatives in 1418, the court made progressively clearer its support for the doctrine specified in the ordinances of 1407. Any other course of action would have forced it to deny the validity both of an existing law, against which it had raised no objections at the time of registration, and also of its own jurisprudence which, erected upon the appeal *en nouvelleté*, bound the court to respect and maintain the rights and liberties of the French Church.

When the official notification of Martin V's election reached Paris at the end of February 1418, the king requested his Parlement, together with leading prelates and royal counsellors, to advise him as to what policy he should adopt towards the new pontiff. After half a dozen consultations in the *Grand' Chambre*, the court with its supernumerary colleagues, drew up a long document in which the Gallican liberties were restated, and which subsequently formed the basis of the royal ordinance dated March 1418 and registered by the Parlement in the following month.

This Gallican decree ordained that French churches and clerics were to be re-established for ever in their ancient freedom; vacancies in bishoprics, abbeys and other elective benefices, secular and regular, were to be filled by the votes of chapters, convents and colleges, and the successful candidate's election was to be confirmed by his competent superior in France. Non-elective benefices were to be granted to worthy candidates by those entitled by common law or custom to make the presentation, in conformity with the ancient discipline established by the general councils of the Church. Finally, financial exactions derived from papal intervention into beneficial matters in France were to cease entirely, although the king

[1] Du Boulay, op. cit., V, 309 et seq.

intended to render reasonable financial assistance to the Holy See whenever necessary.[1]

Immediately after the publication of this ordinance, the dauphin, on behalf of the kingdom, formally recognized the validity of the new pope's election. The Parlement was well satisfied with the royal enactment, which owed a great deal to its advice and included three of the articles, numbers one, two and four, recommended by the court in its proposals of the preceding November.

At this juncture, however, political events altered the situation. At the end of May 1418, the Burgundians re-entered Paris and a decree of John the Fearless, couched in terms of the utmost respect for the papacy, revoked the recent Gallican ordinance. Despite the changes in personnel introduced by the duke of Burgundy to make it more amenable to the new regime, the Parlement refused to publish and register this document. John himself was suspicious enough of the court's reaction to include in the revocation a clause forbidding the *Procureur-Général* to speak on the subject, and his fears were fully justified, for his ordinance, drawn up in September 1418, remained unpublished in February 1419. In that month representatives from Charles VI and the duke appeared before the court and demanded that it should proceed with the enactment's publication and registration. They received the evasive reply that since the *Procureur-Général* opposed it, the Parlement had to carefully consider his arguments before reaching a decision. Subsequently, the *Procureur-Général* developed his opposition before the duke's emissaries in a plenary session of the court and some outspoken counsellors went so far as to declare that all those who for motives of personal profit sought to injure the common weal, and the Gallican Church, by supporting this revocation against the dictates of the law and of custom, should be banished from the kingdom.

At the height of this impasse the court emphasized its intransigence by objecting to the pope's proposal that his legate in France should be allowed to hold the bishopric of Chartres *in commendam* against the electoral principle. A month passed and on 27 March the king sent further orders to the Parlement, requiring it immediately to publish and register the new revocatory ordinance. Once more the *Procureur-Général* signalled his opposition and once more a majority of the magistrates supported him. Finally, on 31 March 1419, the chancellor and a number of supporters of John the Fearless arrived at the court and succeeded in browbeating the unwilling magistrates into publishing the ordinance. The chief clerk

[1] Martin, op. cit., II, 219–20.

was ordered by the chancellor to inscribe on the back of the document the customary legend, '*lecta, publicata et registrata*'. However, the members of the Parlement, meeting the next day to draw up the official record of what had transpired, made it plain that the decision had been taken *contra deliberationem curiae.*

It is one of the first examples to be found in the court's registers of an enforced registration.[1] Nor did its attitude waver during the years of the English occupation. Indeed, it acted consistently as though the ordinance of 1418 remained in force. An agreement dated August 1418 between Charles VI and the pope over the method of appointing to benefices was only registered after six months of government pressure in July 1422. Two years later, when the duke of Bedford, who was acting as regent for the infant Henry VI, consulted the court on a beneficial issue, his attention was drawn to the existing ordinances concerning the liberties of the Church. In 1425 Bedford produced a second agreement with the papacy, which he presented for the court's opinion. The *Gens du roi* adjudged it prejudicial to the Gallican liberties and protested against the breaking of ordinances made after weighty deliberation by prelates, chapters, universities and clergy in the presence of princes, nobles and counsellors of the king. They suggested that registration should be withheld. Discussions followed between Bedford and representatives of the Parlement, which resulted in the court's decision to publish and register the agreement with certain modifications and without prejudice to preceding ordinances; in that way another enforced registration was avoided. Seven years later, in 1433, the government did have to resort to that means to have registered yet another beneficial arrangement with the Holy See.[2] The Anglo–Burgundian Parlement, therefore, despite considerable political pressures, remained firmly wedded to the principles enunciated in 1407 and 1418. That was not only because its task of law enforcement made it sensitive to the needs of consistent legislation, but also because these particular laws, most solemnly enunciated as the *Procureur-Général* had pointed out, represented a long judicial tradition which could not readily be flouted.

The royal Parlement which Charles VII, exiled from his capital, gathered together at Poitiers, followed precisely the same policy as its Parisian counterpart. Charles VII was not unfavourably disposed towards the Gallican position but he was prepared to negotiate and compromise with the papacy. In 1425 he composed the ordinance of Chinon, which

[1] Ibid., 225–9.
[2] Maugis, op. cit., I, 532–6

restored the pope's authority via the nomination of benefices. This proposition was predictably opposed by the *Procureur-Général*, for the Parlement at Poitiers had continued to observe as law the Gallican ordinance of March 1418: it was neither published nor registered and it remained a dead letter. In the following year, 1426, the king concluded another concordat with Pope Martin V, which again abrogated the conclusions of 1418. This time the Parlement ceded to *lettres de jussion* and registered the royal ordinance which ratified the agreement '*de expresso mandato regis*'. Nevertheless, it remained the opinion of many barristers pleading their clients' suits before the court that this latest royal decision could not replace the ordinance of 1418, an opinion which most of the judges undoubtedly shared.[1]

Martin V died in 1431, shortly after summoning another ecumenical council, which met for the first time at Basle in July that year. It very quickly reached a position of deadlock with Martin's successor, Eugenius IV, who proclaimed its dissolution at the end of the same year. The council fathers refused to accept the papal decision, and a bitter struggle developed between the pope and the council that was to last for almost ten years. A climax was reached early in 1438, when the council declared that it had suspended the pope and had itself taken over the government of the Church. This decision was conveyed to a harassed king of France, who had pursued a temporizing policy towards the papacy during this period of religious dissension. To discuss the implications of this conciliar decree, Charles VII summoned a council to meet at Bourges in June 1438 under his chairmanship. Its members included four archbishops, twenty-five bishops, abbots and priors, and many representatives of the universities and chapters, the dauphin, princes and noblemen and members of the *Grand Conseil* and of both Parlements, for by this time Charles had regained possession of his kingdom. At this assembly the text of various reforms passed by the council at Basle was discussed and certain amendments were made. The king was then asked to convert the corrected text into a law of the kingdom. The result was the celebrated edict of 7 July 1438, the Pragmatic Sanction of Bourges.[2]

The first two articles confirmed the authority of ecumenical councils over the papacy in matters of faith and discipline; both were based upon

[1] Martin, op. cit., II, 255–68.

[2] Ibid., 293 et seq; the text of the Pragmatic Sanction is printed in *Ordonnances des Rois de France*, XIII, 267–91; and N. Valois (*Histoire de la Pragmatique Sanction de Bourges*, 1–260) has printed a valuable selection of documents including many extracts from the Parlement's registers.

decrees published by the councils of Constance and Basle. The third article upheld the decision of the council of Basle that the traditional practice of election to major benefices should be restored, though it added the significant rider that the king, provided that he limited his intervention to '*douces et bienveillantes prières*', was entitled to suggest names of worthy candidates to the electors – the old alliance between the king and his clergy was still deeply felt. In the matter of nominations to minor benefices the rights of those who customarily exercised them were safeguarded and the possibilities of papal intervention were strictly limited. The council of Basle had abolished all papal taxation levied upon the holders of benefices. The prelates at Bourges took a more reasonable view of the pope's needs and recommended that Eugenius should receive a proportion of the revenue from French benefices. However, they affirmed the principle enunciated at Basle and the royal edict made it clear that the revenues granted to Eugenius were in the nature of a gift, to cease at his death and made without prejudice to the liberties of the French Church. The concluding articles related to matters of ecclesiastical discipline, all of them endorsing the decrees of the council of Basle.

This, then, was the Pragmatic Sanction, generally considered to be the quintessential statement of Gallican doctrine. Many of its articles – particularly those relating to benefices and to the papal tax on benefices, the annates – simply restored the situation to that applying before the Great Schism. It is true that it did abolish certain taxes of more ancient origin, too, but in the broad view, even taking into account its support for the authority of a general council over the papacy, the Pragmatic Sanction was not a revolutionary document: it contained much that was accepted in contemporary ecclesiastical thought and much that was traditional in France. Besides, since it was generally admitted that the council of Basle, whose decrees had inspired most of its contents, was truly ecumenical, and that the king, presiding over a council of the French Church, could modify conciliar decrees in the light of his kingdom's traditions, the Pragmatic Sanction seemed to conform to canon law requirements as well as to French custom. Finally, the Pragmatic Sanction was not irremediably hostile to the Holy See and in this it reproduced a long-standing Gallican trait, illustrated for example by the fourth article drawn up by the Parlement in November 1417 and subsequently incorporated into the ordinance of March 1418: Gallican doctrine never embraced the possibility of schism between the French Church and Rome.

The Parlement registered the Pragmatic Sanction in July 1439. To the magistrates it offered ample revenge for the humiliating day twenty years before when they had been forced to revoke the Gallican ordinance of the previous year. Like that ordinance, the Pragmatic Sanction reiterated principles that were embodied in the court's jurisprudence and were in perfect conformity with the customs of the kingdom. Like that ordinance, too, and unlike its revocation and subsequent royal arrangements with the papacy, it had been composed after solemn deliberation with royal advisers, princes, nobles, prelates and lawyers, and finally published and registered without duress by the Parlement. Indubitably, the magistrates accepted it as a law to be observed, in the king's own phrase, 'inviolably and for ever'. However, the king was not as steadfast as his court and for the rest of his reign he was embroiled with successive popes in fruitless negotiations.[1]

Relations between Paris and Rome improved, however, with the accession of Louis XI in 1461, who promptly abolished the Pragmatic Sanction. His motives were partly personal – a deep animosity towards his father inclined him to reject the policies that he had inherited – and partly political, for he sensed that his own authority over the French Church would be greater if he accepted the sovereignty of Rome and then used it to control appointments than if he allowed the traditional regime to continue. The Parlement opposed the king's policy in remonstrances presented in 1465. They contained eighty-nine articles, the first seventeen offering a résumé of the quarrel between France and Rome from 1407 to 1439, the seventeenth alleging that the Pragmatic Sanction, in the twenty-three years that it had been applied, had brought prosperity to the king and his kingdom and lustre to the French Church, and the remaining articles prognosticating the evils that would follow its abrogation. In particular, the court defended the Gallican principles of free election to benefices and the non-payment of annates.[2]

However, Louis was unwilling to listen to the Parlement, and with the accession to the papal throne of Sixtus IV in 1471 the *détente* with Rome was carried further. In August 1472 a papal bull promulgated a new concordat with the French kingdom, whereby the Pragmatic Sanction was to be abandoned. The pope was to make appointments to minor benefices becoming vacant during the months of January, March, May, July, September and November, while the customary benefactor was to

[1] Details of these relations may be found in sections of vols III to V of the extremely detailed work of G. du Fresne de Beaucourt, *Histoire de Charles VII.*

[2] Maugis, op. cit., I, 707–8.

exercise his right in the alternative six months. Appointments to major benefices were also to be by the pope, but on the recommendation of the king, and the pope's financial privileges were to be restored. The Parlement was not shown the text of the concordat until 1475, at which time the king was again bitterly hostile to the pope. Then it was fleetingly invited to make whatever modifications to the agreement it deemed necessary. This was Louis's method of putting pressure on Sixtus IV, by raising the spectre of the Pragmatic Sanction once more, for he knew perfectly well, as did the pope, that the Parlement did not consider the concordat to be a valid substitute.

Louis XI had given the court few opportunities before 1475 to express its opposition to the concordat, though one or two judicial decisions had made its position clear. In May 1474, for example, the bishopric of Mende had become vacant, and according to the traditional rules of the Church a successor, one Jean Petitote, was elected by the monks of the cathedral chapter, and his name was then submitted for approval to the immediate superior, who in this case was the archbishop of Bourges, again in keeping with the procedure confirmed by the Pragmatic Sanction. The archbishop, however, refused to give his approval and the case was brought before the Parlement on the grounds of the monks' appeal *en nouvelleté*. The archbishop asserted before the magistrates that the king required absolute obedience to the Apostolic See. He recalled his own earlier experience when an abbatial benefice in his archdiocese had become vacant and his vicar-general in his absence had confirmed the candidate elected by the monks. In consequence the archbishop had been summoned to Rome and there made to promise that in future he would refer all such matters to the Holy See. The monks, for their part, maintained that the king had gone further in bolstering the authority of the pope in beneficial matters than the law allowed. If indeed the law had been abrogated, the revocation had not been published and registered and therefore, the plaintiffs argued, the Parlement must surely judge as it had always done, according to the traditional rules. The *Procureur-Général* and the court upheld the monks' plea, condemned the archbishop's attitude as 'very scandalous' and alleged divine, canon and civil law in support of the electoral principle. However, such openings came rarely. The Parlement's apparent opportunity in 1475 disappeared almost at once, and in the late 1470s Louis was dictating the court's decrees for it, restoring the rights of clerics appointed by the pope or nominated by the king.[1]

[1] P. Ourliac, 'Le Concordat de 1472', XX, 203.

When Louis XI died in 1483, there was a violent reaction in favour of Gallicanism, proclaimed by the Estates-General meeting in the following year and actively pursued on the judicial level by the Parlement. In December 1483, in the first relevant case pleaded before the court in the new reign of Charles VIII, the king called upon the archbishop of Bourges to confirm an election made in his archdiocese, an intervention interpreted by the Parlement as a repudiation of his predecessor's concordat; henceforth it enthusiastically challenged all papal provisions.[1] Although Charles VIII's government and subsequently that of Louis XII reverted to a policy of co-operation with the papacy and of implicit rejection of the Pragmatic Sanction, the magistrates continued to observe it as a legitimate guide in reaching judicial decisions in those cases involving relations between the French Church and the Holy See.

It is especially in regard to the issue of Gallicanism that the changing relationship between the king and his court may be observed. At the close of the fifteenth century, nobody denied, least of all the members of the Parlement, that the king was the sole source of law in the state, but equally it had never been considered that the exercise of that sovereignty should be totally uncontrolled. The necessity for the monarch to act in accordance with what was customary, through channels that were legal and after due consideration of the opinions of his counsellors, was as deeply felt in the fifteenth century as in any that preceded it. The great French divine, Gerson (1363–1429), chancellor of the University of Paris and the country's leading representative at the council of Constance, distinguished in a number of treatises between the tyrannical state, which tended to the destruction of all political life, and the monarchical state, submitted to legal restraint, wherein, as he put it, even the king cannot slay any man except by process of law.

Almost a hundred years later, in 1519, Claude de Seyssel, the Savoyard archbishop of Turin, wrote *La Grande Monarchie de France*, which, although published shortly after the accession of Francis I, reflected opinions matured during seventeen years in the service of Louis XII. Even more than Gerson, Seyssel was actively engaged in political affairs and his comments upon the institution of the monarchy, therefore, were as much practical observations as theories. He observed three limitations in France upon the exercise of royal power: religion, which was fundamental to the whole concept of kingship and which imposed a set of values and a standard of conduct which could be universally recognized,

[1] Ibid., XXI, 136–8.

justice, which ensured that the king obeyed the same laws as his subjects, and lastly, 'police', by which he meant the law and customs of the kingdom made sacred by their enduring observance, the rights of the various estates and the opinions of royal advisers, princes, prelates and magistrates, representing 'the political intelligence of the community'. His view, in other words, was of a monarchy limited by custom and by the law.[1]

Although both Gerson and Seyssel were closely concerned with affairs of state, it may perhaps be argued that what they wrote was essentially political theory, which dwelt rather on principles that ought to be followed than upon politics as they were practised. In fact, however, these opinions did represent a standard of political behaviour which had been accepted for a good many generations by French kings and their advisers. Although it was to be expected that the king, whose theoretical authority was so considerable, would not always resist the temptation to exercise it without respect for traditional limitations, such occasions would be difficult to come upon before the advent of the fifteenth century. If he were consistently to ignore the customary procedures, however, such conduct would be likely to cause friction in government circles and could produce modifications in constitutional practice as a compensation for royal arbitrariness. For that reason the relations between the king and his court in the matter of the Gallican liberties deserve close examination.

The first royal statement of Gallican doctrine was contained in the ordinances of 1407, which confirmed the conclusions reached by an assembly of the French clergy held in the previous year and were themselves published and registered by the Parlement. Their contents were in line with the French Church's tradition of independence from Rome and of close alliance with the monarchy and with the jurisprudence of the Parlement, the chief repository of French law, written and unwritten. These enactments of Charles VI, therefore, bore all the signs of royal legislative authority legitimately exercised. Exactly the same could be said of the ordinance of March 1418, which was drawn up on the advice of an assembly of prelates, members of the *Grand Conseil*, of the Parlement and of the University of Paris, who met over a period of sixteen days to compose their recommendations to the king, and was subsequently registered by the Parlement.

A different matter was Charles VI's revocation of this ordinance, made under pressure from John of Burgundy. Although the duke was careful

[1] Carlyle, op. cit., VI, 140, 219–25; *infra*, 190.

to pay lip-service to the principle of prior consultation, his advisers were politically biased and certainly could not be said to represent a genuine consensus of opinion on the question of the legality of the Gallican liberties. For that reason, and because it contradicted earlier royal legislation enacted in a more proper manner, the Parlement refused to register the revocation though it was eventually forced to do so in the following year.

The contrast between the two forms of registration added to the dubiously valid appearance of the revocatory ordinance. In the years that followed both the English duke of Bedford and the exiled French king, Charles VII, made fresh agreements with the papacy which contradicted the Gallican position established in 1407 and 1418. In every case the Parlement raised objections and either succeeded in modifying the government's proposals, as in Paris in 1425, or only gave way unwillingly before royal *lettres de jussion*. These agreements, which the court opposed, were all *ad hoc* arrangements enforced by the unrestrained authority of the sovereign. The formulation of the Pragmatic Sanction again offers a marked contrast with these preceding agreements. It was composed in an assembly of dignitaries, secular and clerical, which truly represented the whole state; it was published with due ceremony and without recourse to any kind of political pressure; its articles were for the most part strongly rooted in legal tradition. In other words, it offered an example of how royal legislative authority ought to be exercised.

In the reign of Louis XI, however, a more authoritarian attitude was introduced into the king's relationship with the law. Within months of his accession, he abrogated the Pragmatic Sanction not by a formal law but by means of simple letters emanating from his inner council, which were never submitted to the Parlement for registration. Similarly, the magistrates were not allowed to see the concordat concluded in 1472 until three years later and then only to strengthen the king's hand against the pope, and although the royal letters ordering the reception of the concordat mentioned instructions sent to the Parlement to ensure its co-operation, the letters were not themselves published or registered by the court and like those of 1461 they were arbitrarily imposed without previous discussion.

Louis's attitude to Rome and the French Church not only contradicted an earlier legal tradition, it even lacked a consistency of its own. In May 1463 he issued a declaration reaffirming the Parlement's right to concern itself with ecclesiastical cases arising out of appeals *en nouvelleté* or the king's right *en régale* to administer vacant benefices, and in February 1464 he produced an edict denying the pope's right to exact revenues from French benefices; both enactments were registered by the Parlement. Despite the abrogation of 1461 these documents between them in effect restored the Pragmatic Sanction by allowing the court to defend the possession of traditional beneficial rights. But in 1467 he revoked this legislation and once more rejected the provisions of the Pragmatic Sanction. The *Procureur-Général* protested and was promptly dismissed; the Parlement did not register the revocation. After the signing of the concordat, new dissensions arose between king and pope, and in 1476 Louis took action against certain papal bulls which, he alleged, threatened the privileges, immunities and liberties of the Gallican Church.[1] At the time of Louis's death, therefore, the legal position of the Pragmatic Sanction remained disputable and that state of affairs continued during the reigns of his two successors, Charles VIII and Louis XII.

The reason for the uncertainty was quite apparent. Ever since the problem of the Gallican liberties had come to the fore in the reign of Charles VI, royal legislation on the subject had been of two distinct kinds, that supported by broadly-based opinion and by the formality and publicity provided by its registration in the Parlement, and that which depended solely upon the royal will for its efficacy. In addition, the first kind enunciated principles which fitted readily into traditional French law and jurisprudence, while the second proclaimed a policy which, though not without precedents, required at least the same trappings of legality as the other to carry any conviction at all. Because existing law and custom, legal procedure and the taking of counsel still retained their traditional importance in fifteenth-century France, the first kind had a greater aura of legality than the second. Certainly, the members of the Parlement, whose task it was to proclaim and enforce the law, thought so and they stubbornly maintained their support for the principles contained in the Pragmatic Sanction. The position of the Parlement *vis-à-vis* the monarchy changed in consequence.

By the reign of Charles VI it had been established that the Parlement had a political part to play on occasions when the state faced a crisis; at such times it might represent the only source of law and therefore of political stability in the country. Besides, the magistrates remained royal counsellors with an obligation to render advice. Consequently, the system of remonstrance had developed, enabling the magistrates to acquire a more

[1] C. Petit-Dutaillis, *Charles VII, Louis XI et les premières années de Charles VIII*, 413–17.

formal and regular political role. Remonstrances were closely related to the practice of publishing and registering royal legislation and it was this practice which was central to the changing situation. The right of remonstrance itself implied that registration was not a simple formality; rather was it a legal seal of approval, indicating that the law concerned did not offend any of the accepted canons. Laws that were only registered by the Parlement under constraint, therefore, and more especially those that were never submitted to it at all, bore a certain stigma: their validity was not altogether beyond doubt. This fact was closely bound up with the practical implications of publication and registration. Without this procedure how was the Parlement to be sure what the law was that it had to enforce; how was that law to be publicized so that everybody else knew it and recognized it as authentic?

All official copies of ordinances were customarily made under the signature of the chief clerk of the Parlement, with the formula, '*extractum a registris curiae*', their sole guarantee of authenticity. It was with the same guarantee and under the authority of the *Procureur-Général* that they were distributed throughout the court's area of jurisdiction and accepted by the provincial Parlements as the genuine version of a new law.[1] Thus the Parlement was in the best position to attempt to counter royal absolutism. Gerson recognized its importance in that capacity early in the fifteenth century, when he maintained that laws had no force until they were promulgated and unless they conformed with the customs of the country. More specifically, he praised French kings who, although having created the Parlement, did not hesitate to submit to its judgments. Very similar views were expressed by Seyssel a hundred years later, when he maintained that because of the existence of the Parlement, established chiefly to restrain the king's absolute power, there was a greater sense of justice in French government than elsewhere; the monarch as well as his subjects was expected to respect its judgments.[2] It was to be supposed that such views would strike echoes in the court itself: in 1499, the *Avocat-Général* described the Parlement to Louis XII as 'the true senate of the kingdom, where edicts and ordinances of kings take their final form and authority when they are published and registered'.[3]

The members of the Parlement had no intention, of course, of disputing the king's sovereign legislative authority; their views were intended not to

[1] Maugis, op. cit., I, 537–45.
[2] Carlyle, op. cit., VI, 140, 221.
[3] Maugis, op. cit., I, 542–3.

bind the ruler but to enlighten him, to strengthen his authority not to weaken it. The king's role in the constitution was primarily a judicial one and arbitrary conduct on his part could only lessen his authority. It was the Parlement's duty to defend him against that danger by judging each ruler's legislation in the light of the traditional and permanent principles of the monarchy and of its own legal experience. Nevertheless, in the course of the fifteenth century it was possible to detect an increasing rivalry between the king and his court. The more arbitrary the king's legislation became, the more the Parlement cast doubts upon its validity by refusing registration. Louis XI, in particular, was determined to bridle his court and during his reign and that of his successor, Charles VIII, a great many matters were evoked from the Parlement to the King's Council, including those relating to benefices and to the royal domain.[1]

The king's increasing emphasis upon his own unlimited authority caused the court, in defence of the traditional concept of monarchy, to stress its own role in law-making. Relations between king and Parlement were in this ambiguous state in 1515, when Francis I became king, and the equally equivocal position of the Gallican liberties offered the possibility of further conflict.

[1] Petit-Dutaillis, op. cit., 404.

CHAPTER SIX

The Parlement in the Sixteenth Century

Royal sovereignty and its limitations; Francis I and the concordat of 1516; the Parlement's attitude to the Reformation; its relations with the last Valois kings

---

The reign of Francis I has often been interpreted as marking a decisive period in the development of absolute monarchy in France. The king himself has been portrayed as an innovator, hostile to those traditions and influences which served to limit the authority of his predecessors, the chief instigator of a line of absolute rulers who considered their power to be unbridled and the state to be at their personal disposal.[1] Such a view may be challenged, not only on the evidence of Francis's reign, but also on the grounds that absolute monarchy in this sense had little meaning in France at any time before 1789. Support for that argument must be reserved for later chapters, but it is apposite to examine at once whether the developments of the king's reign support a view of French monarchy different from the traditional one.

It would be absurd to maintain that all French rulers possessed identical powers: their authority waxed and waned according to the circumstances of the time and their personal qualities. Francis I indubitably wielded more power than most of his Capetian and Valois ancestors. The prestige and influence of the crown had grown enormously in the last years of the fifteenth century with the increasing homogeneity of the state. Yet, there are good grounds for arguing that his authority and that of his predecessors fitted into a unique context, that, despite changing conditions, the concept of monarchy, unlike the actual power exercised by individual

[1] *See*, for example, F. von Meinecke, *Machiavellianism*, 382; R. Doucet, *Etude sur le Gouvernement de François Ier*, I, 47; G. Pagès, *La Monarchie d'Ancien Régime*, 3; but cf. J. Russell Major, *Representative Institutions*, 3–13, 126–7.

monarchs, remained unaltered until the eighteenth century. Of course, a distinction needs to be drawn between changes in social status, whose ease of accomplishment a study of *parlementaire* origins alone demonstrates clearly enough,[1] and the overriding permanence of the monarchical principle, which gave point to a hierarchical society and identity to the state. Although there was a good deal of movement between social classes, the social structure itself remained rigid under the crown. That fact does not itself prove that the nature of the king's role remained unchanged, though it does suggest a basic continuity. The question of whether or not during the reign of Francis I traditional values ceased to influence royal policy must now be examined.

What those values were has already been intimated in earlier chapters: respect for the law, both statutory and customary, human and divine, for the established processes by which legislation was arrived at, for the advice of counsellors, for the privileges and immunities of the various individuals and groups who were the king's subjects. These were the limitations upon his supreme power of dispensing justice and of making laws, limitations which could be summed up simply as respect for legality, the most desirable virtue in a supreme legislator. However, precisely because these values were traditional, because they had grown out of custom, the limits of the sovereign's freedom of action and of his subjects' right to oppose were never defined, and, according to the vagaries of particular political situations, kings tended to emphasize or play down their sovereign authority, giving more or less weight to restraining influences, but never altogether denying their validity.

Under Francis I, royal authority was in the ascendant. The prestige of the monarchy had soared during the preceding century when the French king had led the country to victory over the English invaders and loosened their long-held domination over a large part of France. The wars had had the effect of increasing the loyalty of the aristocracy and also of considerably reducing their numbers. In addition, in 1482 France acquired most of the extensive lands which had previously formed the duchy of Burgundy, while the marriage between Charles VIII and Anne of Brittany disposed of another danger to French security. By 1515 the country over which Francis came to rule was less liable to disintegration than ever before, a fact that greatly strengthened the king's authority and encouraged him along the path of further centralization and control.

[1] *See supra*, 111.

The powers of the *Estates-General* were already on the wane. Until the late fifteenth century their authority had been considerable and included the right to authorize taxation, to nominate members of the King's Council, and, if the king were a minor, to nominate the regent. After 1484, however, the Estates were rarely summoned, the king named his own counsellors and taxed the people without their consent, by means of a new annual direct levy, the *taille*. He reorganized the central administration of government, making it more efficient in order to profit from the increased authority which had accrued to the monarch.[1] In this context, not surprisingly, the king and a number of political writers, too, placed the emphasis increasingly upon royal authority rather than upon its limitations.[2] The Parlement, however, by reason of its institutional base and its traditional role, remained an effective barrier to royal authoritarianism. Henceforward, it would tend to appear less frequently as the king's ally and more often as his critic.

Not all commentators of the period played down the need for restraint in favour of the glorification of the royal will: it has already been observed that the most celebrated of them, Claude de Seyssel, was chiefly concerned with the limits of royal authority. In his view, the king ought to govern in close co-operation with his counsellors and their chief concern should be the preservation of the state according to the tenets of established law. The king's rights, like those of everybody else, were based in and limited by the law, and therefore, the Parlement judged not only between subjects but between the king and his subjects as well. Seyssel's theory was dominated by a concept of corporate unity; every group occupied certain rights and privileges which the king was obliged to preserve, all united by bonds of law and mutual obligation and respect.[3] His thinking was in line with traditional views of the French state, and it is generally agreed that it also corresponded with the opinions of most articulate Frenchmen in the early sixteenth century.

Even those theorists who gave great weight to the king's absolute power did not abandon certain reservations, which prevented their ideas from marking a basic departure from earlier thinking. With these reservations,

[1] N. M. Sutherland, *French Secretaries of State*, 11–17; R. Doucet, 'France under Charles VIII and Louis XII', 298–301; much greater detail is provided in the latter's standard work, *Les Institutions de la France au XVI^{e}siècle.*

[2] The best analysis of the works of these theorists is to be found in W. F. Church, *Constitutional Thought in Sixteenth-Century France*, 43–73.

[3] The most recent edition of this very important work is the one edited by J. Poujal under its original title of *La Monarchie de France*, 117–18, 133.

the absence of clearly defined constitutional limits left ample scope for such a shift in emphasis within the traditional context. Writers like Grassaille and Chasseneuz, who exalted the sovereign's independence and freedom of action even above the law, were unanimous in asserting that the king ought to consult his advisers, especially when making laws, that he was at all times subject to natural and divine law, to the general dictates of reason and to two fundamental laws, those governing the succession to the throne and the inalienability of the domain. They believed that laws should only be rescinded or amended in wholly exceptional circumstances since otherwise the stability of the state would be threatened. In other words, though they stressed the power of the sovereign, they remained opposed to arbitrary action.

This apparently paradoxical standpoint was entirely at one with earlier constitutional theory, which recognized that the two components, royal sovereignty and its limitations, existed together. The emphasis might change and had changed frequently in political practice – over the royal attitude to the Pragmatic Sanction, for example – but the essential, if undefined bond between the two aspects remained unaltered. The ideas of these absolutists were rooted in the religious aspect of the French monarchy, which was inherent in the whole of Gallican doctrine and was symbolized by the coronation ceremony and by the miraculous power of healing, which Francis I acknowledged no less than his predecessors. This quasi-spiritual role, so it was argued, made the sovereign directly responsible to God and freed him from any terrestrial restraint.[1] At the same time, that very responsibility imposed upon the ruler the obligation of behaving in accordance with Christian principles, at once restoring the idea of limitation and restraint. Even the most venturesome political theorists of the early sixteenth century, therefore, did not chart new worlds for princes to govern, and indeed, in the years that followed, Seyssel's traditional picture remained the generally accepted one. So much for the political theorists; it remains to be seen how Francis I behaved in practice.

From the Parlement's point of view, the reign opened inauspiciously. Since Charles VIII's time, the custom had been established of the king coming to the Palais at the opening of his reign, and in a solemn plenary session exhorting the magistrates scrupulously to interpret to him the wishes of his subjects. In 1515, the new king did not himself visit the Palais, but sent his chancellor, Duprat, himself a former First President,

[1] Church, op. cit., 45–6.

with a message for the court.[1] Duprat delivered it on 4 March. It was in effect an apologia for the prince and his proposed government, with scarcely a reference to the enlightenment to be gained from consultation with his Parlement. His promise to provide wise laws and wise ministers to apply them was couched in vague and general terms. In his reply, the First President, Mondot de la Marthonie, asked that the king should listen to any remonstrances made by the court and he denounced the practice of evoking matters cognizable before the Parlement to another court. Duprat's retort was brief and haughty: the king did not intend his authority to be restricted, though he would permit the Parlement to warn him if it felt it necessary to do so.[2]

In fact, from the first days of his reign Francis did resort to evocation, following the precedent set chiefly by Louis XI and Charles VIII, whenever the Parlement threatened to thwart him. Its hostility was provoked by the need to preserve the sovereign's authority on an entirely legal basis, while the latter's arbitrary reaction only weakened his own position by casting doubts upon the legality of decisions taken without the customary procedural forms in opposition to generally accepted canons. A reference to one such example occurs in the Parlement's registers only eight days after Duprat's visit to the Palais. Francis had chosen to give away part of his royal lands to the duke of Alençon. The Parlement protested that the royal domain was inalienable, an assertion that Francis did not deny, alleging instead that, since these particular counties had come to the crown as a result of the confiscation in 1461 of the Armagnac lands, they did not properly constitute part of the royal domain and could, therefore, be disposed of at the king's discretion. The magistrates were unimpressed by this legal quibble and refused to register the relevant letters-patent. In June 1515 the affair was evoked from the court, and in March 1516 the letters were registered in the *Grand Conseil.* The position adopted by the Parlement had been wholly in accordance with legal custom. Nor was the court's protest concerned only with legal theory; the king's action was clearly prejudicial to the royal finances.[3]

However, the first major clash between Francis and his Parlement concerned not the alienation of royal land, but the thorny problem of Gallicanism which had been looming for a long time as the most likely

[1] Duprat played an important part in the early years of Francis I's reign; the best account of his career, though not an especially valuable one in terms of the crown's relations with the Parlement, is that of A. Buisson, *Le Chancelier Antoine Duprat.*

[2] Maugis, op. cit., I, 548–9.

[3] Doucet, *Etude sur le Gouvernement de François Ier*, I, 60–1.

source of serious friction. The concordat concluded at Bologna in 1516 between the French king and the pope, Leo X, was inserted in the papal bull *Primitiva illa ecclesia* in August of that year, the pope stipulating that it had to be approved first by the Lateran Council then in session and in the following six months it had to be accepted by the French Church and registered by the Parlements. By December 1516 the approval of the Lateran Council had been obtained, and in the same month another bull, *Pastor Aeternus* revoked the Pragmatic Sanction. Francis was faced with the extremely difficult task not only of persuading the court to accept the pope's denunciation of the Pragmatic Sanction and to register the new arrangement, but also of enrolling the support of the French clergy, all within the space of six months. He took informal soundings from a number of counsellors, but they proved inconclusive, and on 5 February 1517 the king himself, accompanied by Duprat and by a number of leading clerical dignitaries and representatives of the university of Paris, came to the court to take up the matter officially. His mood was angry, for the magistrates had just recently held up a decree on the subject of the royal forests, and he began by warning them that it would be as well for them if they showed a greater willingness and alacrity in registering royal orders. His temper was not improved by the speech of the leading cleric present, Cardinal de Boisy, who insisted that it would be necessary to summon a general assembly of the French clergy to ratify the concordat.

The magistrates, for their part, proffered an evasive response, expressing their devotion to the king, but committing themselves to nothing.[1] Their worst fears about the concordat had in fact been confirmed: the two central pillars of the Pragmatic Sanction were to be destroyed, the electoral system for bishops, abbots and priors was to be replaced by a system of royal nomination, and nominees to minor benefices were to indicate to the pope the beneficial revenues that they were already receiving – a stipulation that would hinder pluralism but which also seemed likely to open the way to the restoration of the payments of annates. Although supporters of the concordat argued that this was not the case, the magistrates' suspicions were correct though the papal bull of October 1516, quite clearly saying so, was only published in France in April 1518, after the Parlement had registered the concordat.

A fortnight after the king's visit to the court, Francis deputed Duprat to address the magistrates again on the advantages of the new arrangement with the pope. In mid-May letters-patent ordering the concordat's

[1] Ibid., 84–7.

execution were drawn up, and at the end of the month Duprat made a second and final appeal for the court's support. At last, on 8 June the concordat itself was sent to the Parlement. Upon the advice of the *Gens du roi*, the Parlement decided to appoint a number of commissioners to examine the matter in more detail. This decision meant a delay, and Francis wrote to the court on 21 June to demand immediate registration and followed this by sending his uncle, René of Savoy, to assist at the court's deliberations and to report back on what transpired there. This blatant attempt to intimidate the magistrates angered them, for traditionally the sovereign was expected to respect their independence – was not Seyssel shortly to point out that the Parlement impartially judged even those cases to which the king was a party – and when he refused to countenance their opinions, he at least overcame them with some regard for legal form, by *lettres de jussion* or a *lit de justice*. Consequently, Savoy, who had not been sworn in as a member of the court and had no right to be present at deliberations which were always held in secret, was asked to leave. He agreed to do so. Meanwhile, the magistrates complained to Francis that in seeking to weaken the court's independence he would also risk lessening respect for the monarchy. The king's reply was undisguisedly menacing: if he did not secure obedience, recalcitrant magistrates would have to be replaced. The Parlement decided to yield before the anger and intractability of the king, and it resumed its discussions on the concordat on 13 July in the presence of Savoy.

These deliberations reached their climax in a series of sessions beginning on 24 July, when the court finally decided to refuse publication and registration of the concordat and to reassert the validity of the Pragmatic Sanction. The concordat they condemned comprehensively, as being against the honour of God, the liberties of the Church, the honour of the king and the well-being of his kingdom. In addition, they stated that if the king remained intransigent it would be necessary to summon a council of the French Church, as had happened in the preceding century, for the elaboration of the Pragmatic Sanction, a formality stipulated indeed in the text of the concordat itself.[1]

In view of the king's attitude, which had been extremely threatening ever since the new agreement had been mooted in the court, the magistrates' verdict was a brave gesture of independence. Their arguments, based on their own judicial practice, were traditional ones, supported by ecumenical canons and royal decrees, asserting the French Church's

[1] Ibid., 87–105.

independence from the papacy. They closely resembled the *parlementaire* remonstrances made to Louis XI in 1465 after the first abrogation of the Pragmatic Sanction.[1] The magistrates added a final insult to injury by admonishing the king for his habit of conferring benefices upon his courtiers. The king commissioned Duprat to compose a refutation of the Parlement's objections to the concordat, in which the chancellor denied both the existence of the Gallican liberties and the superiority of a general council over the pope, thereby, in the opinion of a distinguished historian of this controversy, posing a new religious policy, which was contrary to all the traditions of the French clergy and to the Gallican ideals which both Parlement and the monarchy had up to this time accepted.[2]

The new alternative was the submission of the French Church to the twin authority of king and pope. Francis was seeking to capitalize upon the more powerful position in which the monarch found himself, while the Parlement was attempting to defend, as it had always done, those liberties rooted in its own jurisprudence, which limited the king's absolute freedom of action. The situation simply was this: that both the king's policy and his method of procedure were arbitrary, and the Parlement was bound to oppose him on both counts.

The king himself only consented to see the court's delegation on 28 January 1518, and his remarks were predictably outspoken. There was only one king in France, he told them, not a senate as in Venice, and if the magistrates continued to raise difficulties he would make life uncomfortable for them by forcing them to '*trotter après lui*', as peripatetic counsellors.[3] He admonished them to concern themselves solely with the administration of justice. By implying that the Parlement was only a court of law, an implication demonstrably disproved by its past record, Francis was again asserting an extreme view of his own authority, and the Parlement was therefore less disposed than ever to register the concordat. Then, on 6 March, the king sent his First Chamberlain to the court with orders to procure immediate registration; if not, rigorous measures would be taken against the magistrates and rumours emanating from the royal circle suggested that Francis was contemplating the establishment of a new Parlement at Orléans to replace that of Paris. Under this duress, the Parlement was forced to make a decision, and on 16 March, the assembled chambers listened to an address by the *Avocat-Général*,

[1] *See supra*, 180.
[2] Doucet, *Etude sur le Gouvernement de François Ier*, I, 113.
[3] Ibid., 116.

Le Lièvre, who persuaded them that it was possible to proceed with registration without sacrificing their cherished principles. The concordat, so Le Lièvre argued, was a contract between the king and the pope, concluded without the concurrence of the Gallican Church, and therefore incapable of being interpreted as a means of modifying or abrogating its rights. It could not, therefore, be a definite arrangement: in fact, there was already a precedent in Louis XI's suspension and reimposition of the Pragmatic Sanction. Consequently, the opinion of the *Gens du roi* was that the concordat should be registered upon two conditions: that the formula of registration should contain the expression, *de expresso mandato regis iteratis vicibus facto*, and that the publication of the concordat should not entail the abrogation of the Pragmatic Sanction. In its *arrêt* of 18 March, incorporating the conclusions of the *Avocat-Général*, the court was even more specific, stipulating that beneficial cases would continue to be judged according to existing jurisprudence. The concordat was finally published and registered on 22 March. On the same day, the court drew up a protest which it inserted in a secret register, in which it reiterated that registration of the concordat was not the will of the court but of the king, and that the court intended to continue to pronounce its judgments according to the dictates of the Pragmatic Sanction.

This equivocal procedure did not, of course, solve the problem. It has been described as a capitulation on the magistrates' part, the sacrifice of political principles and of the Gallican liberties to the sovereign's whim.[1] However, it is difficult to envisage what else they could have done: they had no further sanctions with which to hinder the king's authoritarianism, if he was determined to act against tradition. On the other hand, their submission was clearly equivocal. They intended to respect their own legal precedents and to view the concordat as a purely temporary expedient. The form of registration itself was intended to cast doubts upon the document's authenticity. In the words of one commentator, they could scarcely have submitted with a greater show of independence.[2] Though their solution was legalistic and ambiguous, though it caused confusion rather than enlightenment, it is significant that Francis accepted it as sufficient. Although the magistrates were unable to resist the pressure of the king's command, neither was he able to dispense with his Parlement's

[1] Ibid., 118–24; the text of the concordat is printed in *Ordonnances des Rois de France. Règne de François Ier*, I, 434–65. There is an interesting evaluation of the historical significance of the concordat by R. J. Knecht, 'The Concordat of 1516: a reassessment', *University of Birmingham. Historical Journal*, IX, 16–32.

[2] Maugis, op. cit., I, 552.

registration, however equivocal it might be. The whole episode, therefore, strengthened the court's political role and deepened the impression created in the previous century that royal legislation enforced against *parlementaire* advice or without recourse to customary processes was of doubtful validity.

After the quarrel over the concordat, Francis continued to treat his court arbitrarily, and remonstrances, *lits de justice* and enforced registrations were day-to-day occurrences. Although the Parlement was always forced to cede in the end, it reserved its position over the concordat as over other controversial matters in a number of ways, for example, by incorporating into the formula of registration the precise articles or the general tenor of remonstrances previously made in vain, or references to the enforced nature of the registration, all of which became part of the edict's text, and gave an appearance of precarious authenticity. In May 1523, when the magistrates were finally constrained to register an edict creating the office of bailiff to safeguard the privileges of the university of Paris, their formula was as follows: '*lecta, publicata et registrata ad onus et absque prejudicio oppositionum de expresso mandato domini nostri regis, pluribus et reiteratis vicibus, tam per litteras missivas quam per nuncios facto*'.[1] However, the situation altered dramatically in 1525 after the disastrous defeat of Pavia, when Francis I became a captive of the emperor, Charles V, and France was temporarily deprived of a monarch.

In his stead, the king's mother, Louise of Savoy, became regent. At once, she wrote to the members of the Parlement, asking them to take all necessary measures to ensure the security and well-being of the kingdom. The chief threat was to the northern frontier, now exposed as a result of the Italian disaster, and then to Paris itself. The magistrates responded loyally and with alacrity. They decided to convene a general meeting of delegates from the Parlement, from among the Parisian clergy, the other sovereign courts, the aldermen of the city and other leading citizens, with the aim of setting up a committee of defence. The First President summoned the leading preachers in the capital and ordered them to do what they could in their sermons to instil confidence into their congregations and respect for law and order. Finally, the military commanders in the threatened area, the Duc de Vendôme and the Comte de Guise, were asked to report daily to the Parlement upon the situation. Shortly afterwards, Vendôme himself made an appeal before the Parlement that in the existing critical situation its advice should be regularly sought.

[1] Ibid., 554.

Meanwhile, the Parlement did its utmost to enlist men and arms for the defence of Paris, to curb the marauding bands of soldiery – remnants of the defeated French army – which had begun to infest the capital and threaten the morale of the citizens and to see that the soldiers were promptly paid. In Picardy, in particular, more money was required to pay the troops and the Parlement took measures of its own, which, strictly speaking, were usurpations of the king's authority, disposing of royal revenues, issuing orders to the king's financial officials and to the *Chambre des Comptes*. In Picardy too, it made itself responsible for recommending the appointment of a new military commander. In a word, the Parlement was organizing and co-ordinating the country's defences, at the same time representing the sole source of law and order in the kingdom. The political authority which Francis had sought to deny it had been regained with a vengeance.[1]

In the first weeks of the crisis the court had shown itself completely loyal to the king, though it certainly hoped to use its unexpectedly authoritative position to reverse some of his earlier actions. In this it received the regent's support in so far as she indicated that the magistrates' advice on political matters would be acceptable. On 13 April, on the Parlement's behalf, the First President presented a long list of remonstrances to Louise of Savoy at Lyons. They included a request for the restoration of the Pragmatic Sanction, now with the additional argument that experience of the working of the concordat confirmed the magistrates' prognostications that it would lead to financial extortion by the papacy and the nomination of unworthy prelates by the king. They contained, too, pleas for judicial independence, on the grounds that justice being the source of the sovereign's own authority he should not jeopardize it by tampering with established judicial practices, for the diminution both of evocations and of the alienation of royal land. The whole emphasis of the document was upon the need to restore the traditional equilibrium by eliminating the excesses, which Francis had practised in the early years of his reign. To secure the sort of reforms that they sought, to increase their influence near the throne and to gain revenge upon their old adversary, Duprat, the magistrates added a final section requesting the regent to delegate to her council a number of members of the Parlement who could share with the chancellor the burden of proffering advice.

The regent's reply was read out to the assembled chambers on 2 May; in most respects it proved to be a conciliatory document. She refused to abolish the concordat in the king's absence but promised that upon his

[1] Doucet, *Etude sur le Gouvernement de François Ier*, II, 15 et seq.

return she would do all in her power to persuade him to restore the Church's ancient liberties. In the matter of evocations, she announced that the chancellor had already been instructed not to continue the practice and similar promising assurances were given on almost every other article.[1] However, this apparently amicable relationship quickly dissolved into bitterness when a real issue arose between the two sides.

The quarrel began with the chancellor's nomination to two beneficial offices, those of archbishop of Sens and abbot of Saint-Benoît-sur-Loire. At both places the majority of the monks, invoking certain reservations contained in the concordat itself, had proceeded by way of election, a procedure supported by the Parlement. The matter had been evoked from the court's jurisdiction some three months before its remonstrances were presented to the regent. The latter's conciliatory response encouraged the magistrates to ignore the evocation, and they pressed for the replacement of Duprat by the bishop of Paris, who had been elected to fill both offices. The regent warned the Parlement against flouting either the concordat or the decision to evoke the whole matter. Nevertheless, emboldened by a speech from Lizet, the *Avocat-Général*, who attacked the judicial power of the King's Council as 'cursory and extraordinary', comparing it unfavourably with that of his own stable and well-informed court, the magistrates decided to remonstrate once more. This time they emphasized that the monks were being deprived of their seisin, against which deprivation they had appealed *en cas de saisine et nouvelleté* to the Parlement, a perfectly legitimate means, indeed the only means by which they could seek redress. Here was the real paradox left over from the court's registration of the concordat: if it were to uphold the precedents in its own registers, it would have to uphold the petitions of appellants whose beneficial rights had been taken away by the terms of the concordat. The remonstrances also contained a vitriolic attack upon the person of the chancellor, the culmination of ten years' deepening animosity. 'Doubtless,' they ran, 'the chancellor is a wise and prudent man with many good qualities, but he also has other characteristics of which the court does not approve . . . the court would have preferred him to conduct the affairs of the kingdom with mildness and humility and without personal interest.'[2]

These outspoken remonstrances sparked off a duel between Duprat and the Parlement that was only settled after the king's return. The chancellor persuaded the regent to summon the *Procureur-Général* to answer for the

[1] Maugis, op. cit., I, 560–7.
[2] Ibid., 568–9.

Parlement's conduct, and the Parlement passed a decree forbidding the *Procureur-Général* to obey the summons. That was in June 1525. Early in July, the court was notified that the dispute over the two benefices had once again been removed from the magistrates' jurisdiction, to which news it responded by solemnly reaffirming its right to judge such matters. At the end of July, the Parlement instituted an inquiry with a view to indicting the chancellor himself for his refusal to respect the court's judicial decisions. At the same time, despite the formal prohibition of the regent, it accepted an appeal by the religious of Saint-Euverte of Orléans, whose election of a new abbot had been followed by the intervention of the *Grand Conseil*. On 5 September, the Parlement issued a decree prescribing the immediate implementation of its own instructions and declaring those of the council null and void. In succeeding months, however, tempers cooled, the regent's attitude became firmer and less conciliatory, and in November 1525 the court suggested that existing disputes should be suspended until the king's return.

In December 1526, Francis suspended the *Procureur-Général* from the Parlement for six months and gave judgment over the disputed benefices in favour of Duprat. In the following month, he demanded the court's register so that those extracts in which the chancellor was personally criticized could be erased. Then on 24 July 1527, the king came to hold a *lit de justice* at the Palais. There he heard a courageous and outspoken speech delivered by President Guillart, in which the *parlementaire* view was firmly and clearly set out. The magistrates had no desire, he assured the king, to limit or dispute his authority, but they did have an obligation to preserve just laws and traditional principles. The king ought not to will all that he was able, but only what was good and equitable. He should always show himself willing to obey the law and to take into account the laws of his predecessors. Then his argument went a step further. The Parlement, he maintained, held its power from the nation, being in origin a public assembly, a sort of Estates' convention. This was an unhistorical assertion, made in an endeavour to raise the court's political status, in response to the king's own excessive acts. But it was itself an arbitrary and dangerous claim, likely to cause renewed difficulties with the crown if pursued further.

Francis remained unimpressed by this speech, forcing the court to register an edict in his presence which forbade the Parlement to concern itself with affairs of state, or to add reservations to its form of registration, which could permit of a jurisprudence contrary to the law itself. Yet, at the same time, Francis forbade the court to concern itself with causes involving archbishoprics, bishoprics and abbacies, thereby undermining a long judicial tradition by which the Parlement, on the king's behalf, had been accustomed to exercise its secular authority at the expense of the spiritual courts.[1] The king did not trust his court to judge beneficial matters according to the new law, so he was evoking them in advance to his own council. In so doing, he was adding point to the magistrates' old argument, which they had maintained consistently since his accession, that the king's chief task was to dispense justice, but that his judges could not perform their role satisfactorily and therefore maintain the king's authority unless they supported traditional values against the caprice of individual sovereigns.

Nevertheless, as regards the appointment to benefices and the payment of annates, the king got his way and these traditional liberties of the French Church disappeared. Thereby, Francis consolidated his authority over the Church to a greater extent than his predecessors had done, but there is no doubt that in so doing he acted arbitrarily by depriving the Church of long-held privileges which it had long been adjudged the monarch's obligation to defend. It may well appear, therefore, that the quarrel over the concordat demonstrated the king's determination to tread new ground, to establish an unbridled control over the state and to reject the ancient view of monarchy, restricted by laws, privileges and immunities. Yet such a view would be misleading. It had always been assumed that if the king chose to act thus there were no sanctions that could prevent him, but the stubborn opposition of the Parlement did serve to underline the authoritarian nature of his conduct and the general belief that the king ought not to act in that way.

In other words, although the Parlement failed in this particular matter, the traditional idea of kingship limited by law was by no means abandoned. Francis himself, by insisting upon the importance of *parlementaire* registration, contributed to its survival, but perhaps the most striking testimony was provided by the subsequent history of the Pragmatic Sanction, which continued to find more favour among clergy and lawyers than the concordat. Despite the papal condemnation of the Pragmatic Sanction in the bull *Pastor Aeternus*, it appears that even Francis I himself did not consider that the concordat totally replaced it. The introduction of the new agreement referred only to the abrogation of those articles of the Pragmatic Sanction which offended the dignity of Rome and the

[1] Doucet, *Etude sur le Gouvernement de François Ier*, II, 251–7.

canons acceptable to the Church of Rome. In 1586 the *Gens du roi* strongly supported the opinion that the Pragmatic Sanction, save for those articles subsequently revoked, remained in force, and indeed a whole series of *parlementaire* decrees dating from 1535 and ending only with the Revolution testified that the court's jurisprudence was wedded to that opinion. Assemblies of the French clergy in 1560, 1576, 1579, 1582, 1585, 1588, 1598 and 1610 asked the king to reimpose in full the provisions of the Pragmatic Sanction; in Louis XIV's reign, the great lawyer and future Chancellor d'Aguesseau, acclaimed it as more respected and more worthy of respect than the concordat, and in the closing decade of the *ancien régime*, the editors of the *Ordonnances des Rois de France de la troisième race* gave it an honoured place in their catalogue. In 1722 a volume was published at the instigation of a general assembly of the French clergy held in 1705, dealing with the sources of beneficial legislation in which the legitimacy of the Pragmatic Sanction was defended and the thesis was upheld that many of its articles remained in force. Neither the authoritarian measures of Francis I nor those of his predecessor, Louis XI, were sufficient in themselves to reverse what had become customary doctrine.[1]

Having borne the brunt of royal displeasure for leading the opposition to the concordat, the period of the king's captivity had provided the Parlement with a fortuitous opportunity to demonstrate once more that its importance and prestige in the state entitled it to more than the purely judicial role which Francis was seeking to impose upon it. In fact, late in 1527, having just previously employed a *lit de justice* to reduce the court to impotence, Francis himself was again consulting the magistrates in a political capacity. On 15 November he told a deputation of magistrates that the unsettled times made good justice more necessary than ever; that he intended to see that the Parlement's justice was enforced, since otherwise his own authority as king would be set at nought. Subsequently, he consulted the court on a variety of political affairs. Sometimes, as in 1540, when a financial edict was completely remodelled by the king after consideration of his court's remonstrances, he readily accepted its counsel. On other occasions, as in 1532, when he sought to abolish certain exceptional electoral privileges allowed by the concordat, he had recourse again to summary methods to enforce his will.[2] Nevertheless, at the end of his reign, the Parlement's political authority had survived, had even been strengthened by the constant disputes with the sovereign which made

[1] Martin, op. cit., II, 316–23.
[2] Maugis, op. cit., I, 583–8.

each side more aware of the authority of and the respect owed to, the other.

One new area in which the Parlement and the king tended to clash requires separate consideration: the Reformation. Although there were a few exceptions, the magistrates for the most part were basically opposed to that movement. This was not surprising, since it posed a threat to the unity of the state and to the traditional social and legal structure, and since its appearance in France became linked increasingly with subversion and disorder, a state of affairs of which a supreme court of law could scarcely approve. Nor was the king himself willing to risk chaos in his kingdom by advocating or supporting a new church, as Zwingli suggested he should in the preface of *De Vera et Falsa Religione*, and he was a severe critic of Luther. However, he drew a sharp distinction between the German reformers and Frenchmen like Lefèvre d'Etaples, having been greatly influenced during his early years as ruler by humanists such as he, and by the great Erasmus. His policy was hair-splitting when it came to protecting the more audacious reformers against the Parlement and the faculty of Theology, and it was equivocal too, for, from time to time, when he was anxious to obtain papal or imperial support, he adopted a more repressive policy. The Parlement's policy, on the contrary, was one of consistent hostility to doctrinal innovation, though it showed itself well aware of the need for moral reform.[1]

Lutheran works began to appear in Paris in 1519, and in 1521 Francis, who was on the point of war with the emperor and the king of England and who wanted to demonstrate his good faith, forbade their publication without the approval of the faculty of Theology. Nevertheless, support for the new faith continued to grow, and the Parlement decided to take action against one Louis de Berquin, a translator of Luther, Erasmus and Hutten, and at the same time, to begin an examination of the works of Lefèvre d'Etaples. These decisions antagonized the king, who was favourably disposed towards both men. In May 1523, after an order to search Berquin's home had revealed books by Luther and Melanchthon, the faculty of Theology pronounced them, and therefore Berquin as well, tainted with heresy, and the Parlement committed him to prison. It was then prepared to act against Lefèvre, but royal letters-patent evoked the matter to the *Grand Conseil.* Shortly afterwards the Berquin affair was similarly evoked to the same court, a procedure by which his release was effected, for Francis had no intention of instituting a retrial. He

[1] Doucet, *Etude sur le Gouvernement de François Ier*, I, 319–25.

intervened again several weeks later when the faculty of Theology threatened to raise the same issue and in the following year he forbade the Parlement to examine the writings of Lefèvre.[1]

Once more the disaster of Pavia gave the Parlement the opportunity for action. In October 1525 it issued a decree announcing that not only Lefèvre but Briçonnet, the bishop of Meaux, the friend and protégé of the Duchesse d'Alençon, the king's sister, were to be prosecuted for their religious unorthodoxy. The captive king wrote from Madrid ordering a suspension of the proceedings until the regent intimated to the court what was to be done. The magistrates decided to ignore the letter, justifying themselves to the regent on the grounds that the king, having expressed his desire for the maintenance of orthodoxy, must see the justice of their present action. Briçonnet's episcopal position made him fairly secure against the Parlement's attack, but he certainly modified his public pronouncements, while Lefèvre who felt no such security fled to Strasbourg. Encouraged by these successes, the Parlement again took up the case of Berquin. After his arrest in January 1526 his books were seized, witnesses were interrogated, once more he was declared heretical. It only remained for sentence to be passed, at which critical juncture Francis returned to his kingdom. His first message to the court forbade it to proceed further against Berquin and a little later he secured his release from prison.[2]

The king continued to favour those advocates of reform who sought to establish a closer contact between Holy Scripture and the individual, though he was opposed to reformers who wanted to abolish the mass and the sacraments and thereby threatened to overturn the social order. By the mid 1530s, however, the rapid growth of Protestantism in France was making Francis fearful of the consequences and he commanded the Parlement to pursue the Protestants without pity, giving his unequivocal support to its efforts. Thus in this matter, after indulging his tergiversations, mocking the law and customary procedures, the king ultimately acknowledged the Parlement's role and relied upon its support.

In the Parlement's conduct, especially during the king's captivity, there may well have been an element of injudicious antagonism, a rash desire to capitalize upon the king's absence. It was not easy to draw the line between reform and heresy and personal rancour may have played too great a part. The king retained the right to judge in person if he wished

[1] Ibid., 336 et seq.

[2] Ibid., II, 191 et seq.

and his evocations, therefore, were not necessarily detrimental to the cause of justice. But his willingness overall to take arbitrary action forced the magistrates to emphasize, sometimes perhaps to abuse, their own restraining role. The effect of that was partly to produce excessive claims on both sides, which presaged more serious conflicts for the future, but partly too to underline the traditional principle of restraint in the exercise of power. Despite the king's frequent recourse to arbitrary methods, that principle remained strong, largely because of the Parlement's persistent and consistent opposition, and Francis himself was forced from time to time to acknowledge it. His reign in this respect, therefore, was not one of innovation, though the king's emphasis was laid more sharply upon his authority than upon its limits, for the ancient balance was restored by the opposing weight given by the Parlement to the limitations of power. It is true, however, that in this reign, more than in any preceding ones, a sense of conflict emerged between the sovereign and his court. As the king's freedom of action grew, only the Parlement remained powerful enough to guard against the abuses of power.

The Parlement remained a political force in the reign of Francis I's successor, Henry II, and its relations with the new king were a good deal more harmonious than they had been with his father. Early in 1552, for example, the king attended the Palais to explain that the war against Spain would force him shortly to leave the country, and to brief the magistrates about important matters of state. Throughout his life he eschewed the violent language and the haughty attitude that Francis had adopted towards the Parlement and permitted it regularly to make known its opposition to proposed legislation. However, this apparently amicable relationship was in fact misleading, for the king paid little or no attention to the magistrates' remonstrances, and consequently towards the end of his reign, the court's language became more outspoken, particularly among the younger magistrates of the chambers of *Enquêtes*, whose criticism of the arbitrary and equivocal conduct of Louis XI was an indirect way of accusing Henry of similar lapses.[1] Nevertheless, the court certainly enjoyed a more continuous involvement in affairs of state than during preceding reigns; the Parlement's long struggle against Francis I had consolidated its political reputation.

The most important single problem with which the court was concerned remained the spread of the Reformation in France, which reached a

[1] Maugis, op. cit., I, 680.

critical stage during Henry's reign. The Parlement was gravely disturbed not only by the threat to the king's authority posed by the new faith, but also by the danger implicit in his methods of seeking a solution. In 1549 he produced the edict of Saint-Germain, by which both diocesan prelates and secular judges were given jurisdiction over matters involving false doctrine or errors against the faith: to the former were prescribed cases concerning the fact of schism and heresy, to the latter cases of sedition and perturbation arising out of schismatic or heretical beliefs. The *Gens du roi* expressed the magistrates' concern about the vagueness of the boundary between secular and spiritual jurisdiction and the consequent likelihood of disputes, though the court, anxious to support the measures against the Huguenots, did not force the issue. Subsequently, however, it twice refused to register an edict establishing the Inquisition in France, giving its reasons in remonstrances read out to the king by Séguier, the First President, in October 1555. The magistrates objected to the stipulation that all judgments on matters of heresy were within the province of the ecclesiastical authorities, without right of appeal to the Parlement, whose sole responsibility was to be the application of penalties against those found guilty by the Church. They argued that in France the king, being the sovereign source of justice, could scarcely deprive his subjects of their right to appeal to him and they pointed out that the court's jurisprudence supported the right of boy laymen and clerics to be judged in the last instance by the king's supreme court, the Parlement.

Their contentions were well grounded in law and their support for the sovereign's judicial independence *vis-à-vis* the spiritual authorities was in keeping with the Gallican tradition and was intended to underpin the king's authority. They also took the opportunity, in these remonstrances, to criticize the application of the concordat in the appointment of prelates. What was needed, they maintained, were zealous pastors living permanently in their dioceses, preaching and working among their people, virtuous enough to resist the bright lure of Paris and the royal court. The king, as was his habit, promised to give earnest consideration to his court's opinions, and in fact the Inquisition was not formally established in France, though some of its practices were introduced.[1]

The Parlement was also opposed to the extraordinary tribunals which sprang up, even within the confines of the Palais de Justice, including the *Chambre des Luthériens* or the *Chambre de la Reine*, which included a number of magistrates from the Parlement. There were also examples of

[1] Ibid., II, 2–6.

individual magistrates taking the law into their own hands and imprisoning suspected heretics. Whatever their religious views, most members of the Parlement, as magistrates, were unwilling to tolerate such extra-legal activities, and in November 1558 the court forbade its presidents and counsellors to sit upon any irregular commissions. This action and the Parlement's earlier opposition to the Inquisition was interpreted to the king as proof of the court's support for Huguenotism. In June 1559 Henry came to the Palais to preside over one of the most dramatic sessions recorded in the Parlement's records.[1] The king challenged each magistrate in turn to state his opinions frankly about how the heresy could best be extirpated. Most of the responses were unremarkable but those of three counsellors caused consternation. Two of them, Paul de Foix and Loys du Faur, appealed to a future ecumenical council to resolve the religious differences, demanding in the meantime that the penalties against the Huguenots should be suspended. The third counsellor, Anne du Bourg, was even more audacious. He denounced the persecution of those whose only crime was the dauntlessness of their faith, comparing them favourably with those who committed grave offences against religion and went unpunished. One of the offences mentioned by Du Bourg was adultery, a reference which Henry chose to take personally. The three magistrates were arrested and sent to the Bastille. The first two, having abjured their heresy, were temporarily suspended by the court. The brave and reckless Du Bourg was condemned to death and executed shortly after his judge, President Minard, had himself succumbed to an assassin's assault.

The repercussions of this dramatic episode were felt for years to come. Much of 1560 was taken up with *parlementaire* discussions of how the court could assert its moral unanimity, but the damage was done and doubts about the magistrates' orthodoxy continued to grow, nourished by the climate of suspicion and delirium which accompanied the outbreak of civil war. During 1562 and 1563, there were frequent popular demonstrations, some within the walls of the Palais itself against counsellors suspected of Huguenotism. In an effort to assuage public discontent, the Parlement decided in June 1562 to exact from all its members, presidents, counsellors, *Gens du roi*, clerks and ushers a solemn oath of Catholicity, a gesture which did much to restore confidence. It also persuaded the few remaining Huguenots in the Parlement to resign their offices.

In fact the Parlement as a body had never wavered in its opposition to

[1] Ibid., 9–10.

the Huguenot cause, which since the 1530s had become identified with tumult and armed revolt. The court's registers were regularly punctuated with accounts of such outbreaks, particularly among the student body: brawls during theology lectures, violent scenes in the streets during formal university processions, vandalism, pillage and murder. By the mid 1550s the police of the *Châtelet* were powerless against the plundering mobs roaming the capital, and *parlementaire* decrees issued against them failed for lack of executors. In September 1554, the *Avocat-Général* testified before the court that more than a thousand students had been marauding through Paris for a fortnight, wrecking orchards and vineyards, killing or wounding those who dared to oppose them. Religious revolt was not always at the root of such activities: the chancellor, L'Hôpital, pointed out in 1561 that the conclusion of war with Spain had left many Frenchmen without a trade, unaccustomed to the ways of peace, restless and discontented. Such men were easily inflamed by Protestant preachers who were declaiming their turbulent sermons from pulpits throughout the capital. The Parlement tried to eliminate this irritant by ordaining that all those who wished to preach had first to give sufficient notice to the bishop in order that he might satisfy himself as to their suitability.

Despite this precaution, the influence of Huguenot preachers and the violence grew apace. Early in 1562 the Parlement was informed that the clergy of Notre Dame had asked for armed guards for protection, while those of Saint-Pol demanded a cannon. It heard, too, that on Christmas Day 1561 a number of worshippers attending vespers in the church of Saint-Médard, later to be the centre of Jansenist hagiolatry, were set upon and killed by a Protestant band. The court itself was not immune from threats. A plot to fire the Palais was uncovered at about the same time as President Minard's assassination, and thereafter the town was virtually in a state of siege as religious disorder spilt over into civil war.

Whatever private doubts may have remained among the counsellors, the Parlement's commitment to the defence of royal authority, traditional beliefs and law and order, placed it firmly in the ranks of the enemies of Huguenotism and gave it a leading political function once more in the beleaguered state.[1]

The magistrates intervened increasingly with remonstrances upon a variety of subjects during the reigns of Francis II and Charles IX. Indeed, one of the latter's envoys to the Parlement remarked sardonically that the king found it strange that his court should prefer to correct rather

[1] Ibid. 14–23.

than to observe his edicts. During the minority of Charles IX (1560–3), the influence of the chancellor, Michel de L'Hôpital, became predominant and considerably affected the political attitudes of the Parlement. His intention was to reconcile the court's restraining influence upon the government with an atmosphere of mutual respect and moderation. He believed too, that the initiative should always rest with the sovereign. In June 1561 he told the magistrates that their duty was to act as judges even in great matters of state, always provided that the king sought their assistance.[1] He frequently returned to this theme of prudence and moderation, not least because the relations between the sovereign and his court were becoming anything but cordial. The friction was caused by a series of edicts of pacification, intended to bring to an end the civil disturbances in one way or another. The first of them, the edict of Amboise, was sent to the court in March 1560, accompanied by royal orders requiring immediate publication and registration, without recourse to remonstrances. The magistrates bowed before this authoritarian gesture in the hope that it would lead to peace. It did not do so, and in June 1560 a second edict, of Romorantin, was sent to the Parlement. This legislation met fierce opposition from the court on the grounds that, in placing the emphasis for the repression of heresy upon the Church courts it offered, as had earlier attempts at introducing the Inquisition into France, the opportunity for the spiritual authorities to override royal jurisdiction, and remonstrances were drawn up insisting that the sole right of ecclesiastical judges was to declare the fact of heresy; judgment should appertain to the king as the guardian of law and order.

These remonstrances were of no avail, though in August of the same year a royal declaration modifying the edict did go some way towards satisfying the magistrates' complaints. However, the edict failed in its essential purpose of quelling the religious revolt, and it became clear that further measures would have to be introduced. L'Hôpital convened an assembly consisting of representatives of the Parlement, the clergy and the University to debate the problem, and after ten days of discussion it was announced that a great council was to be held at which the Parlement, prelates, princes and members of the King's Council would be invited by the sovereign to propose their remedies. Out of this assembly came the famous July Edict of 1561. However, when the time came for the Parlement to register this edict, in whose composition it had already played such a prominent part, it agreed to do so only provisionally, on the

[1] Ibid., I, 603–4.

grounds that the text had undergone numerous alterations in the intervening weeks. Six months later, a new edict of pacification appeared, this time preceded by deliberations between magistrates from a number of provincial Parlements and members of the King's Council. The Parlement was asked for its registration without remonstrances. Predictably it refused to co-operate; if magistrates from the provinces were given an opportunity of participating in the edict's composition, it was unthinkable that the members of the Parlement of Paris should be prevented from expressing their opinions also. The Parisian magistrates were further antagonized by the news that certain provincial Parlements had already published the edict. In addition, however, the contents of this particular edict of Saint-Germain were more favourable to the Huguenots than the Parlement would condone. As a result, a *parlementaire* deputation bearing remonstrances was dispatched to the king at Saint-Cloud in February 1562.

In these remonstrances the court spoke eloquently of the impossibility of two religions co-existing in a single state, a situation which could only result in the dissolution of the state itself: by allowing Huguenots to assemble for common prayer, by approving of Protestant synods and consistories, at least by implication, the edict was in fact supporting the new religion. The queen mother, Catherine de Medici, tried to humour the magistrates by offering further clarification of the edict and small concessions, but they remained hostile and in due course royal *lettres de jussion* ordered obedience. On 18 February 1562, notwithstanding the king's command, a plenary session of the court refused to verify the edict.

The king and the queen mother decided at this stage to allow the Parlement to take the initiative, and five days after its refusal to register, the king ordered it to produce alternative proposals. The magistrates' response was a text almost identical with the original version of the July Edict. They pointed out that in the closing session of the great council which had produced the edict, each article had been drawn up and approved with great precision and solemnity, and they argued that such decisions, emanating from an assembly invested with great authority, and specifically constituted by the sovereign to make these decisions, should have been valid and binding. Yet within the space of a few days, they had been gravely compromised and shortly afterwards the edict of Saint-Germain appeared to contradict much of what had been solemnly decreed in the July Edict. The Parlement objected to the government's flouting of traditional procedure in allowing provincial courts to publish as a law an edict which had not been registered in Paris. It objected, too, to the inconsistency in the law which was the product of such vacillating policy.

All these objections sprang from the court's belief that the effectiveness of laws depended upon the formality and correctness of their institution. Its persistent hostility to the Huguenots caused it at this moment to reaffirm emphatically the original text of the July Edict, which was not only legally the most soundly based, but also, in its opinion, offered the best means of restoring peace to the realm. It proposed, therefore, that ministers of the new religion should be forbidden to preach, that houses suspected of harbouring Huguenots should be razed to the ground, that preachers should be carefully designated by the bishops and the faculty of Theology, that royal officials and prelates should sign a profession of Catholicity, that all moral catechisms and books of instruction should be seized and the printing or sale of them forbidden, and that all insurgents should disperse to their own homes within a fortnight of the publication of these articles or be considered rebels.

Having heard the Parlement's proposals, the queen mother decided to ignore them because of growing Huguenot pressure, and at the beginning of March the court received new orders to register the edict of Saint-Germain. The Prince de la Roche-sur-Yon who brought the message to the court was instructed to remain so that the procedure might be quickened. The First President promptly protested at the prince's presence, and the counsellors refused to offer opinions until he left. On the following day, 4 March, *lettres de jussion* arrived, accompanied by the queen's warning, that 5,000 or 6,000 armed Huguenots were converging on Paris and that the country's security rested upon their decision. For three days the magistrates debated the matter while outside in the courtyard of the Palais angry Protestant students kept up a continuous demonstration. Eventually the Parlement capitulated and resolved to register the edict, though with the sort of reservations – because of the necessity of the times, without approving the new religion, until the king reached a contrary decision – that were intended to cast serious doubts upon its validity. In fact, with the outbreak of civil war shortly afterwards, the time had passed when a legal solution of any kind could be enforced.

At the beginning of the wars, both sides appealed to the Parlement as an arbiter. In April 1562, the Duc de Guise came to clear himself of the accusation that he had fomented trouble by entering the capital with a large armed following; on four occasions around the same time, the

Prince de Condé asked for a hearing for his point of view before the court. However, the Parlement's attitude towards the Huguenots did not change, even though it was unable to persuade the government to act accordingly. Thus its registrations of the peace of Amboise (1563), of Longjumeau (1568), of Saint-Germain (1570) and of La Rochelle (1573), all of them favourable to the Huguenot cause, were carried out without the usual ceremony and before the *Grand' Chambre* alone.[1] The king, Charles IX, complained constantly about the Parlement's lack of co-operation: about its refusal to receive Huguenot counsellors, about its continued hostility towards Protestant citizens, about its unenthusiastic attitude towards all attempts at reaching a *rapprochement* between the opposing factions. The consistency and logic of the magistrates' position was indisputable, even though the political situation made it appear increasingly that a compromise would have to be found. They argued that the prince had no right to compromise, that by his coronation oath he had sworn to extirpate heresy and that that obligation remained with him as with all his predecessors since Clovis.

The expression of such sentiments, of course, clearly indicates that the Parlement's political authority was once more considerable. Its opinion had been sought by all the leading figures in the quarrel, including the king himself. Its approval of the various proposals for a settlement and subsequently of the peace treaties ending each bout of the conflict had been considered vital by Huguenot and Catholic alike; its steadfast and inflexible position again provided the focal point for lawful government, as it had done during the troubles of Charles VI's reign, when the role of the crown itself had been compromised.

Yet the attitude of the government remained paradoxical, for while it recognized the court's political importance and indeed encouraged it on the one hand – Charles IX stated quite openly that the Parlement had the right to examine royal legislation – it also resorted to quite arbitrary procedures in order to restrict the Parlement's role on the other. In April 1561, for example, L'Hôpital produced an edict forbidding the use of the terms 'papist' and 'Huguenot' as an incitement to religious dissensions and ordering the immediate release of prisoners held for their religious opinions. That he was inspired by political considerations and not by a spirit of tolerance does not alter the fact that his assessment of what was required at that time may well have been accurate. However, he vitiated the proposition by sending the edict directly to the provincial governors

[1] Ibid., II, 24–40.

and to the subordinate judicial officers in the localities without having it registered in the Parlement. For the chief legal officer thus to ignore the accepted legal procedure, however apt the terms of the edict itself might have been, was to encourage a general disregard for the law and to quicken the deterioration of lawful government already undermined by religious friction. Besides, how was the supreme court of appeal to deal with cases concerning a law of which it had not been seized and which contradicted previous legislation of which it had been seized? The Parlement protested that an edict which had not been registered could not be a law of the kingdom. Faced with this opposition, L'Hôpital allowed the edict to be forgotten.

The magistrates were again angered in August 1563 when the king, Charles IX, was persuaded to declare his majority at Rouen, in the Parlement of Normandy.[1] The ordinance proclaiming the king's majority in this way caused the Parlement to draw up remonstrances in which the magistrates made far-reaching assertions about their own authority: they declared that all royal ordinances had to be verified and registered by the Parlement of Paris before any other Parlement could have cognizance of them, on the grounds that the Parisian court represented the Estates-General. Such an assertion had no historical validity and it produced from the king an equally unrealistic response: the Parlement existed, so he maintained, only to dispense justice and not to concern itself at all with political affairs. Once again both sides were resorting to excessive claims and once again it was the arbitrary and vacillating attitude of the government that had provoked the court. The king on this occasion also took the opportunity to forbid the practice of iterative remonstrances once the first complaints had been rejected and to threaten the magistrates' freedom of discussion by demanding to see the list of counsellors who had voted against registration.[2]

In such a climate more and more outspoken and excessive claims were being made by both sides: to L'Hôpital's assertion that the superior political wisdom of the King's Council made it necessary for the Parlement to accept its legislation after remonstrances had been made, one of the

[1] The king's speech on this occasion is printed in the Prince de Condé's *Mémoires*, IV, 574–80; this valuable source reproduces many documents relating to the Parlement's activities between the years 1559 and 1569.

[2] E. Glasson, *Le Parlement de Paris*, I, 27–30; H. Amphoux, *Michel de l'Hôpital*, 174–5, 288–92; Maugis, op. cit., I, 608 et seq. According to Glasson, L'Hôpital was responsible for the decision to proclaim the majority at Rouen. Amphoux, on the other hand, ascribes the decision, probably correctly, to the queen mother, Catherine de Medici.

court's presidents replied that the king sent his laws to the Parlement to ascertain whether they were just and reasonable, and if remonstrances were necessary, the law was presumably unjust. It was the remonstrances, not the law, which should be observed. To the chancellor's plea that remonstrances should always be prudent the First President retorted that to approve unjust enactments would always be to oppose the king's real interests.[1]

Against the backcloth of civil war which was gravely weakening the sovereign's authority, there was less scope for him to act in an unrestrained fashion than had been the case under Francis I, and in consequence, the Parlement was better able to assert its limiting role. Only the emphasis changed however: despite the exaggerated claims emanating from both camps, the basic situation of the monarchy was not affected. The Parlement showed no signs of allowing its extreme claims to be carried to their logical conclusion – a division of royal sovereignty – and the king's position was too hazardous to allow him to reduce the court's role to a purely judicial one.

Thus within three months of the royal order prohibiting iterative remonstrances, the magistrates were once more presenting them in December 1563, on the subject of the costs involved in obtaining justice. A further attempt to enforce this prohibition was contained in the ordinance of Moulins, the first two articles of which repeated that the Parlement must not defer the registration and application of edicts when remonstrances had been made and the king's wishes indicated. Before the text of the ordinance was sent to the court, in March 1565, it had been debated at length by royal advisers, princes and magisterial representatives, including the First President and the *Avocat-Général*. Nevertheless, the assembled chambers insisted upon remonstrances which were presented in the following June; a month later, the king produced a declaration ordering the court to proceed to registration without iterative remonstrances. The Parlement still equivocated, however, and a deputation of magistrates explained the position to the chancellor by means of a novel formula, affirming that remonstrances were concerned with two sorts of enactment, those which raised problems and those which were impossible to approve. When it was constrained to register enactments of the latter sort, the compulsion in whatever form freed the Parlement from its responsibility. It obeyed orders without approving the contents of the document that it was thus forced to register. The magistrates made it clear that the first

[1] Maugis, op. cit., I, 604–7.

two articles of the ordinance of Moulins fitted into that category. The king eventually gave way, and another declaration of December 1565 ordained that the Parlement could make and reiterate whatever remonstrances it thought necessary in royal enactments sent to it for registration. The declaration further decreed, however, that after publication such enactments should be obeyed without reserve, even if the publication followed the king's express orders or included qualifications incorporated by the court into its act of registration. This stipulation was intended to counter the indisputable fact that royal legislation thus hedged with *parlementaire* modifications had a somewhat dubious aura. The magistrates registered the royal declaration but neatly reiterated their point of view by adding all the customary formulae of constraint. In fact, the Parlement never ratified articles 1 and 2 of the edict of Moulins.[1]

Both Charles IX and Henry III tried in a variety of other ways, none of them effective, to reduce the Parlement's freedom of action in political matters: by forbidding deputations of magistrates to approach the king unless specifically summoned; by insisting that remonstrances should be drawn up quickly, within a period of three days and sent in writing to the king; by forbidding the chambers to assemble together so that the government could deal with the magistrates of the *Grand' Chambre* alone, the most malleable and conservative element in the court; by sending edicts to the Parlement at the very end of the session so that under the threat of prorogation the magistrates might prove more tractable; finally, by bargaining over the payment of the judges' salaries. The Parlement was kept in session, for example, all through the summer of 1578, when the king was trying to enforce the registration of some twenty financial edicts, though in showing concern about whether registration carried out during the months of the vacation had the same force as usual, he was emphasizing the need for the Parlement's support. Again, in April 1580, Henry III tried the manœuvre of sending an enactment to be discussed by the *Grand' Chambre* and senior members of the *Enquêtes* and *Requêtes* only; the *Procureur-Général* led the protest against this new procedure and the edict was eventually withdrawn.

The one method of enforcement which remained open to the sovereign, the validity of which was not disputed by the court, was the *lit de justice*. In 1580 and again in 1581, when Henry announced his intention of coming to the Palais to publish his edicts, a deputation of magistrates begged him not to adopt that procedure, but to send a prince or a nobleman to act

[1] Ibid., 615–19.

in his stead. The reason for this plea was that the court made a clear distinction between the king's own orders given in person or in his presence by the chancellor, and the king's orders issued by a royal nominee. However distinguished the latter, the Parlement considered the decisions of such sessions less binding than those of a *lit de justice* and therefore infinitely preferable when it came to registering legislation of which the Parlement disapproved. In August 1572 for example, when the king's brother, the Duc d'Alençon, came to the court with a large following of princes and peers to insist upon the registration of a financial edict which the Parlement had held up for some months, the magistrates were willing to accept a formula of registration which emphasized that the orders came from the king's brother rather than from the king himself.

But even after *lits de justice* the Parlement frequently inserted phrases in the official record which indicated the magistrates' own unwillingness to support registration save at the king's express command. This happened in July 1581, when every counsellor in turn refused the chancellor's offer to express an opinion on the grounds that they had not been given any opportunity to do so before the *lit de justice*, a response that was subsequently incorporated into the court's register. An alternative procedure was the inclusion of various reservations about which the magistrates felt deeply into the court's secret registers, a procedure that provided an alibi for enforced acquiescence and strongly underlined the idea that the Parlement's role was not ultimately one of simple obedience to the sovereign's will.[1]

At the conclusion of Henry III's reign, therefore, despite numerous attempts on the part of the government to restrict the Parlement's political authority as exercised through its scrutiny of royal legislation, the court may be fairly said to have held its own. Its right to reiterate remonstrances on two or more occasions was accepted by the sovereign, and although the latter could impose his authority in the last resort, the Parlement's habit of adding its own reservations or the details of compulsion emphasized the precarious and conditional character of the registration as something enforced without due regard to legal forms.

In a wider sense, too, the political authority of the court was confirmed during this period. The power of the Estates-General had been diminishing for almost a century, and the king's traditional noble counsellors were deeply divided by the religious wars. The Parlement became increasingly the only effective guarantor of the traditional constitution, offering the

[1] Ibid., 620 et seq.

king counsel and reminding him of the legal obligations inherent in the French monarchy. More and more the Parlement was inclined to stress its independence from the Estates-General, a fact of great significance in view of the latter's abrupt decline. The Parlement had been summoned to attend meetings of the Estates in 1484. On that occasion although it had nominated deputies, they did not in fact attend the meeting. The argument subsequently invoked by the magistrates with this precedent in mind was that the Parlement, bearing the double responsibility of acting for the king in his capacities of sovereign judge and supreme legislator, could not prejudice either function in advance by taking part in the elaboration of proposed reforms.

In 1560 the king, Francis II, sent to the Parlement for registration the various recommendations recently drawn up by the Estates-General at Orléans. He was anxious for a speedy verification since he needed the promised subsidy that went with it and he suggested to the magistrates that a detailed examination was not necessary on the grounds that the Parlement formed part of the Estates-General and would therefore have no reason for holding up its recommendations. This piece of sophistry, historically baseless, was indignantly repudiated by the First President, who insisted that the court should be allowed to examine proposals emanating from the Estates-General in exactly the same way as it scrutinized royal enactments. The Parlement supported its chief, and when the ordinance was finally registered in September 1560 it contained revisions inserted by the court; in this way its superiority and distinction from the Estates-General was emphasized. By its acceptance of the registration the government tacitly acknowledged the situation. Again in 1579 the king – this time Henry III – sent to the Parlement the ordinance drawn up from the recommendations made three years earlier by the Estates' meeting at Blois and once more the magistrates insisted on their right to examine, criticize and suggest alterations.[1]

Thus the Parlement successfully resisted the government's attempt to link its authority with that of the Estates-General. Instead, it succeeded in asserting its legal and therefore political dominance over that body by stressing its own separate responsibilities. Indeed, the court had already widened its authority at the expense of the Estates-General, particularly in the financial sphere. The sovereign himself had assisted the magistrates by offering matters of financial administration which were not strictly

[1] Ibid., 655 et seq., but note J. Russell Major, *The Deputies to the Estates-General*, 186, n. 15.

within the court's competence for their consideration: exactly this point was made to L'Hôpital in November 1561 by a magistrate seeking to demonstrate the prestige enjoyed by his company.

The Parlement's interest in financial affairs had originally gone no further than its efforts to prevent alienations of the royal domain or of the king's revenue, but during the civil wars, when the monarch was driven to a variety of expedients to obtain more money, the Parlement became much more immediately concerned. In a number of ways it sought to limit the flow, by long delays ending in *lits de justice*, by attacks on prominent financiers, by attempts to persuade the king to appropriate certain sorts of revenue for specific ends. In September 1578, Henry III sent twenty-two financial edicts to the Parlement, two of which the court registered and twenty it rejected on the grounds that they were of an oppressive nature. In the face of an extremely angry royal reaction, the magistrates agreed to register some of these twenty, but successfully held out against total submission. In July 1580 eight more edicts were drawn up on similar lines to those previously rejected by the court. This time the king only overcame the opposition by going in person to the Palais. Similarly, a year later, a further *lit de justice* was needed to ensure the registration of nine more financial edicts creating new taxes, on which occasion the First President argued that, though the king could use his absolute authority to force through these enactments, if the laws of the kingdom based on reason and equity were to have any effect, these edicts should not be published. It was another way of saying that the king ought to act according to what was customarily lawful. A final *lit de justice* in March 1583 effected the Parlement's unwilling publication of eleven edicts, all of them creating new offices from which the king could obtain additional revenue, though its formula of registration included the familiar qualifying phrase, '*de expresso mandato domini regis*.'

The Parlement's attitude to financial exactions by the crown was that they should depend upon the support of the subjects concerned. In 1489, for example, when Charles VIII invited his court to help him to collect a tithe from the French clergy, the magistrates replied that an assembly of the French Church should meet first to approve the levy, adding that if the king tried to exact the tithe without such approval, the Parlement would maintain its right to receive judicial appeals from the clergy against such royal action. The idea of consent to financial exactions was a long-established one arising out of the king's obligation to respect the rights and privileges of all classes and communities in the state. This consent had been given formerly by local assemblies, by town councils and especially by the Estates-General. As many of these institutions declined, it was natural enough that the Parlement should take over their role. There was of course no question of the magistrates, whose offices were tending increasingly to become hereditary, having a genuinely representative status; yet, their court was the only institution which could cite the customary limits of royal authority in the financial sphere and by its opposition could protect the people against arbitrary taxation in general and against inequitable or otherwise disadvantageous levies in particular. The king's increasing reliance upon the magistrates' support for his financial enactments was an indication of the court's political weight. It also offered an opportunity for the Parlement to consolidate its influence in representing to the government the otherwise inarticulate complaints of the people.[1]

Although the court's intermediary role between the monarch and his subjects was implicit in its right of remonstrance, from the reign of Henry III it began to pay much more attention to its representative responsibilities. The remonstrances drawn up in 1579 upon the subject of the recommendations of the Estates-General made at Blois in 1576 were transcribed into the court's registers 'in order to provide a perpetual memory for posterity of how the Parlement had sought to do its duty'. In the summer of 1581, when the magistrates heard of the king's intention to hold a *lit de justice* for the purpose of registering certain edicts creating new offices in the Parlement, they asked the First President to plead with the king either to leave his court free to debate the matter as was customary, or, if he insisted upon attending himself not to require the magistrates to speak *so that the people may know that they had not given their consent.** Despite its growing concern with its public image, however, the Parlement was frequently forced to fall back upon its secret registers to proclaim its opposition in the hope that at some future date it could justify its conduct by producing that evidence. That was what happened in March 1575 and again in January 1580.[2]

This growth in the court's political prestige, coinciding with the decline of the Estates-General and with the protracted weakness of the monarchy itself, encouraged political writers of the time to try to redefine the Parlement's role in the state. The Huguenot author of the *Vindiciae contra Tyrannos* claimed, like most contemporary pamphleteers, that royal

[1] Maugis, op. cit., 674–703; Russell Major, *Representative Institutions*, 127–30.
*Author's italics.
[2] Maugis, op. cit., I, 628–31.

legislation could only be considered valid after the Parlement's ratification: the difficulty was to decide the significance of that fact. The author of the *Vindiciae* implied that the magistrates thereby acquired considerable power to control despotic acts. But where did that power end? According to Pasquier, whose *Recherches de la France* appeared between 1561 and 1565, the Parlement was the direct successor to the Carolingian assemblies, the *champs de mai*, at which all the great political decisions of that epoch had been taken. The purpose of this spurious genealogy was to demonstrate how ancient and continuous was the Parlement's political life, and therefore how significant was its contribution in the process of law-making. Yet, he too acknowledged the court's ultimate impotence in the face of royal insistence.

His contemporary, Du Haillan, wrote in a very similar way, affirming that when a royal decree had been registered by the court, the people at once gave their adherence without a murmur, as if the Parlement formed the bond which knotted the subjects' obedience to the king's command. Nevertheless, he did not doubt that the court's constitutional role depended in the last resort upon the crown's co-operation. Neither did Bodin, whose idea of sovereignty was to contribute substantially to the re-emergence of a strong monarchy, but nor did he underestimate the influence of the Parlement. Though he maintained that the king could override the court's objections by attending in person and having his enactments registered by his express command, he considered that if that procedure was necessary, there was a strong possibility that the law in question would be badly observed.[1]

There was thus a fair measure of agreement among political writers in the second half of the sixteenth century that ultimate sovereignty lay with the king and that the Parlement's practice of registering royal edicts added an important seal of validity, but that whatever limitations this practice imposed upon the monarch's actions, the magistrates had no absolute right to refuse registration. This attitude was very much that adopted by Claude de Seyssel several generations earlier, though it conformed less well with the political practice of his day than with that of the last Valois kings. In the course of the century the Parlement had in fact consolidated its position and had succeeded in maintaining a concept of kingship that was not only implicit in the writings of contemporary

[1] G. Weill, *Les Théories sur le pouvoir royal en France*, 114, 177–80; J. W. Allen, *A History of Political Thought in the Sixteenth Century*, 280 et seq; J. Bodin, *Six Livres de la République*, Bk III, Chapter IV, 418.

commentators, but was also traditional. In the light of that idea the need to delineate precisely the limits of the Parlement's control over royal policies disappeared; what mattered was the belief that French monarchy was not arbitrary but was regulated and controlled by legal rules. Although both crown and Parlement had on occasion taken up extreme positions, such positions remained transient, for to make laws and to enforce them were functions too closely connected for either king or magistrates to claim total independence.

The last of the Valois rulers, Henry III, frequently acknowledged his dependence upon the court: on almost every occasion that he sent legislation to it he confessed that if the Parlement did not obey him, nobody else would either, and his frequent menaces were qualified by an awareness of that fact. This continued dependence of the sovereign enabled the Parlement to strengthen its political role by taking the place of other institutions which were no longer able to limit the king's actions: in a word, to further secure the fundamental traits of traditional French monarchy. So far the excessive claims of each side had not basically undermined these traits, and the writings of contemporary theorists for the most part accurately reflected that fact. It must now be seen whether or not the situation altered in the later stages of the civil wars, when the emergence of the Catholic League brought both the crown and the Parlement to a critical moment in their history.

CHAPTER SEVEN

The League, Henry IV and Richelieu

The Catholic League; the Day of the Barricades and its consequences; the Committee of the Sixteen; the Parlement's support for Henry IV; the financial disputes; the edict of Nantes; Gallicanism and Ultramontanism; Marie de Medici's regency; the Parlement and the king's council; Cardinal Richelieu

---

The Parlement's attitude to the religious problem had been entirely consistent since the outbreak of hostilities, indeed since the influence of Protestantism had first become a serious problem in the country. 'France has been Catholic since the days of Clovis,' the magistrates reminded the king in remonstrances against the comparatively tolerant edict of January 1562, 'and the king must respect the faith.'[1] The government's increasingly moderate policy towards the Huguenots was at this time provoking a violent Catholic reaction. In the previous year a young bachelor of theology, one Tanquerel, defending his thesis before the Sorbonne, had argued without contradiction that the Holy See could depose heretical rulers, a view which threatened the treasured Gallican doctrine, that in matters affecting the kingdom the monarch was independent of the pope. The Parlement, for all its orthodoxy, was not going to allow such opinions to gain favour; it intervened to quash the thesis and to extract a public disavowal from the university authorities. About the same time a French priest appealed to the Spanish king, Philip II, to take action against the Huguenots.[2] Such isolated expressions did not as yet embarrass the magistrates, but they did suggest the serious dilemma which could result if the monarchy began openly to favour the Huguenot cause. On the one

[1] Weill, op. cit., 58.
[2] Ibid., 54–5.

hand, they were committed to the view that the French monarchy was Catholic; on the other, they supported with like conviction the idea that the king of France was subject to no other power on earth. The difficulty would arise if a choice had to be made between these two basic doctrines, a possibility that was brought considerably nearer in 1570 with the formation of the Catholic League.

Leagues of Catholic noblemen and prelates had appeared much earlier in various localities, but Henry III's concessions to the Huguenots made in that year at the peace of Monsieur caused them to be fused into a single nation-wide organization. It was an organization consisting largely of Catholic nobility, formed around the house of Guise, and looking to Rome for its spiritual needs, and to the rulers of Spain and Savoy for material aid. The power of the League first became apparent at the meeting of the Estates-General of Blois in 1576. Its opposition to the king represented in one respect a feudal reaction; it sought to revitalize the Estates-General and to restore old provincial privileges fallen into desuetude – but it was in addition a thinly disguised assault upon the king's authority in the state. The League's manifesto made it clear enough that religion came before hereditary right and that its members' obedience to the ruler was conditional upon his uncompromising Catholicism. That fact, allied with the League's close links with the king of Spain, persuaded Henry III of the need to control its development with the utmost care and to that effect he declared himself its chief early in 1577. He had the satisfaction later in the same year of presiding over its disintegration.

When it was revived in 1585, after the death of the duke of Anjou had opened the way to the throne for the Protestant Henry of Navarre, it was a much more revolutionary organization, centred in Paris and dominated by middle-class professional men rather than by the nobility.[1] The Parlement had been hostile to the League since its inception, and in 1577 it had resisted the king's own command to join it. In 1584 it was quick to register letters-patent forbidding all practices that would lead to the re-formation of the League, including the signing of any memoranda tending to conspiracy against the state, all under pain of high treason. In the dilemma posed by the uncertainty of the succession, the Parlement was moving away from the principle propounded by the League that hereditary right had to cede to religious orthodoxy.

It was encouraged in this direction by the fact that the League was by this time a threat to the king's security, as disruptive an element in the

[1] H. G. Koenigsberger, 'The Organization of Revolutionary Parties', 346–7.

state as the Huguenots had been in the early years of the wars, and from the Parlement's point of view, therefore, as little worthy of approval. Henry of Navarre and the Huguenots, on the other hand, were no longer adhering to the extreme opinions expressed by the author of the *Vindiciae* immediately after the Saint Bartholomew Day massacre. Instead, they were increasingly stressing the original Calvinist doctrine of obedience to the sovereign, whatever his religion, and condemning sedition in whatever guise it appeared. Henry of Navarre told a Protestant assembly at La Rochelle that he was sure that the respect owed by them to the king had grown since His Majesty had become a captive in the hands of the state's enemies (the League).[1]

Predictably taking precisely the opposite point of view, the pope intervened in September 1585 with a bull levelled against the Protestant leaders, claiming that the authority of St Peter's successors was greater than that of any French king, and depriving Henry of his right to the throne. The threat of interference from without was thus crystallized in the reassertion of papal claims over France, which challenged the Gallican tradition. Nothing could have succeeded better in forcing the Parlement to move away from the League and towards the acceptance of a Protestant successor. The magistrates refused to register the bull, adding that they would sooner lose their offices. In addition, they stated the court's opposition to 'a league joined against the state, in arms against the king's person, which commanded fathers to desert their children and friends to betray one another'.[2] At a *lit de justice* in June 1586 the First President, Harlay, categorically affirmed the Parlement's support for the existing law of succession and therefore indirectly its support for Henry of Navarre's claim to succeed Henry III. There were two kinds of law, he asserted, those proclaimed by the sovereign and those appertaining to the kingdom. The latter, he told the king, were immutable and inviolable, and they controlled, among other things, the succession to the throne.

In thus supporting the customary concept of the fundamental nature of the law of succession at the expense of that governing the king's religion, the Parlement apparently made its own attitude clear, though events were to show that the court's position was not as firm as it seemed to be at this time. The President also used this opportunity to make a further attempt at consolidating his court's political role by claiming that its right freely to

[1] Weill, op. cit., 202–3.

[2] Glasson, *Le Parlement de Paris*, I, 42–3; Weill, op. cit., 204.

register royal edicts was also a fundamental law.[1] In so doing, he seemed to be elevating the Parlement's function to a completely new level by demanding for it a constitutional status which it had never possessed. In less troubled times, the government would have reacted very vigorously against such a suggestion, but the monarchy's position was becoming more critical with each succeeding month. The Parlement's attitude in general, however, was one of complete loyalty to the crown. Even this last exaggerated claim, when viewed in the context of kingship under the law and of the Parlement's long struggle to maintain its political role, lost much of its menace. It certainly did not reflect a new attitude to the monarchy; on the contrary, in supporting the secular and spiritual independence of the monarchy, the court was entirely faithful to its own legal precedents.

The pace of events in Paris, however, was quickening as the League, with the help of the mob, strengthened its hold over the capital. The climax came in May 1588, the Day of the Barricades, when Henry III and his mercenary troops were driven out of the city by the Duc de Guise and his supporters. Having become effective chief in the capital, Guise tried in vain to win over the Parlement. In a dignified and noble speech, the First President, Harlay, firmly rejected his overture: 'My company,' he told the duke, 'is founded on the fleurs-de-lis and since it has been established by the king it can only function in his service; we would all rather sacrifice our lives than consent to act in a different manner'.[2] Shortly afterwards, the court sent a delegation to the fugitive Henry III which returned with royal instructions, authorizing the Parlement to continue dispensing justice on the king's behalf. At this point it seemed that the magistrates were entirely united in their support for the king, and in their antipathy to the League. But this façade was about to crumble.

In reality not all the magistrates were willing to support the accession of the Huguenot champion, even though he was the legitimate heir. The crucial choice between legitimacy and catholicity – both until this time basic attributes of the French monarchy – had not been universally resolved in their minds in favour of the former and that fact weakened the Parlement's resolve to have no truck with the League, whose avowed aim was to extirpate Protestantism in France. The Duc de Guise now began to play upon this potential rift in the court by persuading the mayor, aldermen and leading civic figures to put pressure upon the magistrates

[1] Lemaire, *Les Lois Fondamentales*, 148–9.
[2] Glasson, *Le Parlement de Paris*, I, 46–7.

to join the League, at the same time inciting the Parisian mob to make suitably threatening gestures outside the Palais de Justice. In July 1588 the Parlement yielded and published its opposition to Henry of Navarre, denying his right to succeed to the throne. Meanwhile, the king offered to summon another meeting of the Estates-General, which broke up in disorder at the end of the year after the assassination, at royal instigation, of the Duc de Guise and his brother, the cardinal of Lorraine.[1]

This latest bloody act ushered in the final stages of the civil wars and also brought the Parlement's dilemma to its most cruel stage. There was no doubt now that support for the League meant not only implacable hostility to Henry of Navarre and the Huguenots; it also constituted an act of rebellion against Henry III. The king had shown himself incapable of eliminating the Huguenot threat and had been virtually replaced, therefore, by the Guises and their candidate for the throne, the Cardinal de Bourbon, uncle of Henry of Navarre. Henry III's connivance in the murder of the Guises only drove the League's supporters further along their rebellious path. Until this moment the Parlement, whilst rejecting the Protestant heir, had with some success maintained its loyalty to the king. Now it was to be called upon unequivocally to oppose the king and to rebel against the legitimate sovereign. Magistrates who had been willing to denounce Henry of Navarre would not go so far as to support the principle of deposition against a king who had shown himself insufficiently hostile towards his Huguenot subjects. Such a principle was not only without precedent – the problem was after all a novel one – but it tended towards the destruction of monarchical authority as the Parlement had always understood it. Besides, behind the frail figure of the old Cardinal de Bourbon, already a prisoner in the hands of his nephew, loomed the menacing form of Philip of Spain, who had long been intimately connected with the League and who cherished hopes that one day the French crown might be his. If that were to happen, the very independence of the state itself, with which the Parlement's whole history was bound up, would be in pawn.

The rejection of Henry of Navarre possessed exactly the same implications but they were sufficiently disguised for those who took that step to baulk the real issue. When applied to Henry III, however, there could be no more evasion. A claimant's catholicity could not fix his title to the throne as surely as the law of succession, and if the latter were to be

[1] Ibid., I, 47–8; G. Picot, *Histoire des Etats-Généraux*, III, 83–151.

waived in favour of the former, the essential character of the monarchy, perhaps even the independence of the state, would be undermined. Possibly upon becoming king, Henry of Navarre would refuse to uphold the traditional faith of the country, and in that way equally reject the monarchy's ancient role, but such an eventuality was unlikely. Henry was well aware of the fact that as the Protestant leader he represented only a minority group in the country, but that as king he would have to satisfy the Catholic majority as well. Indeed, he had already given indications of his willingness to move in that direction.[1]

Such reasoning could only add to the magistrate's doubts in the days following the assassination of the Guises, and the authorities in Paris decided to take quick action before doubts could be translated into articulate opposition. The governor of the Bastille was ordered to arrest and imprison those magistrates who were suspected of being unco-operative. The First President was among those named, and a number of magistrates who were not indicated chose nevertheless to follow their chief into prison.[2] The remainder, entirely devoted to the League, continued to sit and act in the name of the Parlement of Paris. In March 1589 the king transferred the Parlement to Tours, a decision which in effect meant the setting up of a second, rival institution. In August, not long after nominating the king of Navarre to act as his chief lieutenant in the struggle against the League, Henry III was himself assassinated, leaving his Protestant successor, whose very existence had added greatly to the divisions in the country, to cope with the difficult task of reunification.[3]

Three days after the assassination, France's first Protestant king solemnly swore to maintain the country's Catholic faith, a gesture which had the immediate effect of rallying a good many moderate Catholics to his side. In Paris, the League Parlement registered a declaration proclaiming the Cardinal de Bourbon king, with the title of Charles X, to which Henry responded by granting formal recognition to the loyal court at Tours, now under the presidency of Harlay and numbering almost two hundred magistrates, in comparison with fewer than eighty who sat in Paris.[4] The new king faced a more critical situation than any French sovereign since the days of the English domination in the reigns of Charles VI and his son. The future of the monarchy was at stake, for its prolonged inability to

[1] *Mémoires de la Ligue*, III, 245.

[2] P. de l'Estoile (*Journal pour le Règne de Henri III*, 606–8), has left a famous account of these events.

[3] *Mémoires de la Ligue*, III, 300–8.

[4] Glasson, *Le Parlement de Paris*, I, 55–6.

provide law and stability and to represent the unity of the state was causing widespread disintegration, as a thousand local interests dissociated themselves from the body politic, while the revolutionary element in the Catholic League, which wanted no king at all, was gaining ground at the expense of the conservative aristocratic element. Provincial governors were seeking to make themselves independent; a faction in Dauphiné was considering the establishment of a separate state; small towns like St Malo were setting up their own governments in imitation of the larger ones; bands of poor citizens were overthrowing their middle-class officials in towns like Angers and Amiens. A pamphleteer, writing in 1593, noted: 'in time there will not be a single village left in France which does not claim sovereignty for itself.'[1]

The situation in Paris, the nerve centre of the League's activities, reflected the growing chaos in all parts of the distracted and leaderless kingdom. The rift between the committee of the Sixteen, representing the most violent revolutionary elements in the League, and the members of the Parlement still sitting in Paris grew, as the terrorizing activities of the former were turned increasingly against the latter. Whatever the magistrates' feelings about Henry IV, there was no doubt about their basic support for the monarchical principle and for the maintenance of the traditional social order, a fact which made them increasingly unpopular with the more extreme elements. In addition, the Parlement insisted upon following normal legal forms in executing its role despite the pressures from the Sixteen to condone partial judgments and to admit their protégés to seats in the court.[2]

The pope, Gregory XIV, added to the magistrates' discomfort by publishing a bull in March 1591 proclaiming the solemn annulment of Henry's claim to the throne and excommunicating those who continued to support him. The Parlement's strong Gallican tradition, under different circumstances, would have prompted the magistrates to reject papal interference in the purely French problem of the succession to the throne. That was certainly the reaction of the loyal Parlement at Tours which condemned the bull as 'null, abusive, seditious, damnable, full of impiety and deception, contrary to the holy decrees, rights, privileges and liberties of the Gallican Church'.[3] Henry's own reaction was to issue letters-patent reiterating his promise to maintain the Catholic faith in its entirety and

[1] Weill, op. cit., 256–8; J. H. Mariéjol, *La Réforme et la Ligue*, 342–3.
[2] Mariéjol, op. cit., 360.
[3] Ibid., 327.

emphasizing the dual threat posed to the French Church and state by the actions of Philip II of Spain and of the pope. Meanwhile the Parlement sitting in Paris welcomed the papal announcement, going so far as to include in its declaration the words, 'Our Holy Father, in accordance with the jurisdiction which should be his in matters relating to the preservation of the crown of France . . .', a phrase which sat uneasily upon the consciences of true champions of Gallicanism.[1] In fact, possibly because members of the court were becoming increasingly aware of the fundamental nature of the *volte-face* which was involved in their support for the League and possibly too because of the great friction which now existed between the Parlement and the Sixteen, the magistrates' welcome for the papal initiative was considered by many extremists in Paris to be only lukewarm.

In November 1591, the Sixteen at last acted against the court: the First President Brisson and a member of the *Grand' Chambre*, Larcher, were arrested and summarily executed.[2] It is uncertain to what extent the accusations of the Sixteen against the Parlement were based on genuine information, but there is no doubt that this brutal action had the effect of forcing many of the magistrates to face the fact that their conduct was undermining the very foundations of kingship in France and imperilling the corporate identity of the state itself. Although they were not yet ready to support the claims of Henry IV, they were not willing any longer to subordinate the interests of the French crown to the dictates of Rome or Madrid.

An indication of this changed attitude came with the Parlement's registration, in October 1592, of the bulls brought into France by the new papal legate, a registration once again accompanied by the traditional reservations in favour of the rights of the crown and the liberties of the Gallican Church. Even more significant was its attitude to the proposal by the League's leaders to summon a meeting of the Estates-General with the object of electing a new king. In an ambiguous decree of December 1592, the magistrates defined the role of the forthcoming assembly as that of declaring and establishing a Most Christian king, a Catholic and a Frenchman, in accordance with the laws of the kingdom. In addition, they insisted that, in accordance with precedent, their court should not be bound by the decisions of the Estates-General, but should retain its right to verify whatever conclusions were arrived at by that body. Therefore,

[1] Maugis, op. cit., II, 76.

[2] P. de l'Estoile, *Journal pour le Règne de Henri IV*, I, 135–7.

although a number of magistrates did attend this meeting of the Estates-General, which opened in Paris in January 1593, they made it clear that their presence did not in any way limit the Parlement's freedom of action. Thus for the first time in many years, the Parlement in Paris was regaining a position from which it could play a decisive part in shaping the country's fortunes, a development that was not lost upon some of the League's supporters: in February 1593 the papal legate paid a visit to the Palais in order to assure the counsellors of the pope's favourable dispositions towards them. He was too late, however, to turn back the tide of opinion in the court that was moving rapidly away from the position it had maintained for some time. Of the sixty or seventy survivors of the Parlement who were still meeting at this time, no more than ten were obstinate opponents of Henry of Navarre. Of the remainder, some were already convinced supporters of the king, and the others, if less enthusiastic, were no less certain of the direction in which their duty now pointed.[1]

The debates of the Estates-General only reinforced their conviction. Opinion was moving swiftly towards a reconciliation with Henry IV and, shortly after the meeting of the Estates had begun, it was agreed to accept Henry's suggestion that a deputation should be nominated to meet royalist representatives with a view to finding a mutually satisfactory means of ending the discord. The deputies met at Suresnes, in the first days of May 1593. Their conversations made it abundantly clear that only Henry's religion barred his way to the throne, since, in every other respect, it was agreed that his claim was far superior to that of any other candidate. Having achieved this degree of agreement, the archbishop of Bourges, speaking on Henry's behalf, chose exactly the right moment to announce, on 17 May, the king's imminent conversion. Realizing that time was short, the Spanish supporters suggested that the Estates should proceed at once to the election of a new sovereign, and they nominated Isabella, the daughter of Philip of Spain and the granddaughter of the French king, Henry II. The crucial debate began before the Estates-General on 20 June. Soon it became apparent that the Estates were neither disposed to elect Isabella without reservation, nor capable of resisting Spanish pressure altogether. At this critical juncture, the Parlement at last took the initiative.[2]

On 28 June the magistrates attended a plenary meeting of their court, a

[1] Maugis, op. cit., II, 95–9.
[2] Picot, op. cit., III, 241–2.

meeting which was to pass into history as one of its most famous sessions. The chief spokesman was Guillaume du Vair, a clerical counsellor, who later in Henry's reign became keeper of the Seals. In a speech of great power and fervour, he left his listeners in no doubt about what was at stake or about what the Parlement's attitude should be. The issue, he told his colleagues, was whether or not the Salic law, the first among all French laws, which for twelve hundred years had preserved the unity of the state by causing the succession to be handed down in the royal line from male to male, and which was the adornment of the kingdom and the guarantee of its security, should be preserved or sacrificed to the ambitions of a foreign ruler. If the latter were to happen, the French state would lose its identity and its independence. He begged the magistrates to condemn such a grievous step before it had been taken, reminding them of their obligation to defend the rights of the crown and the laws of the kingdom: 'Therefore arouse yourselves, Sirs, and display today the authority of the laws which are in your keeping! For if this evil admits of any remedy, you alone can provide it.'[1] It was an emotional yet a reasoned speech and it received overwhelming support. The court resolved to draw up a decree demanding that the crown should not be handed over to a foreign line and that the fundamental laws of the country should be observed. There could be no doubt now that the Parlement was firmly committed to supporting Henry of Navarre.

The magistrates' final choice had been made less difficult for them because the alternative had become increasingly untenable. There was no credible substitute for Henry IV, no Frenchman once or twice removed from the direct line; there was instead only a foreign princess whose claims, according to French law, were baseless and who could therefore be foisted upon the kingdom only at the expense of the law. Better than most, the magistrates knew that; they knew too that if Spain succeeded, the pope also would succeed and not only the rights of the crown but the Gallican liberties as well would be betrayed; they knew, finally, that their court was traditionally bound to defend them both. Therefore, the magistrates in Paris began at last to give more weight to the law of succession and to stress the need rather to persuade the legitimate ruler to change his religion than to reject him altogether on the grounds of his religious beliefs. Of course, they already knew of Henry's intention to embrace catholicism, but that knowledge only crystallized the change in emphasis which had been shaping in their minds for some time.

[1] Maugis, op. cit., II, 112; *see also* R. Radouant, *Guillaume du Vair*, 326–38.

The Parlement's decree had an immediate effect upon the Estates-General and upon public opinion. The power of the League was gravely diminished by this single act, and a month later with the news of Henry IV's formal conversion, its morale was totally undermined. When the Parlement reassembled in November 1593 it concerned itself with a number of measures intended to reduce the influence of Spain in France: it ordered all Spanish detachments of troops billeted in Paris to leave the country forthwith and protested against the replacement, as a result of Spanish pressure, of the city's governor. The desperate efforts of the committee of the Sixteen to stiffen the capital's resistance were countered by a *parlementaire* decree dated 14 March 1594, forbidding public assemblies under pain of capital punishment. Eight days later, Henry IV entered his capital and the unity of the kingdom was restored at last.[1]

The preceding decades of civil disorder had demonstrated very clearly that this unity depended totally upon the authority of the monarchy and would speedily dissolve if that authority were challenged. Because the king was the embodiment of the state, it was impossible to envisage one without the other, or to change the nature of one without similarly affecting the other. It is in this context that the Parlement's conduct, after its decision to ally itself with the League, is open to the most serious criticism. The dilemma facing the magistrates should not be minimized: the acceptance of a Protestant king would have placed enormous stresses upon a monarchy whose traditional role required it to maintain the Catholic faith and whose authority and prestige were so intimately involved with the fulfilment of that role. Even Henry's assurances could not assuage serious doubts about the results of such an acceptance. Where those magistrates who chose to support the League erred, however, was in failing to realize that, by opposing Henry III in the closing years of his reign and subsequently by refusing even to consider the claims of Henry of Navarre, they were propagating the anarchy and disorder which it was their primary function to dispel. They forgot that the hereditary principle was also a fundamental law which could not be overthrown without serious damage to the king's authority. Only when the pressure from Rome and Madrid became intense did they realize that their emphasis was misplaced, that they should acknowledge Henry's claim to the throne and seek to secure his conversion.

[1] L'Estoile, *Journal pour le Règne de Henri IV*, I, 387–95; Glasson, *Le Parlement de Paris*, I, 74–7.

It should be remembered of course that a large number of magistrates did oppose the League and left Paris to serve as members of the Parlement at Tours, either *en bloc* in 1589, when the rival court was established, or one by one, month by month, during the ensuing years. Ironically, however, it was the Rump Parlement in Paris that played the most valuable card on Henry's behalf with its famous decree of 28 June 1593. That action demonstrated once again the great weight and influence of the court's political authority, and underlined the dangerous consequences that could have ensued for the monarchy from the Parlement's lack of unity and from its failure, as guardian of the nation's laws, to take full account of their significance. When Henry IV's reign proper began, both the king and the Parlement had to live down the factious image which they had acquired in the course of the wars. It must now be seen what each of them had gained and lost in political terms *vis-à-vis* the other.

The reunification of the Parlements of Paris and Tours took place smoothly and with few signs of rancour, and the king at once showed himself aware of the importance of the court's right of registration.[1] But the financial state of the kingdom was desperate and there was a war to be fought against Philip II of Spain, so Henry was forced to have recourse to a number of novel measures in order to raise revenue, a fact which caused concern and opposition in the Parlement. In June 1594 the impatient king issued a *lettre de cachet* reiterating the pressing financial needs especially of his army, and commanding the court to register the various measures forthwith, measures which included a new tax on corn and the repudiation of part of the debt owed by the government on state loans or *rentes*. Otherwise he promised that his wrath would be directed against them no less fiercely than against the Spaniards.

Nevertheless, the whole tenor of the *lettre de cachet* made it evident that Henry accepted the need to obtain the court's registration, if the money was to be forthcoming; he had no illusions about the importance of its political role. Indeed, when the edict concerning the repayment of *rentes* was registered by the Parlement at the beginning of August, it had been greatly modified by the king on lines suggested by his court. In the following month, a whole series of financial edicts were sent to the Parlement, which, despite a variety of manœuvres by the king – *lettres de jussions*, threats of enforced registration, messages and audiences, promises, appeals in the name of the state security – were held up for months while the court negotiated with Henry a royal declaration, registered on

[1] *Mémoires de la Ligue*, VI, 82–4.

26 November, guaranteeing the inviolability of contracts concerning the payment of *rentes*.[1] Meanwhile the king's financial position deteriorated further. On 20 February 1595 he summoned a deputation of magistrates and told them simply, 'Your deliberations are lengthy. This delay does me great harm. You are not weighing sufficiently the results of a refusal. It will lead to the absolute ruin and destruction of my policies.'[2] Bitterly, he reminded them that if the Spaniards made inroads into France, they would not be halted or frightened by the decrees of red-robed judges, but only by the swords of the royal army. He offered to provide exact details of where the money was required and to what use it was to be put. Still the Parlement raised objections and agreed to verify the financial edicts only one by one, after prolonged resistance.

The critical state of French finances and of the international situation added greatly to the Parlement's influence and responsibility. In this situation both its strength and its weakness as a political force was apparent. Its strength lay in its role inherited from the Estates-General of vetting royal attempts to raise extra financial resources, querying the justice of additional burdens placed upon the subject and opposing the infringement of legal contracts already in existence. The Parlement was thus able to offset the danger of extortion and subject royal policies to criteria of legality and equity. That was its traditional and most valuable political role. Its weakness, however, was also revealed at this juncture. The king urgently required additional funds if the very real threat to the state's security was to be averted, and while the magistrates could find objections in law to his measures, they were not so well-equipped to judge the urgency of the situation on a national level. Only the king could do that and he was constantly thwarted by his court.

In the Parlement's favour it should be said that the concept of the state was still very much that of an association of groups and individuals, as Seyssel had described it, united by the crown, but by no means committed to a creed of complete subservience to the king's interests. In introducing a whole series of *ad hoc* measures, he was not automatically entitled to support without making out a good case for what he was proposing. In fact, his case was a good one – the fall of Cambrai in October 1595 was directly attributable to a lack of funds[3] – and the situation in which he found himself required as much emphasis upon his

[1] Maugis, op. cit., II, 246–51.
[2] Ibid., 252.
[3] Glasson, *Le Parlement de Paris*, I, 91.

ultimate authority as upon the limiting role of the Parlement. It was important, however, that he should exercise that authority in a legal fashion, if it were to be thoroughly effective and in that he did not altogether succeed.

Frustrated by the court's dilatoriness, Henry decided in March 1595 to rescind the declaration of the preceding November, guaranteeing the payment of *rentes*. Though in his straitened circumstances such a step was understandable, it was unwise, partly because it cast doubts upon the reliability of the king's word, but more especially because of the manner by which the abrogation was effected. The king chose as his instrument a simple *arrêt de conseil*, lacking the weight and formality of the original declaration, which had been verified by the court. To allow such a solemn piece of legislation to be annulled by an *ad hoc* decision of the King's Council would make the law a plaything of the government, deprived of its dignity and consequently of its effectiveness. It was not the first time that the magistrates had made such points to the sovereign. On this occasion they were emboldened to annul the council decree with a decree of their own, on the grounds that the king's authority, by which the original declaration had been drawn up, could be harmed by such an irregular act. The king might well have interpreted the Parlement's action as an affront and a challenge to his legislative authority, but he chose not to do so, and his moderate reaction suggests that the court's point had been taken. Certainly, its opposition in this matter had more to commend it than its stubborn refusal to concede Henry's financial needs.[1]

Henry now decided to try another means of obtaining money, by summoning an assembly of Notables. Although the magistrates were well represented at this meeting, which took place at Rouen in the autumn of 1596, the Parlement as a body remained aloof and disapproving. Nevertheless, on 8 November, a royal *lettre de cachet* was sent to the court with an edict approved by the assembly of Notables, authorizing the king to levy a tax on all trading transactions irrespective of the privileges of individuals or communities. Henry demanded the Parlement's immediate registration without discussion, and indeed he had already begun to put the edict into effect. The magistrates at once expressed their opposition to a measure which the public would be expected to observe yet which lacked the trappings of legality. In February 1597, carrying on the battle, the Parlement issued a decree forbidding the execution of edicts which had not been registered in the court. Again, it was overstating its authority to the point

[1] Maugis, op. cit., II, 254–6.

of temerity, and again Henry did not react violently, partly no doubt because he well knew that his own provocative action had weakened the legality of what he was trying to do and partly because shortly after the appearance of the court's *arrêt*, Amiens fell to the Spaniards and the war entered an even more critical stage.[1] However, the fall and recapture of Amiens were the last significant events of the conflict, peace being signed at Vervins in May 1598.

The débâcle of Amiens added point to the king's criticisms of the Parlement's lack of urgency and understanding in dealing with requests for money. It also underlined one of the implications of the Parlement's growth in political authority at the expense of the Estates-General, that in certain circumstances it might no longer be sufficient for the magistrates to concern themselves with the rights of individuals, to reach decisions in their traditional leisurely fashion, on a narrowly judicial basis; they would have to consider the whole political spectrum. Their objections to Henry's financial expedients, alienations of the royal domain and the prodigal sale of offices in particular, were supported by formidable legal arguments, but they were arguments which baulked the most pressing issue. The magistrates' failure to comprehend the seriousness of the situation endangered the existence of the state itself, though their intention was quite the reverse.

After the treaty of Vervins, the king's financial obligations were reduced and friction between himself and his court diminished in consequence. On a number of occasions in the last twelve years of Henry's life, there were serious conflicts, but though the king resorted to the usual threats and insisted that the magistrates' function was purely judicial, in fact he continued to accept the principle of the Parlement's political authority. For example, in April and May 1604, the Parlement resisted five *lettres de jussion* commanding the registration of a financial edict dealing with the creation of certain offices in the *Châtelet*. Its resistance was all the more unrelenting since Henry had already acquired part of the money from the sale of these offices, without waiting for the court's verification. For his part, the king remained anxious to have the edict registered and a further order to that effect was brought before the court in June. The Parlement again justified its opposition on the grounds that such creations added unnecessarily to the public's financial burden. It gave way ultimately but its registration was hedged with qualifications that clearly indicated the court's disapproval and added to the edict an aura of transitory legality:

[1] Ibid., 259 et seq.

'de très exprès commandement et sur sixième jussion, après remontrances faites....'[1]

Incidentally, in this particular dispute, the magistrates showed an awareness of the lesson to be learnt from the events of the preceding years of war. Harlay, the First President, pointed out to the king that what may be justifiable when the country's security was threatened by a foreign power, had an altogether different aspect in peacetime. The general pattern of these years, as far as disputed financial edicts were concerned, was of the king cajoling or threatening the magistrates, sometimes succeeding, sometimes deciding to give way himself, most frequently seeing his measures suspended from one year to the next whilst he sought to persuade the court to proceed with registration.

The other abiding problem with which Henry IV had to grapple was that of religion. His attempts to reconcile Catholics and Huguenots had perforce been muted, whilst the war with Spain continued, but shortly before the signing of the peace at Vervins, the king signed, in April 1598, the celebrated edict of Nantes, guaranteeing the Huguenots liberty of conscience and the right to practise their religion publicly in certain prescribed areas of the country. As a surety against attack, they were granted a number of fortresses, some of them like La Rochelle and Montpellier being extremely formidable strongholds. As individuals, they were to be eligible to hold the same offices as Catholics and to attend the same schools and universities. Finally, to ensure impartial justice for them, the edict established in the Parlement of Paris a new chamber, the *Chambre de l'Edit*, consisting of a president and sixteen judges, of whom six were to be members of the Reformed Church, which would judge all cases in which Huguenots were involved.

Henry was far from sanguine about the Parlement's reaction. He knew that the magistrates as a body were not disposed to countenance the formal recognition of two religions in the state, however much their individual views may have moderated since the days of the League and he took the immediate precaution of appointing one of the court's most respected and eminent judges, Séguier, who was known to be inflexibly hostile to the edict, as his ambassador in Venice. Before sending his proposals to the Parlement he did introduce certain modifications, at the request of the French clergy, in particular he promised that the exercise of the Catholic religion in the Huguenot strongholds would be guaranteed and he restricted the calling of synods to those occasions on which his

[1] Ibid., 271.

express permission had been granted. Nevertheless, the Parlement's hostility was not tempered by these concessions and after a three-day scrutiny of the edict, the magistrates agreed, on 5 January 1599, to draw up remonstrances. Henry at once responded to this decision by summoning the Parlement to appear *en bloc* before him two days later at the palace of the Louvre. There he explained the edict of Nantes in terms of the urgent need for peace within the kingdom and called for registration in language alternately reasonable and authoritarian.

Negotiations between king and court continued for some weeks, including a second meeting at the Louvre, before the Parlement agreed to register the edict of Nantes on 2 February 1599. To obtain the magistrates' adherence, Henry had conceded that the *Chambre de l'Edit* should contain only one Huguenot judge, instead of six, and that the remaining five Huguenots should be allocated places among the chambers of *Enquêtes*.

The negotiations reflected credit upon both sides: the Parlement, despite its deep suspicions of the principle of religious co-existence contained in the edict of Nantes, was persuaded of the overriding national importance of Henry's proposals, whilst on his part the king recognized the need to procure the court's unforced co-operation if the edict was to have its maximum effect. The Parlement's prestige and authority benefited from the episode and in the sphere of political good sense its somewhat tarnished image was much improved.[1]

In the dangerous state of religious uncertainty persisting in the country at the end of the religious wars, the Parlement was as much concerned about the threat of ultramontane influence which had been growing at the expense of traditional Gallicanism, as about the problem of Calvinism. The court itself was partly responsible for the spread of ultramontanism, for in the days of the League its opposition to the claims of Henry of Navarre had made it an ally of the papacy, in its attempt to alter the French succession. Henry's triumph stimulated a revival of the Gallican spirit, for it symbolized the reassertion of independence *vis-à-vis* Rome as well as Geneva and the independence of the French crown was a basic Gallican tenet. The wars of religion had produced pamphlet skirmishes as well as military campaigns; political theorists argued over the rights of resistance to an oppressive sovereign, the merits of passive obedience, the ideas of sovereignty and of divine right, and not least over the role of the Gallican liberties.

The most influential statement on the latter appeared in 1594: Pierre Pithou's *Les Libertés de l'Eglise Gallicane*, in which the author, the

[1] Mariéjol, op. cit., 418–22; Glasson, *Le Parlement de Paris*, I, 94–9.

Procureur-Général in the Parlement, flatly denied that the pope had any temporal authority in France and insisted that even in spiritual matters his authority was strictly limited. Another jurist, Guy Coquille, pursued similar arguments, declaring, for example, that the French clergy owed obedience primarily to the king, not to the pope.[1] Against this background of legal opinion and reconciled with the king, it was to be expected that the Parlement would resume its role of defender of the Gallican liberties, which it had consistently upheld before the appearance of the League. In this context, it is important to examine in particular its attitude to the Society of Jesus and to the decrees of the council of Trent.

The Parlement's new awareness of its ancient responsibility was clearly indicated in January 1596 when it registered letters-patent lifting the prohibition forbidding candidates to go to Rome for the reception of benefices. It added to its registration the following explicit reservations:

> 'without prejudice to the immunities and liberties of the Gallican Church, the rights, prerogatives, pre-eminence and ancient liberties of the Crown and kingdom of France, and without the king or his successors being subject to papal excommunication, by which his subjects would be absolved from their obligation of obedience to their sovereign.'[2]

This was not only an echo of Pithou's recently published opinions; it was basic Gallican doctrine, already two and a half centuries old. In view of the court's attitude in this matter, it was to be expected that when the Parlement was asked later in the same year to verify certain papal bulls brought into the country by the cardinal of Florence, which implied that the decrees of the council of Trent were enforceable in France, though not yet approved there by the Gallican Church, there would be considerable opposition. And so it turned out. The bulls were registered with all the customary safeguards for the Gallican liberties and without approval of the decisions of the council of Trent.

Henry, who was extremely anxious at this moment to preserve his recently acquired accord with the pope, intervened to assure the magistrates that no papal bull would be considered binding in France unless it was approved by the whole Gallican Church and verified in the Parlement,

[1] Weill, op. cit., 244–5; the text of Pithou's treatise is printed at the beginning of Volume III of *Traitez des Droits et Libertez de L'Eglise Gallicane.*

[2] Maugis, op. cit., II, 281.

but insisting that that qualification was sufficiently catered for in the other clauses guaranteeing the Gallican liberties; there was no need to make any specific reference to the council. The Parlement, again revealing an appreciation of political needs, yielded to the royal request and modified its registration.[1] The court was once more firmly committed to its Gallican precedents and the fact that the king was willing to stipulate that *parlementaire* registration of papal bulls was a prerequisite of their acceptance only confirmed its importance as the traditional and chief defender of the crown's independence in spiritual as in temporal affairs, a role that it had temporarily abandoned during the years of civil and religious war.

The magistrates' attitude to the Society of Jesus, which included in its ranks the most eloquent critics of Gallicanism, became one of deep suspicion once the court had committed itself again to the Gallican cause. After the attempted assassination of Henry IV in December 1594, by Jean Châtel, a former pupil at the Jesuit Collège de Clermont, the Parlement took action against a number of his teachers, whose papers were found to express opinions in favour of regicide, and decreed that all pupils and teachers of the college, together with all other members of the Society, were to be banished forthwith from the kingdom as enemies of the king and of the state, guilty of corrupting youth and disturbing public order.[2] Henry did not object to the court's decree at the time, but in 1603, when his gratitude for papal support once again required him to make a suitable gesture, he introduced an edict permitting the society to re-enter the country. It was greeted with fierce and prolonged opposition from the Parlement and only eventually approved, when certain restrictions drawn up by the magistrates themselves were incorporated into the edict. They included a prohibition to establish houses without express royal permission and a curious obligation to provide a permanent preacher at court, who was intended to be a sort of hostage to guarantee the good conduct of the Society, but who frequently succeeded in becoming the king's confessor, thereby exerting a far greater influence than the Parlement had foreseen.[3]

By the end of Henry IV's reign, the Parlement had succeeded completely in the task of restoring its political reputation. Despite the king's authoritarian gestures, his threats and his menaces, he, more than almost any of his predecessors, had respected the political traditions of his court

[1] Ibid., 283–9.
[2] *Mémoires de la Ligue*, VI, 231–46; L'Estoile, *Journal pour le Règne de Henri IV*, I, 439–41.
[3] Glasson, *Le Parlement de Paris*, I, 104–6.

and relied upon it to help him to stabilize his kingdom. As a result, the Parlement was able to play its part in re-establishing the crown's independence and reuniting the country under one sovereign. But the Parlement's role had always been dichotomous: not only did it stand for the unity of the state under the king, it was also the guarantor of the privileges and immunities of all the king's subjects. Its jurisprudence was in part based on the recognition of such privileges, whether applied to local bodies, to groups or to individuals, secular or spiritual, and whether based upon customary law or upon royal enactments. In the purely judicial context, although the king might well raise difficulties from time to time, the court's jurisprudence provided a plain and obvious guide, but in political matters the situation was less clear-cut. With the eclipse of the Estates-General and of other provincial and local bodies, with the decline of seignorial judicial and political independence, the Parlement remained not only the surest guarantor of royal authority, but also the only body capable of opposing the excesses of that authority.

In the interests of a long judicial and political tradition of exemptions, privileges and immunities within the state, and of the limitations of royal power, the Parlement was bound to take the place of those failing elements. Yet in thus reaching the pinnacle of its political authority, the court ran into serious difficulty, for in Henry IV's reign it faced political decisions, especially involving finance, which demanded a wider grasp of affairs and a speedier procedure than the magistrates were able to provide. The king might be tempted, therefore, to rely solely upon a small group of immediate advisers, the members of his council, who had both the political expertise and the facilities to expedite decisions, and to relegate the Parlement to a merely judicial status. Such a development, if it were to take place, would certainly threaten the long-established concept of French monarchy which now depended for its survival upon the Parlement's ability to retain political authority. However, as the seventeenth century opened, the court was showing a good deal of political vigour and there were no indications that the king contemplated a radical change. Nevertheless, the events of Henry IV's reign, though they had strengthened the Parlement's political authority, had also raised some doubts about its effectiveness.

The circumstances of the king's death strongly underlined the Parlement's importance, for his son, now Louis XIII, was still a minor and a period of regency would have to follow. On the very afternoon of Henry's assassination, 14 May 1610, following the request of the Duc d'Epernon,

Colonel-General of the royal infantry, the Parlement announced that the queen mother, Marie de Medici, should exercise the office of regent, and on the following day the youthful king held his first *lit de justice*, to confirm and solemnize his mother's title. At this moment, the essentially judicial nature of the French monarchy was once more revealed, with the supreme court of law taking the lead in ruling upon this vital political issue. Nor was the magistrates' function a purely formal one. The episode not only confirmed but greatly strengthened the court's political power, for existing precedents upon the subject of claims to the office of regent were not particularly favourable to the queen mother, who in consequence leant heavily upon the Parlement's support. Indeed, her obligation was at once apparent at the *lit de justice* of 15 May, when she told the magistrates that she intended that in the conduct of affairs the king would be guided by their advice, which they were encouraged to proffer as and when their consciences demanded. After the king's death, the Parlement's prompt and efficient conduct had done much to dissipate the dangerous situation and its political prestige stood deservedly high as the new reign began.[1]

In view of what was to transpire, it is most important that the full significance of the Parlement's part in the inauguration of the regency should be appreciated. It was without precedent. Never before had the regent leant so heavily upon the court's support. Earlier regencies had sometimes been confirmed by the Parlement after the previous sovereign had intimated his wishes – as happened after the death of Charles IX in 1574. Frequently the office had been claimed as of right by the prince who stood nearest in order of succession to the throne. Sometimes it had been ratified, as was the case in 1561 after the death of Francis II, by the Estates-General.[2]

It was in keeping with the developments of the previous century that the Parlement should once more assert its superiority over the Estates-General, but the political significance of what it had done on this occasion was sufficient to convince the court that its political function should be both central and permanent. There was nothing novel about this conviction save the emphasis, and the new emphasis was all-important, for it could no longer be doubted now that the Parlement alone shouldered the responsibility for representing to the king the myriad rights and privileges of his subjects, for offering the only constitutional form of opposition to royal actions, for preserving the traditional balance of the French state.

[1] Ibid., 117–19.

[2] Lemaire, op. cit., 299–302; Mariéjol, op. cit., 153–4; Picot, op. cit., II, 188.

The Parlement was now more determined than ever to maintain its position, and the threat of serious conflict with the government came closer in consequence.

The court's first reaction after Henry IV's murder was to restate its opposition to the ultramontane ideas which had lodged in the confused mind of the assassin; to this end it condemned, in November 1610, the recently published work of the Jesuit, Robert Bellarmine, in which the doctrine of the pope's temporal supremacy over all secular rulers was proclaimed. The Parlement's action called forth bitter protests from the Papal Nuncio and the regent was forced to intervene, though not with sufficient effect to satisfy the pope's representative.[1] In fact, relations between Marie de Medici and the Parlement remained reasonably tranquil until the declaration of Louis XIII's majority at a *lit de justice* held in October 1614. However, such an air of tranquillity was not characteristic of the period, for the great princes, headed by Condé, had proved far from amenable to the regent's policies, and some five months before the king's majority they had made her promise to summon a meeting of the Estates-General in the same year at which their grievances could be freely aired. The Estates duly met in Paris, shortly after the proclamation of Louis's majority; they were disbanded in March 1615 and were not to meet again until 1789. The meeting was vitiated by the inability of the three Estates to reach agreement on any line of policy whatsoever, thus enabling the crown in the end categorically to assert its overriding authority.[2]

The attitude of the Parlement was thoroughly predictable: its frequently expressed belief that whatever the Estates decided required the court's confirmation made it adopt an independent and superior attitude. One of the issues upon which the Estates found it impossible to agree was the proposition put forward by the Third Estate that no power on earth, spiritual or temporal, could deprive the king of France of his kingdom. This proposition was entirely in keeping with the Gallican tradition preserved by the Parlement and the magistrates decided, therefore, in January 1615 to issue a decree of their own reiterating the opinion expressed by the Third Estate. The execution of this decree was subsequently suspended by order of the royal council on the grounds that the Parlement had no right to decide on matters under scrutiny by the Estates-General, but the court had once more made the point which it was shortly to underline more boldly,

[1] Glasson, *Le Parlement de Paris*, I, 120; G. Pagès, *Les Institutions Monarchiques*, 7–8.
[2] R. Mousnier, 'L'Evolution des Institutions Monarchiques', 58–63.

that as a political force it did not intend to follow the lead of the Estates-General.

The Parlement offered a hint of its determination to pursue its political role in March 1615, when it addressed to the king these words: 'Laws, ordinances, creations of office, peace treaties and other very important affairs of state are sent [to the Parlement] for discussion so that their merit may be weighed and reasonable modifications introduced *in complete freedom*'.*[1] A few days later, it summoned a joint meeting of the magistrates and the princes and peers, in order to debate what ought to be done for the good of the kingdom, in the light of the recommendations emanating from the recent assembly of the three Estates. Although the Parlement of Paris was also the *Cour des Pairs* and there was nothing irregular, therefore, about the composition of this plenary session, the court's decision to initiate political discussion in this way was certainly novel and suggested that it was now vying with the Estates-General in seeking to represent the nation.

One of the reasons for its intervention at this stage was the recommendation of the three Estates, already accepted in principle by the crown, that sale of office and the ability to make office hereditary should be abolished. This decision directly affected the magistrates who were strongly antagonistic to the idea of losing the independence which the purchase of an hereditary office afforded them. Indeed, that sense of independence, strengthened by the introduction of the *paulette* in 1604, helps to explain the self-confidence of their latest political gestures. In an attempt to divert the court's opposition, Marie de Medici, who was still the effective ruler of the country, had a council decree issued on 13 May 1618, putting off any decision on the problem of venal and hereditary office for three years, but this conciliatory gesture had no effect upon the magistrates who, on 22 May, presented a long list of remonstrances complaining about a variety of quite different matters.[2]

In the first place, they asserted the Parlement's right to play a part in public affairs. They repudiated the implication contained in the First and Second Estates' attitude towards papal authority, that the king in certain circumstances should be deprived of his sovereignty. They denounced the introduction into the royal council of favourites, whose presence there did not serve the best interests of the state, and the excessive influence among

* Author's italics.

[1] Glasson, *Le Parlement de Paris*, I, 123.

[2] J. H. Mariéjol, *Henri IV et Louis XIII*, 179–82.

the clergy of the Papal Nuncio. They complained against instances of justice being flouted, of trespass by the royal council upon the preserves of the sovereign courts, of waste, extravagance and malpractice in the government's fiscal affairs, especially in the large-scale distribution of gifts and pensions. They demanded that benefices should be filled by worthy rather than ambitious men, that the edicts against gambling and duelling should be enforced and that the liberties of the Gallican Church should be respected.

These remonstrances in no way represented an attempt by the Parlement to inaugurate a new theory of limited monarchy; on the contrary, the concern with which the magistrates defended the king's independence against possible papal assault indicated that they retained their traditional view of the unshakeable nature of royal sovereignty. In most respects, the remonstrances reflected basic *parlementaire* dogma: respect for the law and its regular application and for rights customarily held. The court's dislike for the repudiation of the *paulette* for example, by the First and Second Estates, has to be seen against the background of law and custom: the edict had been regularly approved a short time before and it was the Parlement's task to enforce the law. It is all too easy to view individual privileges from the standpoint of the central government rather than from the genuinely detached position adopted by contemporaries. Of course these remonstrances were extraordinary, both in their scope and in the manner of their appearance, prompted by no prior royal legislation and lacking royal consent. They were much more reminiscent in style and content of petitions emanating from the Estates-General, and this was in fact the first occasion on which the Parlement's role clearly comprehended that of the Estates as well. These remonstrances have been accurately described as '*de véritables cahiers des Etats-Généraux*'.[1]

Yet there is nothing even in this to suggest that the Parlement's intention was innovatory. Its own obligation was to defend the multifarious rights of the French nation, to preserve, in other words, the traditional concept of kingship, limited by the law, a law which protected the subject's property, whether in the form of land or privilege or office. Although this function certainly involved the Parlement in political affairs, there were many political matters which, within the customary framework, were considered the concern of other institutions, notably of the Estates-General. The latter was concerned with the Parlement in enforcing another ancient limitation upon the monarchy, that involving

[1] Glasson, *Le Parlement de Paris*, I, 125.

the right to offer counsel. By the early seventeenth century, however, only the Parlement remained powerful enough to assert these customary values and in seeking to maintain them it added to its own essentially judicial role the political functions of an obsolescent institution.

The queen mother, however, was adamant that the Parlement was trespassing upon royal authority and a royal council decree duly appeared, condemning the court's action and declaring that since the Parlement's role was purely judicial it was not authorized to intervene in political affairs, unless explicitly invited to do so by the sovereign. This was a highly equivocal statement, which only persuaded the magistrates to renew their complaints. There were, however, other problems confronting the government, notably the revolt of the princes, headed by Condé, and Marie de Medici was persuaded that at this juncture the support of the Parlement was preferable to its animosity. Consequently, a veil was drawn over the dispute.

Shortly afterwards, the king set out for Bordeaux, where he was to marry Anne of Austria, the daughter of Philip III of Spain, having first charged the Parlement to watch over his subjects' loyalty during his absence. The court responded by solemnly forbidding subjects of whatever quality or condition to take up arms under pain of treason. Some eighteen months later, in the spring of 1617 the queen's favourite, Concini, was murdered with royal connivance, and Louis XIII, who took this opportunity to assert his own authority at his mother's expense, appealed to the court for advice as to whether any action was needed to justify the attempted arrest and assassination. The Parlement issued a declaration to the effect that Concini had been killed while resisting a royal order; in June 1617 it also condemned his wife to death as a sorceress.[1]

Therefore, in spite of the council decree limiting the Parlement's function to the purely judicial sphere, the court was almost immediately restored to a position of great influence and authority in political affairs. Whether or not the sovereign sought the court's intervention, the close relationship existing between political and judicial matters made it unrealistic to assert that the one could ever be totally separated from the other. It was no less unrealistic and provocative, of course, to argue that the Parlement had the ultimate right to limit the exercise of royal sovereignty, yet that was the theory propounded in 1617 by a magistrate in the Parlement of Toulouse, Bernard de la Roche-Flavin. In his *Treize Livres des Parlements* he maintained that it was a fundamental law of the

[1] Ibid., 126–31.

French state that without the Parlement's free registration, no royal enactments could be considered valid.[1] Such a statement echoed ancient ideas about the need for the king to act with restraint, but the new emphasis upon constitutional limitations, no doubt stimulated by the Parlement's prominence under Henry IV and especially under the regency of Marie de Medici, found little response in the court itself, where the traditional view of royal authority remained unshaken.

However, the conflict between these two extreme views of the Parlement's function helped to aggravate, and indeed was itself aggravated by, another antagonism which was now coming rapidly to the fore, that between the Parlement and the King's Council. This was not a new quarrel, of course but one which had been for a long time implicit in the court's political role. The Parlement and the council had been frequently at odds in the reign of Louis XI;[2] the magistrates had tried to influence the membership of the regency council when Francis I was a prisoner of the emperor; in 1597 they had suggested to Henry IV that he should choose his council from among men of known integrity from a list of nominees put forward by each Parlement. In the remonstrances of 1615 they bitterly attacked the introduction of favourites into the royal council, and in 1617 when they condemned the wife of their arch-enemy, Concini, they stipulated, with the king's approval, that no foreigner should henceforth be admitted to the King's Council.[3]

It is not difficult to find an explanation for the Parlement's attitude. The king's immediate advisers were responsible for day-to-day administration and, because the king was the source of law, he could make legislative and judicial decisions in his council, which represented *ad hoc* decisions often at variance with the court's jurisprudence, sometimes indeed specifically designed to circumvent *parlementaire* opposition, and therefore undermining, in the magistrates' opinion, the structure of judicial authority. The rivalry between the two institutions quickened about this time, however, as each of them sought to acquire greater control over political affairs.

Mention has already been made of the Parlement's efforts, with the decline of the Estates-General, to speak for the nation; the role of the council was also changing. No longer was it the sole preserve of those great figures, peers and princes of the blood and high officers of state, who

[1] B. de la Roche-Flavin, *Treize Livres des Parlements*, Bk XIII, especially Chapter XVII, 920–1.

[2] *See supra*, 187.

[3] Maugis, op. cit., I, 566; A. Chamberland, *Le conflit de 1597*, 12–13.

through birth or the dignity of their office were customarily entitled to advise the sovereign. The triumphant conclusion of the Hundred Years War had given the French king unequalled prestige, and from the reign of Charles VII successive rulers succeeded in underlining the monarch's pre-eminence. This emphasis – already referred to – upon the power of the sovereign enabled him to rely less than formerly upon the opinions of his relatives and of his aristocratic advisers, who had a vested interest in limiting his freedom of action.

Instead, he employed private secretaries, whose role grew in political significance, especially after 1547, when Henry II established the office of secretary of state.[1] The traditional advisers were not replaced but the secretaries represented the kernel of the bureaucratic conciliar organization that was to be established during the reigns of Louis XIII and his successor. In the sixteenth century the importance of the office of secretary depended largely upon the personality of the holder, and some men – notably Villeroy, who served four kings as secretary of state – succeeded in raising the office to a position of very great authority. These new administrators, emerging from middle class or lesser noble backgrounds to pursue influential political careers in the King's Council, were unlikely to be popular with the magistrates in the Parlement, who were also trying, at precisely the same time, to extend their own political power. From their point of view, these men, whose only interest was to serve the king, were bound in consequence to increase the dangers of unbridled royal authority. They represented a shield behind which the king could shelter from the admonitions of his customary advisers and such a novel development was anathema to the traditionalists in the Parlement.

For their part, the new men in the King's Council could have little patience with the Parlement's cumbersome political machinery, the inadequacy of which had been revealed on more than one occasion during the reign of Henry IV. Certainly, an administrator like Villeroy, who had played a considerable part in the reconstruction of the kingdom after the religious wars and had seen at first hand the grave problems created for the king by the Parlement's reluctance to subordinate legality to political necessity, was likely to encourage his last royal master, Louis XIII, to rely less upon his Parlement in such matters, than upon his council. Increasingly, as the king consolidated his control over the state, the chief cause of tension in the kingdom was to become the struggle between two

[1] The development of this office and the careers of the early office-holders have been traced by N. M. Sutherland, *The French Secretaries of State in the Age of Catherine de Medici.*

opposite needs, that of the sovereign to take whatever political measures were deemed necessary by his professional advisers and that of the Parlement, which sought to maintain the king in his obligation to respect the law. The crown's future was to be bedevilled by the pull of these opposite forces and ultimately its inability to solve the dilemma was to decide its fate.[1]

The first trial of strength between the court and the new-style council came with the rise to power of Cardinal Richelieu. His lengthy period of office coincided with a time of great international tension, when the chief concern of the king's ministers was to eliminate the grave threat of Habsburg encirclement. In such critical circumstances, it was not surprising that the cardinal should stridently proclaim the needs of the state at the expense of the subjects' rights, especially since the recent reign of Henry IV provided numerous examples of the risks involved in rejecting prompt government action in the name of traditional liberties.[2] Richelieu, therefore, was hostile to the Parlement and was prepared to circumscribe its political power. He could scarcely hope to achieve that end, however, without also damaging its judicial authority, thus clearly exposing the arbitrariness of his own policy. Thus, in October 1624, Richelieu established a special court to deal with administrators accused of financial malpractice, before which he also arraigned some of his political enemies, secure in the knowledge that they would be found guilty. The decisions of this irregular and partial body were grounded not in the law, but in what the cardinal considered to be the needs of the state.[3]

More notorious still was Richelieu's establishment in September 1631 of the *Chambre de l'Arsenal*, another extraordinary commission intended to judge certain crimes, counterfeiting and the removal of money from the country, in which state security was involved. Notwithstanding the Parlement's refusal to register the royal edict creating the new court, it commenced its proceedings and began to produce verdicts which paid no regard to established legal practices. The Parlement drew up a series of remonstrances pointing out the irregularities involved in the procedure adopted at the *Arsenal* and the harm done to the king's justice. Its complaints were in vain, for Louis XIII confirmed the commission's authority and forbade his court to discuss the matter further.

Not only was the Parlement's judicial authority being damaged; its

[1] R. Mousnier, 'Le Conseil du Roi', 60–7.
[2] Richelieu, *Testament Politique*, 247–9; 330–3.
[3] Glasson, *Le Parlement de Paris*, I, 133–4.

political role was also coming under attack. Over two years before the establishment of the *Chambre de l'Arsenal*, the keeper of the Seals, Marillac, had warned the magistrates that their task was to dispense justice to individual Frenchmen, not to concern themselves with matters of state while the celebrated Code Michaud of 1629 specified that remonstrances had to be made within two months of receiving proposed royal legislation after which time registration was to be automatic. In May 1631, a council decree was published expressly forbidding the Parlement to deliberate upon royal declarations involving political matters, a prohibition repeated personally to the magistrates by Châteauneuf, who had succeeded Marillac as keeper of the Seals in the previous year. Shortly afterwards, in January 1632, in response to the Parlement's remonstrances against the setting up of the extraordinary commission of the *Arsenal*, the king summoned a deputation of magistrates to Metz and informed them himself: '*Vous n'êtes établis que pour juger entre maître Pierre et maître Jean.*'[1]

But in fact, as in the case of the *Chambre de l'Arsenal*, the Parlement's judicial authority frequently involved it in political affairs, and in seeking to curtail its involvement in the latter, Richelieu was damaging both its judicial role and also the fundamental idea that French government was based upon respect for the law. An example of this sort of arbitrariness in action was provided in the aftermath of the Duc de Montmorency's unsuccessful revolt in Languedoc, when, in January 1633, the king deferred to judgment by the Parlement the case of one of its own members, who had supported the rebellion and subsequently taken refuge abroad. In his absence he was condemned to perpetual banishment and deprived of his office in the court. Louis claimed the right to dispose of the office at once, although both the great ordinances of Moulins and Blois had stipulated that five years should elapse before the king could exercise that right. The Parlement refused to give in on this point of law. One of the presidents *à mortier*, Mesmes, had been largely responsible for persuading the magistrates to remain firm and in March 1633 he received orders to leave Paris within twenty-four hours and go to Blois, where he was to remain during the king's pleasure. In April Louis held a *lit de justice* to register a declaration waiving the five-year interval and ending the Parlement's opposition.

The friction between the government and the Parlement reached a climax in 1635 when the outbreak of war with Spain forced the king to seek further financial resources. He chose the established method of selling offices, holding another *lit de justice* in December 1635 for the registration

[1] Ibid., 144.

of a number of edicts creating new offices, twenty-four of them in the Parlement itself. After a judicious speech by the *Avocat-Général* deploring the corruption consequent upon the multiplication of offices, yet recognizing the urgent military needs of the kingdom, all the edicts were registered. A little later, however, the members of the *Enquêtes* tried in vain to persuade the First President to summon a plenary session of the court to discuss them further. The First President, backed by the king, resolutely refused to give in to the repeated demands of the *Enquêtes* and the dispute culminated in the arrest and exile of a number of the most outspoken counsellors in January 1636. The members of the *Enquêtes* reacted to this measure by ceasing altogether to dispense justice from January until March, when peace between the king and his Parlement was finally restored. The *Enquêtes* emerged from this conflict with some cause for satisfaction, because the king agreed to reinstate the exiled magistrates and to reduce the number of new offices in the Parlement from twenty-four to seventeen.[1]

It is worth considering the significance of this dispute in a little more detail. When judged against the financial needs of the state at war it may appear that the attitude adopted by the members of the *Enquêtes* was unreasonable. However, such a view would gravely oversimplify the situation. Offices were an investment and no investor could be expected to welcome a move that would undermine his own financial assets, particularly in a society which by no means accepted the view that the requirements of the central government took precedence over the rights and property of the individual. In other words, the issue was once again that of whether the king had the authority to poach, in the name of state necessity, upon areas which traditionally he was expected to preserve from trespass.

However, there was something more involved as well. Not for the first time since Richelieu had come to power, the king had been persuaded to abuse his authority, to resort to arbitrary decisions, in order to achieve his aims. In the first place, he had ordered the controversial edicts to be registered unread, at the *lit de justice*, so that the magistrates did not know what in fact they were verifying and subsequently he had forbidden all discussion on the subject. This sort of arbitrary conduct on the part of the king's government was always likely to cause friction so long as the idea persisted that the authority of the king derived its justification from the authority of the law.

[1] Mariéjol, *Henri IV et Louis XIII*, 395–7.

Another similar conflict broke out in 1638, presaged by the bitter complaints of investors in Paris at the government's latest reduction in the payment of *rentes*. Again, the magistrates protested at the violation of valid contracts overthrown in the cause of the government's financial needs. Five counsellors were exiled from the capital and another judicial strike ensued before the Parlement gave way, this time without extracting any concessions from the king. Early in 1640, two more magistrates were exiled after the Parlement had again opposed an edict creating more new offices.

Richelieu was becoming increasingly intolerant of magisterial opposition and in February 1641 the king came to the Palais to hold a *lit de justice* at which an edict was registered defining and drastically curtailing the court's political rights. The Parlement was categorically forbidden to concern itself with affairs of state and ordered to confine its attention solely to judicial matters. Edicts and declarations relating to the government of the kingdom were to be published and registered without prior deliberation, although the magistrates were still to be allowed to complain about financial measures.

Immediately after the registration of this restrictive edict, the *Procureur-Général*, Molé, was appointed to the vacant office of First President, but only after satisfying Richelieu's condition that he should guarantee in writing not to permit any plenary sessions of the court to be held under his presidency. Faced with such ruthless tactics, from this time until the cardinal's death in December 1642, the Parlement was persuaded to acknowledge its impotence.[1]

Yet this arbitrary aspect of royal policy under Louis XIII is only half the story. No attempt was made in this reign to alter fundamentally the role or the nature of the monarchy. The king, who remained indisputably in control of affairs for all Richelieu's authority, was well aware of the various rights of his subjects, both individual and corporate. He recognized their validity though he overrode them when necessity demanded. For the most part, however, he insisted that they should be respected.[2] He knew too that the king should not place fresh burdens upon his people without strong justification. Thus his chancellor explained to the Parlement the king's motives for creating new offices:

[1] Ibid., 398–400; Glasson, *Le Parlement de Paris*, I, 164–71; Isambert, *Recueil des Anciennes Lois Françaises*, XVI, 529–35.

[2] O. Ranum, *Richelieu and the Councillors of Louis XIII*, 14.

> The king was well aware of the great expenses with which the people of his kingdom were burdened; he regretted that they had been imposed and that they were continuing; but the well-being of the state and the preservation of his kingdom had forced him to act thus, and of the mildest remedies available he had been advised to create new offices, which would not seriously strain his finances or seriously trouble the people.[1]

Nor was this traditional attitude always contradicted in the government's relations with the Parlement. Dramatic interventions against the court were few and far between, and for the most part the king and Richelieu left to their lieutenants the task of negotiating with the magistrates over the problems raised by royal enactments sent to the Parlement for registration.[2] Despite occasional dogmatic denials of the court's political role, therefore, in practice it was usually accepted and respected; indeed, both the king and his chief minister considered the Parlement important enough to require them to keep constantly in touch with its changing moods.

Even when rigorous measures were undertaken against the magistrates they were usually followed by a conciliatory gesture: in 1632, for example, the king lifted the suspension upon a number of counsellors who had opposed his policy over the establishment of the *Chambre de l'Arsenal*; in 1636 he reduced the number of new *parlementaire* offices from twenty-four to seventeen. But the most striking example of the government's unwillingness to pursue a genuinely novel policy towards the Parlement is to be found in the edict of 1641, which, it is generally assumed, was intended to break finally the court's political authority. In the first place, remonstrances were still in order on financial matters and a close scrutiny of the edict's clauses reveals that they were also permitted on all legislation registered in the king's presence at a *lit de justice*. In addition, there were provisions for repeated remonstrances in certain circumstances and the edict explicitly mentioned the Parlement's right to discuss political affairs if asked to do so by the king.

In other words, the king sought on the one hand to reduce the Parlement to the status of a judicial court, and on the other he continued to recognize that it was far more than that. This was not a new departure in the relations between the sovereign and his chief magistrates. The tension

[1] Ibid., 14, *n.* 3.
[2] Ibid., 132.

brought about by the clash between the needs of the central government and the rights of the subject was not new either, but it was exacerbated by the growing demands of the former and in particular by the fact that these demands were still being contained within the traditional political framework. Because of that fact, some of Richelieu's measures were clearly revealed as arbitrary, and the tension already existing between the two conflicting tendencies in the state was greatly increased thereby.

Shortly after the cardinal's death, the king once more acknowledged the Parlement's authority in important affairs of state, by requesting it to register a declaration naming the queen mother as regent in the event of his early death, and a second declaration pardoned and restored the offices of five of the court's members who had been exiled from Paris in 1641 for their opposition to government policy. Both declarations were registered in April 1643, less than a month before the king's death.[1] When Louis XIV succeeded his father on 14 May he had not yet celebrated his fifth birthday.

[1] Glasson, *Le Parlement de Paris*, I, 172–5; though giving little prominence to the affairs of the Parlement itself, V. L. Tapié (*La France de Louis XIII et de Richelieu*) provides a valuable backcloth against which to assess them.

CHAPTER EIGHT

The Reign of Louis XIV

Conflict with Anne of Austria and Cardinal Mazarin; the Chambre Saint-Louis; the Parlement's role in the Fronde; the Parlement under Louis XIV; the continuity of the monarchist tradition.

The early years of Louis XIV's reign were dominated by the Fronde, that series of civil disturbances which lasted from 1648 to 1652. The Parlement's part in these events, though clearly important, remains a subject for debate among historians. It has been variously portrayed – to cite only the extremes of opinion – as a revolutionary role involving the denial of absolute monarchy in favour of constitutional kingship, and a reactionary one, in which the magistrates' own narrow interests were alone at issue.[1] In fact, the Fronde was a complex phenomenon and neither the objectives nor the motives of those concerned are readily reducible to such simple formulae. What is certain, however, is that the Parlement's attitude cannot be assessed outside the context of its prior relationship with the crown, both in the immediate past and in broader historical terms.

It is preferable in the first instance, therefore, to examine step by step the problem of the deteriorating relations between the court and those who governed on behalf of the new and youthful sovereign.

At the first *lit de justice* of the new reign, held on 18 May 1643, the queen mother, Anne of Austria, assured the magistrates that she would avail herself of their advice, and, echoing the words of Henry IV's widow in 1610, she invited them to proffer whatever counsels their consciences directed for the good of the state. In return, the Parlement voted to amend Louis XIII's will in order that the queen mother should have sole authority as regent.[2] Although the court was not able, on this occasion, to play as influential a part as it had done after the assassination of Henry IV, it was given the responsibility of solemnly enunciating the conditions

[1] E. H. Kossmann, *La Fronde*, viii–x, 2.
[2] M. Molé, *Mémoires*, III, 56–65.

which would govern the regency and it did receive from the regent herself an assurance that its political authority would be restored.

It was but a short time, however, before the harmony thus established between the court and the government broke down. A council decree of March 1644 ordered that all occupants of buildings built in Paris, in contravention of a sixteenth century ordinance forbidding further construction within the precincts of the capital, should pay a fine fixed according to the area occupied by each residence. This measure, which was simply another expedient in the government's desperate search for revenue to promote the war with Spain, fell upon one of the poorest sections of the Parisian populace and provoked bitter opposition. On the face of it, the Parlement had little right to intervene, since the law in question did exist and had been approved by the court itself. However, the council decree went on to ordain that disputes arising out of this matter should be heard on appeal from the *Châtelet* by the King's Council, not by the Parlement. The magistrates saw in that decision to deviate from the normal legal procedure a continuation of the arbitrary methods of Richelieu's regime, so that when some of the victims of the decree appealed to the Parlement for redress, it was not unwilling to respond. Against a background of popular disorder in the most affected districts, those of Saint-Antoine and Saint-Germain, the magistrates sought to make their voices heard and succeeded to the extent that in July 1644 a second council decree appeared, reducing the total tax to be levied on the householders from eight million *livres* to one million. This satisfied the magistrates and helped to restore calm in the capital.[1]

This affair underlines the division at the very heart of the government, which had been deepening during Richelieu's time in office, that between the Parlement and the council, between traditional methods and concepts and the idea of state necessity. It is significant that the regent's justification for ignoring the Parlement in this matter was that the money was urgently needed and the court's procedure was too slow.

Having been persuaded to yield seven million *livres* of its expected profits, the government was forced to look elsewhere for funds. In August the regent warned the *Avocat-Général* that a *lit de justice* would be held early in September, at which an edict would be registered forcing the wealthiest citizens of Paris to lend money to the government by investing in new *rentes*. The Parlement deeply resented the element of compulsion once again introduced by the government. Not only was this a forced

[1] Kossmann, op. cit., 36; Glasson, *Le Parlement de Paris*, I, 185–91.

loan, it was also to be ratified in a *lit de justice* without any opportunity for prior debate. The Parlement reacted against this threat by claiming that there was no precedent for such an authoritarian act during a period of regency. In the words of Omer Talon, the *Avocat-Général*, 'it was an extraordinary and unparalleled act for a king who was still a minor to hold a *lit de justice* and have edicts verified by the exercise of his absolute power'.[1] This was a constitutional assertion of very dubious validity and a predictably extreme response, at a time when the Parlement's political authority was considerable, to the equally extreme and arbitrary measures employed by the regent and her minister, Mazarin. It did have an effect, however, and a compromise was arranged, whereby the *lit de justice* was abandoned, on condition that the Parlement would immediately nominate a commission to choose the unfortunate citizens who were to support the scheme. The queen also agreed that the magistrates themselves need not contribute, and the blow fell upon the financiers and wealthy middle class merchants. Because the government leant so heavily already upon the former, this measure, too, failed even temporarily to solve the financial crisis.

Meanwhile the Parlement continued to be assailed by requests for justice from householders who had been forced to make contributions by the council decree of March 1644. A number of *parlementaire* petitions seeking the restoration of the court's jurisdiction in this matter were rejected by the regent. The affair came to a head in March 1645, when the young counsellors of the *Enquêtes* and *Requêtes* demanded a plenary session of the court to discuss the issue, despite the regent's specific prohibition. Anne responded by exiling three of the chief malcontents and imprisoning a fourth. A period of strained relations between the government and the court followed, when each side was guilty of abusing its authority. The *Enquêtes* had flouted the regent's orders (though provoked in the first place by the arbitrary council decree), but the regent's retribution in the form of the summary arrest, followed by the exile or imprisonment of a number of counsellors had nothing to commend it either. The First President complained to the queen mother:

> The interest of public order is not served by the imprisonment of an officer of the king nor of any other person simply on suspicion and not according to established procedures, which enable the judges to arrive

[1] Ibid., I, 193.

at the truth of the matter and are intended both to avenge crime and to act as a guarantee against calumny.

In this instance, however, action had been taken '*sans plainte, sans information, sans procédure*'.[1] Nor was that the last of the drastic measures resorted to; the members of the *Enquêtes* and *Requêtes* decided in their turn to stage a judicial strike until their incarcerated colleague was restored to them. Not until 7 September 1645, when the young king held another *lit de justice* was the dispute temporarily settled. The two unpopular taxes of 1644 were both dropped but the magistrates had little cause for satisfaction, for in their place a series of new financial edicts, creating more offices and taxing various professions, were registered at the king's behest, without any opportunity for the court to examine them first. The king did promise to end President Barillon's imprisonment, but even that concession was frustrated by the president's death before he could be released.

In these first years of the regency, the arbitrary expedients of the government, its authoritarian methods, the magistrates' concern for ancient legal rights and also the bellicosity of the *Enquêtes*, all these factors were aspects of the ideological conflict about the nature and extent of the state's authority which Richelieu's ministry had helped to bring into focus. The issue was put succinctly by the chancellor at the *lit de justice* in September 1645 in his reply to the magistrates' affirmation that their consciences did not permit them to support the registration of edicts which they had not previously examined; he asserted that there were two sorts of conscience, one to weigh private matters and the other to judge the needs of the state.[2]

There followed a year of comparative peace between the Parlement and the government, a peace once more broken by the latter's pressing financial needs. In September 1646 a new tax was established, this time a duty upon merchandise entering Paris, either by land or water. It was intended to be a universal tax, applicable to privileged and unprivileged alike, and as such would certainly be resented by the magistrates on the grounds that it interfered with lawfully established rights. Here was one clear reason for their opposition, but there was another one, too, which contributed to persuading the Parlement to react against the tax, namely the fact that the edict was not sent to the court, but was registered instead in the *Cour des Aides*. In maintaining that a tax of such general application needed to be

[1] Ibid., 201–2.
[2] Ibid., 204.

verified in the Parlement, the magistrates had a strong case on the grounds of precedent. Their animosity was again aroused by the government's willingness to resort to other than traditional methods in the application of its policies. Such irregular acts, argued First President Molé, which are at variance with the ancient custom of the kingdom and the jurisdiction of its supreme court, cannot be considered sound and sufficient.

Comments of this sort, if taken out of context, might indeed sound novel, even revolutionary, but in fact they were firmly grounded in the magistrates' traditionalism, a traditionalism which also caused them to question the validity of extraordinary taxes raised to wage a war which was no longer necessary in the interests of national security and which aroused no enthusiasm in France.[1] Though this attitude was traditional, and though it was expressed in narrowly judicial terms, it was still deeply felt by the magistrates and to their mind was still of fundamental political importance. Mazarin failed to recognize that fact and his comment upon the Parlement's claim to register the new tax, that the court was concerning itself with trifles, deeply angered the magistrates.[2] It also demonstrated the extent to which the government's pragmatic attitude was threatening to undermine well established concepts.

During the long-drawn-out discussions between Mazarin and the court's representatives over the introduction of the new duty, the latter also attacked the appointment of royal intendants to administer the provinces on the government's behalf. The intendants, with their overriding authority in a variety of spheres, represented the same sort of threat to the existing order on the periphery of government as did the secretaries of state at the centre. As for the tax, Mazarin offered to repeal it if the Parlement could produce a satisfactory alternative. Its only suggestion, that the financiers should be the people penalized by new taxation, was rejected because the government relied too much upon their support to risk alienating them. Finally, the regent and her chief minister agreed to send the disputed edict to the Parlement, where it was registered in September 1647 with the reservation that it would only remain in force for two years, and only that long if peace had not been concluded earlier. This was a satisfactory arrangement for the court, for its right of registration was safeguarded and also the long-standing principle that additional taxation could only be a temporary expedient to be levied in times of extraordinary national need.

[1] Kossmann, op. cit., 38–9.
[2] Ibid., 39; Glasson, *Le Parlement de Paris*, I, 213–14.

The final act, however, in this particular dispute was the cardinal's: some weeks after the Parlement's decree was published, he had a royal council decree issued, annulling that of the court, though not quashing the tax itself. Once more, Mazarin was demonstrating his lack of respect for normal legal procedures. The remark of a nineteenth-century historian of the period, that the public, though still forced to pay, could now choose between two conflicting pronouncements on the subject, underlines the potential danger for royal authority of such arbitrary conduct.[1]

Almost immediately, however, before the magistrates could make an issue of this matter, the government decided to introduce yet more financial legislation, including the creation of twelve new offices of *maître des requêtes*. It was decided to register these various edicts at a *lit de justice*, to be held on 15 January 1648, a date which for some historians marks the beginning of the Fronde.[2] They single out this event as especially significant because of the speech delivered on that occasion by the *Avocat-Général*, Omer Talon. In a famous oration, he attacked the regent's decision to use a *lit de justice* as a means of avoiding discussion of contentious legislation. He claimed that *lits de justice* were traditionally concerned with great affairs of state and were occasions on which the sovereign could inform the magistrates of his intentions or seek their advice. The presence of the king was not considered a barrier to free speech until 1563, when the existing view was first adopted. Talon condemned in particular the preceding twenty-five years,

> 'when in all public affairs, in the feigned or true necessities of the state, this course has been pursued. [He went on:] And in fact, Francis I . . . having complained in this place of the difficulties made in registering certain edicts which ordered the creation of new offices, did not cause the letters to be published in his presence because he knew well that verification consists in liberty of suffrage, and that it is a kind of illusion in morals and a contradiction in politics to believe that edicts, which by the laws of the kingdom are not susceptible of execution until they have been brought to the sovereign companies and there debated, shall pass for verified when Your Majesty has had them read and published in his presence. And so all who have occupied our places, those great personages who have preceded us, whose memory will be always honour-

[1] The historian in question is A. Bazin, whose account of this period is cited by Kossmann, op. cit., 40.

[2] *See*, for example, P. R. Doolin, *The Fronde*, 3.

able because they defended courageously the rights of the king their master and the interests of the public, which are inseparable, have on like occasions cried out with much more vigour than we could possibly do; the Parlement has made remonstrances full of affection and fidelity. . . . You are, Sire, our sovereign Lord; the power of Your Majesty comes from above, who owe an account of your actions, after God, only to your conscience; but it concerns your glory that we be free men and not slaves; the grandeur of your state and the dignity of your crown are measured by the quality of those who obey you.[1]

It is most important that this speech should not be considered out of context, for it would be perfectly possible then to assume that Talon was propounding a revolutionary doctrine, that he was denying the king's exclusive legislative authority and therefore his ultimate sovereignty. This he was certainly not doing, as the final sentence quoted above makes abundantly clear. He was, however, complaining bitterly against the continuation of the government's authoritarian line, which had now caused it to invoke a formal and extremely solemn procedure in order to register a number of unremarkable edicts, to deny to the individuals concerned – mainly the *maîtres des requêtes* – the possibility of redress of any injustices contained therein. To the *Avocat-Général* this seemed a ludicrous excess of authority and the culmination of an increasingly arbitrary policy. What was significant about Talon's speech, however, was the fact that the tactics of the successive regimes of Richelieu and Mazarin had finally driven him to make some attempt at defining the Parlement's political strength *vis-à-vis* the crown. It was by no means the first time that the Parlement had reacted in this way to the government's adoption of extreme positions. Yet every move of this sort, from whichever side it came, was potentially a source of serious conflict, for the traditional French ideal of sovereignty lawfully exercised by the monarch could only function effectively when the boundary between the authority of king and Parlement remained imprecise.

The French constitution had never been rigidly fixed; its two basic components, the sovereignty of the crown and the rights of the subject, frequently moved in opposite directions, producing a dynamic situation necessarily less subject to definition than a static one. An overall equilibrium was maintained through the acknowledgement of the law as the universal arbiter. To attempt a narrower definition, to seek to establish a

[1] O. Talon, *Mémoires*, 209–12.

fixed position out of an essentially fluid situation, would invite distortion. That was the danger of the *Avocat-Général*'s speech, that in seeking to maintain his court's authority against the assaults to which it had been subjected under Richelieu and Mazarin he risked over-precision; and even though his remarks were along strictly traditional lines, they were likely to widen the rift which already existed between the Parlement and the crown.

The *maîtres des requêtes*, whose offices had been greatly diminished in value as a result of the new creations, were unwilling to leave matters as they stood, and they appealed for the Parlement's support. The latter decided, notwithstanding the fact that the edicts had already been registered at a *lit de justice*, to examine them in the customary way. This decision was taken on 18 January, and on the 20th the regent intervened. The magistrates defended their action by citing the clause of Richelieu's restrictive edict of 1641, which permitted the court to make remonstrances even upon legislation registered in the king's presence. They also pointed out that the edicts had a better chance of being obeyed if the public saw them accepted by the Parlement. Both arguments carried great weight. Nevertheless, the magistrates could scarcely have expected the concession which they were accorded: so long as the king's authority was not endangered, the queen mother and the cardinal announced themselves ready to allow the Parlement to continue its scrutiny of the edicts.

This vacillating attitude reflected the government's own doubts about the course of action taken and to some extent vindicated the arguments of the *Avocat-Général*. Talon himself was surprised at the change in government policy, commenting: 'It will render useless all verifications of edicts which the king may make hereafter, for this right of deliberation will bring with it the right to modify.'[1] Certainly, it seemed to deny the conclusiveness of the *lit de justice*, the very feature which had been its chief attraction for the government in the first place, but although the court could examine and presumably remonstrate upon legislation registered at the *lit de justice*, it was extremely doubtful whether it could introduce its own modifications. That was now the principal issue before the Parlement, and on 15 February without any great enthusiasm, for they were divided over the proper course of action, the magistrates decided to modify one of the edicts under consideration.

The regent reacted to the court's decision by demanding that the Parlement should state categorically whether or not it was asserting the

[1] Doolin, op. cit., 4.

right to alter an edict previously verified in the king's presence. If that were so, she would consider it an unprecedented and illegal act and would proceed accordingly. On the other hand, she was willing to consider remonstrances if the magistrates chose to present them. By issuing this ultimatum, the regent was carrying a stage further the dangerous exercise of seeking a precise definition of royal and *parlementaire* authority, already tentatively essayed by the *Avocat-Général.* The result, as she had anticipated, was to throw the magistrates into a state of alarm and uncertainty, and although some of them were ready to defend the court's stand, Talon accurately reported the views of the majority to the queen mother when he told her: 'They confess that they neither can nor should decide a question of this sort which could involve them in piercing the ultimate mystery of government.' The Parlement signified its submission by adding to its decree authorizing the publication of the modified edict the phrase, '*sous le bon plaisir du Roi et de la Reine*'.[1] A week later, the court returned to the fray by rejecting altogether another of the controversial edicts, but almost at once it retracted its position in favour of remonstrances in which it complained bitterly at the excessive level of taxation and the authoritarian handling of the court. The regent's reply brought no satisfaction for the magistrates, who nevertheless accepted defeat without further resistance.

By this time mutual suspicions had reached a high pitch. The government's unpopular financial expedients continued to provide the occasion for dispute, but on a deeper level the old constitutional issue was becoming sharper. Traditionally it had concerned only differences of emphasis; the danger now was that the scope for manœuvre might be seriously curtailed. Within a week of the Parlement's final acknowledgement of defeat in its dispute over the *lit de justice*, it found itself at loggerheads with the government again, this time with far-reaching results. Once more it was a financial matter which caused the trouble. Since January 1648 the office-holders in the sovereign courts had been awaiting the renewal of the *paulette*, the right to transmit their offices to their heirs. On 30 April this right was duly confirmed for the Parlement but not for the provincial *parlements* nor for the *Cour des Aides*, the *Grand Conseil* or the *Chambre des Comptes*. If the members of these courts wished to retain an hereditary claim upon their offices, they had to sacrifice four years' salary. This proviso simply disguised another of the government's financial expedients. Predictably, it produced a furious reaction among the officers concerned

[1] Talon, op. cit., 217; Doolin, op. cit., 6.

and the three Parisian courts having joined together to examine the implications involved, decided to seek the Parlement's support. On 7 May, the latter agreed to send deputies to discuss the matter with the deputies from the other courts in the *Chambre Saint-Louis*, and six days later it agreed to unite with the other three in order to pursue a common course of action against this latest financial threat. The Regent's reaction was to withdraw the offer altogether, so that none of the officers could be certain that the *paulette* would be renewed at all and to instruct the *Avocat-Général* to warn the court of her grave displeasure. On 23 May Talon addressed the magistrates as follows: 'to make of four sovereign companies a fifth without order from the king and without legitimate authority is a thing without precedent and without reason, the introduction of a kind of republic in the monarchy, of a new power which could pose a dangerous threat to the established government order'.[1]

Language of this sort was provocative, for though what the magistrates had decided to do was unprecedented, it had none of the revolutionary political undertones which the government was now suggesting. Only weeks before, when financial squabbles had led to a constitutional crisis of conscience, the magistrates had firmly rejected any innovatory notions. It was inconceivable that they could have undergone such a fundamental change in attitude in so short a time. Their method of opposition upon this occasion was indeed novel, though the Parlement itself had not been responsible for initiating the union, but there is no evidence whatever to suggest that the novelty was inspired by other than traditional aims. In fact, the Parlement's opposition was directed entirely against what it conceived to be another example of the government's abuse of the property rights of a section of the community in the cause of financial necessity, and was not essentially different from its opposition to earlier taxation measures. Of course, this meant that the Parlement was continuing to assert a political point of view, which was hostile to the dogmatic attitude of the government. As with the previous dispute, the regent and the cardinal once more over-defined as well as over-dramatized the situation. By seeking to cast the magistrates in a revolutionary role, which they had no intention of playing, they hoped to reduce their real authority to manageable proportions. The magistrates, however, refused to be bluffed into submission. It was at this point, though the court had no thought of leading a revolt against the crown, that the Fronde really began.[2]

[1] Talon, op. cit., 225.
[2] Cf. Kossmann, op. cit., 49.

Despite the summary arrest of a number of magistrates from the *Cour des Aides* and the *Grand Conseil* and a royal prohibition to hold further joint sessions, the Parlement insisted upon such a meeting, which was duly held on 16 June. Though the conference itself proved an anti-climax – the magistrates 'used this occasion to congratulate each other, without discussing any business' – that it took place at all is testimony to the Parlement's stiffening determination which had the effect of causing the queen mother and Mazarin to have second thoughts.[1] On 21 June they climbed down entirely, offering to restore the *paulette* to the office-holders' complete satisfaction, to release the imprisoned magistrates and to permit the assemblies in the *Chambre Saint-Louis* to continue, provided that the companies limited their discussion to their own private affairs. The offer came too late. Its effect was not only to demonstrate the uncertainty and weakness of government policy but also to underline how arbitrary had been the standpoint adopted by the government when the crisis began.

As a result, the Parlement was encouraged to press its own case further by insisting that in the assemblies in question it should be permitted to debate public affairs. The court had an excellent case to argue: its long political tradition, boosted during the preceding century by the decline of the Estates-General whose role it had to some extent adopted, had been confirmed as recently as the beginning of the regency in 1643 by no less a person than the queen mother herself. The Parlement was not making an excessive demand, therefore, but was simply seeking to redress the balance. To do so, however, it had to react against the excessive policies and assumptions of the government, without defining its own authority to the extent of distortion, and that would be possible only if a more co-operative spirit replaced the attitude of mutual antagonism existing between government and court. For the moment, the government was on the defensive; at the end of June the queen mother gave the magistrates permission to embark upon the political debates for which they were clamouring.

The first recommendation to emerge from these joint discussions, was that the office of *intendant* should be abolished, and on 4 July the Parlement issued a decree to that effect, revoking 'all extraordinary and unverified commissions' besides ordering the *Procureur-Général* to institute inquiries into the 'bad administration of the finances'.[2] Again the question

[1] Ibid., 51.
[2] Doolin, op. cit., 11.

arises of whether the Parlement was encroaching upon the king's executive authority. The magistrates argued that on the contrary they were defending legitimate government, a task with which the sovereign himself had habitually entrusted them. It was their old argument restated and for the moment at least the government was prepared to go some way towards meeting it. On the other hand, it could not view with equanimity the possibility of a series of independent *parlementaire* decrees. Mazarin therefore persuaded the Parlement on 18 July to accept a royal declaration abolishing the office of *intendant* in all areas save those on the country's borders, where military needs dictated its survival. In this way he was able to prevent the initiative from passing entirely to the magistrates.

The Parlement's hostility towards the *intendants* seems to have been prompted by judicial and financial considerations, the two being intimately connected. They were regarded by the magistrates less as the king's representatives than as agents of the unpopular tax-farmers.[1] Since the reign of Henry IV, the latter had acquired great fortunes by making loans to a government desperate for ready money, receiving in return the right to raise specific taxes for themselves. This practice was universally unpopular, partly because it invariably involved extortion, and partly because those being forced to pay saw their money going not to the king, but directly into the pockets of the tax-farmers. It seemed to many, not without justification, that the king and his kingdom were being held to ransom by a handful of profiteers. Hence the Parlement's fierce and unavailing pleas that new taxes should be levelled against the financiers.

The magistrates complained that the *intendants*, in order to secure a ready flow of money for the crown, put their authority at the tax-farmers' service. They also objected to the irregular institution of the offices: the regent herself acknowledged that the commissions of *intendants* of justice and all others not verified in the sovereign courts were forbidden by certain ordinances. Finally, they maintained that because of their liaisons with the tax-farmers, these royal officials could never act impartially in their judicial capacity; one of the presidents, Novion, called them 'partisans and contractors with a stake in the cases to which they were assigned as judges'.[2] The Parlement's antagonism therefore was compounded of its dislike of the financiers and its mistrust of extraordinary royal commissioners operating outside normally accepted judicial rules. These twin aspects of its opposition were grounded in the same fundamental attitude:

[1] Mme de Cubells, 'Le Parlement de Paris pendant la Fronde', 183.
[2] Kossmann, op. cit., 54–5; Doolin, op. cit., 11–12.

its hostility to the government's arbitrariness, both in its financial policies and in its methods of enforcement.

Exactly the same attitude motivated the other recommendations of the *Chambre Saint-Louis*, to which the Parlement gave its support, most of which were hastily turned into royal declarations by the harassed regent and her favourite, and promptly registered by the court. On 11 July, the level of the *taille* was reduced by an eighth for the years 1648 and 1649, and all taxes still outstanding before 1647 were waived; on the 16th, a *chambre de justice* was established, whose members were drawn from the sovereign courts in Paris and the provincial Parlements and whose function was to try any financiers accused of using violence to extort taxes, or of any other sort of financial malpractice. On the 20th the Parlement registered another royal declaration forbidding the levy of taxes for the future, unless they were authorized by edicts previously registered in the court. The magistrates decided on this matter to add a modification of their own, however, revoking all earlier impositions made in virtue of council decrees and limiting the effectiveness of declarations registered in the *Cour des Aides* and the *Chambres des Comptes* to two years, stipulating, too, that such registrations should not constitute a precedent. This modification once more threatened to take away the government's initiative in this protracted argument, and at first glance it seemed to pose a dangerous threat to the king's legislative sovereignty. However, that was not necessarily the case, for the magistrates' concern was with reaffirming a traditional emphasis. Nevertheless, the danger of over-definition once more loomed and could not but alarm the regent. More alarming still was the subsequent trend of *parlementaire* demands: the repudiation of all that the government owed to the tax-farmers, followed by the latters' prosecution.

The queen mother decided to cut short the Parlement's debates by holding a *lit de justice*, at which the king would solemnly confirm some at least of the magistrates' demands. In this way she hoped to persuade them to drop their more extreme claims. She remarked to her entourage: 'I shall go to the Parlement and scatter roses over their heads but after that if they are not prudent I shall punish them.'[1]

The *lit de justice* was held on 31 July. It was acknowledged in the preamble of the royal declaration that abuses had crept into government administration in the preceding years and that the Parlement's chief task was to authorize the justice of royal acts. The point was more explicitly

[1] Glasson, *Le Parlement de Paris*, I, 242.

made by the *Avocat-Général* in a classical exposition of traditional *parlementaire* theory:

> Formerly the king's wishes were never executed by his subjects without being first approved by all the great men of the kingdom, by the princes and officers of the crown; today this political jurisdiction is vested in the Parlement; our possession of this power is guaranteed by a long tradition and respectfully acknowledged by the people. The opposition of our votes, the respectful resistance which we bring to bear in public affairs must not be interpreted as disobedience but rather as a necessary result of the exercise of our office and of the fulfilling of our obligations, and certainly the king's majesty is not diminished by his having to respect the decrees of his kingdom; by so doing, he governs, in the words of the Scriptures, a lawful kingdom.[1]

Such a thesis was not unacceptable to the government, while for its part the Parlement was content to respect the assertion made in the king's speech, that all reform had to be initiated by the sovereign. As to the reforms themselves, the declaration went on to decree that encroachments by the royal council upon the jurisdiction of the sovereign courts were to cease; that the *taille* was to be reduced by one quarter; that no new taxes were to be imposed except by edicts 'well and duly verified', though the taxes then in force were to continue until circumstances permitted reduction; and that abuses in the administration of the *rentes* were to be remedied. In addition, the king assured the magistrates that the *paulette* would be unconditionally restored to members of the sovereign companies.[2]

The magistrates were by no means satisfied with this *lit de justice*: their modification on the subject of unregistered financial edicts was rejected, and some doubt remained about what the precise form of registration of future acts of this sort would be; also, it took no account of certain other recommendations of the *Chambre Saint-Louis*. In particular, the demand that

> no subjects of the king, of whatever quality and condition they may be, shall be held prisoner longer than twenty-four hours without being interrogated according to the ordinances, and given over to their natural judges, and the jailors, captains, and all other who shall hold them, shall be

[1] Talon, op. cit., 260.

[2] Molé, op. cit., III, 236–9; Glasson, *Le Parlement de Paris*, I, 242–4.

> held responsible for infractions of the law in their own and private names,

had been ignored.[1] Nevertheless, the queen mother had made great concessions. The whole tenor of the *lit de justice*, the acts emanating from it, together with the royal declarations promulgated earlier in the month, represented a drastic change in the government's attitude; it was now apparently willing to act in accordance with that ancient concept of French government of which the court was the supreme champion. This gesture it had made without seriously diminishing the crown's authority. The basis existed, therefore, for a reconciliation between crown and court. Yet the Parlement failed to respond. As its sense of political power grew, its momentum carried it beyond the middle ground of moderation and compromise; now it was the magistrates' turn to go to extremes again.

On 4 August, the most militant member of the *Grand' Chambre*, Broussel, demanded that the *Procureur-Général* should instigate proceedings against the tax-farmers on the charge of embezzlement, and that the Parlement should begin discussions upon those recommendations of the *Chambre Saint-Louis*, which had not been incorporated into the royal declaration. Realizing that her efforts at placating the court had so far been in vain, the regent deputed the king's uncle, Gaston d'Orléans, to attend the Parlement and speak for the government. This he did, pointing out that Broussel's demand concerning the financiers contravened the declaration establishing a *chambre de justice* specifically to deal with such matters, and warning the magistrates that their conduct towards the government would jeopardize the war effort, undermine the people's sense of obedience to the crown and destroy French credit abroad. His plea went unheeded. On 19 August the Parlement countermanded the article of the royal declaration by which only future taxation edicts were to be 'well and duly verified', substituting its own original modification to the effect that any such edict which had not been registered by the Parlement was invalid, save for those registered in the *Cour des Aides* or the *Chambre des Comptes*, which would remain valid for two years only. The magistrates refused to add to their decree the expression, '*sous le bon plaisir du roi*', which would have given it the character of a petition. Three days later, they issued a second decree inaugurating judicial proceedings against three leading tax-farmers.

For the government's reeling finances, still grievously overburdened by

[1] Doolin, op. cit., 18.

the demands of the war against Spain, these two acts together promised the *coup de grâce*. They also offered the most direct challenge yet to the king's authority, and for both reasons the regent decided to resort to force. On 26 August, two of the court's most outspoken judges, Broussel and Blancmesnil, a president in the *Enquêtes* and the bearer of a famous *parlementaire* name, were arrested.[1] The effect was immediate and dramatic. The poorer people of Paris rioted in support of the arrested men, and from the 26 to 28 August, the Days of the Barricades, the capital was in a state of disorder and confusion. The frightened regent was forced to release Broussel and Blancmesnil before order could be restored.[2]

With the advent of serious civil disturbances, the question must be asked whether at this time the Parlement was assuming the leadership of elements in society which were hostile to the established order; whether, in other words, the Parlement was placing itself at the head of a revolutionary movement.[3] There is no evidence in favour of such an idea. The fact was that the magistrates alone were in a position to offer a serious and legitimate challenge to the government's unpopular policies. They had opposed a series of financial expedients which oppressed various groups, office-holders, *rentiers*, affluent middle-class merchants and also the very poor. Their opposition was too universal for them to be accused of acting as the mouthpiece of one or other of these groups alone, and besides, it is evident that, though the magistrates' attack was directed in the short term at particular financial measures, in the long term it had a deeper traditional aspect.

This involved the Parlement's claim to speak on behalf of all the classes in the kingdom; it was not asserting any right of representation but only its ancient due to preserve and defend the rights and privileges of the various elements in the state. That was what President de Coigneux intended in February 1648 when he declared that the Parlement had been established by the king partly to authorize his legislation, 'in which the people's consent was formerly necessary, and now that of the judicial officers'.[4] It was what lay behind President Molé's speech at the *lit de justice* on 31 July 1648: 'Your Majesty some day would reproach us justly if, having been committed by you to employ all our vigils for the salvation

[1] Molé, op. cit., III, 250 et seq; Talon, op. cit., 261 et seq.

[2] R. Mousnier ('Les causes des journées révolutionnaires', 33–78) has analysed the role of the various elements involved in this episode.

[3] Mousnier (ibid., 55) describes the Parlement's role as revolutionary but denies that it stood at the head of a revolutionary movement.

[4] Cubells, op. cit., 174.

of your people, we concealed the ills of the state, the oppression of the officers, the dissipation of the finances, the despair of the poor people'.[1] Although it was not surprising, therefore, in the midst of extreme financial hardship, that the poor of the capital should revolt in support of those who had championed them, the magistrates neither instigated nor led the disturbances of those days. On the contrary, Broussel's first act after his triumphant return to the Palais de Justice on 28 August, was to propose a decree ordering the barricades in the streets to be pulled down. The Parlement was certainly helped in its argument with the government by the popular support it received, but it did not pretend to use that support as a basis for novel demands.

Nor could the more wealthy Parisians be identified with the Parlement; indeed, they were scrupulously careful to keep themselves apart from the fray. Even the narrow union of sovereign court officers, which produced the *Chambre Saint-Louis*, did not provide a permanent alliance, for the members of the Parlement very quickly asserted their court's superiority over the registration of edicts.[2] The Parlement's opposition, therefore, did not depend upon the support it gave to, or received from a particular social or economic group; nor did it have a revolutionary programme of its own, though its provocative conduct during the weeks of August contributed to the atmosphere of crisis in the capital. There is one further point. The concessions which the Parlement had elicited from the government at the end of July, prior to the Days of the Barricades, were not given under the threat of force. To the government's generally weak position caused by the minority was added an awareness of the fact that it was less able than the Parlement to justify its policies.

Having forced the regent to recall the exiled magistrates the Parlement was not disposed to lose the initiative thus gained. It decided, therefore, to pursue its prosecution of the tax-farmers. In the circumstances it was an impolitic decision, unlikely to lower the political temperature, though far less injudicious than the attitude now adopted by Mazarin: the familiar story of one excess provoking a greater was once more to be enacted. On 13 September the king and the royal court abruptly departed from Paris, and it seemed that Mazarin intended nothing less than a full-scale war against the Parlement, using troops under the command of Condé. Five days later two former ministers, the Count de Chavigny and the Marquis de Châteauneuf, who were known to have friendly contacts with the

[1] Doolin, op. cit., 75.
[2] A. L. Moote, 'The Parlementary Fronde and Robe Solidarity', 347–52.

court, were arrested. The next step evidently was to be the ordering of the Parlement out of the capital, but before that move could be made, the magistrates retaliated. On 22 September, they petitioned the regent to conduct the king back to Paris and the princes of the Blood – Condé included – to come to the Parlement to deliberate upon the decree of 1617, which forbade foreigners to take any part in government. A council decree was issued, forbidding any such discussion, but the magistrates were unwilling to shift their position and ordered the mayor to make the necessary arrangements for the defence and victualling of the city.

The magistrates' decision to attack Mazarin personally was not surprising; in a sense it was simply a recognition of the fundamental issue at stake. The cardinal represented a barrier between the king and his Parlement, a new and uncontrolled influence in the state. What they resented was not the fact that he was a foreigner but that his role was alien; that like Richelieu, his predecessor, he could not only use the evolving administrative machinery to carry through *ad hoc* policies, but that he could relieve the king of much of the actual business of government. The last thing that the Parlement was willing to contemplate was the removal of the monarchy from the centre of the stage. At this juncture, however, the attitude of the government suddenly altered. A conference was proposed between its representatives and those of the court, out of which an agreed declaration emerged which was registered in the Parlement on 24 October. This declaration represented further concessions on the government's part, on matters originally raised in the *Chambre Saint-Louis*. No new offices were to be created for at least four years, abuses in the administration of the *rentes* were to be remedied, the salaries of royal officials were to be safeguarded and reductions were to be made in the amounts levied from the *taille* and the *gabelle*. Other clauses again were not concerned with financial issues at all, but with judicial and jurisdictional matters. In particular, there had been a long argument with the government on the issue of arbitrary arrests. Speaking on the regent's behalf the chancellor had informed the court

> that there was a great difference between public and private justice, between the government of the state and the distribution of justice to individuals . . . in the conduct and administration of the state . . . it should be in the discretion of sovereigns to arrest those upon whom suspicion falls . . . in the government of states it is more expedient that a

hundred innocent persons suffer than that the state perish by the fault of an individual.[1]

Here was a clear statement of the doctrine of *raison d'état* according to which the normal rules of justice had to be waived if the interest of the state was involved. It was a doctrine which justified arbitrariness and which the Parlement had consistently opposed. However, the regent refused to give way altogether and eventually a compromise was arrived at and incorporated into clause fifteen of the new declaration:

> We desire also that none of our subjects of whatever quality and condition be treated criminally in the future except in accordance with the forms prescribed by the laws of our kingdom and the ordinances and not by commissions and chosen judges and that the ordinance of King Louis XI . . . of October 1467, be kept and observed according to its form and tenor; in interpretation and execution of which none of our officers of our Sovereign Courts or others shall be troubled or disturbed in the exercise and practice of their charges by *lettres de cachet*. . .[2]

Finally, the normal processes of law were to be restored and the irregular jurisdiction of the King's Council and of the various commissions appointed by it, was to disappear.

The declaration was not revolutionary. It was concerned in part with immediate financial considerations, in part with judicial matters and its basis was constitutional; it was entirely consistent with the Parlement's attitude throughout the regency period. The attitude of Mazarin, however, who was determined to interpret the Parlement's role as a direct challenge to the crown and to act accordingly, makes it easier for the historian to emulate the cardinal and to lose his sense of proportion.

Early in January 1649 the royal court once more slipped out of Paris and the Parlement once more took measures to prevent supplies being cut off from the capital. On 7 January royal letters-patent were issued, transferring the Parlement from Paris to Montargis. The magistrates' reply was to issue a decree of their own, ordering Mazarin, whom they called the enemy of the king and his state, to leave France forthwith. Royal troops encircled Paris: civil war was now imminent. What Mazarin intended was a repudiation by the government of all the concessions extracted by the

[1] Doolin, op. cit., 18–19; Kossmann, op. cit., 72–5.

[2] Doolin, op. cit., 20.

Parlement since June 1648. In order to succeed he was willing to resort to force and he relied for a quick victory upon the increasing isolation of the court within the capital.[1] In this he miscalculated, for although the city corporation refused for some days to support the magistrates, the rioting Parisian mob came to the rescue and frightened the municipal authorities into co-operating with the Parlement. Once this united front had been established, dissident members of the nobility including princes of the Blood also rallied to the Parlement's support. However, the tense situation thus arrived at quickly turned to anti-climax, for within a few weeks negotiations had begun between the government and the Parlement. Threatened respectively by the prospects of Spanish invasion and by fears of the militant Parisian mob, the government and the court agreed terms which were incorporated into the treaty of Reuil, registered in the Parlement on 1 April 1649, bringing the magistrates' Fronde to an end.

During this final stage, the Parlement was completely on the defensive. Mazarin bore the responsibility for prosecuting a policy which forced the magistrates unwillingly into acknowledging that a situation of civil war existed. In the critical weeks they carefully eschewed any revolutionary postures, making it clear that their antagonism was reserved for the cardinal, and in no way affected their respect and loyalty for the king. Their remonstrances of 21 January 1649 declared that

> it is always shameful for the Prince, and injurious to his subjects that an individual should take too great a share of either his affections or his authority, since the former should be communicated to all, and the latter belongs to him alone [and again,] It was necessary . . . to declare Cardinal Mazarin the enemy of Your Majesty and of the public . . . if we were to defend ourselves it should be notorious . . . that it was against a tyrant and not against our master before whose name we prostrate ourselves and for whom we have only sentiments of obedience.[2]

Here once more, in a nutshell, was the fundamental cause of the Parlement's opposition: the evolution of a system in which power was no longer directly wielded by the sovereign but was moving into uncharted and illegal areas. For its part, the court resolutely resisted the temptation when the siege was at its height to claim new powers for itself. It refused,

[1] Kossmann, op. cit,. 80 et seq.
[2] Doolin, op. cit., 73–4.

for example, to take the title of *Parlement de France,* which would have enabled it to extend its jurisdiction across the whole kingdom.[1] Proof of the magistrates' basic social conservatism is provided by their horrified reaction to the ugly mood of the Paris mob, which promptly persuaded them of the need to make peace with the regent.[2] The treaty of Reuil, confirming that the royal declarations of May, July and October 1648 were to be observed, represented a triumph for the Parlement's point of view.

Its triumph did not endure, however, for the diminishing prestige of the government now gave the princes their opportunity for rebellion, and a second period of civil war began. This time the Parlement's role, for the most part, was passive; the situation had passed beyond its control, and the magistrates' chief concern was to prevent themselves from being forced to support a revolutionary movement. Unwilling to pursue the battle and unable to stop it, the magistrates fled the field.[3] For three months, from March to May 1652, they resisted all Condé's efforts to persuade them to speak out definitely in his favour. Only at the end of July – when Condé controlled the capital – did the Parlement yield before the threat of force, and by then many of its members had left Paris or ceased to attend the Palais de Justice. By then, in any case, the Fronde was virtually over, Louis XIV entering his capital in triumph on 21 October. For all its attempted neutrality, the Parlement's antagonism towards Mazarin and its record of opposition to the government condemned it in the king's eyes and caused him to deprive it of all the hard-won gains of 1648 and 1649. At a *lit de justice* held immediately after his return to Paris he ordered a declaration to be registered, prohibiting the magistrates from taking cognizance of any matters of state or of finance, and from taking action against any person in whom the king chose to confide the administration of the kingdom; and declaring null and void all contrary measures taken previously by the court on these matters.[4]

In what sort of context, then, ought the Parlement's role in the Fronde to be judged? Was it a revolutionary role? By no means, for in its actions and pronouncements the court remained basically loyal to the idea of monarchical sovereignty, resisting contrary pressures both from above and below, from the princes and from the Parisian mob. It had no alternative political philosophy: the laws and traditions written into its

[1] Kossmann, op. cit., 95.
[2] Ibid., 111–12.
[3] Ibid., 238.
[4] Glasson, *Le Parlement de Paris*, I, 379–81.

registers made it an unlikely candidate to seek to undermine the crown's authority.

Nor does it seem to be the case during the Fronde that the Parlement acted as the spokesman for one class of society or another. The evidence points rather to the continuing isolation of the court for a large part of the time.[1] The relations between the magistrates and the Paris mob were never close and they very quickly turned sour. Nor had the Parlement a strong *rapport* with the bourgeois municipal authorities, who seem to have been allies from duress as much as from conviction. As for the *noblesse de race*, its increasingly revolutionary demands in the later days of the Fronde met little response from the conservative benches of the Palais de Justice. Even within the *robe* hierarchy itself, there were few signs of solidarity. Not only was the union of the *Chambre Saint-Louis* short-lived; but the Parlement was not on close terms either with the provincial courts.[2] Its isolation was emphasized by the First President in February 1651 when he spoke of 'the excellence of the Parlement of Paris and the pre-eminence which it has over all the other Parlements.'[3]

What then did the Parlement stand for during the Fronde? The magistrates were defending a concept of the state in which the law was sovereign. According to that law, the subjects' rights – particularly those of privilege and property – should be respected. There should be no arbitrary commissions or arbitrary arrests, no evocations to the royal council, and the normal legal processes and the accepted rules of procedure should be observed inviolate, even by the sovereign. One of the magistrates, Coquelay, remarked at the end of 1650, 'Kings are obliged to observe the laws as well as their subjects, but with this difference, that the people must observe them through a sense of natural obligation and kings through the duty imposed by their own consciences and through love, as fathers towards their children.'[4] In other words the magistrates were defending a very old political tradition, the only one consistent with their court's own registers.

It is not intended that the Parlement's policies should be viewed as irreproachable simply because it claimed the backing of the law. The government had pressing financial problems to solve and commitments to meet which the magistrates were in no position to assess. Nor is it suggested that traditional values in every sphere can or ought to be maintained.

[1] Cf. *supra*, 270–1.

[2] Moote, op. cit., 337–8; Kossmann, op. cit., 80–6.

[3] Doolin, op. cit., 70.

[4] Cubells, op. cit., 175.

Yet the government had shown no signs of contemplating a veritable reform of the state: and because the established order remained, the *ad hoc* changes which it introduced bore the stamp of illegality. Hence the Parlement's antagonism, an antagonism which caused grave political problems to which it could offer no solution, yet an antagonism which was based on the defence of the law and was a valuable deterrent against despotism. It is quite possible that a solution could have been found to the problem of reconciling the Parlement's traditional role with the requirements of state security if a spirit of moderation between the crown and the court had been restored. But both sides had defined their positions too closely and had left too little room for manœuvre. Extremism had once more vitiated their relations. In 1653 Claude Joly published his collection of *Maximes* in which he claimed that free registration of royal enactments by the Parlement was a necessary part of law-making and that where justice and the law were concerned the king was subject to his magistrates.[1] Joly was not himself a member of the Parlement and few of the magistrates would themselves have dared to voice such views, though many may well have found them attractive. Louis XIV was equally determined, on his part, to demonstrate the completeness of his authority. The auguries for future co-operation between the king and his Parlement were not good.

Until his death in 1661, Mazarin continued to dominate government policy and he regularly employed the practice of evocation to the royal council in order to deprive the Parlement of its authority. The magistrates complained to the king, who, on one occasion at least, responded with unexpected sympathy. In August 1656 Denis Talon, the *Avocat-Général*, was assured by Louis that he considered the Parlement to be the chief company in the state and that he would be pleased to receive remonstrances on the subject of evocations. Later, he restored the court's jurisdiction over the matters in dispute.[2] But this was an isolated and uncharacteristic gesture. For the most part, the cardinal was permitted to use the weapon of evocation at will. After his death in March 1661, the king decided to govern without the assistance of a chief minister and from the beginning of his personal rule the Parlement was subjected to ever more stringent controls. The magistrates had consistently opposed government by ministers since the days of Richelieu, and the fact that Louis was now obliging them by taking the reins into his own hands to some extent muzzled their opposition in advance. Thus they meekly accepted a

[1] C. Joly, *Recueil des Maximes*, 149–50, 392–3.
[2] Glasson, *Le Parlement de Paris*, I, 401–3.

council decree, dated 8 July 1661, ordering the Parlement to recognize the validity of such enactments, no less than royal edicts, ordinances and declarations. From time to time, as in December 1665, the magistrates attempted to carry their opposition not to extremes but further than the king thought permissible, and on such occasions, the weight of royal authority was decisive. Since the Fronde and the king's victory, the balance of power in the state had swung decisively back to the royal side, and with the king willing, as Louis was, to exercise that power in person, he was likely to encounter but muted opposition.

The decisive moment of this reign came in February 1673, when Louis produced regulations which stipulated that the Parlement's remonstrances against royal enactments sent to the court could only be made in future after registration.[1] By this decree, the Parlement's registration would become no more than a clerical device and its influence over royal policies, therefore, would be negligible. However, several reservations needed to be made. Louis did not feel himself free to waive altogether the ancient right of remonstrance, which traditionally modified the excesses of royal sovereignty. Nor did he intend his decree to be permanent. War had recently been declared against the Dutch, and the king's object was to prevent the Parlement from pursuing obstructive tactics, especially over urgent financial measures, whilst the international situation remained unsettled. It was intended to be a wartime measure, but because France remained at war, or on a war footing, from 1673 to 1715 it assumed the appearance of a permanent innovation.[2] The Parlement's feeble objections were brushed aside, and no more remonstrances appeared during the remainder of Louis's reign.

However, the Parlement's role was not entirely confined to routine judicial matters. Over certain religious issues the king had need of its support, and, when the occasion demanded, he was perfectly willing – like many of his predecessors – to rely on his court's political authority,whilst at the same time denying its existence. The authority of the Parlement was a useful weapon to be used in defence of the crown's rights, particularly against the pope.[3] In 1665, a decision of the faculty of Theology in Paris opposing the spread of ultramontane doctrines was condemned by a papal bull, and, prompted by the king, the Parlement forbade the bull to be received in France. Later, it enthusiastically supported the four Gallican

[1] Isambert, op. cit., XIX, 72.
[2] F. Hartung and R. Mousnier, 'Quelques problèmes concernant la monarchie absolue', 10.
[3] H. G. Judge, 'Church and State under Louis XIV', 220.

articles drawn up by the assembly of French clergy in 1682 as a result of the king's long feud with Pope Innocent XI, which had originated over the right of *régale*. These articles stipulated that the king was not subject to the pope in temporal matters, nor could he be excommunicated and his subjects freed from their obligation of obedience; that the pope's authority was not superior to that of a general council of the Church; in matters of faith his decisions required the Church's approval; finally, that the rules, usages and customs of the Gallican Church – which were not further defined – were to remain inviolate.[1] They were in perfect accord, though for the most part rather vaguely expressed, with the Parlement's Gallican tradition, and when the king incorporated them into the form of an edict, the magistrates had no qualms about registering it as a law of the state.

The quarrel between the king and the pope flared up again in 1687 over the matter of ambassadorial franchises in Rome. Innocent XI maintained that the freedom from arrest enjoyed within foreign embassies was being abused and he demanded that the countries represented should agree to waive the right. Louis refused and the pope threatened to excommunicate him. Once more the king sought the court's assistance, and the *Procureur-Général* lodged a formal appeal in the Parlement to a future general council of the Church against the pope's abrogation of the right of franchise. The Parlement duly supported him.[2] This too was a customary Gallican manœuvre and one which the magistrates were most willing to employ, for the principle at stake was that already enunciated in the articles of 1682: the king's immunity from excommunication and his independence in all temporal matters.

However, from the French point of view the international situation soon showed signs of deterioration; in particular, the success of William of Orange in procuring the English throne in 1689 was an unexpected and grievous blow for Louis who decided that the time had come to make peace with the pope. Innocent XI died in 1689, and it was with his successor, Innocent XII, that the king finally reached a compromise settlement in 1693.[3] In that year Louis agreed to suspend the various disputes which had disturbed his relations with the papacy for two decades: he assured the pope that the edict of March 1682 – proclaiming the four Gallican articles – would no longer be enforced. This decision was not

[1] The Gallican articles are printed in L. Mention, *Documents relatifs aux Rapports du Clergé*, I, 26–31.

[2] The whole issue is analysed by J. Orcibal, *Louis XIV contre Innocent XI, passim.*

[3] Innocent XI was succeeded by Alexander VIII whose pontificate lasted from 1689 to 1691.

well received in the Parlement, for it was an entirely arbitrary one, dictated by the contemporary political situation. The king had not even formally countermanded the edict: he was simply allowing it to lapse, despite the fact that it had been registered as a law of the state with all due solemnity, and despite the fact, too, that in the magistrates' opinion at least the Gallican articles proclaimed therein summarized an ancient legal tradition. They were hostile, therefore, both to the form and to the implication of Louis's decision, and for the first time for a number of years they showed signs of resistance. Despite contrary orders transmitted to the court via the *Procureur-Général*, they insisted on maintaining the legality of the law of 1682.[1] This show of independence, provoked, as had frequently been the case in the past, by the government's inclination to sacrifice legal traditions and procedures to the interests of the moment, was the precedent for a more serious conflict with the king during the last years of his reign. Again it was a religious matter which was at the root of the dispute, the problem of Jansenism, whose austere adherents, whilst seeking to remain within the French church, had, since the middle of the seventeenth century, criticized conventional standards of morality.

With the support of the king, the pope – by this time Clement XI – renewed his attack on the Jansenists in 1705, with the publication of the bull, *Vineam Domini*. Although he had solicited a formal condemnation of this kind, Louis was not anxious to weaken the Gallican position and he again had recourse to the Parlement, instructing the magistrates to register the bull only if they were satisfied that it contained nothing contrary to the rights and pre-eminences of the crown or to the liberties of the Gallican Church. The Parlement carefully conformed with his stipulation.[2]

However, Jansenism survived the publication of *Vineam Domini*, and Louis pressed Clement XI to promulgate a second, final condemnation, assuring the pope that such a pronouncement would be accepted without opposition throughout the kingdom. Finally, Clement concurred, publishing the bull *Unigenitus* in September 1713.[3] At once the king found himself in difficulties for, despite his assurances to the pope, there was a great deal of suspicion among the clergy and the magistrates, on the grounds that the Gallican liberties had been jeopardized in part by the

[1] E. Préclin and E. Jarry, *Les Luttes Politiques et doctrinales*, I, 163–4.
[2] Judge, op. cit., 230–1.
[3] The bull is printed in Mention, op. cit., II, 2–40.

bull's contents and also by the alliance between king and pope out of which this authoritarian document had been born.

It was a deeply held Gallican belief that papal decisions in matters of faith required the approval of the French Church before they could command unequivocal observance in France. That was the implication of the fourth Gallican article. It followed from that tenet that such pronouncements could not become laws of the state until they had been proclaimed as laws of the French Church, and indeed, in 1682, the king had been careful to obtain the support of the assembly of French clergy before enacting the Gallican articles as a law of the state. In the matter of *Unigenitus* he paid lip-service to these beliefs, but his determination to fulfil his promise to the pope made him impatient of the normal procedure. He did summon a council of bishops, comprising less than half of the episcopate, yet even from this specially selected body he could not extract a unanimous acceptance of *Unigenitus*. A small group of bishops, headed by Noailles, the cardinal archbishop of Paris, demanded that qualifications should be added to the bull. With this very dubious majority support from the bishops, Louis consulted the *Gens du roi*, his representatives in the Parlement. Both D'Aguesseau, the *Procureur-Général*, and Joly de Fleury, the *Avocat-Général*, maintained that according to the Gallican articles no papal pronouncement could be considered a law of the Church until it had been accepted by the French bishops, and that the episcopal support so far received fell far short of that requirement. On the basis of the Gallican articles, they also opposed proposition ninety-one of the bull, by which the pope claimed the right to excommunicate the king and to free his subjects from their duty of obedience. Finally, because *Unigenitus* was not yet a law of the Church, they denied that it could be enforced as a law of the state, since the state had no right to decide matters of faith or arbitrate between bishops.

Louis was adamant, however, and despite these objections of his legal advisers, he sent the bull and letters-patent enforcing it to the Parlement for registration in February 1714. A stormy debate ensued in the court and for the first time since 1673 a demand was heard for remonstrances, and the First President was forced to intervene in order to deflect this audacious proposal. In the end, the Parlement registered the bull, not purely and simply as the king required, but with a series of qualifications preserving the authority of the bishops and the liberties of the Gallican Church. This did not satisfy Louis, who was determined to have *Unigenitus* accepted as a law both of the Church and of the state. He intended to summon a national council of bishops as the next step in his attempt to enforce acceptance of *Unigenitus*, but before the council could be convened Louis XIV died, on 1 September 1715.[1]

On the issue of *Unigenitus* the Parlement finally abandoned the docility which had characterized its conduct towards the king since 1673. The magistrates bowed unwillingly before his authoritarian policy, yet he was their sovereign and they were less inclined to oppose him than to oppose a chief minister. Nevertheless, his decision to flout not simply traditional Gallican doctrine and procedure, but a law embodying that doctrine which he himself had been instrumental in procuring, was too much for them; they resented his arbitrary and inconsistent attitude more than his authoritarianism. They also resented the fact that Louis appeared to be undermining one of the traditional and most important bulwarks of the French monarchy, the Gallican tradition of royal independence *vis-à-vis* the papacy, a tradition which, until 1705, he had shown himself most anxious to preserve. On the occasion of the publication of *Vineam Domini* Louis had given the magistrates explicit instructions in that regard, but only eight years later he was concerned solely with the enforcement of the papal bull. In 1714 the Parlement qualified its registration of *Unigenitus* against the king's wishes but on his behalf. In doing so, it was defending both the traditional rights of the French crown and the traditional concept of kingship under the law.

However, the Parlement's real opportunity to reassert its political authority arose not from its opposition to *Unigenitus*, but out of the uncertainty surrounding the succession to the French throne. If Louis XIV died before 1723 – the year of his great-grandson's majority – a period of regency would intervene and both Louis's grandson, Philip V of Spain and his nephew, Philip, duke of Orléans, coveted the position of regent. In August 1714 the king attempted to solve the problem by drawing up a will in which Orléans was nominated as head of a council of regency, yet without any real power. The will was deposited in the Parlement. Its precise terms were not widely known, but Orléans, suspecting them to be unfavourable to his own ambitions, began to negotiate secretly with some of the magistrates. He offered to restore to the court its right of remon-

[1] A. Le Roy, *La France et Rome*, 560 et seq.; *l'Abbé* Dorsanne, *Journal*, I, 101–3; G. Rech, 'Daguesseau et le Jansénisme', 122–3; J. Carreyre, *Le Jansénisme durant la Régence*, I, 7. The magistrates' opposition was scarcely affected by the influence of Jansenism itself; during the first half of the eighteenth century there were no more than a dozen of them who adhered to the religious traditions of the movement, *see* A. Gazier, *Histoire Générale du Mouvement Janséniste*, I, 297.

strance in return for greater powers as regent than the king's will stipulated. Thus, when Louis XIV died in 1715, the Parlement found itself once more, as in 1610, the virtual arbiter of the regency.

More than any of his predecessors, Louis XIV maintained the principle that needs of state always justified the abrogation of customary rights and privileges. More than any of his predecessors, therefore, he adopted an authoritarian attitude towards the Parlement, the chief defender of those rights, reducing its political role to negligible proportions. Yet, significantly, he did not destroy it altogether. Besides continuing to permit an emasculated form of remonstrance to be made, he also recognized the abiding importance of registration itself, and indeed, his reliance upon the backing of the Parlement in his quarrels with the papacy and with the Jansenists, and the deposition of his will with the court, implied that despite the restrictive legislation of 1673, he did not regard the Parlement as simply a judicial court.

In fact, Louis was no less aware than his predecessors had been of the restricted nature of royal authority in France, of the need for the king to take counsel and then to act in accordance with the dictates of justice and legality. Of course, this represented an ideal, which was quickly tarnished by the strident and urgent demands of reason of state, but it was an ideal, nevertheless, which Louis never repudiated and which remained at the heart of the political system. His firm belief in the divine right of kings gave him a sense of responsibility which undermined his own most authoritarian attitudes. The long reign of Louis XIV did not mark a fundamental change in the concept of French kingship; indeed the strong element of continuity has recently been stressed by two distinguished historians of the *ancien régime*, Fritz Hartung and Roland Mousnier, who point out that during the sixteenth, seventeenth and eighteenth centuries in France a notion of absolutism existed, from which despotism was excluded.[1] This notion oscillated around a point of equilibrium between the concept of a power less limited and that of a power more limited; according to circumstances, to the king's personality or that of his ministers, or to the international situation, one or other of these nuances of absolutism became more important, without any profound change in the notion of absolutism itself. They observe that even Louis XIV was forced to discuss the application of his edicts with a variety of bodies: clergy, towns, craftsmen's guilds, the nobility in certain provinces, provincial estates, Parlements. Only within the royal domains was he entirely the

[1] Hartung and Mousnier, op. cit., 12.

master and even there he was restricted to exercising his customary rights.

It is even possible to widen the period in which this element of continuity deserves to be stressed to include the fourteenth and fifteenth centuries as well, for although relations between the monarchy on the one hand and those groups and orders of which society was composed on the other, were gradually modified with the consolidation of royal power, the change was one of emphasis, not of kind. The continuing and universal regard for the ancient principles of French kingship, whose roots lay beyond the fourteenth century, was a source of great strength for the crown and helps to explain why even the capricious and excessive policies in which Louis XIV indulged from time to time did not seriously jeopardize the position of the monarchy. But in the eighteenth century the crown eventually lost the prestige which had so far enabled it to reconcile traditional values with the demands of an increasingly bureaucratic state.

CHAPTER NINE

The Parlement in the Eighteenth Century

Law's bank; the bull *Unigenitus* in dispute; financial crises; relations with Cardinal Fleury; increasing friction between the Parlement and the Crown; the Chancellor Maupeou's judicial reforms; suppression of the Parlement

---

The excesses and failures of Louis XIV's reign did not undermine the monarchic ideal itself, but they did provoke a reaction in favour of a renewed emphasis upon the limitations which had traditionally restricted the exercise of royal power.[1] Thus Fénelon wrote that 'the king can only believe his subjects to be well-governed if they all obey the law. He too must obey the law and set a good example'.[2] Similar views were expressed by Jean-Baptiste Massillon, the bishop of Clermont, in a sermon preached before the young king, Louis XV in 1718: 'The liberty owed by princes to their people,' he warned, 'is the liberty provided by the law . . . the law must have more authority than the ruler.'[3] The only instrument still capable of implementing these views, which were neither revolutionary nor novel, but lay at the roots of French monarchy, was the Parlement. Its permanent corporate identity, its strong political and judicial tradition, its *esprit de corps*, its central role in law-making – that of registering and publishing royal legislation – all gave it a unique opportunity once more to defend that principle which gave point to its own existence, that kings should rule under the law.

Its opportunity came on the morrow of Louis XIV's death, when in a

[1] The first half of this chapter is based upon two articles: J. H. Shennan, 'The Political Role of the Parlement of Paris, 1715–1723', *Historical Journal*, VIII, 179–200; J. H. Shennan, 'The Political Role of the Parlement of Paris under Cardinal Fleury', *English Historical Review*, LXXXI, 520–42.

[2] Fénelon, 'Lettre au Marquis de Louville', 164.

[3] J-B. Massillon, *Oeuvres Complètes*, VI, 125.

solemn session, attended by the princes and peers, the court annulled the dead king's will and proclaimed Orléans regent, with undivided authority. In return he at once restored the Parlement's right of remonstrance to the form in which it had existed before 1673. In addition, he promised the magistrates an even wider political influence: 'whatever my title to the regency I assure you that I shall earn it through my zeal for the king's service and through my love for the public good, being chiefly assisted by your advice and by your wise remonstrances, both of which I ask for in advance'.[1] At one bound, the Parlement had regained the centre of the political stage. From a strictly legal viewpoint, Orléans's claims to the regency by birth and through Louis XIV's will had some force: yet the one depended upon the validity of Philip V's renunciation of his right to the throne, which few Frenchmen considered binding, and the other Orléans himself had been instrumental in destroying. Consequently, he leant heavily upon the Parlement's support, a fact of which the magistrates were well aware.

The two chief domestic problems confronting the new regent were religious and financial. Louis XIV's reign had further exacerbated the already serious problem of inadequate financial resources and after a series of expedients had failed to provide relief, Orléans turned for help to the Scottish financier and adventurer, John Law. Law's basic idea was to set up a state bank and establish a great commercial and industrial company which in time, financed by the bank, would take over the management of the state's commerce and industry. He was a strong believer in the use of paper money, though his fundamental mistake was to attribute intrinsic value to a means of exchange. His first venture was the establishment of a private bank in May 1716. It prospered to such an extent that in April 1717 the state was made solidary with the bank, and henceforth banknotes were accepted in payment for all taxes. While he was enjoying this success, Law worked to realize the second part of his scheme, the creation of a commercial company. A declaration carried before the Parlement in August 1717 promised to fulfil that ambition too.

The Parlement had thus far exercised its newly restored authority with moderation, but the hold which Law and his novel ideas were acquiring over Orléans caused increasing resentment among the magistrates. The first signs of serious trouble came in January 1718 when the Parlement drew up remonstrances censuring in particular the non-payment of *rentes* and Law's bank. The Scotsman was not mentioned by name, but the

[1] Isambert, op. cit., XXI, 5.

king was requested to restore the management of his revenues to the anciently established form and was warned against '*un genre de billets jusqu'à présent inconnus*'.[1] These complaints were remonstrances only in name since they were not in response to royal legislation, yet they could be justified not only by Orléans's previous invitation already referred to, but in a broader context by the long tradition of *parlementaire* involvement in political matters, which went far beyond the mere right to respond to royal enactments. Indeed, the fact that Orléans agreed to receive the remonstrances and even to answer them, confirms that he, too, accepted this wider interpretation of *parlementaire* influence. As for the points made in the remonstrances, they were mostly valid enough: criticisms of the continuing waste of money and of the government's refusal to adhere to its legal promises, especially in the non-payment of *rentes*.

But potentially the most explosive criticisms were those of the new bank. The Parlement had always been resentful of any individual other than the sovereign assuming control of affairs, and its long history of support for the independence of the French crown made it especially resentful of foreigners like Concini and Mazarin, who had succeeded in monopolizing government policies. Now John Law threatened to do the same thing and the magistrates feared as a result that the government would implement financial schemes which would prove harmful to the king's interests and those of his subjects. It was a fact, too, that these were innovatory and unproved ventures advocated by a man of very dubious reputation. It should also be added that Law's proposals were reviewed with suspicion by the councils of State and Finance, and by worthy theorists like the chancellor, D'Aguesseau, and that the magistrates themselves took expert advice from the mayor of Paris, who was in charge of the administration of *rentes*, from shareholders of commercial companies and from merchants and bankers.[2] It cannot be argued, therefore, that the Parlement opposed Law simply because of a doctrinaire refusal to contemplate change; it is true on the other hand that the Parlement's traditional role made it unwilling to approve untried policies, especially in this sort of situation when they stemmed not from the king, but from a foreigner of questionable repute.

The Parlement's new-found militancy seemed unlikely to survive the regent's firm rejection of its complaints, but in May 1718 Orléans himself

[1] J. Flammermont, *Les Remontrances du Parlement*, I, 56–64.

[2] P. Harsin, *Les Doctrines Monétaires et Financières en France*, 158, 189, 225.

provoked a resumption of the quarrel by producing an edict ordering a devaluation of the currency, which he had registered in the *Cour des Monnaies*. It was less the contents of this measure than the manner of its publication that antagonized the Parlement. Indeed, a very similar enactment sent to the court at the end of 1715 had been registered without protest.[1] That measure, however, had been presented to the Parlement for scrutiny; the second one had not. Although the *Cour des Monnaies*, as a superior court, gave publicity to the edict, in matters of such widespread public interest it was generally accepted that it was the Parlement's registration that provided the necessary complement to legislation; even Louis XIV had implicitly recognized that fact. By ignoring the court, Orléans was flouting the traditional method of law-making, thereby running the risk that his edict would be less well obeyed than the comparable enactment which had been duly registered by the Parlement less than three years before. Moreover, he was threatening to dislodge the cornerstone of the court's political edifice and for that reason too his action was bound to provoke fierce opposition from the magistrates.

Their response, no doubt inspired by the precedent of the Fronde, recollection of which was being currently revived by the *Memoirs* of Cardinal de Retz, was to invite deputies from the other sovereign courts to meet and discuss the situation with the Parlement. Under pressure from the regent, these courts refused the offer and by mid-June it was clear that the magistrates would have to stand alone in their opposition to the government. Then, in response to a more conciliatory attitude by Orléans, the Parlement sent a deputation to remind him of his obligations in the business of law-making: 'Our fathers have taught us that every law which contains a government regulation applicable to the whole kingdom must be registered in the Parlement.'[2] However, Orleans's attitude at once hardened again and these representations proved fruitless. The Parlement now took the matter into its own hands, issuing a decree forbidding the distribution and circulation of the new money and calling for a revocation of the controversial edict. Orléans at once annulled this decree, and the magistrates retaliated by ordering it to be observed and copies to be sent to the superior courts, as well as to the inferior tribunals within the Parlement's jurisdiction. The regent's response to this defiance was to send soldiers to seize the printing press supplying the court, at the same time

[1] Ibid., 162.
[2] Flammermont, op. cit., I, 71.

expressing his willingness to receive remonstrances. The magistrates decided to conform; their paper revolt was over.[1]

In this crisis the Parlement had sought to place its own legislative authority above that of the regent. In so doing it adopted an extreme position which it could not justify and from which it very quickly withdrew. Examples of such extreme conduct were not, of course, without precedent in the Parlement's history. Usually, they were caused by the crown's adoption of similarly excessive claims, or to put it another way, by one side or the other choosing to overdefine its authority. What these extreme claims ought not to obscure is the fact that both the king and his Parlement had a part to play, the one in making laws, the other in enforcing them; and these functions, it has already been observed, were too closely connected for either to be totally independent of the other.

In the following weeks remonstrances and the regent's responses to them allowed both sides to reiterate their extreme points of view, though this time within an acceptable constitutional context. In fact, Orléans's authorization of remonstrances, a gesture which had persuaded the magistrates to end their revolt, was itself an implicit admission of the fact that normal processes of law could not be arbitrarily ignored. Yet, within several days of the presentation of these remonstrances on 25 June 1718, the regent evoked all matters concerning the execution of the contentious edict to the king. By thus distinguishing between royal and *parlementaire* justice, he was weakening the authority of the law and underlining the capricious nature of his own policy. The court's remonstrances, submitted on 27 June, claimed that in a matter of such universal importance there could be no substitute for registration in the Parlement, '*cette formalité nécessaire pour rendre une loi publique*'.[2] Speaking through the voice of the young king, Orléans gave his reply on 2 July, declaring that laws existed only by the will of the sovereign and that registration added nothing to their validity.

This categorical statement of the extreme monarchical theory of government provoked further remonstrances presented on 26 July. In them the magistrates asserted that only royal enactments registered in the Parlement were valid and that they had the right freely to examine them first.[3] Here was the extreme *parlementaire* view emerging, echoing the opinions expressed by Claude Joly in his *Recueil des Maximes*. Yet once again the

[1] E. de Barthélemy (ed.), *Gazette de la Régence*, 264–5.
[2] Flammermont, op. cit., I, 78.
[3] Ibid., 85–105.

extremes adopted by government and Parlement were more apparent than real. Orléans had already recognized, and was increasingly to recognize in the future, the importance of the magistrates' function, while the latter, in remonstrances which seemed, at least in part, to threaten the king's legislative sovereignty, could still say with truth, 'we recognize you as sole ruler, sole legislator'.[1] In keeping with a long-standing tradition, they were opposing the exercise of royal authority when it paid no regard to the law, whether traditional law or the day-to-day enactments copied into the Parlement's registers. However, because they could not call upon sanctions for the law's enforcement, they endeavoured to give great weight to their own part in registering royal legislation.

While they awaited a reply to their remonstrances, the magistrates' frustration grew. They had achieved nothing by their opposition and there were no indications that the regent intended to become more amenable as a result of their pressure. The continuing activities of John Law in particular antagonized them and they saw themselves now confronted with a situation in which government policy was apparently not even controlled by the regent, but by a financier twice removed, as it were, from the centre of power, and a foreigner into the bargain.

In the middle of August, in a bitter mood, the magistrates met to discuss Law's bank and the decree that they drew up and published once more placed them clearly beyond the limits of their authority. They ordered the bank to be reduced to the bounds prescribed for it in 1716 and they forbade all foreigners under threat of legal summons to take part in the administration of the royal revenues. In a more comprehensive way than before, this decree attempted to dictate government policy in defiance of the regent. By legislating independently the Parlement went far beyond the limits indicated in its own remonstrances and its action was made less creditable by the attitude of personal antagonism towards Law himself, which was evident on this occasion among the magistrates. On both counts its decree was bound to provoke stern reprisals.[2]

Orléans reacted strongly and quickly. A royal council decree forbade the Parlement to meddle in financial affairs or take cognizance of any matter of state unless the king requested its advice. All acts of the court considered inimical to royal authority were annulled; remonstrances on measures sent to the Parlement were to be made within eight days or they

[1] Ibid., 94.
[2] Saint-Simon, *Mémoires*, XXXV, 30–1; Dangeau, *Journal*, XVII, 356; Flammermont, op. cit., I, 106–7.

would be presumed registered; and judicial decisions of the court contravening any enactment presumed registered in this way would be declared null and void.[1] Orléans thus adopted an authoritarian policy towards the Parlement, although, like Louis XIV, he was now insisting upon the necessity of registration. On 26 August, Louis XV held a *lit de justice*, at which this decree was registered by the king's express command. Ironically, the *lit de justice* provided excellent support for the magistrates' original point of view. Orléans clearly appreciated that if the council decree was to be effective, it would have to be registered by the Parlement, yet it was precisely his refusal to do likewise with the financial edict of the previous May that had provoked the storm.[2]

After the defeat of the Parlement, John Law was able to develop his financial schemes further. In December 1718 his bank became a royal one, administered in the king's name. The Parlement refused to register the edict, but, because it had not presented remonstrances within eight days, the edict was considered registered. Next Law turned to the other feature of his dual system – commercial expansion – and in May 1719 his *Compagnie de l'Occident* acquired a monopoly of maritime commerce, becoming the *Compagnie des Indes*. When this measure was sent to the Parlement, the magistrates decided to consult expert opinion; among those interviewed were directors and shareholders of the trading companies involved in the proposed merger. Having heard their views, the magistrates decided to draw up remonstrances. These Orléans refused to accept, three weeks having already passed since the Parlement's receipt of the enactment, and from this time for almost a year he omitted to send any new financial measures to the court.

In the last months of 1719 Law's system reached its zenith. His company's shareholders acquired immense fortunes and the triumph of paper money seemed assured. Yet the boom was illusory, and soon the system began to groan under the weight of growing inflation. Law tried to retain public confidence, but one of his measures, the reduction of the legal interest rate from five to two per cent, raised fresh hostility among the magistrates. Orléans's decision to send the measure to the Parlement indicated his growing concern over the economic situation and also the importance that he attached to *parlementaire* support in a time of crisis. Realizing that the system was beginning to fail, and that the regent might

[1] Isambert, op. cit., XXI, 159-62.

[2] A famous – though highly coloured – account of this *lit de justice* is to be found in Saint-Simon, op. cit., XXXV, 210 et seq.

be prepared, therefore, to heed their opinions, the magistrates decided to present remonstrances, on 17 April 1720.[1] The state of panic which gripped Paris during the following months amply demonstrated that the Parlement was speaking for a great many people whose property, in the shape of government investments, had been put in jeopardy. Such people could customarily expect legal redress. However, the remonstrances were unsympathetically received, and the king forbade the Parlement to carry the matter further.

By this time the financial position was critical, and on 21 May 1720 Law caused a council decree to be issued drastically devaluing both the bank-notes and the company's shares. Its publication, heralding the breakdown of the government's fiscal policy and the bankruptcy of many private investors, caused consternation in Paris.[2] The magistrates shared the general alarm and agreed to draw up remonstrances. Before they could do so, however, Orléans intimated on 27 May that he would welcome an immediate conference with their representatives. On the same day, he repealed the week-old decree. Seriously perturbed by the financial crisis, and by the resulting public unrest, the regent was now prepared to reverse his policy of the preceding two years and consult the Parlement in a political capacity. A series of meetings was held in July. It was scarcely to be expected that they would succeed in solving the grave economic problems facing the government, but from Orléans's point of view, they were a means of preventing the Parlement from adding to his difficulties. The two sides could find little on which to agree: the government declined to elaborate on a new edict shortly to be sent to the Parlement, by which the *Compagnie des Indes* was to be made perpetual in return for financial aid, and relations were further strained by the magistrates' demands that Law should be dismissed. When the edict in question was presented for registration, the court decided to demand its withdrawal since the government had not provided sufficient details. Orléans's patience was now at an end and on 18 July he decided to exile the Parlement as a body to the village of Pontoise, some twenty miles north-east of Paris.

During the preceding two months the regent's attitude had been capricious. In a moment of financial crisis he had turned to the Parlement for support, having ignored it for almost a year, only to revert abruptly to an authoritarian attitude when he found the court unwilling to co-operate.

[1] Flammermont, op. cit., I, 126–39.
[2] Saint-Simon, op. cit., XXXVII, 314; M. Marais, *Journal et Mémoires*, I, 265.

His decision to exile the Parlement was unjustified; the magistrates found the proposed edict insufficiently explained, and, in view of the financial chaos in the capital, they did not feel able to approve the measure. The declaration transferring the Parlement, registered at Pontoise on 27 July 1720, indicated that the magistrates were being exiled for deferring the execution of a royal decision on the financial administration of the kingdom. Thus, indirectly, their earlier opposition to the edict of May 1718 was vindicated. For that edict, quite as important a financial regulation and affecting every individual in the state, was registered only in the *Cour des Monnaies*. The serious view taken by the regent of the Parlement's latest refusal suggests that he was well aware of the need for registration in that court, if the edict were to have its full effect. Despite its own excessive claims and the excessive restrictions imposed upon it by the regent, the importance of the Parlement's political function was once again demonstrated.

While the magistrates were at Pontoise, the religious disputes which had surrounded the bull *Unigenitus* ever since its publication came to a head. In March 1717 four bishops had solemnly appealed from the bull to a future general council.[1] The appeal was in accordance with Gallican doctrine and the bishops received considerable support. The faculties of Theology in Paris, Rheims and Nantes all followed their example, as did a number of individual clerics. On 8 September 1718, the sixth anniversary of the publication of *Unigenitus*, the pope responded with the promulgation of the letters *Pastoralis Officii*, excommunicating all those who withheld their unqualified submission to *Unigenitus*. On 3 October the *Procureur-Général* denounced the letters in the Parlement and they were declared invalid, a decision in line with Gallican belief, and one which Orléans did not dispute. Instead he renewed his efforts at effecting an agreement, and early in 1720, when John Law's system was tottering on the edge of disaster, the long sought after religious settlement appeared to be imminent. By May of that year, about a hundred prelates had signed a body of doctrine interpreting the sense in which the bull's condemnations should be understood.[2] However, Cardinal Noailles, the chief of the dissentient bishops, was wavering in a characteristic state of indecision, uncertain whether to confirm his adherence until a royal declaration, embodying the explanations, had been registered by the Parlement. The regent, too, accepted that registration in the Parlement was necessary to

[1] The bishops of Senez, Montpellier, Boulogne and Mirepoix.

[2] Carreyre, op. cit., II, 291.

give the greatest possible weight to the compromise and he also appreciated that Noailles's support was vital. He decided, therefore, to send the declaration to the recalcitrant magistrates, who by this time had begun their sojourn at Pontoise.

In 1714 the Parlement had pointed out that both *Unigenitus* and its mode of acceptance contradicted the Gallican liberties and the situation had not changed fundamentally since then. The agreed body of doctrine was not a law of the Church and it could not therefore be approved unequivocally as a law of the state. Consequently, most of the magistrates opposed registration unless accompanied by adequate qualifications. What precisely these modifications were to be remained a matter of dispute. The *Procureur-Général*, Joly de Fleury, an unenthusiastic supporter of the proposed compromise, stated them in the most general terms on 10 August 1720, when he wrote: 'We must register the bull, therefore, but with safeguards which . . . will protect the laws of the kingdom, the right of appeal and the appellants themselves.'[1] When the declaration was finally brought before the court, on 2 September, evidence of further considerable opposition from the four appellant bishops, from the University of Paris and from a number of *curés*, came to light, and the Parlement decided not to register the declaration at once but to nominate commissioners to examine the matter further. The commissioners wanted modifications of a more specific nature than Orléans was willing to allow and on 7 September he countered their stubbornness by sending one of his secretaries to Pontoise to bring back the unregistered declaration to Paris.[2]

Orléans now decided to have the declaration registered in the *Grand Conseil*, and although he encountered opposition there too, he was finally successful on 23 September. Letters-patent were registered at the same time, granting the *Grand Conseil* cognizance over all actions arising from *Unigenitus* within the Parlement's jurisdiction. The position of the exiled court became more perilous with this curtailment of its jurisdiction. Noailles remained unwilling to take the initiative and the regent, who wrongly suspected that the Parlement and the cardinal were acting in collusion, finally lost his patience and ordered *lettres de cachet* to be expedited, transferring the Parlement to Blois. It was to convene there on 2 December 1720.[3]

This more rigorous exile could be interpreted as the first step in a plan

[1] Shennan, 'The Political Role of the Parlement of Paris, 1715–1723', 195.
[2] Dorsanne, op. cit., II, 16 et seq.
[3] Shennan, 'The Political Role of the Parlement of Paris, 1715–1723', 197.

to suppress the Parlement altogether, for the distance from the capital would make even the routine administration of justice difficult and it was strongly rumoured at the time that Orléans did intend to abolish the court. Whatever his intentions, he succeeded in forcing the cardinal's hand. As soon as the regent had secured Noailles's formal support for his declaration he countermanded his earlier orders banishing the Parlement to Blois. Instead the magistrates were required to assemble at Pontoise once more to examine the declaration on *Unigenitus*. On 4 December the Parlement registered it almost unanimously and ordered its execution with the same conditions as had applied in 1714 to *Unigenitus* and in conformity with the maxims of the kingdom on the authority of the Church, on the power and jurisdiction of the bishops, on the acceptance of papal bulls and on appeals to a future council.[1] Immediately afterwards, the *Gens du roi* brought letters-patent before the court, restoring the Parlement's jurisdiction over all actions arising out of the bull. They were registered by general acclaim.

The closing months of 1720 had been a time of difficulty for the magistrates, but not of disaster. The eventual registration was not simply an act of obedience; the accompanying qualifications, though they were vague enough, did safeguard the appellants and the Gallican liberties. The Parlement's attitude was consistent with the one it had adopted towards *Unigenitus* at the time of its publication. On both occasions it asserted, though in a minor key, that there were certain laws and legal procedures which neither the king nor the Parlement should disregard. Orléans's conduct was less consistent, yet his attitude in these months, and more especially the attitude of Cardinal Noailles, emphasized again the significance of the Parlement's role in registering laws of general public importance.

On 16 December 1720, the magistrates received their official recall to Paris, two days after John Law had driven inconspicuously from the city and from the French scene. The magistrates intended that the juxtaposition of these two events should give the impression of a *parlementaire* victory over the Scotsman, though in fact there was no direct connection. The system had long been moribund, and at least since June 1720, Law's erratic star had been dimmed by that of a more successful careerist, the Abbé Dubois.

During the last two years of the regency, there was comparative peace between Orléans and the Parlement. The religious rift had been healed, at

[1] Mention, op. cit., II, 60.

least temporarily, and Law's system, the other great source of friction, had vanished. On 10 February 1723, Louis XV celebrated his thirteenth birthday, and on the 22nd a *lit de justice* marked the formal end of the regency. The king still occupied a unique place in the hearts of most Frenchmen, and for the magistrates as for the country in general, it was a time for rejoicing. At the ceremony on 22 February, the keeper of the Seals observed that regencies were always stormy seasons.[1] However, the significance of the preceding eight years was not to be found in the Parlement's abuse of power at the expense of a weakened government. On the contrary, it was the regent's subjection of the laws and traditions of the kingdom, as well as the accepted procedures of law-making, to arbitrary and inconsistent treatment that had exposed the government to attack. In opposing his vacillating policy, the Parlement was defending that long-held principle of the French monarchy, which was reflected in the first remonstrances of the regency, those of May 1716, 'The majesty of the law demands inviolable observance.'[2] It was a principle which could be ignored, as Louis XIV and the regent had ignored it on occasion. But as the eighteenth century progressed the prestige of the monarchy would become less adequate to support such limitless authority.

When Louis XV had reached his majority, he did not take over the direction of the government; that task fell eventually into the hands of another Cardinal First Minister, Fleury. Although already an old man when he took office in 1726, Cardinal Fleury remained the dominant political figure in France from that time until his death in 1743. During this period, as in the years of the regency, financial and religious affairs constituted the main sources of conflict between the government and the Parlement. Financial differences were less acute than the religious ones, but they deserve prior consideration, because it is principally the magistrates' attitude towards fiscal immunities which have coloured historians' views of their political motives and actions and have caused them to he condemned as 'the obscurantist defenders of vested interests'.[3]

Two points need to be made in this connection. In the first place, the social structure of the country, founded upon privilege, was traditional. The medieval idea that the king should live off his domain persisted in the view, still current in the eighteenth century, that extra taxes, considered necessary to meet the state's expenses, should be levied on a purely tem-

[1] Flammermont, op. cit., I, 165.
[2] Ibid., 43.
[3] A. Cobban, *In Search of Humanity*, 164.

porary basis.[1] The extent to which the government itself respected this outlook may be estimated from its own pronouncements. Towards the end of his reign Louis XIV was desperately in need of funds, yet even he maintained this traditional point of view. His declaration of 1695, ordering the levy of a capitation tax, stated in the preamble: 'We have resolved . . . to establish a general capitation tax, payable only while the war lasts.' Similarly, in establishing the *dixième* of 1710, Louis specified its limits: 'and since we are only calling for this tenth in order to provide means for continuing the war, it will cease to be levied three months after the proclamation of peace'. The same qualification was contained in the declarations of 1733 and 1741, also ordering the levy of a *dixième*.[2]

The explanation of the government's acquiescence lies in the nature of the *ancien régime*. The French state was not monolithic; the various groups of which it was composed were not constituted for its service. Each group was concerned with maintaining its own privileges, its own status, its own traditional liberties. Even Louis XIV could only invoke the doctrine of *raison d'état* as a temporary and abnormal expedient. For their part, the magistrates of the Parlement inherited the belief that privilege belonged naturally in the world in which they lived; indeed, they knew that the possession of privilege was recognized and safeguarded by law.

There is a second point, however, which must qualify the first. In the first half of the eighteenth century, few voices were raised against the one-sided financial system, and those that were – including Voltaire as well as Vauban – were concerned with strengthening the king's authority.[3] The threat to the privileged classes came in fact from above, not from below, for although the king had no wish to destroy the social hierarchy over which he presided, the financial situation became so desperate for the government from the close of the seventeenth century that successive ministers were forced to take measures which tended to undermine the principle of tax exemption. The first of these measures was the capitation tax of 1695, described by the leading financial historian of the period as 'the first step taken under the *ancien régime* towards equality of taxation'.[4] The capitation was suppressed in 1698, re-established in 1701 to provide money for the war of the Spanish Succession, augmented in 1705 and again in 1747, by which time it had become a permanent direct tax. The

[1] J. Meuvret, 'Comment les Français voyaient l'Impôt', 59–78.

[2] M. Marion, *Les Impôts Directs sous l'Ancien Régime*, 242–3, 270, 284–5.

[3] *See*, in particular, Vauban, *Projet d'une Dixme Royale*, 23.

[4] Marion, *Les Impôts Directs sous l'Ancien Régime*, 49.

privileged classes found ways and means of paying less than their share, yet the theory of a universal tax system had been at least tentatively enunciated. The declaration of 1710 ordering the levy of a *dixième* marked a further step by the government towards the reduction of financial privilege. The *dixième* taxed all sources of income and all classes of the population, though in practice, because of administrative inadequacies and the non-co-operation of the privileged orders, the *dixième* yielded far less than it should have done.

The attitude of the Parlement of Paris towards these developments was unenthusiastic yet not irreconcilably hostile. Following Louis XV's majority, the first occasion on which financial matters reached a new crisis occurred in June 1725, when the government introduced the *cinquantième*. Like the *dixième*, this was a tax on income, to be paid by all sections of the community, clerical and lay, noble and non-noble, privileged and unprivileged. However, in several aspects this tax was innovatory. It was not introduced as an emergency war-time measure. France was at peace in 1725, yet the *cinquantième* was to be levied, nevertheless, for a period of twelve years. Its greatest novelty lay in the fact that, whenever possible, it was to be paid in kind. This new departure indicated that the privileged groups would have more difficulty in avoiding their obligations than had been the case with the *dixième*, and that the government was making a more determined attempt to scrutinize and control its sources of revenue.[1]

A majority of the king's advisers, fearing that the tax would arouse widespread hostility, suggested that the declaration announcing the *cinquantième* ought not to be sent to the Parlement for discussion, but should be registered there by royal command, at a *lit de justice*. This advice was duly followed. Afterwards, the magistrates contented themselves with passing a form of resolution customary in such circumstances, protesting against the authoritarian means employed in registration. There they allowed the matter to rest, despite the expected wave of opposition from provincial Parlements, from the clergy and from privileged individuals.[2] The first collection of the tax was scheduled for the summer of 1726, and the government seemed determined to press ahead with its plans. However, in June 1726, Louis XV dismissed his first minister, the Duc de Bourbon, and with him Paris-Duverney, the effective head of government finances and the man responsible for the *cinquantième*. From this time Cardinal Fleury was in charge, and at once

[1] M. Marion, *Histoire Financière de la France*, I, 130–1.
[2] Ibid., 132–4; Flammermont, op. cit., I, 211–19.

the government's attitude to the new tax changed. Ten days after the dismissal of Paris-Duverney a royal declaration condemned the principle of payment in kind and substituted the more pliable regulations which had governed the collection of the *dixième*. In July 1727 the levy was suppressed altogether. The conduct of the Parlement of Paris throughout this period had been restrained, even passive. Not only had it done nothing itself to champion the forces of opposition to the tax, but its example of obedience had also helped to reduce the resistance of the provincial Parlements.[1] The Parlement did not support the idea of radical financial reform, but it did seem possible that so long as the king maintained his prestige in the court the magistrates might be persuaded to accept the need for some modification of existing immunities. Fleury's decision, however, was bound to weaken the authority of the government in the eyes of those who had opposed the introduction of the *cinquantième*, and to make it more difficult, therefore, for it to overcome such hostility in the future.

The Parlement next took an active part in the state's financial affairs in December 1733, when it presented remonstrances against a declaration re-establishing the *dixième* in order to finance the war of the Polish Succession, in which France had recently become involved. This measure, based on the *dixième* of 1710, was, like its predecessor, open to abuse and manipulation by influential bodies and individuals and it did not, therefore, produce the furore which had accompanied the introduction of the *cinquantième*. In addition, it was intended to meet a specific, extraordinary crisis. The Parlement's remonstrances were moderate in tone; the magistrates accepted the tax in principle, though they would have liked it to be less than ten per cent. They were particularly concerned that the tax should be assessed justly; they sought to ensure that property holders and investors, merchants and traders would not be taxed disproportionately.

As a whole, the remonstrances did not suggest that the magistrates were willing to give up the principle of financial privilege; but they did confirm that the court was not willing to adopt an inflexible position against the government's financial policies.[2] In the end the Parlement registered the declaration without substantial alteration. Again, in September 1741 the magistrates presented brief remonstrances on the subject of Fleury's decision to reimpose the *dixième* because of the threat of war. As in 1733,

[1] A. Renaudet, *Les Parlements*, 132.
[2] Flammermont, op. cit., I, 314–27.

the magistrates agreed that the exceptional circumstances made the imposition necessary, but they asked that it should be delayed for three months and that its duration should be clearly stated.[1] The king refused to suspend the operation of the levy, however, and the Parlement registered the declaration imposing it without further protest.

It has been argued that the sole reason for the comparative indifference with which the privileged classes accepted the *dixième* was the knowledge that they would be able to avoid some, if not all, of their obligations.[2] In general terms, this may well be true. The members of the Parlement, however, were in a special position. They had the task of affirming the legality of this sort of levy, of sanctioning a principle whose implications – as demonstrated by the abortive *cinquantième* – were inimical to all privileged interests. They also had the opportunity to make vigorous protests. Their attitude, in fact, was reserved and suspicious, yet far from rebellious. Whatever private reservations the magistrates may have had, they were not anxious to oppose the crown uncompromisingly over the issue of financial privilege. The idea of a universal tax which the government had tentatively propounded in the years between 1695 and 1741 marked a real break with the past, yet it met with far less hostility from the magistrates than did the schemes of John Law. However, by the end of Fleury's ministry that respect for royal authority, which was the vital element in deciding the court's attitude, had been jeopardized, partly as a result of the prolonged quarrel between the Parlement and the government which began in the early days of the cardinal's ascendancy and concerned, at least in the beginning, the bull *Unigenitus*.

The religious agreement of 1720 had demonstrated the extent to which the episcopal enemies of *Unigenitus* had fallen away; the defection of Noailles was a particularly grievous blow to those bishops who continued to dispute the bull's validity. Nor could they hope for support from the new chief minister, Fleury, described by Noailles many years before as '*moliniste à vingt-quatre carats*'.[3] In 1727 a provincial council of bishops suspended one of the appellant leaders, the bishop of Senez, from all priestly and episcopal functions and exiled him to a lonely abbey in the Auvergne mountains; it also pronounced *Unigenitus* to be a dogmatic judgment of the Church from which there could be no appeal. These decisions were confirmed by a papal brief in December 1727. The decision

[1] Ibid., 379–83.
[2] Marion, *Histoire Financière de la France*, I, 131.
[3] G. Hardy, *Le Cardinal de Fleury et le Mouvement Janséniste*, 10.

to exile Senez was of far less significance than the assertion that the bull was a dogmatic judgment of the Church. If that were so, *Unigenitus* was a rule of faith, which, by its nature, could not be subjected to qualification, and therefore, the restrictions with which the Parlement, with government support, had hedged its registration in 1720, could not apply.

There were other signs, too, of Fleury's intentions. Vintimille, the archbishop of Aix, who succeeded Noailles in 1729 as archbishop of Paris, was a supporter of *Unigenitus*. In October of that year, Fleury moved against the faculty of Theology in Paris excluding all those doctors who had opposed the acceptance of *Unigenitus* since 1720. By the end of the year, the cardinal felt that the time had come to introduce a royal declaration recognizing *Unigenitus* unequivocally as a law of the state. Such an action would bring him into direct conflict with the Parlement.[1]

Since its exile in 1720 the court had not been in a militant mood, though it had continued to concern itself with religious affairs, invoking its right to safeguard the laws of the kingdom, and in particular the Gallican liberties. Thus, in January 1726 the *Avocat-Général* asked the Parlement to condemn a letter emanating from an assembly of French clergy held in 1725, attacking the compromise of 1720. For this act he received a written reprimand from the government, which concluded with a sentence that the magistrates were bound to consider ominous: 'Since the declaration of 1720, the king has several times recognized the Bull [*Unigenitus*] as a law of the Church and of the state.'[2] This statement, shortly to be echoed in the condemnation of Senez, convinced the magistrates that Fleury intended to erase the qualifications, which in 1720 had brought the quarrel to a halt. For their part, they strove to maintain the position established in 1720, but the cardinal proved to be adroit at deflecting and blunting their criticisms. On a number of occasions before March 1730, Fleury intervened to hinder the Parlement from taking action over matters concerned with *Unigenitus*.

His tactics, though successful in the short term, neither enhanced the king's authority nor clarified the status of the bull. The king was perfectly entitled to judge matters himself if he so chose, yet in these instances the intention seemed less to uphold the law than to obscure or evade it. Nor could Fleury's attitude be explained on the grounds that he was seeking to reduce the friction between the two sides; on the contrary, the best explanation is to be found in his increasing determination to introduce

[1] Ibid., 178 et seq.
[2] Shennan, 'The Political Role of the Parlement of Paris under Cardinal Fleury', 528.

fresh legislation commanding unqualified submission to the bull. On 28 March 1730, a royal declaration was duly presented to the Parlement. Its third article ordained 'that *Unigenitus* be inviolably observed . . . and that, already being a law of the Church . . . it should be regarded too as a law of our kingdom'.[1] In that context the use of the appeal *comme d'abus* was also prohibited.

It was clear from the magistrates' initial debate that their opposition would be formidable. Fleury's reaction was to command that the declaration should be registered only by the *Grand' Chambre*, traditionally the least rebellious of the Parlement's chambers. This the First President refused to contemplate, because he believed that such a registration, differing from those of 1714 and 1720 on the same subject, and indeed completely out of line with customary legal procedure, would create hostility and suspicion among the public, and would run the risk of being ignored. The events of 1720 had recently confirmed the traditional view that in a law affecting the general public, registration by the whole Parlement added a weighty seal of legality. Fleury, however, had already revealed his willingness to circumvent normal legal practice in order to stifle opposition.[2] To this end he now signalled a *lit de justice* for 3 April 1730.

At this assembly a number of magistrates spoke out vehemently against *Unigenitus*, reiterating the familiar Gallican objections to article ninety-one. The most trenchant argument was one which pointed out that a judgment of the universal Church was incapable of modification; yet the Parlement had already modified *Unigenitus*, and in 1720 the king had given his consent to its modifications.[3] However, the *lit de justice* reached its expected conclusion with the registration of the declaration by royal command.

Both by its content and by the manner of its enforcement, the new declaration antagonized the Parlement. As in 1714 and 1720, it based its stand on the Gallican liberties and certainly if these traditional rules were still to apply, nothing had happened since 1720 to alter the status of the bull. The magistrates were particularly incensed by the way in which the declaration had been registered. The religious cleavage caused by *Unigenitus* had troubled the kingdom for a generation and any settlement of the problem, to have a chance of success, required the maximum show of

[1] Mention, op. cit., II, 66.
[2] Shennan, 'The Political Role of the Parlement of Paris under Cardinal Fleury', 530.
[3] *Nouvelles Ecclésiastiques*, 5 April 1730; Barbier, *Journal*, II, 106–8.

legality. Fleury's authoritarian method, so obviously designed to forestall magisterial criticisms, was bound to reduce the effectiveness of the new law, especially since that law contradicted a royal declaration approved only ten years previously. Fleury's subsequent conduct enraged the magistrates further. When the court reassembled the First President announced that he had received instructions forbidding the magistrates to discuss the declaration. He added that the cardinal had assured him that the declaration would not be strictly enforced, and that the Parlement would be permitted to receive appeals *comme d'abus* if the bishops resorted to excessive measures. This opportunistic and vacillating attitude towards the law could only weaken respect for the legislator and make it impossible for the Parlement, whose main duty after all was to administer the law, to know precisely what that law was.[1]

It was not surprising, therefore, that even the *Grand' Chambre*, despite its subservient reputation, should show no inclination to enforce *Unigenitus* as a rule of faith. In May, it suppressed a thesis to that effect written at the Sorbonne; during July it received appeals *comme d'abus* from priests in Amiens and Paris. All these matters and others arising during the summer of 1730, Fleury was forced to evoke to the King's Council. The magistrates' frustration grew, partly because of the evocations, partly because they were still prevented from commenting upon the original declaration. A situation now existed whereby the law was being enforced on two contradictory levels, by the King's Council and by his Parlement. Eventually, the magistrates had recourse to remonstrances which were presented to the king early in 1731. They were moderate in tone, acknowledging the king's right to evoke suits to his own council, yet making it clear that this practice had always been regarded as exceptional, and that the Parlement was the law's traditional guardian. Fleury, however, having committed himself to the declaration of March 1730, was forced to eschew traditional legal procedure. In his reply to the remonstrances the king relegated the court to the level of a simple instrument through which he dispensed royal justice.[2] Yet again, it was an extreme and unrealistic position for the government to adopt.

Fleury's policies were increasingly forcing him into such a position. His declaration of March 1730 disregarded the Gallican liberties with their traditional support for the independence of the French crown, and his policy of evocation disregarded the appeal *comme d'abus* which had

[1] *Nouvelles Ecclésiastiques*, 1 May 1730.

[2] Flammermont, op. cit., I, 232-43.

customarily protected the individual and the Gallican Church against ultramontane intervention. By rejecting these traditional aspects of French law and by refusing to allow the magistrates to make any comment whatsoever upon the declaration, in a word, by resorting to authoritarian methods, Fleury invited a conflict, not simply on the religious issue, but on the fundamental constitutional one of whether the king should act within the law or independently of it.

There was more yet to follow. Underlying the procedure of the appeal *comme d'abus* was the complex problem of disputed jurisdiction between the spiritual and secular powers. In March 1731 this issue suddenly flared into the open when Fleury had a council decree published guaranteeing the Church's right, independently of the secular power, to enforce its spiritual censures. By this *ad hoc* measure, '*dont la teneur déroge nettement aux traditions juridiques du royaume*',[1] the cardinal destroyed the long-standing equilibrium which had existed between the two powers and gave a decisive advantage to the spiritual order.

The Parlement's response to this latest move and to the continual use of evocations by Fleury was to draw up a decree, early in September 1731, stating its views of the respective limits of the authority of the secular and spiritual powers. The decree contained four articles: first, temporal authority is entirely independent of any other; secondly, the ecclesiastical authority cannot fix the boundaries between the powers; thirdly, only the temporal authority has the power of coercion; fourthly, ministers of the Church are accountable to the king and his court if, in the exercise of their jurisdiction, they should disturb public order or give offence to the laws and maxims of the kingdom. For some time the Parlement's legal pronouncements had been diverging from those of the King's Council, a state of affairs that could only weaken the king's authority, especially since the Parlement's judgments were more solidly based on precedent. Certainly this decree was entirely at one with traditional Gallican principles. However, in contradicting the royal decree of March 1731 it encroached upon the king's prerogative of law-making, and Fleury was bound to take immediate action. On 8 September, a royal council decree ordered the offending *arrêt* to be erased from the Parlement's registers.

The summer vacation intervened at this stage, and when the magistrates reassembled they were informed that Fleury had forbidden any further discussion on the matter. From November 1731 to January 1732 the

[1] Hardy, op. cit., 234.

magistrates sought furiously but in vain to regain their freedom of speech. Their case was an impressive one. The complete independence of the crown in temporal matters and its quasi-spiritual role in the Gallican Church had been for centuries a recognized aspect of royal rule, and the magistrates could claim with justice that they had only reminded the king of laws which hitherto it had been in his own interests to support. In any case, a simple council decree, like that of March 1731, that took account only of the advice of the current ministers and was essentially an *ad hoc* decision to cope with particular circumstances, lacked the formality and solemnity that should have accompanied the reversal of such important principles if the decision was to have any permanence. Indeed, it seemed that the cardinal tacitly recognized the validity of the magistrates' point of view in part, for in December 1731 the chancellor assured the First President that the prohibition to discuss the authority of the two powers was not to be perpetual but provisional. Meanwhile, another serious dispute was already at hand.

An ascetic and saintly young deacon, called Paris, had been a bitter opponent of *Unigenitus*, against which he registered a formal appeal. This last fact became of paramount importance after his death in 1727, for within a short time a rash of so-called miraculous cures broke out around his grave in the little Parisian churchyard of Saint-Médard. Soon, however, these activities deteriorated into a series of hysterical frenzies and convulsions, and in January 1732 a royal ordinance commanded the churchyard to be closed. Though the Parlement as a body was disposed to concur with the government's attitude, the king now forbade the court to concern itself with any subject connected with *Unigenitus*. This further quite arbitrary curtailment of the Parlement's jurisdiction, intended to prevent it from reaching decisions which would be unpopular with the government, provoked the magistrates into adopting new tactics. They decided upon a judicial strike, to last until the government lifted its prohibition. Fleury retaliated by arresting and exiling a number of leading malcontents. In their turn, all the magistrates save those in the *Grand' Chambre* at once offered to resign their offices.

They immediately found Fleury in a more malleable mood and were promised free debate and the opportunity to remonstrate about their grievances. The magistrates drew up remonstrances containing a strong plea for independence in the execution of the law. The king's reply was in the form of a declaration ordaining that only the *Grand' Chambre* should have cognizance of matters relating to the maxims of the kingdom and it strictly forbade judicial strikes. In direct defiance the magistrates forthwith went on strike and the declaration was only registered at a *lit de justice* on 3 September. The magistrates remained defiant and this time a hundred and thirty-nine of them were exiled to various provincial towns or to more isolated parts of the country. However, that drastic action solved nothing; the judicial services were disorganized and public order was threatened. Eventually a compromise was reached: in return for a show of servility from the court, the unpopular declaration was suspended, though not revoked, and the exiled magistrates returned to the capital. The suspension of a declaration which had been registered with all the solemnity of a *lit de justice* represented more than a setback for the cardinal in his quarrel with the Parlement; it was also damaging to the prestige of the law and to the king's authority. Once again, Fleury had shown himself willing to bend with the wind, to use the king's legislative power pragmatically as a tactical weapon. In that connection, an early historian of the period has commented, 'Who cannot detect here the progressive decline of royal authority?'[1]

Despite this apparent victory, however, the Parlement had no real success in the concluding ten years of the cardinal's rule. Whenever it sought to withhold unqualified recognition from *Unigenitus*, Fleury produced a council decree forbidding the court to interfere. What rendered this policy so arbitrary was the fact that the cardinal did not base his own policy squarely upon the controversial declaration of 1730. Between 1731 and 1736, by means of royal decrees he suppressed a series of episcopal Instructions which were too outspoken in favour of unreserved support for the bull. In fact, his chief concern was to prevent either side from stating clearly and dogmatically its own point of view; he now sought to end the controversy by the imposition of silence.

In the course of his ministry, Fleury effected a revolution. By ignoring or contradicting Gallican traditions, which hitherto had safeguarded the king and individual Frenchmen against ultramontane pressure, he not only reduced the authority of the crown *vis-à-vis* the spiritual powers, he deprived it of one of its firmest supports. Although the theory of divine right was rapidly losing its hold over men's minds after 1715,[2] a deeper-rooted tradition remained of legitimate kingship supported by, and functioning under, the law. The Gallican tradition formed an important

[1] C. Lacretelle, *Histoire de France pendant le XVIIIe siècle*, I, 111.
[2] Cobban, *In Search of Humanity*, 101.

part of the legal inheritance of Louis XV, and it could only be rejected at the risk of undermining the monarch's prestige. Certainly, the continued observance of long-held principles may sometimes cease to be a virtue, and then it may be preferable to run the risks inherent in enforcing radical change. Fleury's revolution, however, could not be justified on these grounds: it was both unnecessary and irrelevant. It was unnecessary because the status of *Unigenitus* had already been settled in 1720 and in reopening the matter Fleury simply aroused fresh antagonisms without offering a more permanent solution. It was irrelevant because the future security of the monarchy did not depend on whether or not *Unigenitus* was a rule of faith. It depended rather upon whether a more equitable and efficient system of taxation could be arrived at; yet almost Fleury's first act upon assuming power in 1726 had been to undermine the effectiveness of the *cinquantieme*.[1] It depended principally upon whether respect for the monarch's authority, based upon his role of supreme executor and defender of the law, could be maintained. In that context, Fleury's attitude was especially disastrous for not only was his religious policy novel in itself; it was carried through in a thoroughly arbitrary manner with little respect for the normal processes of law. It demonstrated not the power but the impotence of the law in the face of royal authoritarianism.

How may the role of the Parlement be assessed under this regime? Generally its attitude has been condemned by historians as negative and damaging to royal authority.[2] It is true that from the early 1730s the court began to publish its remonstrances and its more controversial resolutions, despite its members' oaths of secrecy. However, there is no evidence to suggest that the magistrates intended thereby to encourage sedition or rebellion; on the contrary, the nature of the Parlement's activities made it hostile to any such idea. Its concern was with the enforcement of law and the preservation of public order. The formal, legalistic and on the whole restrained language of the court's remonstrances and resolutions which were distributed piecemeal, were not likely to inspire public outbreaks. Yet the disorders at Saint-Médard, which could well have been used to support *parlementaire* demands, were quashed and the churchyard closed, with the approval of all in the Parlement save a handful of followers of the deacon Paris. The court publicized its opposition not to stimulate a crisis among the public, but to convince the cardinal that it had an important part to play as the upholder of the established law, the enemy of arbitrary

[1] *See supra*, 298–9.
[2] Shennan, 'The Political Role of the Parlement of Paris, 1715–1723', 179–80.

government. The magistrates were not questioning the king's ultimate authority, but they were seeking to persuade the government always to act within the law. The importance of this traditional duty had been diminished under Fleury's regime. By making public their concept of government, the magistrates were making it more explicit and giving it more force than was otherwise possible. Similarly, the Parlement's demands for freedom of speech and for independence in the enforcement of the law, forced upon it by the cardinal's policy of evocation and by his impositions of silence, was not intended to dispute the king's authority, but rather to underline the sovereignty of the law.

Almost six years after Fleury's death, Montesquieu published his *De l'Esprit des Lois*. In his work he made no attempt to challenge the king's overall supremacy in the state. His was the last and the greatest defence under the *ancien régime* of the ideal of legitimate royal authority, exercised under and not outside the law. Montesquieu saw the Parlement as the depository of the laws, both fundamental and statutory, with the duty of proclaiming new laws and recalling old ones when they had been overlooked. He dismissed the claims of the King's Council to fulfil this function because its decisions only represented *ad hoc* wishes of the ruler. He believed that the magistrates had their part to play in curbing the excesses of royal sovereignty in so far as they could maintain their resistance. Ultimately, the ruler's will had to prevail, though the frontiers up to which the magistrates could advance in countering royal arbitrariness, Montesquieu left ill-defined.[1] There are many echoes of his ideas in the history of the Parlement's relations with the government of Cardinal Fleury, in the magistrates' attempt to eliminate what Montesquieu called '*la volonté momentanée et capricieuse d'un seul*'.[2]

In the second half of the eighteenth century, the Parlement became far more militant. It was certainly inspired by Montesquieu's *De l'Esprit des Lois* – the so-called 'Grand Remonstrances' of April 1753 contained much of Montesquieu's own language and vocabulary – but in addition, the magistrates had clearly lost their sense of awe for the king's authority. In retrospect, the years in which first Orléans and then Fleury governed the country appear critical ones in terms of this serious decline in royal prestige. During these years, the king himself played little or no role in decision-making; his authority was enforced by the regent or by the cardinal. As a result, that authority was weakened, partly because the monarch was seen

[1] Montesquieu, *De l'Esprit des Lois*, I, Bk II, Chapter IV; Bk V, Chapter X, *passim*.
[2] Ibid., Bk II, Chapter IV, 20.

not to be governing the country himself, partly because those who were exercising power on his behalf were doing so in an arbitrary and inconsistent fashion. This was all the more serious for the crown because the era of divine-right monarchy was passing. Although Louis XV still touched his scrofulous subjects, the ceremony was fast becoming a meaningless charade. In France, as Montesquieu ironically noted in his *Lettres Persanes*, the king was a great magician.[1] Shorn of his supernatural support, the king needed to buttress his authority by exercising his traditional and basic role of chief justiciar, of supreme guardian of the law, but that function had been seriously compromised in the first half of the eighteenth century. When Louis XV at last took over the task of governing himself, only to pursue similar arbitrary and variable policies, he was fiercely opposed by the Parlement; and because that opposition was aimed directly against the sovereign and not against a minister, it was doubly dangerous.

It was a religious dispute again connected with the enforcement of *Unigenitus*, which provoked the renewal of serious conflict between the king and his Parlement. A number of *curés*, influenced by the strongly anti-Jansenist archbishop of Paris, Christophe de Beaumont, were once more refusing the last sacraments to opponents of *Unigenitus*. In April 1752 the Parlement forbade any priests to refuse the sacraments on such grounds and proceeded to indict those *curés* who continued to defy it. The king was forced to intervene frequently to frustrate the court's offensive, eventually evoking to the *Grand Conseil* all disputes arising out of refusals to administer the sacraments. This was the signal for the beginning of a series of disputes with the crown which lasted for almost twenty years.[2]

The Parlement refused in its turn to register the letters-patent and in April 1753 it produced its Grand Remonstrances. It did not in fact make any revolutionary claims in this famous document, though it did push its traditional function to the limit:

> If there are times when the court's unshakeable attachment to the laws and to the public good seems to accord ill with a limitless obedience, then it would be wrong . . . to forget . . what the Parlement told the sovereign in 1604: if we disobey by serving you well, then the Parlement is frequently guilty of this fault. When there is a conflict between the king's absolute power and the good of his service, the court respects

[1] Montesquieu, *Lettres Persanes*, Letter XXIV, 44.

[2] B. de Lacombe, *La Résistance Janséniste et Parlementaire*, 102–7.

the latter rather than the former, not to disobey but in order to discharge its obligations.

The magistrates also quoted the words of Bossuet: 'Arbitrary government, where the only law is the Prince's will, does not exist in well ordered states; it has no place amongst us; it is manifestly opposed to legitimate government'.[1] These remonstrances touched upon the constitutional, as well as the religious issue, a sign of the court's self-assurance; more strenuously than ever it was demanding that the king should not exercise his authority in an unrestricted manner, and in a more positive way than usual it was defining its own rights and obligations in the matter.

Louis XV refused to receive these remonstrances. The Parlement retaliated by staging a judicial strike, to which the king's response was to order the magistrates into exile either on their own estates or in towns far removed from the capital. In Paris, a 'royal chamber' was set up to take the Parlement's place. However, it lacked the latter's aura of legitimacy and long-standing, and was boycotted both by the professionals, barristers and solicitors, and by the parties. The government, thus faced with a difficult situation, decided to give way. A reconciliation was worked out, according to which both bishops and Jansenists were to be forbidden to publicize their differing points of view, while the Parlement was to guarantee and enforce this mutual silence. A royal declaration was published to that effect in September 1754. The magistrates were of course recalled from exile and reinstated in the Palais de Justice. It was a victory for the Parlement, which gave the magistrates a feeling of great self-confidence and underlined the deterioration of the king's authority.

Almost at once, the king suffered another setback at the Parlement's hands. In December 1756 Machault d'Arnouville, a former finance minister and the strongest man in the government, was appointed chancellor. He immediately supervised the drawing up of a number of royal acts, which were ratified in the Parlement by the authoritarian means of a *lit de justice*. These acts forbade the court to make iterative remonstrances or to hold judicial strikes, and gave the least combative *Grand' Chambre* the right to control the plenary sessions of the court, at which political matters were debated. In addition, two of the five chambers of *Enquêtes* were suppressed. This was a brave counter-attack by the government, but one which it proved unable to sustain. The members of

[1] Flammermont, op. cit., I, 526.

the *Enquêtes* resigned *en bloc* and almost half the *Grand' Chambriers*, surprisingly, did likewise.[1] This action disconcerted the king, but far more disconcerting was the support given to the Parlement of Paris by its provincial counterparts. Since 1755 the theory of *parlementaire* unity had been gaining ground. The Parlement of Paris borrowed the idea from the argument originally propounded by L'Hôpital in 1560, stating it for the first time in 1755 in remonstrances opposing the powers exercised by the *Grand Conseil*: 'the Parlement of Paris and . . . the other Parlements form a single body and are only different divisions of the royal Parlement'.[2] Now, in this moment of crisis for the Parisian Parlement, the Parlements of Rouen, Rennes and Bordeaux invoked the same principle, a principle already officially applauded by the Parlements of Toulouse, Metz, Grenoble and Aix.

There could be no doubt now that the Parlement was taking the offensive. This idea of a united magistracy implied less a royal court than a nation-wide institution with positive powers of its own, virtually independent in the exercise of them. In the days of Orléans and Fleury, the court had felt itself unable to do more than decry the arbitrary and inconsistent exercise of authority; by the late 1750s it was close to asserting the right to regulate it. Once again, its claims were becoming extravagant. As one commentator has put it, it was as if the French monarchy was no longer absolute but constitutional, controlled, as in England, by a parliament.[3]

The magistrates' mood, therefore, even in the face of direct royal attack, was one of buoyant optimism, a mood which turned out to be fully justified. The king's position was further weakened by the fact that the Seven Years War was just beginning and, predictably, the government was short of funds. Louis needed the Parlement's support if he was to raise sufficient money adequately to prosecute the war and so, yet again, he capitulated. In February 1757 Machault, the one minister who had dared to humiliate the court, was disgraced; his disciplinary measures against the Parlement, enforced by the *lit de justice*, were suspended, and though two chambers of *Enquêtes* – the fourth and fifth – remained suppressed, their members were shared out between the other chambers, so that no counsellor lost his office. In return for these favours, in 1757 and 1758, the Parlement supported the king's extraordinary war-time financial

[1] L. Cahen, *Les Querelles Religieuses et Parlementaires*, 58–61; Renaudet, op. cit., 153.

[2] Bickart, *Les Parlements et la Notion de Souveraineté Nationale*, 152 et seq; *see supra*, 85.

[3] Renaudet, op. cit., 155.

measures; in terms of royal prestige, however, its support had been dearly bought.

Meanwhile, the war continued and with it the king's financial problems. In 1759 the government was forced to submit a further bunch of fiscal measures to the Parlement; that it was on the defensive was made abundantly clear by accompanying proposals for various economies in the royal household. The magistrates were quickly on the attack. Their remonstrances of September 1759 complaining about the latest impositions received an unusually long, conciliatory reply from the king, which did not satisfy them. They renewed their objections in further remonstrances presented later in the same month, in which they sought in advance to invalidate the authoritarian measures which they knew would be necessary to overcome their resistance, by making a spirited defence of their court's right of free registration. The mechanism of the *lit de justice* was subsequently employed to enforce these fiscal measures, but that act served only to underline the magistrates' challenge, which they were in no mood to withdraw. They returned to the attack with further remonstrances early in 1760.

> All administration in the state [declared this latest magisterial apologia] is founded on the laws. That involves free registration, preceded by verification and examination . . . the people's trust . . . which the supreme power, however just, cannot inspire alone, is a result of this free scrutiny, after which the verification of the law testifies to the justice of its motives and to the need for its execution.

This was not yet a revolutionary doctrine that the Parlement was propounding. Less than a year before, the court had solemnly declared that in the person of the monarch, who was the sole source of law in the kingdom, resided the plenitude of power; it added that it would take severe measures against anyone who tried to limit or divide that sovereignty.[1] The magistrates had certainly not rejected such a fundamental monarchical principle, but a surprising change of emphasis was taking place. Not for the first time the Parlement was stressing the limitations to which the king was subject. But this time its argument left little room for compromise; it was also receiving strong support from the provincial courts, not only through similar arguments put forward in their remonstrances but also through the idea of *parlementaire* unity which the magistrates were con-

[1] Flammermont, op. cit, II, 194–5, 274.

tinuing to canvass. Even more significantly, it was challenging a king whose title to the throne was indisputable and whose reign, undisturbed by any serious crisis, had already lasted for forty-five years.

The magistrates' objections to the government's fiscal expedients were now along thoroughly predictable lines. Gone were their earlier hesitations: they vehemently opposed any new or additional tax burdens, especially levies like the *vingtième*, the successor to the *dixième*, with its implications of tax equality, which was first established in 1749 and twice renewed in 1756 and 1759. They considered such measures difficult to justify even in the most serious emergencies. The basis of their position was the idea that the state should not offend against existing custom, privilege or standards of equity. It was an attitude increasingly unlikely to solve the desperate financial situation, but at least it had certain legal virtues; it was consistent and it was based on a multitude of precedents. The government's policy, on the other hand, had a far less valid appearance, partly because its measures were quite clearly a series of expedients to tide the country over a difficult period, governed by no coherent principle and partly because apparently the king had very little faith in his financial advisers. In 1754 Machault d'Arnouville, the architect of the *vingtième*, was transferred from finance to the navy office. In 1759 Silhouette was made to resign after his financial proposals had been bitterly criticized by the Parlement. In 1763 his successor, Bertin, was similarly sacrificed by the fickle king. It was not surprising therefore, that the Parlement should cling all the more obstinately to its own position which was not based on such shifting foundations.

The fall of Bertin in 1763 illustrates very well the attitudes of the protagonists. With the ending of the Seven Years War, it was widely expected that the extraordinary taxation levied in the war years would be abrogated. When Bertin produced an edict authorizing much of it to continue, the Parlement's reaction was furious. The king could scarcely have been surprised, and indeed he tried to cut short the protestations by holding a *lit de justice*, at which the controversial edict was registered. He did not succeed, however, in preventing the magistrates from composing remonstrances in June 1763, in which they denounced the continued high level of taxation, nor from repeating their objections at great length in August, when the king rejected their initial complaints. To reinforce their point of view they felt it necessary to make further claims on the Parlement's behalf. In June the magistrates attacked the authoritarian procedure of the *lit de justice*. In September, after receiving the king's rejection of their

August remonstrances, the magistrates made further representations, in which they were more specific: 'the magistrates . . . must deliberate freely and maturely over verification: without verification no tax should be levied'.[1] At last Louis gave way, as he had done on so many previous occasions. Bertin lost his office, and a new edict replaced the latter's unpopular measure. The king virtually accepted the validity of much of the Parlement's criticism, declaring in the edict's preamble that he wanted to rule not simply by invoking his authority, but with respect for justice and for the rules and procedures which had been established in the kingdom. He did not repeal all the contents of the previous edict, but he made a number of concessions to the court and invited its advice on all aspects of the government's taxation policy. Finally, the king nominated as Bertin's successor in the office of controller-general of finance a member of the Parlement, Clément de Laverdy, a man with no flair for his office and quite incapable of withstanding the pressures exerted upon him by his former colleagues.[2] It was ironic that the king's acceptance of what was after all a fundamental principle of the French monarchy should have diminished his authority, but that was the case, for his gesture was clearly made out of weakness rather than strength. The Parlement, too, was ensnared in a dangerous irony, for each time that it forced the king to yield ground, however legally justified its stand, it reduced the crown's prestige, and in the last resort the Parlement's own status and authority depended upon the respect which the monarchy commanded.

Meanwhile, the ancient animosity between the Parlement and the Jesuits which had led to the expulsion of the Society in Henry IV's reign was resumed in 1761 and ended in another serious setback for the king's authority. The magistrates' traditional hostility as the chief defenders of Gallican doctrine to the ultramontane Society of Jesus had been further exacerbated by the quarrels arising out of *Unigenitus*. Then, quite unexpectedly, the magistrates were presented with a splendid opportunity to destroy their old adversaries, and they were not slow to seize it. The opportunity centred around one Father Lavalette, who, since 1741, had been in charge of a Jesuit mission at Martinique in the Windward Islands. Besides being a priest, he was a considerable business man, and during his stay there he inaugurated a number of profitable ventures, which he financed through a series of loans. However, with the outbreak of the Seven Years War, the island's economy was seriously damaged, and

[1] Ibid., 411.
[2] Renaudet, op. cit., 156–8.

Lavalette found himself deeply in debt. The financiers who had made the loans sued him and his Order in an effort to recoup their losses. At the first hearing, the case went against the Jesuits, who now decided – and it was a fatal decision – to appeal to the Parlement of Paris.

In April 1761 a counsellor from the *Grand' Chambre*, Abbé Chauvelin, seized the excuse of Lavalette's appeal to make wide-ranging criticisms of the whole Jesuit Order, denouncing its rule as being incompatible with public order. A largely sympathetic court at once decided that this rule should be handed over to the *Gens du roi* to be examined further. In the meantime, the Parlement reached a decision on the narrower matter – the only one upon which its opinion had been called for – of Lavalette's grave debts. In May 1761 it decreed that the Society was responsible for repaying the money, and as a surety it issued an *arrêt de saisin* against the Society, which would provide legal duress if the reimbursement was not forthcoming. Then, at the beginning of July, the *Gens du roi* announced their conclusions on the broader issue of the Jesuits' rule, previously referred to them. They recommended that the court should institute a further inquiry, especially into the Order's attitude to the Gallican maxims of 1682, and into ways of supervising their activities. The portents were growing that the magistrates intended to take drastic measures against the Society and the king was persuaded to intervene on 3 August, with a declaration forbidding the Parlement to make any legal pronouncement upon the Jesuits until a year had elapsed. The court took so little account of this order that three days later it received the *Procureur-Général*'s appeal *comme d'abus* from the papal bull *Regimini*, which had authorized the Society's establishment in 1540. At the same time, it condemned twenty-four books written by Jesuits and forbade them to recruit novices or to teach in France. The king intervened again, this time to impose a further year's delay before the Parlement's latest decrees became effective. The court registered his orders but reduced the period of suspension to six months. Louis then tried to placate the court by a declaration of March 1762, which stipulated that no orders emanating from the Jesuits' General could have effect in the kingdom unless accompanied by royal letters registered in the Parlement. In addition, the Society was commanded to teach in its schools and seminaries the four Gallican articles of 1682. However, the time was approaching – 1 April 1762 – when the six months' period of suspension would be over and the Parlement could enforce its decrees. The magistrates showed little enthusiasm, therefore, for the new measure, and proceeded to employ time-wasting tactics until the critical date. When it came, all the Jesuit colleges and schools within the Parlement's area of jurisdiction were summarily closed, and shortly afterwards the magistrates produced a decree authorizing the sequestration of the Society's property and possessions. Then, by a decree dated 6 August 1762, the Parlement took up the appeal *comme d'abus* which it had received exactly twelve months before. It proclaimed that the Jesuits' rule constituted a threat to the sovereign's person, to the rights of his crown and to the obedience of his subjects, and forbade the members of the Society to practise their rule. The king did not dare to resist the Parlement's actions; indeed, in November 1764 he approved an edict which finally suppressed the order altogether in France. The whole episode reflected little credit on Louis. He had exerted himself just enough to reveal his inadequacy, when faced with the determined court. The latter's rancorous attack on the Society of Jesus, inspired by a very deep and ancient enmity, was unjustified and partial. Yet the king, whose inclination was to defend the Society, not only proved incapable of doing so, but was even forced to assist at its eclipse.[1]

The provincial Parlements, too, were becoming more bellicose in their relations with the central government, particularly the Parlement of Brittany, that most independent of provinces. Since 1763, the magistrates at Rennes had been at odds with the provincial governor, the Duc d'Aiguillon. In 1765 they resigned *en bloc*, and the king set up a new judicial court at Rennes to take their place. At that moment the Parlement of Paris chose to intervene in the dispute, invoking the theory of *parlementaire* solidarity, which had become so popular with the magistrates. Twice, in September and again in December 1765, the court presented remonstrances complaining against the treatment meted out to their colleagues in Brittany; the king ignored both petitions. Shortly before the presentation of the second remonstrances, La Chalotais, the *Procureur-Général* of the Parlement of Brittany, was arrested. Evidently the king had at last decided to compromise no longer, but unequivocally to assert his absolute power. For this purpose he attended a *lit de justice* on 3 March 1766, a celebrated occasion known as the *séance de la flagellation*. At this session, Louis XV's speech achieved a hitherto unsuspected level of eloquence and vigour, as he firmly rejected all the constitutional claims put forward by the Parlement during the preceding decade and a half. He dismissed the idea of a union of all the Parlements, the claim that the

[1] Cahen, op. cit., 64–73; Renaudet, op. cit., 160–3; reference should also be made to the article by J. Egret, 'Le Procès des Jésuites devant les Parlements de France', 1–27.

Parlement was the nation's tribunal, the possessor of sovereign power in the business of registering royal orders. He reminded the magistrates that such power appertained to him alone, '*sans dépendence et sans partage*'. It was certainly the king's most impressive performance and it duly had its effect. But matters had gone too far for one royal gesture to restore all the old prestige, and it was not very long before the Parlement was reiterating its complaints on behalf of the Parlement of Brittany.

That Parlement was finally restored in 1769 but its *Procureur-Général* remained in exile; for that reason the members of the Breton court decided to attack their old adversary, D'Aiguillon. He appealed to the king, who decided that he had the right to be judged by the Parlement of Paris in its capacity of the peers' tribunal, with Louis himself presiding. In April 1770, the court began its examination of the charges against D'Aiguillon, but almost immediately the magistrates shifted their ground from the particular to the general, demanding details of the government's instructions to its agents in Brittany. Louis was no longer prepared to tolerate this sort of interference with its implied challenge to his own authority and he promptly announced that all the proceedings instituted against D'Aiguillon were to be dropped. The Parlement ignored the royal order and issued a provisional judgment against the duke, which was in turn broken by contrary orders from the royal council. Another *lit de justice* followed in September 1770, at which the magistrates were forbidden to take the matter any further and this was followed by an edict drawn up by the Chancellor Maupeou and sent to the court at the end of November. This strongly worded criticism of the court's behaviour forbade the court to quote the doctrine of *parlementaire* unity and stipulated that once laws had been registered the magistrates were obliged to execute them, whether registered in the usual manner or by a *lit de justice*. The magistrates replied with remonstrances, which were silent on the accusations made against them and which did not dispute their ultimate dependence upon the king. Instead they tried to magnify the Parlement's historic past to justify its rights to a major role:

> If the pride of great vassals has been turned to humility before the throne of your ancestors . . . if they have recognized the king as their sovereign . . . if the independence of your crown has been maintained against the unsurpations of Rome . . . if, finally, the sceptre has been preserved in a long and happy succession for the eldest representative of the royal family in the male line . . . all these

services . . . are due to your Parlement, a fact which history can support.[1]

These assertions, though exaggerated, were not entirely without foundation; in fact, the Parlement's position, like the king's, was broadly based on precedent. But the position of each side was hardening and the room for manœuvre was fast diminishing. In particular, the Parlement's actions were beginning to resemble their most extreme theoretical utterances.

Louis XV rejected the Parlement's latest statements out of hand and ordered the edict to be registered on the morrow. The magistrates refused and drew up reiterated remonstrances; the king ordered and held a *lit de justice* at which the edict was registered; the members of the Parlement went on strike. There followed a series of royal orders commanding the magistrates to resume their judicial work, all of them ignored by the Parlement. By this time, January 1771, the situation was almost beyond the king's control. 'This astonishing anarchy cannot last,' commented Voltaire, 'either the Crown must re-assert its authority or the Parlements will gain the upper hand.'[2] Finally, under heavy pressure from Maupeou, who did not esteem the court, though he had once been its First President, Louis asserted his power in the most spectacular and drastic manner possible. On 21 and 22 January, the magistrates' offices were confiscated and they themselves were sent into exile: after five hundred years the Parlement of Paris had ceased to exist.

Maupeou's judicial reforms represented the monarchy's most dramatic attempt to shore up its fast declining authority, by eliminating its most persistent and powerful critic.[3] It may be asked why such a measure had not been tried earlier, since for the rest of Louis XV's reign the new system of courts, devised by the chancellor and composed of royal nominees, worked satisfactorily and caused the king no trouble. The answer lies in the nature of the reform itself. What Maupeou was attempting was nothing less than a reorientation of the monarch's function. In the past, that role had been subject to a good deal of variation, according to the special needs and conditions of the moment, but essentially it involved an ideal of kingship enmeshed by traditional laws, customs, rights and

[1] Flammermont, op. cit., III, 159; the D'Aiguillon-La Chalotais dispute is discussed in Cahen, op. cit., 89–98; Lacombe, op. cit., 188 et seq; Glasson, *Le Parlement de Paris*, II, 307 et seq.

[2] Cited by Lacombe, op. cit., 207–8.

[3] The best analysis of Maupeou's work in this connection is to be found in R. Villers, *L'Organisation du Parlement de Paris et des Conseils Supérieurs d'après la Réforme de Maupeou.*

privileges. Maupeou was destroying the one institution capable of reminding the sovereign of these responsibilities. That is not to say that such a role remained relevant, nor that it was always played with scrupulous fairness. It may well have been that the monarchy's only hope of survival lay in making a complete break of this kind. What is important is the fact that the chancellor had taken a revolutionary step on his king's behalf. The threats of extremism which had periodically vitiated the relations between the crown and the Parlement had this time produced drastic results. The immediate causes of the final breakdown were to be found on both sides – the excessive and uncompromising claims of the magistracy, the vacillating and unpredictable responses of the government – but it was the sharp decline in the king's prestige, for which Orléans and Fleury bore a heavy responsibility, which provided the significant underlying motive.

Having taken such a decisive step, it was of critical importance for the monarchy that it should not retract, but should seek in its new context of authority to strengthen its grip on the country. A reappearance of the Parlement would certainly imply for the crown an obligation to reckon with the old order and for the Parlement freedom to resume its militant attitudes. Yet, when Louis XVI succeeded his grandfather in 1774, he was persuaded to dispense with Maupeou and his reforms and to restore to the Parlement its ancient rights and dignities. He did restrict the court's political role by insisting that plenary sessions of the court depended upon the First President's approval, that such sessions held for non-political reasons – the reception of a new counsellor, for example – could not be used for raising political issues and that no political debate could take place at times customarily set aside for judicial work.

The long history of the Parlement was virtually over; the epilogue had begun. Its return was hailed as a triumph by those who believed that the arbitrariness of the crown was over, and the old legal values and liberties were to be restored. In the light of what was shortly to take place, such people may be labelled as reactionaries. Yet without the benefit of hindsight such tags are misleading. Most people were aware primarily of the fact that royal authority had lost its way, and, that in seeking to recover, it had rejected the traditional path. The need seemed to be to restore some kind of legal equilibrium; few dreamed as yet of a root and branch reform. Many felt that the Parlement could provide the necessary corrective force and therefore its return was popular, not only among those with privileged interests to protect, but with the Parisian poor as well. When the porters and stall-holders at the *Halles* acclaimed the magistrates they did not perceive that they were supporting reaction any more than the magistrates themselves perceived that the hostility to the crown which was implicit in the welcome given to them would, in the long run, extend also to the Parlement.

The magistrates showed at once that their mood had not been softened by exile. They remonstrated against the disciplinary limitations imposed upon the court at its restoration and must have been gratified at the timidity of the new king's response. The real friction, however, was caused by financial difficulties. The magistrates mistrusted the economic ideas of the new finance minister, Turgot, the physiocrat, who advocated a greater freedom of internal trade, the abolition of restrictive guild regulations and of the *corvée*, substituting for the latter a tax on all landowners. Measures to implement these policies were opposed by the Parlement and registered eventually at a *lit de justice*, in March 1776. The magistrates' opposition was based on the need to maintain established rights and privileges and inspired by their abhorrence of the novelty of Turgot's schemes. Turgot had other enemies besides the Parlement and, in May 1776, Louis XVI was persuaded to dismiss him.

His successor, Necker, was able to maintain a far better relationship with the Parlement, basically because he, like it, was opposed to the introduction of new taxes. He ran the country on a series of loans, thereby affecting the illusion that the government's financial resources were more than adequate. However, in 1778 he submitted to the king a secret memorandum, criticizing the Parlement's financial attitudes and advocating a series of provincial assemblies, which, in the fullness of time, would take over the Parlement's financial, and even political attributes. When the contents of this memorandum came to light in 1781, the *entente* between the minister and the magistrates was broken, and Necker was unable to persuade the court to support any further loans. He, too, was dismissed in the early summer of 1781.

The financial problem facing the government could not be solved by a series of expedients. It was becoming increasingly evident that radical steps would have to be taken if the government was to regain its freedom of action. The highly intelligent, but politically inept Calonne, who became controller-general of finance in 1783, tried for some time to run the country along the lines indicated by Necker, by a series of loans, but Calonne was far less popular with the Parlement than Necker had been. Louis XV had nominated him to take charge of the trial of La Chalotais, the *Procureur-Général* in the Parlement of Brittany whose bitter rivalry with the Duc d'Aiguillon had made him a leading figure in *parlementaire* hagiography: it was not an encouraging background against which to endeavour to rehabilitate the country's economy. The Parlement co-operated unwillingly until the end of 1785, when it made a firm stand against the levying of a new loan and against the whole principle of running the economy by this means, at least in peace-time. Calonne now had no alternative but to accept the fact that only profound changes in the taxation system could solve the country's problems. By August 1786 his project was prepared: he could admit of no inequality in tax obligations and the basis of the new order was to be a new tax, the *subvention territoriale*, levied on all property holders. The amount to be collected from the *taille* and from indirect taxes like the *gabelle*, on the other hand, was to be greatly reduced. Because Calonne had no hope of obtaining the Parlement's approval, he asked an assembly of Notables to approve his scheme. The assembly, which met in February 1787, found the project quite as unacceptable as the Parlement would have done, a result which may have surprised the naïve Calonne but was scarcely unpredictable. With his failure to win over the Notables, Calonne's position was undermined and he gave way to Marie Antoinette's nominee, the archbishop of Toulouse, Loménie de Brienne, who saw no alternative but to put Calonne's proposals to the assembly again. This he did, in May 1787, with the same lack of success. Any new tax, the Notables decided, required the approval of the Estates-General, or, whilst the Estates were not in session, of the Parlement.[1]

Brienne was driven, therefore, to seek the support of the Parlement, though, like his predecessor, he could have had few illusions about the sort of reception his measures would receive. For their part, the magistrates were firmly committed to opposing fiscal innovations, which would be so damaging to the interests of the privileged classes, and they now borrowed from the assembly of Notables the idea of an appeal to the Estates-General. In remonstrances opposing the imposition of the *subvention territoriale* in July 1787, they maintained 'that the Nation, represented by the Estates-General, alone has the right to grant to the king the necessary aid'.[2] This move by the court was simply a delaying tactic, another method of resisting the government's policy and of justifying the old order. The king

[1] Renaudet, op. cit., 186–92; A. Cobban, *A History of Modern France*, I, 120–5; J. Egret' *La Pré-Révolution Française*, 5 et seq.

[2] Flammermont, op. cit., III, 676.

held a *lit de justice*, at which the measure was registered, and the Parlement promptly declared this authoritarian registration null and void. The Parisian populace, interpreting the appeal to the Estates-General as an indication of the court's determination to prevent further arbitrary impositions – as indeed it was – was enraptured, and was even more enthusiastic at hearing that the Parlement intended to put Calonne on trial. The government was bound to respond to these frontal attacks. The decree against Calonne was nullified and the magistrates were exiled to Troyes. But by this time public opinion was thoroughly aroused in the Parlement's favour, and Brienne lost his nerve. The edict imposing the *subvention territoriale* was repealed, a guarantee given that the Estates-General would be summoned and the triumphant magistrates were recalled to the capital.

Meanwhile, the financial situation grew more desperate, as Brienne tried in vain to persuade the Parlement to approve further loans, at least until the Estates-General met. He was again forced to invoke the king's tottering authority at a *lit de justice*; again, the registration was declared null and void and this time two of the most outspoken counsellors were arrested. The Parlement again objected to the authoritarian method employed: 'The king's will alone is not sufficient to make a law . . . to be obligatory this will must be legally proclaimed; to be legally proclaimed it must be freely verified; that, Sire, is the French constitution.'[1] Inspired by the popular support they were receiving, the magistrates now further widened the basis of dispute. In remonstrances in January 1788, they condemned the use of *lettres de cachet* by which the counsellors had been summarily arrested. 'Man is born free,' they proclaimed emotively, 'and his happiness depends on justice'.[2] In May they published a decree enunciating the fundamental laws of the kingdom, which included the right of all Frenchmen to be free from arbitrary arrest, of the Estates-General to vote new taxes and of the Parlement to verify the king's orders and register them only if they were in accordance with the laws of the state.[3] Such gestures heightened the court's popularity and dissuaded the government from attempting to repeat Maupeou's action *in toto*. Instead, the Parlement's area of cognizance was reorganized in such a way as to greatly reduce its jurisdiction, and a new plenary court was set up composed of royal nominees, which was to take over the task of registering royal edicts. It

[1] Ibid., 1–27.
[2] Ibid., 714.
[3] Glasson, *Le Parlement de Paris*, II, 472–3.

was a desperate measure taken far too late to improve the situation for the crown. Royal authority was by now breaking down altogether. The *intendants* no longer dared to collect taxes in their localities, and the public outcry on the Parlement's behalf threatened to become a revolution. Louis XVI took what in retrospect was to be a decisive step; he summoned the Estates-General to meet on 1 May 1789, 'handing in his resignation', as one distinguished historian of the revolution has put it.[1] At the same time, Necker was recalled to perform his sleight of hand over an empty treasury.

Yet again – and for the last time – the Parlement came back in triumph to the Palais de Justice, at the end of September 1788. But in its first debate, on the subject of the approaching meeting of the Estates-General, it made a fatal mistake, by insisting that the voting procedure should follow the precedent of 1614 and be by estate only. The Parlement's popularity drained away like water into sand, and overnight the idolatry of the populace turned to bitter resentment. For the magistrates it was a mistake which sooner or later they were bound to make, for just as many who had supported them had done so without comprehending all the implications, so too, the magistrates, with their slogans and their histrionics, had aroused passions of which they were unaware, but which would shortly destroy them. The court never regained the prestige which it had lost so suddenly in September 1788. In May 1789 the Estates-General met at last; in June the Third Estate arrogated to itself the title of National Assembly; in July the Bastille was stormed.

The destruction of the Parlement was a piecemeal process. On 3 November 1789 the National Assembly decreed that the Parlement would remain in recess while its work would continue to be performed by the *Chambre des Vacations*. For another year the Vacations represented the court, until the Assembly finally decided that the Parlement should be suppressed altogether. Its last act was to draw up a secret protestation against the decisions perpetrated by the revolutionary National Assembly . . . 'in the midst of the ruins of the monarchy there still stands a monument preserving the principles by which that monarchy has been regulated for so many centuries'.[2] It was signed by all sixteen members of the chamber, half of whom would subsequently pay with their lives for this defiant gesture. The date was 14 October 1790.

[1] G. Lefebvre, *The Coming of the French Revolution*, 2; the same author has provided a most valuable survey of the events leading to the outbreak of the revolution in *La Révolution Aristocratique*, 74 et seq.

[2] Carré, *La fin des Parlements*, 242.

The attitude of the Parlement in the last decades of its history is made difficult to comprehend because contemporaries tended to misinterpret it. It would be unfair to accuse the magistrates of hypocrisy at this time simply because their criticisms of the regime did not embrace the extreme views which came to the fore in 1789. The Parlement as a whole did genuinely believe that, in reflecting the public's disillusionment with the existing political order, it was fulfilling a vital and a traditional role.[1] For that disillusionment, in the Parlement's view, sprang from the arbitrariness of the king and his ministers, from the novel forms of taxation and the fiscal expedients which they introduced, from their recourse to *lits de justice* and *lettres de cachet* to enforce their measures, from their attempts to destroy even the court itself, the only institution, in the absence of the Estates-General, capable of opposing royal caprice. As the king became increasingly the prisoner of his ministers' varying policies, incapable of consistency or firmness, the magistrates reinforced their own argument, by appealing to the Estates-General, by claiming that registration in the Parlement was a fundamental law, by elaborating the theory of *parlementaire* unity. All these ideas were intended to buttress the court's basic standpoint, that the crown's principal function was to preserve and enforce the law, upon the fulfilment of which role its authority chiefly depended.

Especially after 1774, when Louis XVI restored the Parlement, the inability of this doctrine to resuscitate the state's fortunes became more apparent, and the unwillingness of the magistrates to accept radical changes is that much easier to criticize. The decisive factor was the decline in the king's authority, exacerbated by the weak character of Louis XVI and by his subordination to successive ministers, which allowed the magistrates to push their case to extremes. In doing so they only succeeded in further weakening that authority. Therein lay the irony of the court's position. Once the magistrates' respect for the king's power had been undermined, the traditional order, for whose preservation they were fighting, was immediately doomed, because its maintenance depended essentially upon the existence of a dominant monarchy. Similarly, so long as the Parlement continued to advocate support for the traditional order, the deterioration in the crown's position would of necessity adversely affect its own authority too. One of the court's leading historians,

[1] There were in fact a handful of magistrates whose opinions were radical, who welcomed the ideas of the American revolution and who spoke enthusiastically of liberty and of a new constitution. The Marquis de la Fayette described them as '*des gens honnêtes, instruits et patriotes*', Egret, *La Pré-Révolution Française*, 329.

Edouard Maugis, has expressed that fact in words which may also serve as the Parlement's epitaph:

> *And so they will continue to exist side by side, these twin and complementary powers, united by a keen sense of mutual dependence until at the close of a long and glorious history, equally incapable either of survival without the other or of renewal, both of them will perish together.*[1]

[1] Maugis, op. cit., I, 538.

Conclusion

For five hundred years the Parlement of Paris stood close to the heart of government in France, and an examination of its various functions – judicial, administrative, political – provides the best clue to an understanding of the role of the French monarchy itself. That role was, in the last analysis, a judicial one, based in and bound by the law, which the Parlement had the task of proclaiming, enforcing and preserving in written form. Thus its growing corpus of jurisprudence buttressed the authority of the crown and helped to unify the country under a single legal sovereign. But the Parlement was not simply a mechanism through which the king could subjugate and control his kingdom: the magistrates were equally obliged to protect the privileges of the subject against royal assault. This 'federal' concept of the state, of countless groups and individuals accepting the king's overall headship but by no means yielding their own immemorial rights, was not overthrown before 1789. It was increasingly menaced, however, by the doctrine of *raison d'état*, according to which the crown could invoke the overriding requirements of the state to justify the sacrifice of individual liberties. This was particularly the case with issues of national defence and security which provided the king with powerful arguments in favour of the exercise of unrestricted authority. In this conflict, the Parlement's jurisprudential heritage made it the firm ally of the traditional view.

It is undeniable that opportunities for royal arbitrariness grew, especially from the middle of the fifteenth century, when the prestige of the monarchy was high and royal administration was becoming more sophisticated and efficient. With the emergence of a bureaucratic, ministerial system, it became possible for the king to act as it were in a vacuum, without reference or regard to any external consideration, leaving the official machinery to implement his *ad hoc* decisions. Yet, at no time did the monarch reject the older view out of hand: he simply modified or ignored it when it was not convenient or practicable to abide by it, and therefore his measures often assumed an illegal character. The Parlement, on the other hand, adhered more rigidly to the traditional concept of the state, opposing the king first on the basis of its own legal records, then on behalf of those other institutions, local assemblies and Estates-General, which gradually became powerless to defend the old order.

So long as royal prestige remained high, it was possible for the king to overcome his court's objections. But the extreme positions which both sides adopted on occasion were never long maintained, precisely because they were seen to be extreme in comparison with the accepted norm. It was the decline of royal authority in the course of the eighteenth century which opened the way to drastic change. That decline was primarily the result of the king's failure adequately to fulfil any role at all: he had become totally irrelevant. His chief obligation – to act as the supreme judge – had been obscured and vitiated by the conduct of his ministers and by his own personal eclipse. In the end, ironically, the king might have saved himself by recourse to the despotic role which French kings had always rejected; as it was, the crown stood for neither one thing nor the other and was brushed aside in consequence.

For its part, the Parlement remained loyal to the only concept of government which its own history allowed. In the closing years of its existence its attitude was indeed as irrelevant as the institution of monarchy, with which it had always been intimately bound. It had grave defects: the slowness and the cost of its justice, the excessively cautious, wrong-headed or grievously-misguided nature of some of its political judgments. Yet its achievements and its overall significance in the context of pre-revolutionary France remain outstanding. The Parlement's contribution to the continuity of the French legal and political tradition, and therefore to the unity and stability of the country, and most of all its adherence to the idea that even princes should be governed by the law, deserves to survive the euphoria engendered by slogans of liberty, equality and fraternity.

APPENDICES

*

GLOSSARY

*

BIBLIOGRAPHY

*

INDEX

APPENDIX I—The Organisation of the Parlement

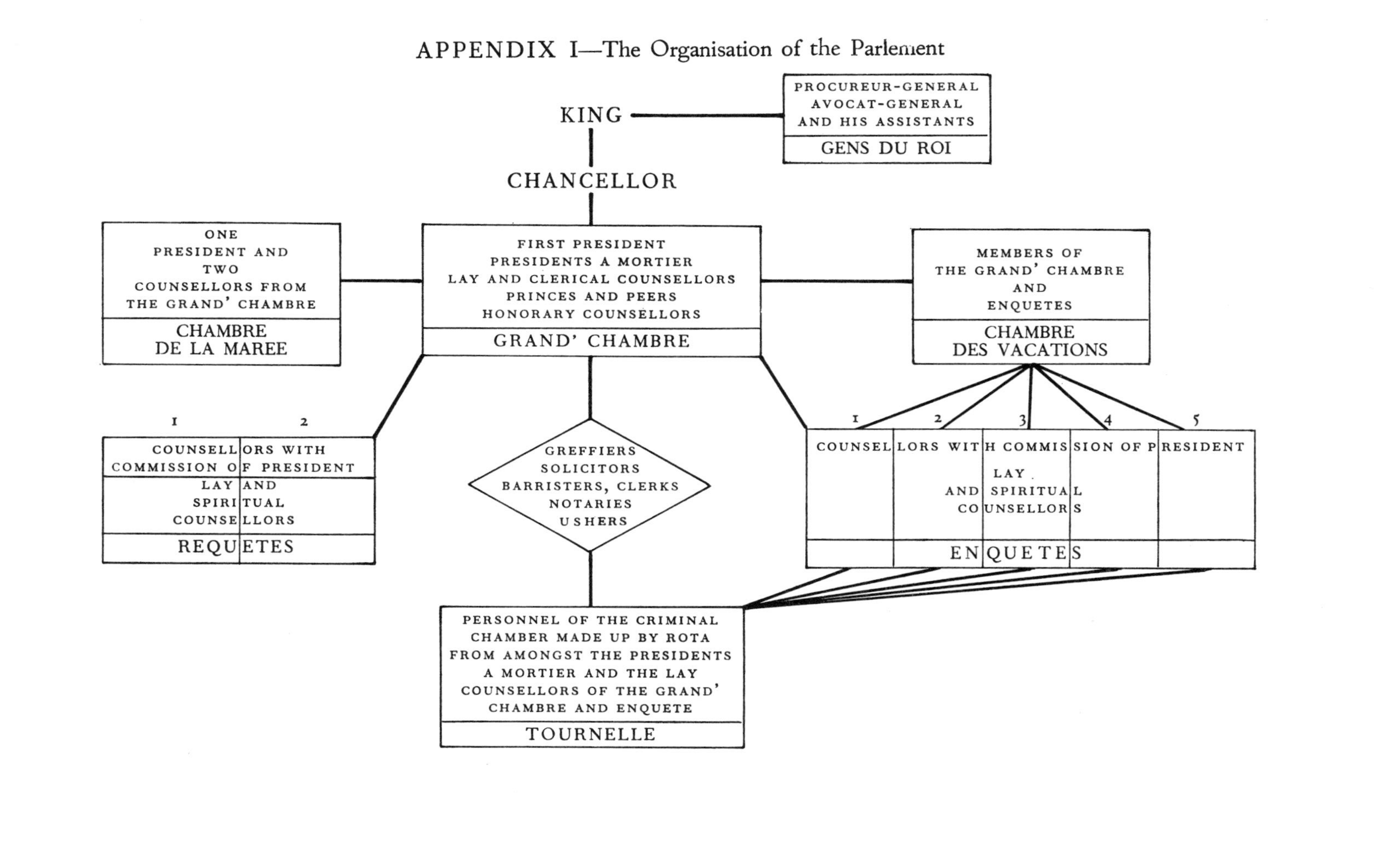

APPENDIX II—The Geneal

GENEALOGY

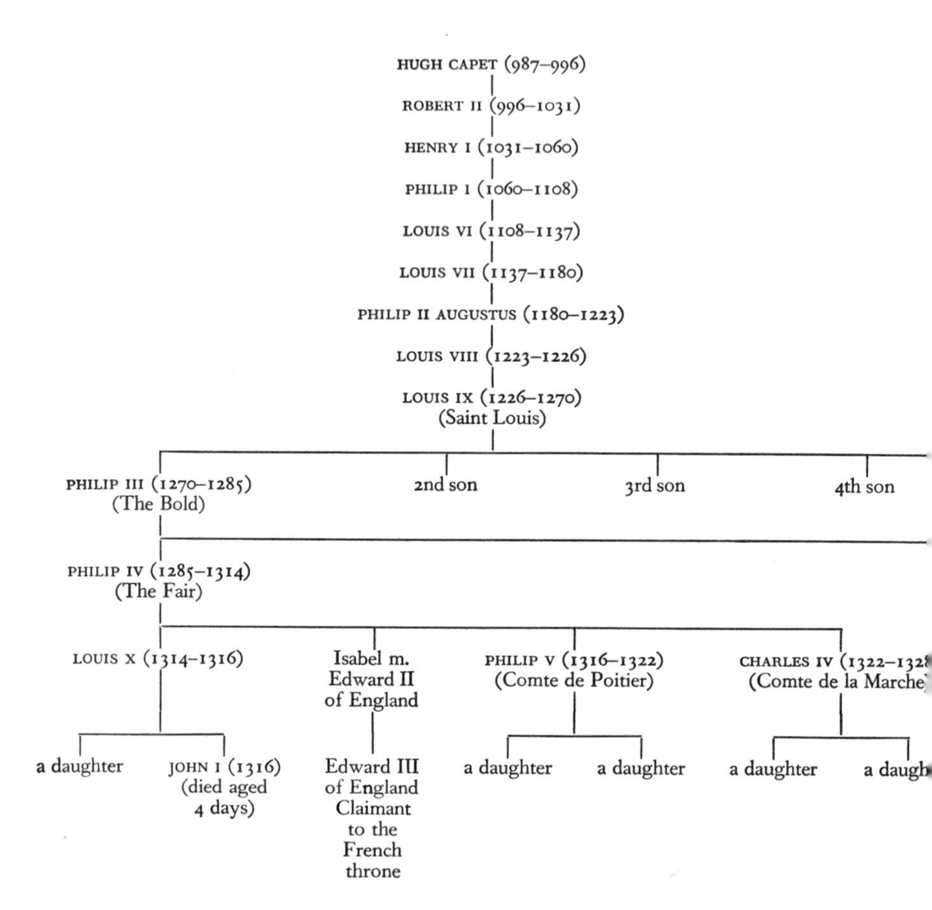

e French Monarchs to 1793

THIRD RACE

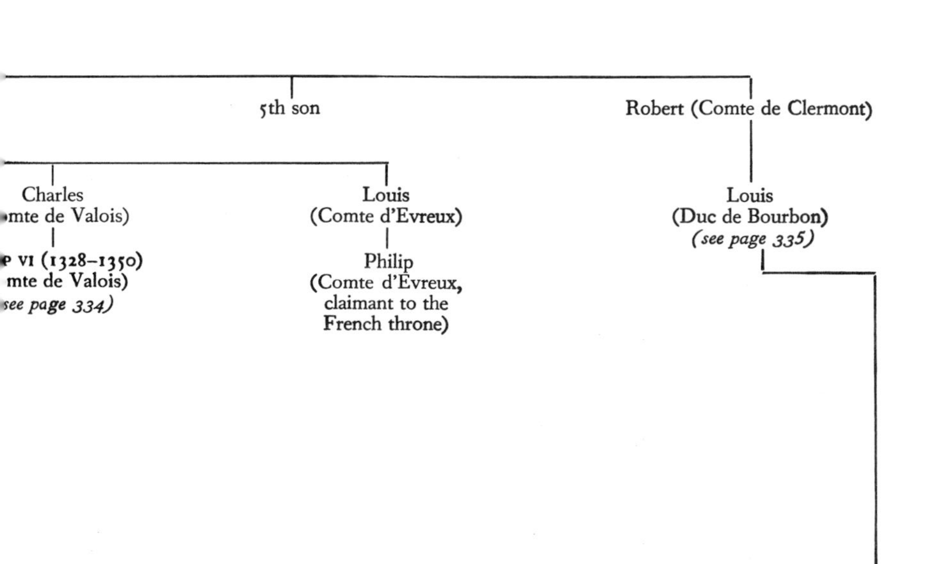

APPENDIX II

THE GENEALOGY OF THE FRENCH MONARCHS TO 1793 (THE VALOIS)

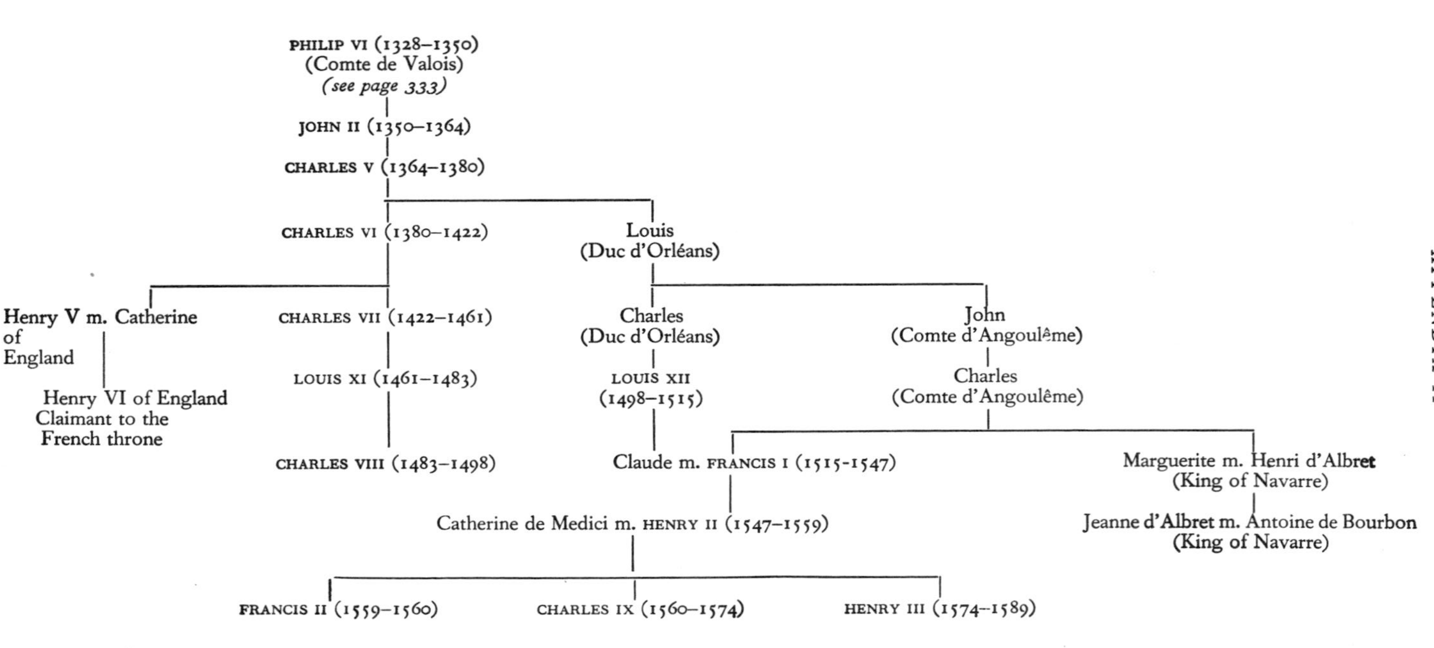

APPENDIX II

THE GENEAOLOGY OF THE FRENCH MONARCHS TO 1793 (THE BOURBON)

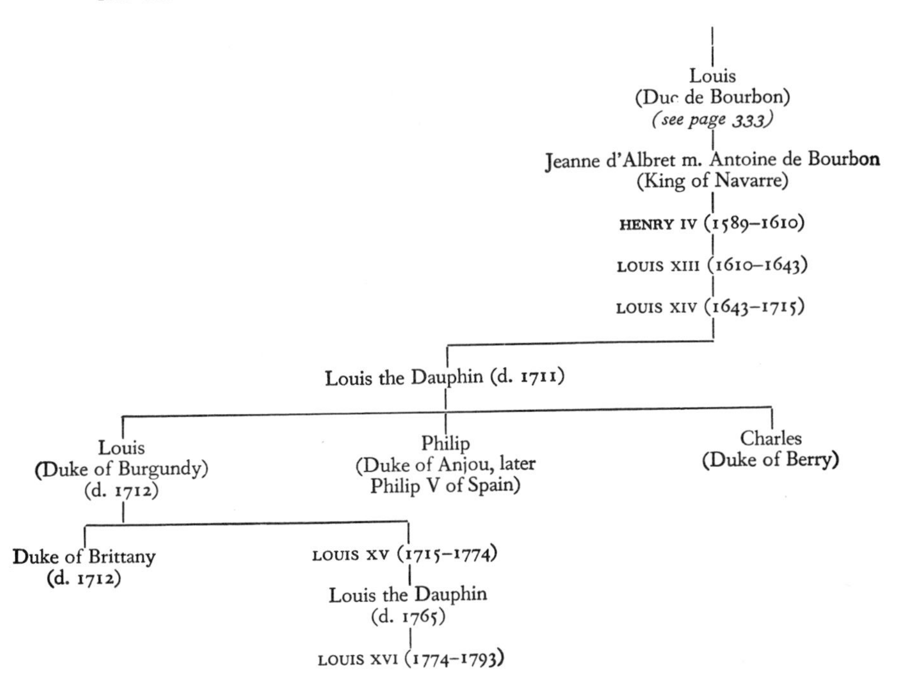

GLOSSARY

Amende honorable	A punishment requiring the prisoner to undergo a degrading public ritual as a sign of his guilt.
Appeal *a minima*	An attempt by the *Procureur-Général* to add severity to a criminal verdict.
Appeal *comme d'abus*	A complaint to the Parlement against an ecclesiastical judge who was accused of exceeding his powers.
Appeal *en cas de saisine et nouvelleté*	A legal channel through which clerics could seek redress in royal courts.
Arrêt	A formal judgment of the Parlement.
Arrêt de conseil	A decree emanating from the King's Council.
Arrêt de règlement	An administrative decree issued by the Parlement which possessed the force of law.
Arrêt de saisin	A decree issued by the Parlement to enforce a settlement previously stipulated by the court.
Basoche	A name applied to the Palais de Justice, particularly in reference to the young clerks who assisted the solicitors and barristers working in the court.
Cas royaux	Cases in which the king's person or his rights were involved and which had always to be tried before a royal court.
Committimus	Letters which entitled the holder to seek justice before the Parlement in the first instance.
Conseil	A private meeting at which the judges discussed cases which had been reserved for further consideration and also those registers of the Parlement containing decisions arrived at in such meetings.

Conseil secret	Those registers of the Parlement containing a variety of matters in which the court as a whole was concerned.
Coutumiers	Volumes in which professional jurists sought to write down the customary law of particular localities.
Enquête	The procedure by which plaintiff and defendant could summon witnesses to give oral testimony before a judge.
Epices	Presents in kind or cash made to the judges for their services.
Grande Audience	The chief judicial session in the *Grand' Chambre*, lasting from 9 a.m. to 10 a.m. on each working day.
Grands Jours	Courts composed of magistrates from the Parlement sitting in various provinces.
Jugés	Civil registers of the Parlement, following immediately upon the *Olim*.
Lettres de cachet	Sealed royal orders.
Lettres de jussion	Orders to the Parlement demanding immediate and unqualified registration of royal legislation.
Lettres de justice	The Parlement's authorization for a case to be brought before it.
Magister or *maître*	A graduate in Roman and canon law.
Maîtres des Requêtes	Distinguished judicial officers, closely associated with the Parlement in its formative years.
Mortier	The ceremonial black velvet cap worn by the presidents of the Parlement.
Olim	The first surviving records of the Parlement.
Order *à vérifier*	Replaced the order *en faits contraires* and was applied to written rather than oral investigations.
Order *en droit*	The preliminary to a further scrutiny of written evidence.
Order *en faits contraires*	The necessary preliminary to an *enquête*.
Parquet	Collective name for the *Gens du roi*.

Patre et avo consulibus	The principle by which personal nobility could be transformed into hereditary nobility in the third generation.
Pays de coutumes	Those areas of France in which customary law was traditionally predominant.
Petit criminel	Cases in which fines only, not physical punishment, could be inflicted.
Petit habit	The magistrates' normal dress for routine judicial occasions in the seventeenth and eighteenth centuries, consisting of a black gown and a broad black hat.
Plaidories	Those registers of the Parlement containing decisions on cases pleaded orally.
Prévention	A legal argument in favour of royal intervention in the sphere of seignorial justice.
Prévôt	A royal judge below the level of the bailiff.
Prévôté	The area of the *prévôt*'s jurisdiction.
Rapporteur	A member of the Parlement appointed to take chief responsibility in the conduct of a specific case.
Régale	The king's right to administer vacant bishoprics and draw revenue from them.
Rentes	State investments.
Séance de rentrée	The opening formalities of the Parlement's year observed every November.
Survivance	The practice of holding an office jointly with a close relative, the survivor to retain the office.

BIBLIOGRAPHY

1. Archival Sources

The official records of the Parlement are located in Paris, *Série* X in the *Archives Nationales*. This series alone represents a vast collection but in the same archives there are also a number of other collections – *Séries* K and U, for example – which offer a mass of additional material. Two catalogues, *Guide des Recherches dans les Fonds Judiciaires de l'Ancien Régime*, published in 1958, and Vol. I, *L'Ancien Régime*, of *Les Archives Nationales, Etat Général des Fonds*, ed. E. Taillemite (1978), provide an introduction to these copious sources.

Besides the *Archives Nationales* there are a number of other Parisian libraries that house an enormous amount of manuscript material relevant to the Parlement's history. They include, among others, the *Bibliothèque Nationale* – the *Fonds des Anciens Manuscrits Français*, the *Nouvelles Acquisitions Françaises* and the *Collection Joly de Fleury* all contain a great deal of information, legal, political, religious and personal – the *Bibliothèque du Sénat* and the *Bibliothèque de l'Institut*. The *Bibliothèque de Port-Royal*, which preserves the library of the eighteenth-century Jansenist barrister Adrien Le Paige, is especially valuable on religious topics; the *Archives de la Seine* provides details of magisterial testaments.

When provincial and private collections are added the volume of manuscript material assumes monumental proportions. The scope and scale of the present volume are such as to render otiose any choice of specific references from these voluminous sources. There is in addition a vast amount of published material.

2. Published Sources

Barbier, E.J.F., *Chronique de la Régence et du Règne de Louis XV, 1718–1763*, 8 vols (Paris, 1857–8)

Baye, Nicholas de, *Journal, 1400–1417*, ed. A. Tuetey, 2 vols (Paris, 1885–8)

Beaumanoir, Philippe de, *Coutumes de Beauvaisis*, ed. A. Salmon, 2 vols (Paris, 1899–1900)

Beccaria, Cesare Bonesana, Marchese de, *An Essay on Crimes and Punishments*, 4th edn (London, 1785)
Beugnot, A. (Ed.), *Les Olim*, 4 vols in 3 tomes (Paris, 1839–48)
Bodin, J., *Six Livres de la République* (Geneva, 1629)
Bossuet, J.-B., bishop of Meaux, *Oeuvres Complètes*, 12 vols (Paris, 1836)
Boulay, C.E. du, *Historia Universitatis Parisiensis*, 6 vols (Paris, 1665–73)
Boutaric, E. (Ed.), *Actes du Parlement de Paris*, with an introduction by A. Grün, 2 vols (Paris, 1863–7)
Breuil, Guillaume du, *Stilus Curie Parlamenti*, ed. F. Aubert (Paris, 1909)
Condé, Louis I de Bourbon, Prince de, *Mémoires, 1559–1569*, 5 vols (The Hague, 1743)
Cosneau, E., *Les Grands Traités de la Guerre de Cent Ans* (Paris, 1889)
Dangeau, Philippe de Courcillon, Marquis de, *Journal*, ed. E. Soulié and M.L. Dussieux, 19 vols (Paris, 1854–60)
Dorsanne, L'Abbé, *Journal*, 2 vols (Rome, 1753)
Douët d'Arcq, L. (Ed.), *Choix de Pièces Inédites relatives au Règne de Charles VI*, 2 vols (Paris, 1863–4)
Estoile, P. de l', *Journal pour le Règne de Henri III, 1574–1589*, ed. L.-R. Lefèvre (Paris, 1943)
——, *Journal pour le Règne de Henri IV, 1589–1611*, ed. L.-R. Lefèvre and A. Martin, 3 vols (Paris, 1948–60)
Fauquembergue, Clément de, *Journal, 1417–1436*, ed. A. Tuetey, 3 vols (Paris, 1903–15)
Fénelon, F. de Salignac de la Mothe, *Ecrits et Lettres Politiques*, ed. C. Urbain (Paris, 1920)
Ferrière, C.-J. de, *Dictionnaire de Droit et de Pratique*, 2 vols (Paris 1740)
Flammermont, J., *Les Remontrances du Parlement de Paris au XVIIIe Siècle*, 3 vols (Paris, 1888–98)
Gazette de la Régence, 1715–1719, ed. E. de Barthélémy (Paris, 1887)
Isambert, F.-A. (ed.), *Receuil Général des Anciennes Lois Françaises*, 29 vols (Paris, 1822–33)
Joinville, Jean, Sire de, *Histoire de Saint-Louis* in *Collection Complète des Mémoires relatifs à l'Histoire de France depuis le Règne de Philippe-Auguste jusqu'au Commencement du Dix-Septième Siècle*, ed. C.B. Petitot (Paris, 1821–7)
Joly, C., *Receuil des Maximes Veritables et Importantes pour l'Institution du Roi* (Paris, 1653)
Kervyn de Lettenhove, *Lettres et Negociations de Philippe de Commines*, 2 vols (Brussels, 1867–8)
Langlois, C.V., *Textes relatifs à l'Histoire du Parlement depuis les Origines jusqu'en 1314* (Paris, 1888)
La Roche-Flavin, B. de, *Treize Livres des Parlements de France* (Paris, 1621)

Marais, M., *Journal et Mémoires*, ed. M. de Lescure, 4 vols (Paris, 1863–8)
Massillon, J.-B., *Oeuvres*, 13 vols (Paris, 1810)
Mémoires de la Ligue, 6 vols (Amsterdam, 1758)
Mention, L., *Documents relatifs aux Rapports du Clergé avec la Royauté de 1682 à 1789*, 2 vols (Paris, 1893–1903)
Molé, M., *Mémoires*, ed. A. Champollion-Figeac, 4 vols (Paris, 1855–7)
Montesquieu, C.-L. de Secondat, Baron de la Brède et de, *De l'Esprit des Lois*, ed. G. Truc, 2 vols (Paris, 1949)
——, *Lettres Persanes*, ed. G. Truc (Paris, 1956)
Nouvelles Ecclésiastiques (Paris, 1728 et seq.)
Ordonnances des Rois de France de la Troisième Race, 22 vols (Paris, 1723–1849)
Ordonnances des Rois de France-Règne de François Ier, 7 vols (Paris, 1902–41)
Richelieu, Armand-Jean du Plessis, Cardinal de, *Testament Politique*, ed. L. André (Paris, 1947)
Saint-Simon, Louis de Rouvroy, Duc de, *Mémoires*, ed. A. de Boislisle, 41 vols (Paris, 1879–1928)
Seyssel, Claude de, *La Monarchie de France*, ed. J. Poujol (Paris, 1961)
Songe du Vergier, Le, ed. J.L. Brunet, *Traitez des Droits et Libertez de l'Eglise Gallicane*, 4 vols (Paris, 1731)
Talon, O., *Mémoires, continués par Denis Talon*, vol. XXX of *Nouvelle Collection des Mémoires relatifs à l'Histoire de France depuis le XIIIe Siècle jusqu'à la fin du XVIIIe Siècle*, ed. J.F. Michaud and J.J.F. Poujoulat, 34 vols (Paris, 1854)
Vauban, Sébastien le Prestre, seigneur de, *Projet d'une Dixme Royale*, ed. E. Coornaert (Paris, 1933)

3. Secondary Works

Acerra, M. 'Les avocats du parlement de Paris (1661–1715)', *Histoire, Economie et Société*, 2 (1982)
Alatri, P., 'Parlements et lutte politique en France an XVIII siècle', *Studies on Voltaire and the Eighteenth Century*, 151 (1976)
Allen, J.W., *A History of Political Thought in the Sixteenth Century*, revised ed. (London, 1961)
Allmand, C.T. and Armstrong, C.A.J., *Fifteen English Suits before the Parlement of Paris, 1420–1426, Camden Society*, Series IV, 26 (1982)
Amphoux, H., *Michel de L'Hôpital et la Liberté de Conscience au XVIe Siècle* (Paris, 1900)
Antoine, M., *Le Conseil du Roi sous le Règne de Louis XV* (Geneva, 1970)
——, *Le Gouvernement et l'Administration sous Louis XV. Dictionnaire Biographique* (Paris, 1978)

——, 'Sens et portée des réformes du chancelier de Maupeou', *Revue Historique*, 288 (1992)
Archel, R., *Crimes et Châtiments au XVIIIe Siècle* (Paris, 1933)
Armstrong, E., *Before Copyright. The French Book- Privilege System, 1498–1526* (Cambridge, 1990)
Aubert, F., *Le Parlement de Paris de Philippe le Bel à Charles VII*: I. *Son Organisation* (Paris, 1887); II. *Sa Compétence, ses Attributions* (Paris, 1890)
——, 'Le Parlement et les Prisonniers', *Bulletin de la Société de l'Histoire de Paris et de l'Ile de France*, 20 (1893)
——, *Histoire du Parlement de Paris de l'Origine à François Ier*, 2 vols (Paris, 1894)
——, 'Recherches sur l'organisation du parlement de Paris au XVIe siècle (1515–1589)', *Nouvelle Revue Historique de Droit Français et Etranger*, 36 (1912)
Autrand, F., 'Culture et mentalité: les librairies des gens du parlement au temps de Charles VI', *Annales, E.S.C.*, 28 (1973)
——, *Naissance d'un Grand Corps de l'Etat, les Gens du Parlement de Paris, 1345–1454* (Paris, 1981)
——, 'Naissance illégitime et service de l'Etat: les enfants naturels dans le milieu de robe parisien, XIVe–XVe siècles', *Revue Historique*, 267 (1982)
Avout, J. d', *La Querelle de Armagnacs et des Bourguignons* (Paris, 1943)
Baker, K.M., 'Public Opinion as Political Invention' in Baker, *Inventing the French Revolution* (Cambridge, 1990)
Beaucourt, G. du Fresne de, *Histoire de Charles VII*, 6 vols (Paris, 1881–91)
Bell, D.A., 'The "Public Sphere", the State, and the World of Law in Eighteenth Century France', *French Historical Studies*, 17 (1992)
——, *Lawyers and Citizens: The Making of a Political Elite in Old Regime France* (Oxford, 1994)
Bickart, R., *Les Parlements et la Notion de Souveraineté Nationale au XVIIIe Siècle* (Paris, 1932)
Bisson, T.N., 'Consultative Functions in the King's Parlements', *Speculum*, 44 (1969)
Bisson de Barthélémy, P., *Les Joly de Fleury, Procureurs-Généraux au Parlement de Paris au XVIII Siècle* (Paris, 1964)
Bloch, M., *Les Rois Thaumaturges* (Paris, 1924)
Bluche, F., *L'Origine des Magistrats du Parlement de Paris au XVIIIe Siècle, 1715–1771* (Paris, 1956)
——, 'Les magistrats des cours parisiennes au XVIIIe siècle: hiérarchie et situation sociale', *Revue Historique de Droit Français et Etranger*, 4th Series, 52 (1974)

——, 'Le role des offices dans la mobilité sociale des familles du Parlement de Paris', *Amterkauflichkeit: aspekte sozialer mobilität im Europäischen Vergleich*, ed. K. Malettke (Berlin, 1980)

——, *Les Magistrats du Parlement de Paris au XVIIIe Siècle, 1715–1771*, revised edn (Paris, 1986)

Bonfait, O., 'Les collections des parlementaires parisiens au XVIIIe siècle', *Revue de l'Art*, 73 (1986)

Bongert, Y., *Recherches sur les Cours Laïques du Xe au XIIIe Siècle* (Paris, 1948)

Bonney, R., *Political Change in France under Richelieu and Mazarin, 1624–1661* (Oxford, 1978)

——. 'La fronde des officiers: mouvement réformiste ou rébellion corporatiste?', *XVIIe Siècle*, 145 (1984)

Bordes, M., 'Les intendants de Louis XV', *Revue Historique*, 223 (1960)

Bossuat, A., 'L'idée de nation et la jurisprudence du parlement de Paris au XVe siècle', *Revue Historique*, 204 (1950)

Bourgeon, J.-L., 'La fronde parlementaire à la veille de la Saint-Barthélémy', *Bibliothèque de l'Ecole des Chartes*, 148 (1990)

Boutaric, E., 'Recherches archéologiques sur le palais de justice de Paris', *Mémoires de la Société des Antiquaires de France*, 3rd Series, 7 (1864)

Bryant, L.M., '*Parlementaire* Political Theory in the Parisian Royal Entry Ceremony', *Sixteenth Century Journal*, 7 (1976)

Buisseret, D., *Henry IV* (London, 1984)

Buisson, A., *Le Chancelier Antoine Duprat* (Paris, 1935)

Burke, P., *The Fabrication of Louis XIV* (New Haven and London, 1992)

Cabourdin, G. and Viard, G., *Lexique Historique de la France d'Ancien Régime* (Paris, 1978)

Cahen, L., *Les Querelles Religieuses et Parlementaires sous Louis XV* (Paris, 1913)

Campbell, P.R., *Power and Politics in Old Regime France, 1720–1745* (London, 1996)

Carey, J.A., *Judicial Reform in France before the Revolution of 1789* (Cambridge, Mass., 1981)

Carlylye, R.W. and A.J., *A History of Medieval Political Theory in the West*, 6 vols (London, 1903–36)

Carré, H., *La Fin des Parlements, 1788–1790* (Paris, 1912)

Carreyre, J., *Le Jansénisme durant la Régence*, 3 vols (Paris, 1929–33)

Chamberland, A., *Le Conflit de 1597 entre Henri IV et le Parlement de Paris* (Paris, 1904)

Cheyette, F., 'La justice et le pouvoir royal à la fin du moyen âge français', *Revue Historique de Droit Français et Etranger*, 4th Series, 40 (1962)

Church, W.F., *Constitutional Thought in Sixteenth Century France* (Cambridge, Mass., 1941)

——, 'The Decline of French Jurists as Political Theorists, 1660–1789', *French Historical Studies*, 5 (1967)

Clément, P., *La police sous Louis XIV* (Paris, 1866)

Cobban, A.B., *A History of Modern France: I. Old Regime and Revolution, 1715–1799* (London, 1957)

——, *In Search of Humanity* (New York, 1960)

Cubells, M., 'Le parlement de Paris pendant la fronde', *XVIIe Siècle*, 35 (1957)

Cummings, M., 'The Social Impact of the Paulette: the Case of the Parlement of Paris', *Canadian Journal of History*, 15 (1980)

Declareuil, J., *Histoire Générale du Droit Français des Origines à 1789* (Paris, 1925)

Delachenal, R., *Histoire des Avocats au Parlement de Paris, 1300–1600* (Paris, 1885)

Descimon, R., 'La haute noblesse parlementaire parisienne: la production d'une aristocratie d'Etat aux XVIe et XVIIe siècles', *L'Etat et les Aristocraties*, ed. P. Contamine (Paris, 1989)

Descimon R., and Jouhaud, C., 'La fronde en mouvement: le développement de la crise politique entre 1648 et 1652',*XVIIe Siècle*, 145 (1984)

Diefendorf, B.B., *Beneath the Cross. Catholics and Huguenots in Sixteenth-Century Paris* (Oxford, 1991)

Dievoet, C. Van, 'La *Somme Rurale* de Boutillier et la jurisprudence du parlement de Paris, *Revue du Nord*, 56 (1974)

Dillay, M., 'Les registres secrets des chambres des enquêtes et des requêtes du parlement de Paris', *Bibliothèque de l'Ecole des Chartes*, 108 (1950)

Dodu, G., *Les Valois: Histoire d'une Maison Royale* (Paris, 1934)

Doolin, P.R., *The Fronde* (Cambridge, Mass., 1935)

Doucet, R., *Etude sur le Gouvernement de François Ier dans ses Rapports avec le Parlement de Paris*, 2 vols (Paris, 1921–6)

——, 'France under Charles VIII and Louis XII', *New Cambridge Modern History: I. The Renaissance, 1493–1520* (Cambridge 1961)

——, *Les Institutions de la France au XVIe Siècle*, 2 vols (Paris, 1948)

Doyle, W., 'The Parlements of France and the Breakdown of the Old Regime, 1771–1788', *French Historical Studies*, 6 (1970)

——, *The Parlement of Bordeaux and the End of the Old Regime, 1771–1790* (New York, 1974)

——, *Origins of the French Revolution* (Oxford, 1980)

——, 'The Price of Offices in Pre-Revolutionary France', *Historical Journal*, 27 (1984)

——, *Venality. The Sale of Offices in Eighteenth-Century France* (Oxford, 1996)
Ducoudray, G., *Les Origines du Parlement de Paris et le Justice aux XIIIe et XIVe siècles* (Paris, 1902)
Dupont-Ferrier, G., 'La formation de l'unité française aux XVe et XVIe Siècles', *Journal des Savants* (1941)
Echeverria, D., *The Maupou Revolution: A Study in the History of Libertarianism, 1770–1774* (Baton Rouge, 1985)
Egret, J., 'Le procès des Jésuites devant les parlements de France', *Revue Historique*, 204 (1950)
——, 'L'aristocratie parlementaire française à la fin de l'ancien régime', *Revue Historique*, 208 (1952)
——, *La Pré-Révolution Française, 1787–1788* (Paris, 1962)
——, *Louis XV et l'Opposition Parlementaire* (Paris, 1970)
Ellis, H.A., *Boulainvilliers and the French Monarchy. Aristocratic Politics in Early Eighteenth-Century France* (Ithaca, 1988)
Esmein, A., *Cours Elémentaire d'Histoire du Droit Français*, 2nd edn (Paris, 1985)
——, *A History of Continental Criminal Procedure*, trans. J. Simpson (London, 1914)
Famiglietti, R.C., 'The Role of the Parlement de Paris in the Ratification and Registration of Royal Acts during the Reign of Charles VI', *Journal of Medieval History*, 9 (1983)
Farge, J.K., *Le Parti Conservateur au XVIe siècle: Université et Parlement de Paris à l'époque de la Renaissance et de la Réforme* (Paris, 1992)
Félix, J., *Les Magistrats du Parlement de Paris, 1771–1790: Dictionnaire Biographique et Généalogique* (Paris, 1990)
Fliche, A., 'Les Origines du gallicanisme', *Journal des Savants* (1942)
Ford, F.L., *Robe and Sword. The Regrouping of the French Aristocracy after Louis XIV* (Cambridge, Mass., 1953)
Fournier, E., 'Le palais de justice et le pont-neuf', *Paris à travers les Ages*, ed. F. Hoffbauer, 2 vols (Paris, 1875–82)
Frostin, C., 'Le chancelier de France Louis de Pontchartrain, 'ses' premiers présidents, et la discipline des cours souveraines (1699–1714)', *Cahiers d'Histoire*, 27 (1982)
Gazier, A., *Histoire Générale du Mouvement Janséniste*, 2 vols (Paris, 1922)
Giesey, R.E., 'The Juristic Basis of Dynastic Right to the French Throne', *Transactions of the American Philosophical Society*, 51 (1961)
——, 'The Presidents of Parlement at the Royal Funeral', *Sixteenth Century Journal*, 7 (1976)
Glasson, E., 'Les sources de la procédure civile française', *Nouvelle Revue Historique de Droit Français et Etranger*, 5 (1881)

——, *Histoire du Droit et des Institutions de la France*, 8 vols (Paris, 1887–1903)
——, *Le Parlement de Paris. Son Rôle Politique depuis le Règne de Charles VII jusqu' à la Révolution*, 2 vols (Paris, 1901)
Godard, C., *Les Pouvoirs des Intendants sous Louis XIV* (Paris, 1901)
Grand, R., 'La prison et la notion d'emprisonnement dans l'ancien droit', *Revue Historique de Droit Français et Etranger*, 4th Series, 19 (1940)
Grellet-Dumazeau, A., *L'Affaire du Bonnet et les Mémoires de Saint-Simon* (Paris, 1913)
Griffiths, Q., 'Les origines et la carrière de Pierre de Fontaines, jurisconsulte de Saint Louis. Une reconsidération avec documents inédits', *Revue Historique de Droit Français et Etranger*, 4th Series, 48 (1970)
——, 'New men among the Lay Counselors of Saint Louis' Parlement', *Medieval Studies*, 32 (1970)
Guerout, J., 'Le palais de la cité à Paris de origines à 1417', *Fédération des Sociétés Historiques et Archéologiques de Paris et de l'Ile de France, Mémoires*, I, II, III (Paris, 1949–51)
Guilhiermoz, P., 'De la persistance du caractère oral dans la procédure civile française', *Nouvelle Revue Historique de Droit Français et Etranger*, 13 (1889)
——, *Enquêtes et Procès* (Paris, 1892)
Habermas, J., *The Structural Transformation of the Public Sphere*, trans. T. Burger (Cambridge, Mass., 1989)
Hamscher, A.N., *The Parlement of Paris after the Fronde, 1653–1673* (Pittsburgh, 1976)
——, 'The Parlement of Paris and the Social Interpretation of Early French Jansenism', *Catholic Historical Review*, 63 (1977)
——, *The Conseil Privé and the Parlements in the Age of Louis XIV: a Study in French Absolutism*, *Transactions of the American Philosophical Society*, 77 (Philadelphia, 1987)
——, 'Parlements and Litigants at the King's Councils during the Personal Rule of Louis XIV: the Example of *Cassation*' in *Society and Institutions in Early Modern France*, ed. M. P. Holt (Athens, Georgia and London, 1991)
Hanley, S., 'The *Lit de Justice* and the Fundamental Law', *Sixteenth Century Journal*, 7 (1976)
——, 'L'idéologie constitutionnelle en France: le lit de justice', *Annales, E.S.C.*, 37 (1982)
——, *The Lit de Justice of the Kings of France* (Princeton, 1983)
——, 'Constitutional Discourse in France, 1527–1549' in *Politics and*

Culture in Early Modern Europe, ed. M.P. Holt and M.C. Jacob (Cambridge, 1987)

——, 'The French Constitution Revised: Reprensentative Assemblies and Resistance Right in the Sixteenth Century' in *Society and Institutions in Early Modern France*, ed. M.P. Holt (Athens, Georgia and London, 1991)

Hardman, J., *Louis XVI* (New Haven and London, 1993)

——, *French Politics, 1774–1789* (London, 1995)

Hardy, G., *Le Cardinal de Fleury et le Mouvement Janséniste* (Paris, 1925)

Hardy, J.D., *Judicial Politics in the Old Regime: the Parlement of Paris during the Regency* (Baton Rouge, 1967)

Hargreaves-Mawdesley, W.N., *A History of Legal Dress in Europe* (Oxford, 1963)

Harsin, P., *Les Doctrines Monétaires et Financières en France du XVI*[e] *au XVIII*[e] *Siècle* (Paris, 1928)

Hartung, F. and Mousnier, R.E., 'Quelques problèmes concernant la monarchie absolue' in *Rapport pour le X*[e] *Congrès International des Sciences Historiques* (Rome, 1955)

Holt, M.P. 'The King in Parlement: the Problem of the *Lit de Justice* in Sixteenth-Century France', *Historical Journal*, 31 (1988)

Hudson, D., 'The Parlementary Crisis of 1763 in France and its Consequences', *Canadian Journal of History*, 7 (1972)

——, 'In Defence of Reform: French Government Propaganda during the Maupeou Crisis', *French Historical Studies*, 8 (1973)

Joynes, D.C., 'Parlementaires, Peers and the *Parti Janséniste*: the Refusal of the Sacraments and the Revival of the Ancient Constitution in Eighteenth-Century France', *Proceedings of the Annual Meeting of the Western Society for French History*, 8 (1980)

Judge, H.G., 'Church and State under Louis XIV', *History*, 45 (1960)

Jurmand, J.-P., 'L'évolution du terme de sénat au XVIe siècle' in *La Monarchie Absolutiste et l'Histoire en France* (Paris, 1987)

Kaiser, C., 'The Deflation in the Volume of Litigation at Paris in the Eighteenth Century and the Waning of the Old Judicial Order', *European Studies Review*, 10 (1980)

——, 'Les cours souveraines au XVIe siècle: morale et contre-réforme', *Annales, E.S.C.*, 37 (1982)

Kaiser, T.E., 'The *Abbé* de Saint-Pierre, Public Opinion, and the Reconstitution of the French Monarchy', *Journal of Modern History*, 55 (1983)

——, 'Money, Despotism, and Public Opinion in Early Eighteenth-Century France: John Law and the Debate on Royal Credit', *Journal of Modern History*, 63 (1991)

Keohane, N.O., *Philosophy and the State in France. The Renaissance to the Enlightenment* (Princeton, 1980)

Kettering, S., *Judicial Politics and Urban Revolt: the Parlement of Aix, 1629–1659* (Princeton, 1978)

——, 'The Causes of the Judicial Frondes', *Canadian Journal of History*, 17 (1982)

——, *Patrons, Brokers and Clients in Seventeenth-Century France* (Oxford, 1986)

——, 'Patronage and Politics During the Fronde', *French Historical Studies*, 14 (1986)

——, 'Patronage and Kinship in Early Modern France', *French Historical Studies*, 16 (1989)

Kicklighter, J., 'Appeal Procedure in the Medieval Parlement of Paris', *Bulletin of the John Rylands Library*, 72 (1990)

Kim, S.-H., 'The Chancellor's Crusade: Michel de L'Hôpital and the *Parlement* of Paris', *French History*, 7 (1993)

Kitchens, J.H., 'Judicial *Commissaires* and the Parlement of Paris: the Case of the *Chambre de l'Arsenal*', *French Historical Studies*, 12 (1982)

Klaits, J., *Printed Propaganda under Louis XIV* (Princeton, 1976)

Knecht, R.J., 'The Concordat of 1516: a Re-assessment',*University of Birmingham Historical Journal*, 9 (1963)

——, *Francis I* (Cambridge, 1982)

——, 'Francis I and the "Lit de Justice": a Legend Defended', *French History*, 7 (1993)

Koenigsberger, H.G., 'The Organisation of Revolutionary Parties in France and the Netherlands during the Sixteenth Century', *Journal of Modern History*, 27 (1955)

Kossmann, E.H., *La Fronde* (Leyden, 1954)

Kreiser, B.R., *Miracles, Convulsions, and Ecclesiastical Politics in Early Eighteenth-Century Paris* (Princeton, 1978)

Krynen, J., 'Le roi "très chrétien" et le rétablissement de la *Pragmatique Sanction*. Pour une explication idéologique du gallicanisme parlementaire et de la politique religieuse de Louis XI' in *Eglises et Pouvoir Politique, Journées Internationales d'Histoire du Droit* (Angers, 1987)

Labatut, J.-P., 'Situation sociale du quartier du Marais pendant la fronde parlementaire (1648-1649)', *XVIIe Siècle*, 38 (1968)

Lacombe, B. de, *La Résistance Janséniste et Parlementaire au temps de Louis XV. L'Abbé Nigon de Berty, 1702–1772* (Paris, 1948)

Lacretelle, C., *Histoire de France pendant le XVIIIe Siècle*, 2 vols (Paris, 1819)

Langlois, C.V., 'Les origines du parlement de Paris', *Revue Historique*, 42 (1890)

Langlois, M., 'Les archives criminelles du parlement de Paris', *Actes du 107 Congrès National des Sociétés Savantes* (Paris, 1984)

Lefebvre, G., *La Révolution Aristocratique* (Paris, 1946)

——, *The Coming of the French Revolution*, trans. R.R. Palmer (Princeton, 1947)

Lehugeur, P., *Histoire de Philippe le Long, Roi de France*: I. *Le Règne* (Paris, 1897); II. *Le Mécanisme du Gouvernement* (Paris, 1931)

Lemaire, A., *Les Lois Fondamentales de la Monarchie Française* (Paris, 1907)

Le Patourel, J., 'Edward III and the Kingdom of France', *History*, 43 (1958)

Le Roy, A., *La France et Rome de 1700 à 1715* (Paris, 1892)

Le Roy Ladurie, E., *The Royal French State, 1460–1610*, trans. J. Vale (Oxford, 1994)

——, *The Ancien Régime. A History of France, 1610–1774*, trans. M. Greengrass (Oxford, 1996)

Lot, F. and Fawtier, R., *Histoire des Institutions Françaises au Moyen Age*, 3 vols (Paris, 1957–62): II. *Institutions Royales* (1958)

Luchaire, A., *Manuel des Institutions Françaises, Période des Capétians Directs* (Paris, 1892)

Maire, C.-L., 'L'église et la nation. Du dépôt de la vérité au dépôt des lois. La trajectoire janséniste au XVIIIe siècle', *Annales, E.S.C.*, 46 (1991)

Major, J. Russell, *Representative Institutions in Renaissance France, 1421–1559* (Madison, 1960)

——, *The Deputies to the Estates-General in Renaissance France* (Madison, 1960)

Mariéjol, J.H. *La Réforme et la Ligue, 1559–1598* (Paris, 1904)

——, *Henri IV et Louis XIII, 1598–1643* (Paris, 1905)

Marion, M., *Les Impôts Directs sous l'Ancien Régime* (Paris, 1910)

——, *Histoire Financière de la France depuis 1715*, 3 vols (Paris, 1914)

——, *Dictionnaire des Institutions de la France aux XVIIe et XVIIIe Siècles* (Paris, 1923)

Martin, V., *Les Origines du Gallicanisme*, 2 vols (Paris, 1939)

Maugis, E., *Histoire du Parlement de Paris de l'Avènement des Rois Valois à la Mort d'Henri IV*, 3 vols (Paris, 1913–16)

McManners, J., 'France' in *The European Nobility in the Eighteenth Century*, ed. A. Goodwin (London, 1953)

Meinecke, F. von, *Machiavellism. The Doctrine of Raison d'Etat and its Place in Modern History* (London, 1957)

Merrick, J.W., ' "Disputes over Words" and Constitutional Conflict in France, 1730–1732', *French Historical Studies*, 14 (1986)

——, 'Subjects and Citizens in the Remonstrances of the Parlement of Paris in the Eighteenth Century', *Journal of the History of Ideas*, 51 (1990)

——, *The Desacralization of the French Monarchy in the Eighteenth Century* (Baton Rouge, 1990)

Mettam, R., *Power and Faction in Louis XIV's France* (Oxford, 1988)

Meuvret, J., 'Comment les français du XVIIe siècle voyaient l'impôt' in *Comment les Français voyaient la France au XVIIe Siècle*, ed. R.E. Mousnier (Paris, 1955)

Moote, A.L., 'The French Crown versus its Judicial and Financial Officials, 1615–1683', *Journal of Modern History*, 34 (1962)

——, 'The Parlementary Fronde and Seventeenth-Century Robe Solidarity', *French Historical Studies*, 2 (1962)

——, *The Revolt of the Judges: the Parlement of Paris and the Fronde, 1643–1652* (Princeton, 1971)

——, *Louis XIII. The Just* (Berkeley and Los Angeles, 1989)

Mousnier, R.E., *La Vénalité des Offices sous Henri IV et Louis XIII* (Rouen, 1945)

——, 'Le conseil du roi de la mort de Henri IV au gouvernement personnel de Louis XIV', *Etudes d'Histoire Moderne et Contemporaine*, 1 (1947)

——, 'Le causes des journées révolutionnaires parisiennes de 1648', *XVIIe Siècle*, 2–3 (1949)

——, 'L'évolution des institutions monarchiques en France et ses relations avec l'état social', *XVIIe Siècle*, 58–9 (1963)

——, *The Institutions of France under the Absolute Monarchy, 1598–1789*, trans. B. Pearce and A. Goldhammer, 2 vols (Chicago, 1979–84)

Muller, D., 'Magistrats français et peine de mort au XVIIIe siècle', *XVIIIe Siècle*, 4 (1972)

Neveu, B., 'Un parlementaire parisien érudit et janséniste: Jean le Nain, 1609–1698', *Paris et Ile-de-France: Mémoires*, 16–17 (1965–6)

Nixon, E., *Voltaire and the Calas Affair* (London, 1961)

Olivier-Martin, F., *Histoire du Droit Français des Origines à la Révolution* (Paris, 1948)

Orcibal, J., *Louis XIV contre Innocent XI* (Paris, 1949)

Ourliac, P., 'Le concordat de 1472 – étude sur les rapports de Louis XI et de Sixte IV', *Revue Historique de Droit Français et Etranger*, 4th Series, 20–1 (1941–2)

Pagès, G., *La Monarchie d'Ancien Régime* (Paris, 1928)

——, 'La vénalité des offices dans l'ancienne France', *Revue Historique*, 169 (1932)

——, *Les Institutions Monarchique sous Louis XIII et Louis XIV* (Paris, 1962)

Pange, J. de, *Le Roi Très Chrétien* (Paris, 1949)
Parker, D., *The Making of French Absolutism* (London, 1983)
——, 'Sovereignty, Absolutism and the Function of the Law in Seventeenth-Century France', *Past and Present*, 122 (1989)
Perrichet, L., *La Grande Chancellerie de France des Origines à 1328* (Paris, 1912)
Perrot, E., *Les Institutions Publiques et Privées de l'Ancienne France jusqu'en 1789* (Paris 1935)
Perroy, E., *La Guerre de Cent Ans* (Paris, 1945)
Petit-Dutaillis, C., *Charles VII, Louis XI et les Premières Années de Charles VIII, 1422–1492* (Paris, 1902)
Picot, G., *Histoire des Etats-Généraux, 1355–1614*, 4 vols (Paris, 1872)
Préclin, E.and Jarry, E., *Les Luttes Politiques et Doctrinales aux XVIIe et XVIIIe Siècles*, 2 vols (Paris, 1955–6)
Prou, M., 'Les coutumes de Lorris et leur propagation aux XIIe et XIIIe siècles', *Nouvelle Revue Historique de Droit Français et Etranger*, 8 (1884)
Radouant, R., *Guillaume du Vair. L'Homme et l'Orateur* (Paris, 1908)
Ranum, O., *Richelieu and the Councillors of Louis XIII* (Oxford, 1963)
——, 'Money, Dignity, and Self-Esteem in the Relations between Judges and Great Nobles of the Parlement of Paris during the Fronde' in *Society and Institutions in Early Modern France*, ed. M.P. Holt (Athens, Georgia and London, 1991)
——, *The Fronde* (New York, 1993)
Rech, G., 'Daguesseau et le jansénisme' in *Le Chancelier Henri-François Daguesseau, 1668–1751* (Limoges, 1953)
Renaudet, A., *Les Parlements. Etudes sur l'Histoire de la France, 1715–1789* (Paris, 1946)
Richet, D., 'Autour des origines idéologiques lointaines de la révolution française: élites et despotisme', *Annales, E.S.C.*, 24 (1969)
——, 'La formation des grands serviteurs de l'état, fin XVIe-début XVIIe siècle', *L'Arc*, 65 (1976)
Roche, D., 'Noblesses et culture dans la France du XVIIIe siècle: les lectures de la noblesse' in *Buch und Sammler. Private und Öffentliche Bibliotheken im 18 Jahrhundert* (Heidelberg, 1979)
Roelker, N.L. *One King, One Faith. The Parlement of Paris and the Religious Reformations of the Sixteenth Century* (Berkeley and Los Angeles, 1996)
Rogister, J.M.J., 'New Light on the Fall of Chauvelin', *English Historical Review*, 83 (1968)
——, 'Louis-Adrien Le Paige, and the Attack on *De l'Esprit* and the *Encyclopédie* in 1759', *English Historical Review*, 92 (1977)

——, 'The Crisis of 1753–1754 in France and the Debate on the Nature of the Monarchy and of the Fundamental Laws' in *Studies Presented to the International Commission for the History of Representative and Parliamentary Institutions*, 59 (Gottingen, 1977)
——, 'A Minister's Fall and its Implications: the Case of Chauvelin, 1737–1746' in *Studies in the French Eighteenth Century*, ed. D.J. Mossop (Durham, 1978)
——, *Louis XV and the Parlement of Paris, 1737–1755* (Cambridge, 1995)
Rowen, H.H., *The King's State. Proprietary Dynasticism in Early Modern France* (New Brunswick, 1980)
Salmon, J.H., 'Venal Office and Popular Sedition in Seventeenth-Century France', *Past and Present*, 37 (1967)
Schnapper, B., 'La justice criminelle rendue par le parlement de Paris sous le règne de François Ier', *Revue Historique de Droit Français et Etranger*, 4th Series, 52 (1974)
Sergène, A., 'Le Précédent judiciaire au moyen âge', *Revue Historique de Droit Français et Etranger*, 4th Series, 39 (1961)
Shennan, J.H., 'The Political Role of the Parlement of Paris, 1715–23', *Historical Journal*, 8 (1965)
——, 'The Political Role of the Parlement of Paris under Cardinal Fleury', *English Historical Review*, 81 (1966)
——, *The Origins of the Modern European State, 1450–1725* (London, 1974)
——, *Philippe, Duke of Orléans: Regent of France, 1715–1723* (London, 1979)
——, 'The Political Vocabulary of the Parlement of Paris in the Eighteenth Century' in *Atti del quarto congresso internazionale della società italiana di storia diritto* (Florence, 1982)
——, *Liberty and Order in Early Modern Europe: the Subject and the State, 1650–1800* (London, 1986)
Soman, A., 'The Parlement of Paris and the Great Witch Hunt 1565–1640', *Sixteenth Century Journal*, 9 (1978)
Stein, H., *Le Palais de Justice et la Sainte Chapelle de Paris* (Paris, 1927)
Stocker, C., 'Office as Maintenance in Renaissance France', *Canadian Journal of History*, 6 (1971)
——, 'The Politics of the Parlement of Paris in 1525', *French Historical Studies*, 8 (1973)
——, 'Office and Justice: Louis XI and the Parlement of Paris, 1465–1467, *Mediaeval Studies*, 37 (1975)
——, 'Public and Private Enterprise in the Administration of a Renaissance Monarchy: the First Sales of Office in the Parlement of Paris, 1512–1524', *Sixteenth Century Journal*, 9 (1978)

——, '*Parti*, Clientage, and Lineage in the Fifteenth-Century Parlement of Paris', *Proceedings of the Annual Meeting of the Western Society for French History*, 13 (Flagstaff, 1988)

Stone, B., 'Robe against Sword: the Parlement of Paris and the French Aristocracy, 1774–1789', *French Historical Studies*, 9 (1975)

——, *The Parlement of Paris, 1774–1789* (Chapel Hill, 1981)

——, *The French Parlements and the Crisis of the Old Regime* (Chapel Hill, 1986)

Strayer, J.R., *The Reign of Philip the Fair* (Princeton, 1980)

Sutherland, N.M., *The French Secretaries of State in the Age of Catherine de Medici* (London, 1962)

Sutto, C., 'Le roi et le parlement dans la pensée et l'action des Jésuites français, 1590–1625' in *Pouvoir et Institutions en Europe au XVIe Siècle*, ed. A. Stegmann (Paris, 1987)

Swann, J., 'Parlement, Politics and the *Parti Janséniste*: the *Grand Conseil* Affair, 1755–1756', *French History*, 6 (1992)

——, 'Parlements and Political Crisis in France under Louis XV: the Besançon Affair, 1757–1761', *Historical Journal*, 37 (1994)

——, *Politics and the Parlement of Paris under Louis XV, 1754–1774* (Cambridge, 1995)

——, 'Le parlement de Paris et la réforme financière au XVIIIe siècle, 1749-1789' in *L'Administration des Finances sous l'Ancien Régime* (Paris, 1997)

Taber, L., 'Religious Dissent within the Parlement of Paris in the Mid-Sixteenth Century: a Re-assessment', *French Historical Studies*, 16 (1990)

Tapié, V.L., *La France de Louis XIII et de Richelieu* (Paris, 1952)

Thompson, D.G., 'The Persecution of the French Jesuits by the Parlement of Paris, 1761–71', *Persecution and Toleration*. Papers read at the 22nd and 23rd Meetings of the Ecclesiastical History Society (Oxford, 1984)

Timbal, P.C., *La Guerre de Cent Ans vue à travers les Registres du Parlement, 1337–1369* (Paris, 1961)

Valois, N., *Histoire de la Pragmatique Sanction de Bourges sous Charles VII* (Paris, 1906)

Van Kley, D., *The Jansenists and the Expulsion of the Jesuits from France, 1757–1765* (New Haven, 1975)

——, 'The Refusal of Sacraments Controversy and the Political Crisis of 1756–57' in *Church, State and Society under the Bourbon Kings*, ed. R.M. Golden (Lawrence, Kansas, 1982)

——, *The Damiens Affair and the Unraveling of the Ancien Régime, 1750–1770* (Princeton, 1984)

——, 'The Estates-General as Ecumenical Council: the Constitutionalism of Corporate Consensus and the Parlement's Ruling of September 25, 1788', *Journal of Modern History*, 61 (1989)

Villers, R., *L'Organisation du Parlement de Paris et des Conseils Supérieurs d'après la Réforme de Maupeou, 1771–74* (Paris, 1937)

Viollet, P., *Précis de l'Histoire du Droit Français* (Paris, 1886)

——, *Histoire des Institutions Politiques et Administratives de la France*, 3 vols (Paris, 1890–1903)

Weill, G., *Les Théories sur le Pouvoir Royal en France pendant les Guerres de Religion* (Paris, 1892)

Wells, C.C., *Law and Citizenship in Early Modern France* (Baltimore and London, 1995)

Yardeni, M., *La Conscience Nationale en France pendant les Guerres de Religion, 1559–1598* (Paris and Louvain, 1971)

INDEX